BEST ENTRY-LEVEL JOBS

The Princeton Review

BEST ENTRY-LEVEL JOBS

RON LIEBER, TOM MELTZER, JULIE DOHERTY, CHRISTOPHER MAIER, AND MARISSA PARELES

RANDOM HOUSE, INC.

NEW YORK

PRINCETONREVIEW.COM

The Princeton Review, Inc.
2315 Broadway
New York, NY 10024
Email: bookeditor@review.com

ISBN 978-0-375-76599-5

Editorial Director: Robert Franek
Editor: Michael V. Palumbo
Production Manager and Designer: Scott Harris
Production Editor: Christine LaRubio

Printed in the United States of America.

9 8 7 6 5 4 3 2 1

ACKNOWLEDGMENTS

I'm grateful to Jeanne Krier, who makes publicity magic wherever she goes, and Tom Russell at Random House, for agreeing to take on this book. Meanwhile, much of the credit for this particular enterprise ought to go to my coauthors: Tom Meltzer, Julie Doherty, Christopher Maier, and Marissa Pareles. And, finally, we should all have people as wise as my agent Christy Fletcher looking after our careers.

The idea for this book came to me in 1998, as my brother, David, and sister, Stephanie, were trying to make the best out of their first jobs. I tried to exorcise their particular demons in the form of a 1999 story for *Fast Company*. I'm grateful to Bill Taylor and Alan Webber for providing that forum. Although I'm not on the career beat full time anymore, I'm so much better at everything I do thanks to intensive attention from the likes of Edward Felsenthal, Jesse Pesta, Neal Templin, and Eben Shapiro at the Wall Street Journal.

Finally, thanks go out to Liebers, Bramsons, Krimstons, and Kantors everywhere. Jodi, as much as I've tried (and failed) to cut down on the number of jobs I've taken on over the years, this husband gig suits me pretty well, I think. I can't wait to see what new projects spring from it.

—Ron Lieber

Thanks to everyone who provided support on this project and without whose tireless efforts this book would have been impossible. Thanks to Ron for coming up with such a swell idea for a book. Lastly, thanks to my wife Lisa for putting up with my grousing and for walking the dogs when it was my turn.

—Tom Meltzer

Three wonderful people here at TPR—Andrea Kornstein, Chaitra Ramanathan, and Jennifer Adams—were instrumental in our effort to reach out to the terrific companies profiled in this book. Many thanks also go to Andrew Baker, Lisa Marie Rovito, and Erica Ciccarone for their help in shaping the final manuscript. And much gratitude is reserved for our production team, Christine LaRubio and Scott Harris—they are always flexible and total pros.

The folks most vital to this book, however, are the contributors—the company officials and the current and former first jobbers who took time out of their busy lives to answer all our questions. To all who participated: Many thanks for your hard work and generosity. We commend you for laying it out there for today's aspiring first jobbers.

—Michael V. Palumbo

CONTENTS

INTRODUCTION

So what do you want to be when you grow up?

If you're about to graduate from college, the best way to answer this question is also the most honest way: I don't know because I'm not a grown-up yet.

Somewhere along the way, people got it into their heads that twenty-two-year-olds should finish school with a clear idea of what they want to do for a living. And nowadays, most parents become anxious if their children graduate and don't immediately find jobs, or find jobs that aren't lucrative, or find jobs that don't sound impressive.

But how on earth can you possibly know what you want to do with your life when all you've ever done is go to school? Sure, summer jobs help. Internships give you a sense of what the real world is like. But the vast majority of internships aren't substantive and don't last long enough to give you a true sense of what it would be like to work for a particular company or in a given industry for years, decades, or through to retirement.

And consider this: In all likelihood, your first job will have little to do with your last job. Taking a job is not an irreversible trip down a one-way career path. In fact, for many twenty-two-year-olds, the function of a first job is merely to aid them in figuring out what they don't want to do. It's an experiment, almost like picking a major, but in some ways less important. After all, you have much longer than four years to figure out what you want to be when you grow up.

Now, about being a grown-up. You hear the word "adolescent" thrown around a lot when you're in high school. But many specialists in human development believe adolescence extends long past the time you're done growing into your body. You're not truly a grown-up until you're done growing into your own head. And that can't possibly happen until you've been on your own for a while, living in your own place, fending for yourself financially, and working for a living.

So we've established that, at twenty-two, you have reason not to know what you want to be when you grow up. College curriculum designers understand this—courses of study in English, history, economics, and countless other disciplines do not point to a single, obvious first job. This is a perfectly fine for your college years, because you should be looking to shape your mind and not trying to scribble the first draft of your resume. Trade-specific study can come later.

At the end of the day, it is you who is responsible for finding your way into the world, and that is as it should be. Through absolutely no fault of your own, however, you may lack some sense about what's possible beyond what older friends and parents' friends do all day. Even if you treat your trips to the career placement office as if they were part of an academic course, you still may not find the real-world stories and nitty-gritty details that tell you where the best first jobs are and, more importantly, what makes a first job great.

That's where we come in. Some time ago, we came to the sad conclusion that most first jobs aren't very good and usually aren't fulfilling by design. The idea of the first job as a rite of passage is nothing new. In the old days, you had to apprentice yourself to a tradesman and work for free in return for an education in how to perform a set of tasks. Needless to say, the most grueling and menial tasks always fell to the apprentice.

Run-of-the-mill first jobs for twenty-two-year-olds in private companies, government offices, and nonprofit organizations are typically built on a philosophy of making workers pay their dues. This isn't bad in theory. Materials must be procured, goods must be counted, numbers must be crunched, facts must be checked, and research must be compiled. There are plenty of mind-numbing details vital to the functioning of any organization. During your first year, your mind may be numb most of the time. But it's important to have context for your work. All too often in first jobs, you don't get to play a role in creating the report that contains your work, going to the meeting where it's discussed, or meeting with the customer who ends up using it.

Consider this: Bruce Tulgan, the preeminent consultant to companies who want to figure out how best to treat younger workers, notes that the whole culture of paying dues is partly based on the idea that there's a club you get to join once you're done shelling out. A generation or so ago, that club was the job-for-life club—the one for which you worked for forty years at one company and got a gold watch and a great pension at the end.

But nowadays few people want to work at the same company for their entire career. Any number of conditions keeps this from happening: Their closest colleagues move on, their spouses get jobs elsewhere, they get new bosses, they want to change careers, or recruiters come after them with great offers. Many potential employers are suspicious of people who stay in one place too long. And there exists the possibility that you'll eventually be laid off if you stick around one place for several decades.

The point of all this is only to state what's now plainly obvious to employees, but doesn't always get through to employers: What's the point of making people pay their dues if there isn't any club for them to join? A lousy first year or two in the workplace shouldn't be the price of admission for people who simply want to earn a living. In that time, you ought to be able to watch a few meetings, go to a conference, meet a few customers, tag along with your boss on a business trip, or learn how to sell something.

Consider this sobering observation from Glen T. Meakem, an Internet entrepreneur who is also a Gulf War veteran: "We won two wars while the current crop of graduates was in college. Both of those were won by platoons of eighteen- to twenty-two-year-olds on the ground being led by commanders who were often just a few years older. If we're capable of defending our country, isn't it insulting that we're shunted as a matter of course in most corporations to some isolated corner to do grunt work for a few years?"

It's ridiculous, of course, but nobody says you must go to work for a company that treats young people this way, either. You may have noticed by now that we haven't yet mentioned the name of a single good place to work. That's because, in some ways, making sure the building blocks of a great first job are present in any position is just as important as the company that offers it and what the company does. So it's crucial to understand the current you're fighting against first—the tendency of most entry-level jobs to revert to mediocrity or worse.

Therefore, before we start naming the employers who offer rewarding entry-level jobs, we'd like to isolate all of the different ways in which many employers fail their entry-level hires. We hope you'll use this list as an evaluative tool. Some of these considerations may be crucial for you, depending on what you want to do, while others could be irrelevant to you for any number of reasons. For instance, advancement doesn't matter much for most investment bank analysts, since relatively few of them stay longer than two or three years at one place. And if you don't have any student loans, salary may not be that important if you're working for Newell Rubbermaid, since you're likely to be stationed in areas where the cost of living is relatively low (they better have a good expense reimbursement system, however, if you're going to be driving to stores all of the time). If you're fortunate enough to get a few job offers, you'll want to consider your opportunities and the people and places they're coming from by using many of the following standards:

- **Are you entering a program or merely taking on a job?** Many big companies have turned the first job into something resembling a degree-granting institution. There's an admissions committee, fellow class members, course work, a dean who keeps track of all the new arrivals, and other such accoutrements. You may like structure like this, or you may find it stifling. Washington Mutual's PACE Program and GE's Corporate Leadership Development Programs, for example, prepare new hires for the challenges ahead with tons of formal training.

- **Will you be doing work that makes you excited (or makes other people excited when they hear you're doing it)?** As a general rule, you have to like what you're doing all day if you want to be truly successful at it. How will your job sound when you explain it to others? Will you be proud of what you do? Occasionally, you may pull weeks of late nights because you know, once a particular project gets done, you'll be able to say you worked on something really cool. Entry-level positions with the Associated Press or the Peace Corps may fall into this category for you.

- **How much responsibility will you have?** Some companies don't let twenty-two-year-olds near the big customers—or even near the boss's boss. Will they trust you to take trips on your own or to send e-mails without having them vetted? One of the best feelings you can have as a young person in the workforce is that a little piece of the business belongs to you—i.e., there's a set of results you're responsible for and actually have some control over. Will they trust you with something like this? They should. Teach for America, Newell Rubbermaid, and Boston Beer have entry-level positions that grant first jobbers an enormous amount of independence and shoulder them with a great deal of responsibility.

- **Who will your mentors be?** This is a tricky one, since you can't always figure this out in advance. Many companies will try to assign someone to look after you before you even arrive. While the thought is nice, these relationships can sometimes feel forced. It's probably better for you to forge such relationships on your own after you arrive by approaching people who have something in common with you (say, an alma mater) or are in a part of the organization you hope ultimately to enter. While evaluating potential jobs, it's important to find out whether most entry-level employees have someone like this. As you'll note in their profiles, Ogilvy and KPMG both value mentor/coach relationships.

- **How will you get your feedback?** Whom will you get it from and how often? Are the bosses themselves evaluated on the basis of how well they give feedback to the people who work for them? The feedback process is a bit like being graded in college in that there will probably be some grading system to give you a sense of where you stand in comparison with your colleagues and against the expectations they have for you. Good feedback is given more than once a year—it happens every day or as often as possible, either on schedule or on demand, and it's thorough enough to cover every aspect of what you do and how you do it. Newbies at Raytheon Company and Wells Fargo learn as much (or more) through feedback from their seniors as they do in formal training.

- **How good are the bosses?** How well they give feedback is only one small part of what makes them effective. Are these people who have volunteered to help younger people along, or are they doing it because they have to? Once you enter the workforce, you'll probably recognize the unique psychological make-up of the entry-level employee in yourself. You have super-high expectations for this first job; you don't want to be disappointed. Yet in many ways, you have no earthly idea what you're doing or what you're supposed to be doing. Who's signed up for the privilege of keeping track of you and why? Did they start at this company themselves? Goldman Sachs' Big Buddy program, for example, pairs a new analyst with an experienced associate who helps him or her negotiate the new, sometimes alien landscape a high-pressure workplace presents to a recent college graduate.

- **Who will your peers be?** How many people tend to get hired each year, and where do they come from? Is it like college all over again, with happy hours and weekend get-togethers? Or is it not a particularly social enterprise? These are crucial yet often overlooked questions for recent graduates. It can be extremely difficult to move to a new city without knowing anyone. So what does the company do to ease the transition? Once you've started, your peers and superiors at the company will become your colleagues; if you stay at the organization or in that line of work, they'll become your network. So what kind of people does the place draw? Will you fit in? In Newell Rubbermaid's Phoenix Program, it won't matter; you won't see your peers on a day-to-day basis once you've completed your initial training because you'll be out on the road. If you don't like happy hours, figuring out how to build a network at Booz Allen Hamilton may take some creative thinking.

- **How much will you learn about how the company works?** Some of the worst organizations put people like you to work without ever explaining to you what they do and how everything works. Other good organizations take weeks to teach you everything. Entry-level jobs like those in Washington Mutual's PACE Program teach you the different aspects of how the total enterprise functions before you finally settle into one position within the business. This is to acknowledge an obvious fact that most first jobbers ignore: Most people graduate from college with no idea whether they belong in sales or in marketing, or whether they function better as an editor or as a web developer.

- **Some of the best companies to work for will continue to give you exposure outside of your own area.** This may take the form of weekly lunch meetings for first jobbers at which different executives talk about what their group does or field trips on which you get to see other teams in action. If this sort of thing doesn't seem to go on at a place you're thinking about working for, ask if you can put something like it together yourself. Doing so will show initiative and curiosity, two traits for which all hiring managers look. Members of the Green Corps spend two months out on their own in the field organizing campaigns and events, but every two months they come together to debrief one another on their most recent events, receive more training, and prepare for their next campaigns out in the field.

- **How much money do you want to make?** How much money do you need to make? These are two different, but equally important, questions. There's no shame in wanting to make a lot of money as fast as possible. If you're a trader or a really good salesman, you can make a lot of money very quickly. Big bucks, however often require working long hours; some supposedly high-paying jobs actually pay less per hour than do other jobs at which the annual salary is much lower. Engineers do well, as you'll see in the profiles for Raytheon and Schlumberger; bankers also do well, as the numbers for Goldman Sachs show. However, one job requires you to be out on an oil rig, far from friends and family, while another will keep you in the office until past midnight on some nights. Are you prepared to give up weeknights out and weekends away to make your desired salary? For many, it's the "need to make" part they have to reckon with before facing down their inner materialists. Although interest rates are still low, the average student loan balance just keeps going up, so you may be facing a payment of several hundred dollars a month. Combine that with a job in a low-paying creative industry in a big, expensive city, and you could be looking at an impossible financial situation. Will your family help you out the first year? You should be calculating your loan payments and talking to your family before you even begin to look for work. Places like Random House don't pay starting salaries that compare favorably with those at big technology companies and investment banks; but if you stick around for a while and show some aptitude for and commitment to the publishing industry, you could become one of those legendary publishers who get to work with the great authors of the age. It's important to figure out your financial situation before you take any job.

- **Perks are out there.** Northrop Grumman offers employees pet insurance. Electronic Arts gives its video-gaming geeks $100 toward a gaming console. And while you may not be worried about child care benefits and health care right now, you should pay careful attention to the retirement plan, even though it might be the last thing on your mind. The fact is, the more you put away in your first couple of years on the job, the better off you'll be at age sixty-seven. That's because the sooner you set money aside, the more time it has to earn interest. If you care at all about retiring comfortably, do not scrimp on this now. And ask tough questions of the companies that don't let you participate in their 401(k) plans right away and instead make you wait a year before putting money aside. What kind of welcome message does that send?

- **Advancement.** You may not want to stick around for a long time at a company. Some entry-level workers at Deloitte want to get a few years of experience and then leave to work for a client company or go back to business school. Then again, you may be like those people who enjoy their entry-level jobs so much, they don't leave for a long time. In that case, talk to people who started working straight out of college and have been at the same company for years. What about the organization has kept them interested and engaged? It's good to keep in mind that the chairman and chief executive officer of Caterpillar started as an entry-level trainee with the company more than thirty years ago; today, he runs an enterprise valued at more than $26 billion.

- **Many organizations have reputations as not only great places to work but also as great places to have worked for.** In many respects, it's like having gone to a really good college. Not having gone there won't shut you out from later success in life, but it'll be easier to get your foot in the door if you're coming from the right place. If you want to build a career as an accountant, for example, experience with KPMG is simply going to get you further than experience with a smaller, lesser-known firm. Try to figure out where alumni of the first jobs you're considering end up. If it's a program that ends after two years, where did last year's "graduates" go next? What kinds of jobs did they get? What graduate schools did they get into?

When choosing the jobs to feature in this book we had no minimum salary or geographical requirements or quotas. Our goal was to profile jobs in both the for-profit and nonprofit sectors, as well as across numerous industries. We wanted to find places at which people were happy, engaged with their work, nicely compensated, well positioned for advancement, getting great preparation for graduate school, doing really interesting stuff, or benefitting from any combination of these things. To profile these organizations, we interviewed not only their official representatives but also—and more importantly—hundreds of the people who were currently holding (or had formerly held) the positions we describe. They're the ones who know the most about what having one of these jobs is like, so we contacted as many of them as we could.

For this edition of the book (the fourth), we offered the organizations that have been featured each year since the book's inaugural edition the opportunity to receive a completely new profile. Twenty-five took us up on it. We also offered every organization in the previous edition of the book the opportunity to directly to update the hard data in their profiles. (Most changes involved salary and benefits, and they tended to be for the better.) Finally, fourteen new companies were added to this year's edition, providing you with a wider breadth of choices within several prominent industries.

Finally, a word about hiring prospects: As we're going to print, they're looking brighter for this year's college graduates than those faced by students who graduated in the 2005–2006 academic year. The National Association of Colleges and Employers (NACE, naceweb.org) regularly releases reports of employer responses to its Job Outlook survey, and one such report said that employers planned on hiring 17.5 percent more college graduates in 2006–2007 than they had hired in 2005–2006[1]. That means you're entering a better hiring environment than the one experienced by your predecessors. It means you'll likely get more in return for your job-hunting efforts than they got. It means you could be offered a higher starting salary than those offered last year to people with similar skills and knowledge as you.

Of course the job market is still very competitive for newly minted college graduates. So the better your grades, the more internship experience you have, and the earlier you start your job search, the better. Early fall of your senior year isn't too soon to start sending out letters and resumes to prospective employers. If you don't have any internship or co-op experience in the industry in which you are interested in working, get some now—freshman year isn't too early, and senior year isn't too late. And network like crazy. Every family gathering, every career fair, and every mixer with faculty and administrators is a chance to get onto people's radar screens. Most people want to help young, energetic people just starting out in their careers. Adjunct professors (part-time professors who have other jobs outside your college or university) are especially valuable in this regard. Impress them; they usually have more immediate "real world" connections than do tenured, full-time faculty.

We consider this book a work in progress. We plan to release further editions, continually adding new companies and dropping those at which the quality of the entry-level experience has declined. You may have worked at an organization you think is even better than the ones we've profiled here. If so, drop us a line at bookeditor@review.com and let us know about it.

---

[1]   National Association of Colleges and Employers. "College Hiring Expected to Increase 17.4 Percent." NACEWeb. http://www.naceweb.org/press/display.asp?prid=242 (accessed November 6, 2006).

SURVIVING YOUR JOB HUNT

Knowing about all of the awesome entry-level positions in the world won't help if you blunder when it counts in the job-hunting jungle. We thought it may help if we provided you with a list of essential job-searching tools: networking, perfecting your resume and cover letters, and acing the all-important interview.

Part One: Networking

You have a great new interview outfit and a killer resume. You've worked hard to investigate possible employers in this book, online, at the library, and at your college career center. You've spent hours sifting through job listings in your field of interest. You've sent out scores of resumes without so much as a nibble from prospective employers. Worse yet, you're running out of ideas and enthusiasm. What's wrong? Many people become so intent on their job searches that they end up conducting them in a vacuum. Networking is one of the most important components of career research and of the job search. The more people you know, the more information you gather, and the more you're out there, the better equipped you will be to find employment.

WHO ARE YOUR CONTACTS?

Even if you're starting with very few connections, you can network successfully. Most people focus their networking on those people immediately surrounding them. "Well, my mother or uncle or cousin doesn't know anyone in my field, so I'm sunk." The trick is to delve beyond that first layer of contacts and to use your imagination. Say you're pursuing a career in the music industry. You may know someone who works at your college's radio station. Although this person probably won't be your contact with the president of Sony BMG, he or she may know someone at an independent label who has been in contact with him or her to promote local bands. In checking out your college alumni directory, you may discover an alumnus who's an entertainment lawyer. Although he doesn't work at a record label, he may very well have contacts in the field. If you think creatively, networking contacts can be found in many different places. Just learn to think outside the box and talk to those you come in contact with in your daily routine. Here's a list of possible resources to start your networking.

FAMILY/EXTENDED FAMILY

Parents, guardians, siblings, grandparents, aunts, uncles, and cousins are all possible resources. Remember: Look beyond the obvious.

FRIENDS/ACQUAINTANCES

This includes friends of friends, parents of friends, and people in your apartment building or neighborhood.

COWORKERS AND EMPLOYERS, PAST AND PRESENT

Past and present colleagues can be good sources of networking information, even if they are in a seemingly unrelated field.

TEACHERS AND PROFESSORS, PAST AND PRESENT

Educators can be excellent sources for contacts, particularly if you have had a good rapport with them.

COLLEGE ALUMNI

In addition to keeping listings of alumni, many schools organize alumni/ae receptions throughout the year, so it's always wise to inquire about such opportunities when contacting your alma mater. Most schools have their graduates categorized by career area and geographic location, so if you're considering moving to another city or state, find out if there are other alums in that area.

COLLEGE COUNSELORS

This could include career counselors, deans, and college activities officers. Make nice with these people if you're still in school!

CLUBS OR ORGANIZATIONS

People who have common interests . . .

HEALTH CLUBS OR SPORTS TEAMS

. . . and participate in common activities often have great information to share with one another.

RELIGIOUS ORGANIZATIONS

Churches, temples, and other religious organizations can be rich resources that offer a wide array of contacts in a variety of career fields.

YOUR DOCTOR, DENTIST, BANKER, AND ANYONE ELSE WHO WORKS WITH YOU

You may also want to contact the local chamber of commerce for a list of employers in your geographic area of interest.

PEOPLE YOU DON'T KNOW BUT WHO DO WORK THAT INTERESTS YOU

Maybe you read an article about a successful civil engineer in your area, and you're interested in entering that field. Write that person a letter. Whether someone enjoys the attention and recognition or is simply interested in helping you out, you could benefit from initiating contact.

PROFESSIONAL ORGANIZATIONS

Organizations such as the American Medical Association, the American Association of University Women, the NAACP, and the Asian American Journalists Association often keep lists of members arranged by geographic location.

TELEPHONE BOOKS

The local phone book for your desired destination is an excellent source of information. Phone books for most major American cities can be found at branches of the public library or at your career development center.

NEWSPAPERS

Check out local papers to get acquainted with key players and organizations, career fair listings, and local job listings.

Online

In addition to the obvious sites like Yahoo, HotJobs, and Monster, bulletin boards, newsgroups, and chat rooms can be excellent resources.

Career/Job Fairs

With nonprofit fairs, business/financial service fairs, and minority career fairs making up but a few of the career fairs out there, these offer frequent opportunities to network with a large number of people without a lot of running around.

The Informational Interview

The most effective way to network is by conducting informational interviews. Usually no more than thirty minutes in duration, they're meant to help you gather information related to a potential career and job search. Through meetings with people, you can find out what a particular job involves and how best to prepare yourself for your job search. Informational interviews are usually limited to one meeting; they're not job interviews and shouldn't be used to ask for a job (though you hope they may lead to one). Rather, they're a way to discover pathways to particular jobs or careers. Research the person, the organization, and the career field ahead of time whenever possible.

Initiating Contact

Once you've acquired your network of names, initiate contact with either a phone call or letter (or e-mail) of inquiry. Don't overlook the importance of phone strategies when seeking out contacts. Since it's often the first communication you'll have with a networking contact, your phone tactics are just as important as your other networking strategies and thus deserve as much attention.

Getting Beyond the Gatekeepers

You have to establish rapport not only with your contact, but also with the people (such as administrative assistants or receptionists) who can connect you with your contact. Your interaction with these people can determine your success in ultimately reaching your contact, so be professional and courteous at all times. If you're making an unsolicited or "cold" call and your contact isn't able to take your call, don't leave your name with the receptionist. Instead, ask when a convenient time would be to call back. If you leave a lengthy message, it may be recorded incorrectly, and you lose the power to call back. Simply leaving your name may put you at the bottom of the priority list for returned phone messages. If you're returning a call to a potential contact with whom you've already spoken, however, it's fine to leave your name, phone number, and a time when you can be reached.

Voice Mail

What happens when you keep getting your contact's voice mail? If you've made several attempts to phone, hanging up each time you hear, "Please leave a message," you should leave a message. Just make sure it's short and concise. If you're calling contacts with whom you've previously had contact and they're not available, leave a time you'll be available. Nobody likes playing phone tag.

And a word about *your* voice mail: Now's the time to have a clear, professional outgoing message. Your name and number will suffice.

MAKING CONTACT

When you speak with your contact, you won't have a lot of time to get your point across, so you want to be sure that you cover some important details.

IDENTIFY YOURSELF

Speak slowly and clearly. You also want to be alert, enthusiastic, confident, and poised.

IDENTIFY YOUR PURPOSE FOR CALLING

Be clear about why you've made contact. You need to set the table for what's to follow.

GIVE SPECIFICS ABOUT WHAT YOU WANT FROM YOUR CONTACT

Be concise. Convey that you're interested in information, not (necessarily) a job. Carefully consider what you want to say and, as cheesy as it sounds, do a practice run before initiating your call.

Letters of Inquiry

An alternative to phoning your contact directly is to send out a letter of inquiry for an informational interview first and then to follow up with a phone call. Some people prefer this more formal method; the letter serves as an introduction before the phone contact. There are no surprises, and your networking contact will be expecting your call.

Get the correct spelling of your contact's name when sending the letter; if you're unsure for whatever reason, call first to verify. If you found your contact's name in trade publications or from what appear to be outdated job ads or organizational materials, call the organization to verify your contact's name and job title.

Use a standard business layout. It should be single-spaced and have a double-space between paragraphs. No grammatical errors, misspellings, or typos in your inquiry letter! Don't just spell-check it; have several people proofread your letter before you send it out.

OPENING PARAGRAPH

Identify why you're writing. Be clear about how you've come to write to your networking contact; mention your referral source—whether it is another person, professional organization, or article in which your contact was cited.

MIDDLE SECTION

This is usually one to two paragraphs in length. Include some personal information. Briefly mention the school you'll be graduating from or your present position of employment as well as your (tentative, in some cases) future career plans. Be clear that you're in the process of gathering information about a particular career field—and that you're not, at this point, looking for a job. Here you can propose an informational interview. Do so politely, and indicate that such a meeting would be at your networking contact's convenience.

CONCLUDING PARAGRAPH

Thank your contact for his or her time and consideration and have a specific follow-up plan at the conclusion of the letter. You may want to suggest an informational interview via telephone; this can be scheduled over the phone or by e-mail.

Part Two: Tips for Making Your Resume Beautiful

Submitting a resume that looks unprofessional is one of the surest ways to eliminate yourself from contention for a job, regardless of how impressive your qualifications may be. You would be amazed at the resumes we've seen with ketchup stains, chewed-off corners, handwritten updates, and illegible print. Fortunately, designing an attractive, eye-catching resume is very doable.

GETTING MARGINALIZED

Margins act like a frame, providing a welcome border of white space around your text, and they serve as a built-in memo pad for employers, many of whom like to make notes directly on your resume. Set your margins at one inch on all four sides to start. If space becomes an issue, you can shrink them down to as little as a half inch, but any smaller and your page will start looking extremely cramped.

TYPEFACES

When choosing a typeface, consider its readability, attractiveness, and appropriateness. It's best to use no more than two typefaces on your resume—one serif typeface for the body of your resume and, if you wish, one sans-serif typeface for your name and category headings. Traditional favorites for the body text include

Times

Palatino

Garamond

Good choices for your name and category headings are

Arial

Helvetica

Futura

Stay away from fancy scripts, decorative typefaces, or any other type that strains the eyes. After all, you're sending out a resume, not a wedding invitation. Size-wise, you'll generally want to go with ten- to twelve-point type for the body of your text, twelve- to fourteen-point type for your category headings, and sixteen- to eighteen-point type for your name:

This is Times 18 point.
This is Times 14 point.
This is Times 12 point.
This is Times 10 point.

LAYOUT

While there are literally dozens of ways to lay out a resume, there are certain basic rules you should follow. Your layout should always be clear, logical, and easy to follow, and there should be plenty of white space. Make sure you're consistent in your layout. Place key information—such as category headings, titles, names, and dates—in a logical order.

FINISHING YOUR STROKES

There are five main text-embellishment techniques to consider: **bolding**, CAPITALIZING, • bulleting, *italicizing*, and <u>ruled</u> lines. CAPS should be used sparingly, as capital letters take up significantly more space than lowercase letters and will leave you severely pressed for room. **Bolding** works well for the items that require the most emphasis, such as your name and category headings. Avoid the use of dingbats and graphics that tend to appear too gimmicky.

PROOFREADING

This is perhaps the most crucial—yet most overlooked—component of the entire resume-writing process. Never send out a resume before you've had it carefully reviewed by at least a couple sets of trusted eyes for typos, poor grammar, awkward or repetitive language, a misaligned layout, and other mistakes. There's no margin for error (pun intended, sorry). A single misspelled word could cost you a desired opportunity.

PAPER AND PRINTING

Use paper that's 8.5" x 11" in size, with a weight of at least twenty-four pounds (which is sometimes referred to as seventy lb. text). Stick with neutral colors—white or a subtle off-white is best. The advantage of white is that it reproduces well when being either faxed or photocopied. Stay away from loud colors.

Laser printing is the only way to go. Never print more resumes than you're ready to send out at one time. Fifteen is a reasonable number unless you're attending a mega-career fair or other special event at which you expect to visit with a large number of prospective employers at one time.

ENVELOPES

Using envelopes that match your resume paper is a nice professional touch, but white envelopes will always do in a pinch. If you really want to impress your prospective employer, send your resume and cover letter in a large envelope (9" x 12" is a perfect size). By doing so, your resume will arrive flat, a definite advantage if it's going to be scanned into a database.

The downside of using a larger envelope is purely economic: They require additional postage compared with standard business envelopes. Whatever type of envelope you use, it's important that you print the recipient's address legibly and correctly, otherwise your resume may never reach its destination. The address can be typed, laser-printed, or hand-written (provided you have good penmanship). And don't forget to include your return address on the envelope!

GETTING YOUR RESUME INTO THEIR HANDS

The only thing left to do is make sure your resume (and accompanying cover letter) reaches your prospective employer in a timely fashion. There are several ways to do this—traditional mail, e-mail, fax, courier, and hand delivery. The method you select should be contingent on a) how badly you want the job, b) how long the job was posted before you heard about it, c) how much of a rush the employer is in to fill the job, and d) the personality type of the prospective employer.

Of course, in most cases, if the position was advertised, the ad will state the preferred method of resume submission. Follow the directions. If the organization won't accept a fax or e-mail submission and time is of the essence, you always have the option of sending your package via FedEx, UPS, or some other courier service. Overnighting a package is an expensive proposition, but, in addition to getting your resume into your employer's hands quickly, you'll be sending the message that you want the job badly enough to spare no expense.

Another alternative, provided the employer is within close proximity, is delivering your package by hand. This approach has the added benefit of enabling you to get a peek at your potential place of employment, as well as providing an opportunity to see some of your prospective colleagues in action.

Sample Resume

Feel free to borrow from this resume to help create your own: Pay careful attention to format, layout, design, and phrasing.

Nada Kendra

1011 Oak Street • Rochester, NY 11111 • (716) 555-5555

OBJECTIVE

Position as a counselor in a group home for emotionally disturbed adolescents.

EDUCATION

BS, Child and Family Studies

Syracuse University, May 2005
- Coursework included education, psychology, and family dynamics.

COUNSELING AND TEACHING EXPERIENCE

Child and Family Counselor

Community Medical Center, Syracuse, NY, Spring 2004
- Interacted with children and parents while children waited for medical treatment.
- Modeled effective childcare techniques and provided feedback to parents regarding parenting behavior.
- Established ongoing relationships with families.

Student Teacher

Syracuse University Early Education Center, Syracuse, NY, Spring 2003
- Designed and implemented instructional activities for children ages 3–6.
- Researched learning styles and cognitive development of children.
- Organized and supervised educational field trips.

Student Teacher

Elizabeth M. Wall Nursery School, Syracuse, NY, Fall 2002
- Coordinated and led educational activities for groups of 4-year-olds.
- Planned new activities daily to teach group interaction skills.

ADDITIONAL EXPERIENCE

Assistant to Director, Creative Services, 2004 to present

Cosmetics 'R Us, Rochester, NY
- Assist art director in coordinating photo shoots.
- Create and organize filing system for directors.
- Identify new products and displays by speaking with vendors.

Sales Clerk

Leigh Barrett Boutique, Rochester, NY, Summer 1999
- Created window displays and performed in-store merchandising.
- Assisted customers in selection of merchandise; maintained inventory.

United Jewish Appeal and American Red Cross, Volunteer

INTERNATIONAL EXPERIENCE

Have lived in Australia and London; traveled extensively throughout Europe.

Part Three: Power Tools for Killer Cover Letters

The trick to writing an effective cover letter is to think things through before you put pen to paper or fingers to keyboard. Once you've completed the five steps below, you'll have all the basic components of your cover letter in place.

POWER TOOL #1: IDENTIFY THE READER'S NEEDS

Far too many job seekers focus on what they want from the people who will read their cover letters, when the better approach is to focus on the readers' needs and objectives. While employers recognize that they may need to train you and that they can offer an environment in which your interests may flourish, they can only justify hiring you if you can add some value to their organization, either right away or down the road. This isn't to say that you can't express some needs, interests, and goals in your cover letters; it's just that there must be a balance between what you ask for and what you can offer, and the scales should tip in favor of what you can offer.

Most readers' concerns fall into five categories:

- Are you the type of person they want in this job and this organization? Do you have the proper educational background and work experience? The right personal qualities?

- Do you have—or can you learn—the skills it takes to perform the day-to-day functions of this job?

- Have you demonstrated a commitment to and familiarity with this career field or industry?

- Have you chosen to contact their organization for a clearly identifiable reason?

- Can you organize your thoughts, express them clearly, and write well?

If you do your homework at the start of your job search, you'll have plenty of information on career fields, specific types of jobs, and specific organizations or companies. Through library, bookstore, and online research, as well as by talking with people, you can learn a great deal about what employers are looking for. You can also find the qualities a specific private-sector company or nonprofit organization is seeking out. Learning about an organization's culture, management style, products and/or services, areas of expansion, problems, and financial status can give you an edge when addressing your reader's needs. It's all right not to mention a specific job title in your letter, but you should at least define a functional area or division in which you'd like to work. You may say something like, "I would like to discuss any entry-level positions available in your marketing department," or "Given my skills and experience, I believe I could make the greatest contribution in your editorial department." These statements show much more focus and maturity than do general statements of interest in any entry-level position with the company.

POWER TOOL #2: IDENTIFY YOUR OBJECTIVES

Be clear about what you want and what action you'd like the reader to take. Your objectives will typically fall into two categories: career goals and immediate actions.

As far as career goals are concerned, you should let your reader know what type of position you're looking for, either generally or specifically. If you have a definite career objective in mind, it's okay to mention a specific type of job as long as your terms aren't so narrow you miss out on any related opportunities the employer may have. Stating your career or job objective is especially important when sending an unsolicited resume because this is how you can direct the reader to particular jobs in which you'd be interested. If you're answering an ad, the job objective is obvious because you're applying for a specific position.

Your immediate-action objective is concerned with letting your reader know you'd either like to be contacted by him or her or that you'll initiate contact soon. Also, let him or her know if your goal is a phone appointment, an exploratory or office interview, or—if he or she is a network contact—merely obtaining some advice.

POWER TOOL #3: PREPARE YOUR JOB-SEARCH SOUND BITE

One way to construct a powerful cover letter is to be concise, and using a job-search sound bite is one way you can achieve that end. A sound bite can serve as the thirty- or sixty-second pitch you give over the phone when you make cold calls to prospective employers or network contacts. It can also be the answer to that dreaded wide-open interview question, "Tell me about yourself." And, with a little restructuring, it can be the profile or summary statement that appears at the top of your resume. So if you prepare a sound bite for your cover letter, you'll also have it ready to use in other parts of your job search.

Who You Are

Give the information about yourself that is the most impressive and relevant to the reader or the job you're seeking. This may include your educational status, school(s) attended, major or specialized program of study, and a brief reference to work experience (including volunteer work, internships, summer jobs, and paid employment).

What You Have to Offer

Include specific experience, specific skills, knowledge areas, and personal qualities.

POWER TOOL #4: DEVELOP YOUR REPERTOIRE

Now it's time to back up the claims you have made in your sound bite and expand on what you have to offer and what you're seeking. Your repertoire is a collection of specific examples that provide evidence of your skills, experience, and accomplishments; every job seeker should have a versatile repertoire to help him or her navigate each twist and turn of the job search.

To develop a repertoire, pick the key points your target reader is looking for in you: personal qualities, specific skills, field or industry knowledge and/or commitment, and anything else. Then think of concrete examples from your work, academic, or extracurricular experiences that demonstrate these points.

POWER TOOL #5: ASK YOURSELF, "WHY THEM?"

The final step is to define for yourself and for your reader why you've chosen to write this letter. Employers want to know you've chosen them for a reason, so flatter them a bit. Doing so also shows something about your character. If you've taken the time and initiative to gather information about a company, you're displaying all sorts of positive characteristics, from attention to detail to good time management, research skills, and intellectual curiosity. And you won't come across as someone who's totally desperate for a job because you will appear to be approaching your job search thoughtfully, rather than just writing to anybody and everybody.

Your reasons may refer to the company's products or services, corporate culture, philosophy, ethics, style, success rate, reputation, or growth and expansion.

Sample Cover Letter for an Exploratory Interview

Here's a cover letter requesting an exploratory, rather than informational, interview. The writer has already made her career decision and is ready to be considered as an actual applicant for a job. To keep the door open should no jobs be available, she asks simply for the opportunity to speak to the reader.

Eva Jackson

34 University Avenue, Apt. 4A

Columbus, OH 11111

(614) 555-5555

Ms. Margaret Ransom

Director, Special Education

The Sterling School

22 East State Street

Akron, OH 11111

March 18, 2007

Dear Ms. Ransom:

I am a senior at Ohio State University majoring in Speech Pathology, and I would like to speak with you about the special education curriculum and possible employment opportunities at the Sterling School. I have taken the liberty of enclosing my resume for your review.

Through a recent internship at the Columbus Speech and Hearing Center, I put my education to practical use in a professional environment and demonstrated my ability to work effectively with both children and adults. The experience also strengthened my commitment to a career in speech therapy with young children.

I plan to pursue a master's degree in speech pathology, most likely on a part-time basis, so that I can make a long-term commitment to a school. I read about the outstanding program at Sterling as recently profiled in Speech Therapy journal and would welcome the opportunity to be a part of such a progressive, professional team.

Whether or not you know of your staffing needs for the upcoming summer or fall terms, I would appreciate the opportunity to speak with you by phone or in person to discuss your department. I will be in Akron in early April, so I will call you soon to see if we may be able to meet. Thank you for your time and consideration.

Sincerely yours,

Eva Jackson

Eva Jackson

Part Four: The Interview—Theme Questions

There are really only a limited number of basic questions an interviewer can ask you—and an unlimited number of ways in which they can phrase these questions. Here's a list of some typical questions, grouped by category, that you can expect.

College Experience Questions

- Why did you choose your major?

- Which classes in college have you liked best/least? Why?

- Why did you select your college? How have you liked it?

- Has your college experience prepared you well for a career?

- Describe your most rewarding college experience.

- If you could do it over, how would you plan your education differently?

- To which teaching styles do you react best?

- Do you plan to go to graduate school?

- Are your grades a good indicator of your potential?

- What have you learned from your extracurricular activities?

- Tell me about one of your papers or your thesis.

Questions About You

- Tell me about yourself.

- How did you choose this career direction?

- What are your strengths and weaknesses?

- How would you describe yourself? How would a friend or your last boss describe you?

- What motivates you to work hard?

- What does success mean to you?

- Of what are you most proud?

- In which kind of environment do you work best?

- How do you handle pressure?

- What's important to you in a job?

- Do you have a geographical preference? Would you relocate? Travel?

- Describe a major obstacle you've encountered and how you dealt with it.

- What have you learned from mistakes you've made?

- What would you do if you won the lottery?

- What else should I know about you?

Questions About Your Experience

- Tell me about your jobs/internships.

- How has your background prepared you for this job?

- What work-related skills do you have?

- What was the toughest job challenge you faced, and how did you deal with it?

Questions About Your Goals

- What do you see yourself doing five years from now? Ten? Fifteen?

- What do you really want out of life?

- Why do you want to work for us?

- Why do you want to work in this industry?

Questions to See If You Know What You're Getting into

- What do you know about this organization?

- What do you think it takes to be successful in this organization?

- Why do you want to work for us?

- What do you look for in a job?

- How can you make a contribution to our organization?

- Where do you think this industry is headed?

SELL YOURSELF, GATHER INFO, AND EVALUATE A JOB BY ASKING GREAT QUESTIONS

Asking good questions throughout an interview helps you sell yourself. In this way, you demonstrate your interest in the organization and position as well as your professional curiosity. Also, you gather key information about the job and organization that will enable you to refine your sales pitch as you go. The more you understand the interviewer's priorities, the more you can tailor what you have to offer to the employer's needs. Finally, the input you get from the interviewer will help you evaluate the job and decide whether or not you want to pursue a potential job offer. Here are some productive questions you can ask.

About the Organization

- How does your organization differ from its competitors?

- What are your company's plans for future growth?

- Is your organization facing any problems?

- What do you like most about working here?

- How would you describe the corporate culture (or work environment) here?

- Does the organization tend to promote from within?

About the Job Itself

- Where does this position fit into the structure of the department and the organization as a whole?

- What are the future plans for this department?

- How much contact is there between departments or areas? (Ask only if it is a large organization.)

- To whom will I report?

- What percentage of my time will be spent in the various functions that this job involves?

- What is a typical career path for people in this position?

- Why is this position available?

- What personal qualities make someone successful in this job?

HOW THIS BOOK IS ORGANIZED

The jobs profiled in the following chapter are listed in alphabetical order according to the name of the company or organization they're with. To make it easier to find specific information on a given job, we use the same format for each profile. (If you are interested in learning more about jobs in a specific industry, please refer to the "Index by Industry" on p. 380.)

The name of the organization at the beginning of each profile is followed by the name of the position(s) or program(s) described. The body of each profile may have as many as ten fields of information. Not every field will appear for every job, as the information driving that field may not have been reported to us, or such information may not be applicable to a particular job. Some companies and nonprofits, for example, do not have data on how many entry-level employees are still with the company after three, five, and ten years simply because they haven't been operating for that long. In a profile that has complete information, however, you can expect to see the following:

THE BIG PICTURE

This is a short description of what the company or nonprofit organization does, and, if appropriate, how entry-level employees fit into the picture.

STATS

This section provides a snapshot of the facts that most job seekers want to know right away: where the job is located; how many applications are received each year and the number of available job openings; the titles of the available positions and the average number of hours worked each week by the people holding these positions; the percentage of entry-level hires who are still with the company after three, five, and ten years; the average starting salaries; the medical and additional benefits offered; and the contact information for those interested in applying for a job or seeking additional information.

GETTING HIRED

Some organizations recruit on college campuses and other organizations don't. Some only recruit new hires from select colleges with certain undergraduate majors, while others are looking for people with specific internship or cooperative work experience. Some will only want to interview you over the phone and others will want to fly you to their headquarters for a battery of interviews (they may even ask you to take a test when you get there). This is the admissions process for the organization and, as with colleges and graduate schools, it's different for every place. Compiled using information provided by employees and the organizations themselves, this section tells what you need to know about a company or nonprofit when you're trying to land the job.

MONEY AND PERKS

Let's face it, remuneration is at the top of almost every worker's mind, young and old. Some jobs offer low salaries, while others offer low salaries with the possibility of making much more in overtime hours. Jobs in finance and a few other industries often offer good salaries and the possibility of large bonuses, but these jobs also usually require employees to put in very long hours. Perks are the things that improve the quality of life, or at least make life a little easier, at no cost (or a reduced cost) for employees. Some jobs offer laundry lists of perks, while other jobs offer none. Some of the most popular perks include 401(k) or similar retirement savings plans, paid time off, and flexible spending accounts (in which you get to use pre-tax dollars to pay for things like transportation and uncovered medical expenses). Additional perks may include gym memberships, tuition reimbursements, and matching donations to charitable causes.

The Ropes

No matter where you go to work, you will receive training. It can be an hour or two spent with a human resources representative talking about benefits and company policies or weeks of off-site classes on the different software technologies in which you will have to become an expert. In this section, we explain the structure and length of the training you can expect to receive before you actually start doing real work.

Day in the Life

Once properly trained, employees are expected to work. Here, mostly in their own words, is what first jobbers do all day.

Peers

What are the people in the position or program like? Are they similar to you in age and background? Do entry-level workers form close friendships with one another, or are they pretty much on their own because the employees with whom they spend most of their time are older? Is there a big after-hours social scene, or do people keep to themselves? Does the company do anything—such as sponsor corporate sports teams—to encourage fraternizing? This is where you'll find answers to all of these questions.

Moving on

When people have drawn all they can from a given entry-level position, what do they do next? Do they head to graduate school, get promoted into positions of greater responsibility within the organization, leave for more lucrative or better positions within the same industry, or launch new careers in completely different lines of work? Many people don't think about what comes after an entry-level job, but they should. This section tries to answer these questions and get you thinking about what your long-term plans may include.

Attrition

We asked employers how many entry-level employees leave their organizations within a year of being hired. In some cases, we're able to report actual percentages; in most cases, we provide an explanation of why people depart from their jobs so early in their tenure.

Best and Worst

We asked employers to tell us who their best and worst entry-level employees were. Some responded with general descriptions of what makes a good or bad employee, while others gave us specific cases.

THE BEST ENTRY-LEVEL JOBS

ABBOTT
PROFESSIONAL DEVELOPMENT PROGRAM

"The job is constantly changing, and we are constantly being challenged and pulled to grow in arenas that make us well-rounded and skilled in several job sets around the company."

The Big Picture

A global health care company, Abbott is "devoted to the discovery, development, manufacturing, and marketing of pharmaceuticals, nutritionals, and medical products, including devices and diagnostics." Abbott offers a wide assortment of entry-level jobs, including positions in science, information technology, finance/accounting, engineering, and sales/marketing. Many employees enter the company through its rotational Professional Development Program (PDP); this allows them to gain valuable industry experience in a number of areas before deciding which one best suits their interests and talents.

LOCATION(S) WHERE ENTRY-LEVEL EMPLOYEES WORK

"Entry-level employees work at Abbott's corporate headquarters in Lake County, Illinois and at most of Abbott's domestic and international sites."

AVERAGE NUMBER OF APPLICATIONS EACH YEAR

About 250,000 resumes are received each year. There is no specific figure available for entry-level positions.

AVERAGE NUMBER HIRED PER YEAR OVER THE LAST TEN YEARS

"More than 5,000 new hires have come on board directly out of college over the last ten years."

ENTRY-LEVEL POSITION(S) AVAILABLE

"They can be grouped into functional areas, including science, engineering, sales/marketing, manufacturing/operations, quality, finance, information technology, and corporate administration (i.e., groups like human resources, public affairs, and purchasing). Specialized opportunities in environmental health and purchasing also exist."

AVERAGE HOURS WORKED PER WEEK

"Employees work around 40 to 50 hours per week."

AVERAGE STARTING SALARY

"It is hard to generalize. We have so many hires per year. Abbott is known to have a competitive salary within the top quartile of the industry for base pay and benefits packages. The average base pay for the Professional Development Program is determined by approximating the median in the external market, with total cash compensation exceeding this amount when the company performs well."

BENEFITS OFFERED

"Every employee starts with three weeks [of] paid vacation, plus medical, dental, and disability insurance; [and] pension plan, 401(k) plan, and profit sharing."

CONTACT INFORMATION

Visit the career center at www.abbott.com.

Getting Hired

The gateway into entry-level jobs at Abbott is through their "five-star, nationally-ranked Internship Program" in which they "convert high-performing interns who are graduating within the next twelve months into entry-level hires." The company also has a robust University Relations strategy and presence on campus; it targets top schools and top talent for all functions throughout the year. "[Abbott] also [has] alumni networks working for [them]; for example, the University of Illinois [at Urbana-Champaign] produces forty entry-level hires per year, many of them referred by the 1,100 alumni working at Abbott." One entry-level employee says, "[Interviews are] mostly behavioral based, and the tone is very relaxed. I was able to ask a lot of questions about the interviewers' career paths and current jobs at Abbott." In all the interview sessions, "Abbott's core competencies (adaptability, initiative, innovation, integrity, and teamwork) were stressed, and questions were geared toward getting candidates [who] showed aptitude in those areas."

Money and Perks

Program participants note that "entry-level salaries are competitive" within the industry and that "Abbott is a meritocracy. High-performing people get ahead quickly here," earning solid raises and development opportunities to advance their careers in the process. Employees enjoy "a ton of special perks," including "flexible work scheduling, telecommuting, 100 percent tuition reimbursement, a relocation package, a sports and activities program [that has] 8,000 employees in leagues and clubs [who] meet outside the workplace, a mentoring program, an employee assistance program, and the Clara Abbott Foundation (scholarship program)."

The Ropes

The specific training Abbott's entry-level employees receive is relevant to their positions. One PDP participant in information technology recalls, "I started with our diagnostics division, which has a dedicated training coordinator for each department. Through her, I was able to complete the training requirements (document reviews, computer-based training, and classroom training)." Some program participants start with a two-day orientation: "The first day is the regular new employee orientation that all new employees go through, where you learn about benefits, payroll, etc. The second day focuses solely on the on-boarding process of your specific Professional Development Program, giving information on people involved with the program, [the company's] expectations, future training [opportunities], important phone numbers, and [relevant] websites." After that, "most of the training you receive is hands-on from members of your department—learning how basic business functions there. Other training consists of soft-skill training through Abbott Training Services." Many new hires are "assigned a mentor, whom [they] regularly meet with to discuss Abbott's business model and the general business of business. This is one of the program's biggest strengths and one of the best learning experiences at Abbott." Abbott also encourages diversity and inclusion through formal employee networks so that employees are able to grow in areas of personal and professional development and build relationships by creating an internal network.

Day in the Life

A company representative says, "All of our new hires jump into meaningful work assignments. Responsibilities are directly related to the success of business. New hires meet periodically with their management team to make sure [they] are properly trained and [are] delivering results. Several areas have structured development programs—rotating assignments that are six to twelve months in duration." Many of our respondents participated in these rotations, and all of them enjoyed the experience. One writes, "I liked the rotational aspect of [my program]. It's great for college graduates who are not set on what they want their career paths to be because it gives them the opportunity to experience several different options within their field[s] while [still] being a part of the company." Another person adds, "As a member of the Professional Development Program, the job is constantly changing, and we are constantly being challenged and pulled to grow in arenas that make us well-rounded and skilled in several job sets around the company." A third employee adds, "I learned more in each of my six month rotations from my bosses than I could have learned in two years' worth of classes at college."

Peers

Because Abbott's Professional Development Programs are mostly geared toward recent college graduates, there is "a lot of contact with first jobbers at Abbott." One recent hire in the finance department writes, "Because of my current assignment, I have three other first jobbers around me who are in their first rotation as well. There are often a lot of invitations to after-hours events, which allow us to socialize and get to know [one another] better." First jobbers also see one another at "monthly staff meetings, bimonthly luncheons, [and] quarterly social events." As mentioned above, Abbott actively encourages employees to participate in intracompany sports and networking groups to build a sense of community throughout the company.

Moving on

Those who leave Abbott are relatively few in number. "Over 80 percent will stay long-term," says one company representative. People who do leave often "go back to school for further education. [They] come to Abbott with expectations of working for a few years, then getting their [graduate or professional] degree. For example, I had two young human resources professionals [whom] I mentored, and both decided to go to law school. Both are now halfway through law degrees. Both want to return to Abbott. That is desirable turnover that we encourage, as we believe in investing in our employees with the intent of future return on investment."

Best and Worst

A company spokesperson describes one of the PDP participants this way: "He joined the company about twenty-five years ago as an entry-level employee and second-generation Abbott employee. His father worked at Abbott. He performed well and was promoted through many functional roles. Today, he is president of one of Abbott's global divisions. That's not a unique story. Our Professional Development Programs have a great track record for producing corporate officers."

ABC News
Desk Assistant

"Every day you are witness to and involved in the incredible process of making the news. It is very gratifying to know that you contributed in some way to a product that millions of people see."

The Big Picture

To get to the top of any skyscraper, you have to enter through the ground floor. In network news, the job of desk assistant is the ground floor; it's where everyone who wants a career in broadcast journalism begins. It's a low-paying, extremely demanding, and sometimes tedious job, but if your dream is to make it in the news biz, well, this is the way to go. The good news is that if you impress your bosses, you will eventually be promoted to a better position.

LOCATION(S) WHERE ENTRY-LEVEL EMPLOYEES WORK

The news organization has major office hubs in Los Angeles, California; New York, New York (most of the jobs are available in New York City); and Washington, DC.

AVERAGE NUMBER OF APPLICATIONS EACH YEAR

ABC News receives 700–1,000 applications per year.

AVERAGE NUMBER HIRED PER YEAR OVER THE LAST TEN YEARS

ABC News has hired 150–200 people per year over the last ten years.

ENTRY-LEVEL POSITION(S) AVAILABLE

Entry-level hires work as desk assistants.

AVERAGE HOURS WORKED PER WEEK

Employees work from 50 to 60 hours per week.

PERCENTAGE OF ENTRY-LEVEL HIRES STILL WITH COMPANY AFTER THREE, FIVE, AND TEN YEARS

Fifty percent, 40 percent, and 30 percent, respectively.

AVERAGE STARTING SALARY

Entry-level hires earn $26,000 base pay, plus overtime.

BENEFITS OFFERED

The company provides medical, dental, life, and disability insurance.

CONTACT INFORMATION

Nissa W. Booker
ABC News Recruitment Coordinator
47 West 66th Street, 6th Floor
New York, NY 10023

Getting Hired

The job of desk assistant is among the most competitive low-paying positions to obtain, so finding some way to distinguish yourself from the pack is crucial. One desk assistant writes, "Once I knew that I wanted to pursue a network job, getting one was quite the challenge. Every desk assistant has become one through a different channel and brings with them different experiences. I believe what got me an interview was that I had a good producer resume tape that showed I had a decent amount of experience writing and editing. Plus, my resume demonstrated my other journalism experiences through internships, summer jobs, etc. I do believe, however, that you must bring something different to the position other than journalism skills. I was a Spanish and journalism double major and had completed a semester abroad. I think traveling and knowing another language helped me in that I could bring a wide variety of knowledge and passion for [a] subject other than broadcasting to ABC." A passion for the news is also crucial, of course. ABC is on constant lookout for good candidates, "even when there are no positions available." Network representatives tell us that "resumes are screened and interviews are conducted on a regular basis. If certain qualifications are met after an initial review of the resume, the candidate is invited to set up an exploratory interview. Resumes of interest are kept on file for one year. Resumes from the strongest candidates are flagged and reviewed again when a position becomes available. A hire is then made from that select group." ABC also holds "several job fairs" that "specific[ally] focus on minority recruitment."

Money and Perks

Desk assistants earn a pretty poor salary, especially considering the big-city location of the jobs. The best desk assistants, however, can earn much more (yet, still at a poor hourly rate), since they "make [a great deal] of their money in overtime earnings, which are largely dependant upon how good they are at the job. The best desk assistants are asked to work more and therefore make more money." Regardless of the pay, all desk assistants are happy to have the job because "in journalism the supply [of qualified candidates] is much greater than the demand [for such candidates]." The biggest perk, according to one desk assistant, "is that every day you are witness to and involved in the incredible process of making the news. It is very gratifying to know that you contributed in some way to a product that millions of people see. This is only amplified when major news breaks. I was a desk assistant during Election 2000, and even though the work wasn't that challenging, I had a front row seat to how this historic event was reported to the public. You are also exposed to a talented array of news professionals and news stars. Simply observing them is an education."

The Ropes

At ABC, orientation is a quick review of "benefits, company policies, company history, etc. It lasts only a few hours with a human resources representative." After that, work begins; you train as you work. One desk assistant explains, "I was trained by my peers on the job. Outside of the heavy packet of information we were expected to study, there was no formal training process." ABC News representatives explain why: "There is no way to prepare an individual for the chaos of covering a breaking news story, so we immediately throw them into an environment [that] helps them to build a level of confidence that will carry them through the chaos."

Day in the Life

Desk assistants' duties depend on their assignments. "If they are assigned to a show like *World News Now* or *World News Tonight*, they are responsible for supporting the show so that it runs smoothly. This means organizing scripts, routing calls appropriately, and collecting editorial information. If a desk assistant works on the assignment desk, the responsibilities include helping to coordinate news coverage, obtaining and retaining very specific editorial information about several important stories, and knowing how stories are staffed." One assignment desk assistant writes, "I had to learn where everyone was at all times and had to be up to speed on all news, especially breaking news, and who from our team was covering what stories. I worked with an assignment editor. Some nights it was so busy, I couldn't get up to go to the bathroom. The phone would be ringing off the hook, and you just have to manage. The night of the blackout [in New York] was crazy but incredibly fun 'cuz I love this stuff!" All of the desk assistants we spoke with agreed that they needed to take on jobs beyond their own to get ahead; one assistant explains, "I took a lot of initiative, and I pitched story ideas that aired, and I got to go on shoots (this is rare). You need to be aggressive or else you could get stuck. Most importantly people have to like you and have confidence in you. Network! If you don't network, you won't move. Talk to anyone who will talk to you, [and] make sure you have mentors."

Peers

Desk assistants get to see a lot of one another at work. "We do not hang out that much after work, since we're here on average sixty hours a week together." One desk assistant writes that because they spend so much time together, "there is a lot of camaraderie among the desk assistants. During the day, we'll discuss the various ABC shows as well as what's happening in our personal lives. I also think we offer a support network for one another since we all have our days of struggling as desk assistants and the stress of worrying about moving up the ABC ladder." Desk assistants like one another, in part, because they are so much alike. One desk assistant interviewed notes that "ABC News—maybe news in general—attracts smart, interesting people with drive and talent. It generally takes a certain type of personality to withstand the [pressure-filled] environment, so while people have diverse interests, they generally share a sense of adventure, humor, and curiosity. The desk assistants I worked with all went to good schools and were your typical overachievers."

Moving on

According to company representatives, "The majority of the people who leave the desk assistant position are promoted to the next level job at ABC News. Some people who leave the company leave to go back to school or for other jobs in the industry." You should be aware that promotions don't always happen quickly. In fact, "promotions among desk assistants typically occur at a glacial pace. There is not a lot of movement among production staff; they don't leave, and they aren't promoted regularly, so people can be desk assistants for some time, maybe a year to two years. The unhappy people were those who had a sense of hopelessness that they would never move on to have greater responsibilities and do more interesting work."

Attrition

"Less than 5 percent" of the desk assistants quit within a year of taking the job; "everyone stays at least a year with the hope [of being] promoted to the next-level job." Employees who leave, as well as many who stay, "complain about working too many hours and not really doing tasks that represent their true capabilities." Ultimately, though, "people know being a desk assistant in New York is a golden opportunity [that] can lead to so much."

Best and Worst

Pick your favorite broadcaster as your own personal "best-ever" desk assistant from ABC's news staff; one first jobber explains, "Everyone has been a desk assistant at one point. All executive producers and vice presidents of news are former desk assistants."

ACCENTURE
CONSULTING ANALYST

"You won't be on your own here, as "many times [older alumni] also make a special effort to ensure that they are progressing. Accenture offers both informal and formal mentoring programs and encourages participation on all levels."

The Big Picture

Consulting analysts are the cavalry of the business world. They save the day by solving problems that businesses can't solve on their own. Accenture is well-known for its consulting work in IT services and technology; with $11.8 billion in annual revenues, there are few areas in the business world in which Accenture isn't a major player.

LOCATION(S) WHERE ENTRY-LEVEL EMPLOYEES WORK

Accenture has locations across the United States.

ENTRY-LEVEL POSITION(S) AVAILABLE

Accenture hires entry-level employees mostly for consulting analyst positions; candidates are chosen according to the company's skill and capability needs, as demanded by individual markets.

AVERAGE HOURS WORKED PER WEEK

Employees generally work more than 40 hours per week, but this varies based on factors such as level and position.

BENEFITS OFFERED

"Accenture offers total rewards packages that consist of professional growth opportunities, competitive compensation, and a broad and flexible range of benefits that include medical, dental, disability, and life insurance; paid holidays; and paid time off. In addition, Accenture provides a range of services to employees that can include financial planning, apartment listings, consumer resources, and many others."

CONTACT INFORMATION

For more details, visit Accenture on the Web at http://campusconnection.accenture.com.

Getting Hired

Candidate screening at Accenture is a four-step process. First, the company begins with a review of resumes and qualifications. Selected individuals may then be scheduled to begin the interviewing process, which consists of three steps. The first round—a twenty- to thirty-minute interview—offers a chance for those who wish to work at Accenture to present their resume in person. "This initial conversation allows us to get to know [one another], understand objectives, and evaluate qualifications. The second round—a forty-five-minute interview—gives the interviewee a chance to share experiences [in] greater detail. This interview will hone in on candidates' educational and personal experiences as they would relate to their potential performance at Accenture. Recruiters may ask for specific examples of situations encountered and how they have been handled. The final step in the process is an office visit. During the office visit, analysts, consultants, and executives further assess qualifications. There will also be presentations to explain further some of the nuts and bolts of working at Accenture." Company officials tell us that "individuals who excel during the interview process are those who are well prepared and demonstrate that they have done research on the company and the position. Many times these candidates have attended an event or talked to company representatives to gain a better understanding of the company and position."

Money and Perks

Accenture offers "competitive compensation"; representatives did not provide further details, but rest assured the pay is pretty good by first job standards. Perks include "many personal and professional development opportunities," a new laptop for business use, personal use of airline miles accrued during business travel, discounts from a variety of vendors, and "a transit transportation program that allows Accenture employees to pay for transportation using pre-tax dollars."

The Ropes

Accenture's orientation program occurs in stages. The first, which lasts several weeks, is called the new employee orientation and the core analyst local course. Once they complete the course, analysts head to core analyst school at the center in St. Charles, Illinois. One analyst describes the experience: "My first few weeks comprised local training with my start group and central training with others from around the world. The local training gave me the opportunity to create instantly a network with my start group and others I met in the office. It also provided an introduction to skills that were very valuable at central training in St. Charles. It was hard work but also fun. The training simulated a real project. It really provided background on what the Accenture culture is like—work hard as a team and play hard as a team." Continuing training is a fact of life for all Accenture employees, regardless of their seniority; "as part of continuous training throughout a career at Accenture, training can be completed either in person or virtually."

Day in the Life

Consulting analysts meet with the businesses they advise, explore the parameters of the problem they are hired to address, and begin solving that problem. One analyst writes, "a typical day at my current project includes meeting with my team leader to ensure all tasks are being addressed, completing those tasks, and raising any issues found along the way. Currently, we are still in the concept phase. The workload will pick up significantly within the next couple of months as we head into the design and implementation phases." The firm adds that "responsibilities can vary across client engagements. On any given day, an analyst may [need to] leverage skills that include building industry skills; developing technology-based solutions; analyzing, designing, and implementing business process improvements; defining user requirements; and specializing in business process design, business validation concepts, testing and quality assurance, system building concepts, programming, and development [skills]." You won't be on your own here, as "many times [older alumni] also make a special effort to ensure that they are progressing. Accenture offers both informal and formal mentoring programs and encourages participation on all levels."

Peers

New consulting analysts at Accenture are "constantly impressed by the people here. Coworkers are intelligent, amiable, helpful, and very committed to the quality of their work. People are always willing to help [one another] out or answer questions. There is a feeling of camaraderie that always develops when working on a team project, and those friendships extend beyond the workplace." One newbie reports, "The people are fantastically motivated and accept nothing but the highest level of work ethic and achievement. That said, most of the employees are very laid-back and down-to-earth, [which creates] a relaxed but productive work environment." Employees also praise the diversity of their coworkers; one employee reports, "When I attended new analyst training in St. Charles, I was astonished by the diversity of backgrounds, cultures, and nationalities represented by Accenture employees. The company is truly a global one."

Moving on

Consulting analysts make tons of contacts in the business world; thus, it is not surprising that some employees leave the firm to join one of Accenture's clients. Others leave to return to school. Representatives note that "Accenture has a well-established alumni program to [stay up-to-date] with the exciting opportunities that many of our alumni pursue."

Attrition

"Globally, our attrition rate (company wide) is below the industry average."

ADMISSION POSSIBLE
VARIOUS POSITIONS

ADMISSION POSSIBLE

"We were the ones students called all the time at any hour of the night, the ones they looked up to, and the ones they ultimately thanked when they got into college. We were the ones who were celebrated when students did well."

The Big Picture

Admission Possible is a respected Minnesota nonprofit that guides low-income high school juniors and seniors through the college admissions and financial aid processes. An independent study found that 98 percent of students who completed the Admission Possible program were admitted to college and that more than 80 percent remain enrolled (a far larger percentage than the national average). Most new hires come in through the U.S. government's AmeriCorps and VISTA programs (sometimes called the "domestic Peace Corps"). Terms of service are ten or twelve months, depending on the position.

LOCATION(S) WHERE ENTRY-LEVEL EMPLOYEES WORK

All employees work in St. Paul, Minneapolis or Robbinsdale, Minnesota. Currently, 38 AmeriCorps members are placed in high schools throughout the Twin Cities, and 8 operate out of the St. Paul office. New hires may request particular placements but are not assigned until after accepting the job.

AVERAGE NUMBER OF APPLICATIONS EACH YEAR

"Admission Possible receives about 150 applications each year."

AVERAGE NUMBER HIRED PER YEAR OVER THE LAST TEN YEARS

Admission Possible hires about 46 full-timers per year.

ENTRY-LEVEL POSITIONS AVAILABLE

This year, 46 entry-level AmeriCorps members have been distributed as college-prep coaches, partnering with other local college access programs, or focusing on Alumni Programming. Other AmeriCorps members tailor student workshops and volunteer activities and coordinate events. The organization adds, "Additionally, about half of our 11-person leadership team holds entry-level positions, all of which are full-time, permanent, and salaried. . . . We will also receive enough funding to fill 46 entry-level positions in each of the next two years in order to serve 1,300 students by 2008–2009."

Getting Hired

Admission Possible "recruit[s] nationally across college campuses" and has a particularly strong relationship with Macalester College and Carleton College, both located in Minnesota, although it seeks students from all colleges and universities. Positions are filled in the spring for the following fall. "To apply, applicants must submit the following materials: cover letter, resume, Admission Possible application (found on our website, AdmissionPossible.org), and an unofficial undergraduate transcript. Once all application materials are reviewed, applicants are invited to a half-day interview . . . which includes a group interview and mock-teaching session. All interviews occur at our main headquarters; however, applicants who are unable to travel from further distances are able to interview by phone and submit a teaching video." The group interview gets high marks: One hire reports, "While we were waiting to be interviewed, there were current coaches to chat [with], get to know, . . . and answer any questions we had about the job." Interviewers look for "people who are confident and provide thoughtful answers that are in line with the mission of our organization. [Good candidates] work well in the group interview situation, making their voice[s] heard without dominating the group or appearing to be too pushy." According to the organization, the ideal new hire has "an interest in working with high school youth, a 'whatever it takes' attitude," and an eagerness to create social change. In addition, "people who prefer a standard nine-to-five workday probably will not be a good fit for our organization, as the demands of students and the requirements of our program require a more flexible approach to scheduling!"

Money and Perks

Successful new hires consider living their ideals to be a major perk. "I am extremely into social justice . . . the fact that there is an inequality in the American educational system is wrong," explains an ex-coach. "Is changing the world considered a fringe benefit?" asks another, echoing a comment we hear often among young teachers. Equally rewarding is a sense that one is taking on serious responsibility and accomplishing something recognizably important. "We were there in the trenches every single day. We were the ones students called all the time at any hour of the night, the ones they looked up to, and the ones they ultimately thanked when they got into college. We were the ones who were celebrated when students did well." All staffers we spoke with considered themselves very important to the organization. "I felt like the backbone of the organization," says one former coach; another says, "The best thing about the job is that you really become the expert on your school and feel a really strong sense of ownership over your school. No one, not even the leadership team of the organization, knows your school as well as you do." The AmeriCorps/VISTA pay may seem grim, but for new hires who pay between $350 and $450 a month in rent and use the food stamps for which they are eligible, living on the stipend is "definitely doable." Some AmeriCorps members report small holiday bonuses, but, officially, AmeriCorps and VISTA staffers are "not eligible for raises . . . or monetary bonuses," although "leadership team members are eligible for raises on a case-by-case basis."

The Ropes

"Orientation for AmeriCorps and VISTA members involves two full weeks of programming and training" with weekly additional follow-up throughout the year. Session topics "range from cultural competence to office skills, financial aid basics to professionalism in the work place, and team-building to essay-editing skills." They "are planned around the understanding that, for most of our staff, this is their first job experience after completing college." Orientation takes place "in various community spaces and [on various] campuses, including an overnight all-staff retreat at a beautiful lakeside retreat center outside of the metro area." New hires learn from the experts. "We had a teaching workshop with a teacher at the Blake School, a private school in Minneapolis. We went to the Hmong Cultural Center to learn about Hmong history and traditions. We had a woman from the state department of education come talk to us about how to fill out the FAFSA."

Day in the Life

The typical AmeriCorps member works at a school four days a week and spends Friday in the office, attending meetings and prepping for the coming week. "Because of the very demanding nature of the job, most coaches would arrive at school anytime between 7:00 and 10:00 A.M. and leave anytime from 7:00 to 9:00 P.M." However, "we were never told that we had to arrive at an official time and leave at an official time." One staffer describes a common routine: "Most of the school days were filled with students dropping by for various needs . . . I would have to plan the after-school session for the day, which might involve creating and photocopying handouts, creating individual action plans for each student, doing online research for various opportunities for students." She continues, "I spent a lot of time on the phone with various colleges, tracking applications, asking about admission policies, talking to the counselors about specific student situations . . . . There were also weekend commitments [that included] college visits, practice ACT [tests], and volunteer activities." As hectic as the week can be, Friday can be just as stressful, albeit for different reasons. "Every week at the Friday morning meeting there is a list of everyone's statistics on [topics including] ACT score improvement, number of colleges applied to/accepted at, [and] amount of scholarship money won. Although no one was ever singled out or made to feel bad about their numbers, and everyone understood that sometimes you just have a bad student, it still feels lousy to have low numbers in something."

Peers

A longtime staffer calls the organization "very youthful [and] open-minded." First jobbers are "ambitious and successful, [qualities they] turn toward their work with their students." New hires "become very close." "There were times at Friday meetings," says an ex-staffer, "when I would think, I am sitting in a room with twenty-five of the smartest people I have ever met." We're told that "it is more common than not that [colleagues] become best friends, travel together, and even find life partners!"

Moving on

After a one- or two-year term of service, AmeriCorps members go on in large numbers to graduate and professional schools [including] "Harvard, University of California—Berkeley, Stanford, and many other top graduate programs across the country." Others move on to nonprofits or "undergraduate admissions or college access programs." A few are promoted to outreach, public relations, or communications positions within the company. One coach turned grad student calls the day that her term concluded "one of the saddest days of my life."

Attrition

"Though our hiring structure is such that entry-level employees are contracted for a term of service that consists of a ten- or twelve-month agreement . . . nearly one-third of our recent college graduates do extend their initial commitment" for at least an additional year. "No full-time entry-level person has ever voluntarily left our organization before completing their term of service."

Best and Worst

"The most successful Admission Possible entry-level employee was an AmeriCorps member who . . . was energetic, self-motivated, and ready to take on an opportunity that she knew would be difficult but incredibly rewarding. She was a relentless advocate for her students [and] a strong leader among her peers, leading not only by the example of her high-quality work, but also by her willingness to step up to additional responsibilities . . . . [S]he was able to keep 'the big picture' vision of our organization, while not losing sight of the details and deadlines of her day-to-day work." In contrast, one employee "was looking for a nine-to-five position that wouldn't require any additional thought after she left work" and "disagreed with the organization's emphasis on results." She was terminated.

ADOBE
VARIOUS POSITIONS

"It's always been extremely busy and I have always had a great deal of responsibility," assures an employee. But, beams a newbie, "if you're up for the challenge, you can really excel—and fast!"

The Big Picture

Easily one of the most recognizable names in computer software, Adobe gives budding developers and engineers the chance to work in an environment renowned for its creativity and out-of-the-box thinking. One recent hire says that prior to taking the job she had "read articles about how it was a great company to work for," and Adobe hasn't disappointed. "Never bored," says a rookie. Another adds, "There's almost always something going on." There's also a sense of community at Adobe, which supplies a support network for young employees as they get used to high-intensity workloads. A developer admits to being overwhelmed on several occasions, but raves, "My team has been awesome in both being patient with me, as well as positive and helping me learn."

LOCATIONS WHERE ENTRY-LEVEL EMPLOYEES WORK

Adobe is headquartered in San Jose, California, where many entry-levelers start. Other locations include San Francisco, California; Newton, Massachusetts; Seattle, Washington; and Ottawa, Ontario (Canada).

AVERAGE NUMBER OF APPLICATIONS EACH YEAR

Adobe's University Recruitment Program receives approximately 875 applications annually.

AVERAGE NUMBER HIRED PER YEAR OVER THE LAST TEN YEARS

The University Recruitment Program brings in approximately 30 new employees each year.

ENTRY-LEVEL POSITIONS AVAILABLE

First-time employees work as software development engineers, software quality engineers, and technical staff members. Occasionally, there are openings in other areas.

AVERAGE HOURS WORKED PER WEEK

New hires put in between 40 and 50 hours each week.

AVERAGE STARTING SALARY

Though Adobe does not report a starting salary range, the new hires we spoke with began at annual salaries ranging from $50,000 to $75,000.

Getting Hired

When Adobe decides to bring in new employees, it not only scouts for those who are technically smart in their discipline, but those who are self-starters—i.e., those individuals who don't look to be given the steps to complete a project, but can ask the right questions to get the project done. The company also seeks candidates with a passion for Adobe products. To find such candidates, Adobe visits a core group of targeted universities each year, attending career fairs, information sessions, and conducting on-campus interviews. Interested applicants from other universities should use Adobe's website to apply. The company's hiring process includes an initial screening by an individual manager or small panel to determine company fit. Candidates who make it past this first stage will begin the interview process. As one recent hire says, "Be prepared for many interviews. If they like you enough, they'll even fly you out so that the recruiter, hiring manager, and each of the hiring manager's teammates can speak with you face to face. Adobe loves to discuss, share ideas, and have many meetings/interviews before they decide, resulting in a thorough but lengthy process." Another newbie, who experienced both telephone and on-site interviews before landing the job, says that in one day he had five half-hour, face-to-face interviews in a row. Interviewers tend to focus on a candidate's real-world experience as opposed to academic accolades. (Take note, potential applicants: Internships are worth gold in this arena.) One question that Adobe asks almost all interviewees—a question that many candidates don't have a solid answer for—is, "why do you want to work for Adobe?" Because there aren't too many entry-level positions available, a first-year employee urges candidates "to really go after it. If you can find a contact and use a name to pass your resume along, do it."

Money and Perks

Initial paychecks vary, but most Adobe newcomers enjoy salaries ranging from $50,000 to $75,000. While this is good scratch for a first-jobber, the cost of living in a place like San Francisco is certainly a financial force to be reckoned with. Pay raises depend on regular performance reviews. Informally, these reviews occur on a quarterly basis. A formal performance and salary review occurs annually. Employees have a hard time settling on the best fringe benefit at Adobe. "Private offices for all employees," says one. An engineer at the San Jose headquarters adds, "To me, the best benefit was, without a doubt, the on-site gym. I would arrive at Adobe around 7:00 A.M., work out for an hour, shower and change, and be at my office at 8:30. No sweat." (Employees at other locations are given free or subsidized access to off-site fitness centers.)

The Ropes

According to the Adobe brass, the company takes "extraordinary steps to ensure that every new employee feels welcome and receives the tools and information they need to be immediately comfortable, productive, and successful. During their first day on the job, new employees learn about Adobe's history, vision, values, culture, business, and future, as well as their own benefits, equity compensation, and productivity tools." As far as job-specific training is concerned, it varies depending on the position. Some new hires spend a week or so working part-time, in order to learn the ropes. Others are assigned a mentor within their department. Across the board, Adobe's young employees report a very supportive working environment. One fresh hire explains, "[I] was encouraged to ask everyone as many questions as I wanted. All team members were very open and very encouraging. In a sense, they all trained me." And training is an ongoing process. "There is Learning and Development training that you can sign up for year round," says an employee. "Just ask your manager if you can miss work on a specific day to take the class, and that's it! Adobe encourages these classes, so there is never a problem. I probably take five to ten days a year to take various classes."

Day in the Life

Just because the position is entry-level doesn't mean it's unimportant. One technical staff member who's been with Adobe for less than two years says, "Being the newest and youngest on the team, I expected my tasks to be the grunt work. . . . But for the most part I didn't do grunt work, and could see how my work directly affected the product and business decisions made by the team's managers. In fact, the first time I realized that, it felt a bit scary to know that business decisions were sometimes based entirely on input or results I provided." While each day can involve a significant degree of independent work—such as testing programs or developing content—employees are often engaged in cooperative endeavors. Many young workers are assigned to a team that meets on a regular basis, while others collaborate closely (via telephone, e-mail, and IM) with colleagues at other Adobe sites. "It's always been extremely busy and I have always had a great deal of responsibility," assures an employee. So yes, hard work and high expectations come with the territory. But, beams a newbie, "if you're up for the challenge, you can really excel—and fast!"

Peers

"I know that practically every company says 'we hire the top people,' but, in the case of my team, they were all top people," boasts an employee. Young workers use words like "smart," "knowledgeable," "easygoing," and "friendly" to describe their colleagues at Adobe. As far as company-arranged opportunities to meet other new employees go, there are new-grad, MBA, and intern luncheons; product showcases; and other related events that happen throughout the year. However, a newcomer asserts, "If I run into a new hire or MBA it is usually by chance rather than having met them at an organized new-grad event." Outside of work, the young employees who've crossed paths find plenty of ways to socialize, such as attending a beer bash every Friday after work.

Moving on

Given the opportunity to brand their career with a two-billion-dollar technology leader, Adobe employees have many choices if they choose to leave. Some seek to diversify their resume by working with another company in the field; some go to grad school.

Attrition

Since 2000, according to company figures, around 98 percent of all recent college graduates working at Adobe have remained with the company for at least twelve months. That said, after a few years some employees begin to think about lateral or upward movement within the industry. The biggest gripes against Adobe are that it's "too bureaucratic (we have a lot of meetings and, as we grow, we become less and less nimble)" and "too corporate." Some complain that it takes too long to move up, while others praise Adobe for its potential for internal upward mobility. The latter viewpoint leads one recent hire to exclaim, "I hope to stay with Adobe for as long as they'll have me."

ÁEGIS LIVING
VARIOUS POSITIONS

Áegis Living
People live here.

"It's a really great place to be. It's challenging, busy, friendly, caring, and funny, and sometimes [it is] better to be at work than at home!

The Big Picture

Named America's third-fastest growing private company by Inc. magazine in 2003, Áegis Living is a business that will likely be creating many new jobs for years to come. If you're interested in working for Áegis, that's especially good news; employee satisfaction levels there result in a turnover rate that's among the lowest in the assisted-living industry.

LOCATION(S) WHERE ENTRY-LEVEL EMPLOYEES WORK

Corporate headquarters are located in Redmond, Washington; regional offices are located throughout Washington, Nevada, and California.

CONTACT INFORMATION

Visit the website at www.Áegisal.com/careers/php.

Getting Hired

Áegis advertises job openings on its website and on Monster.com. Most applicants undergo multiple interviews before the company decides to hire them. One support staffer explains, "The office manager, director of recruiting and retention, chief marketing officer, and accounting manager all interviewed me. My interview process began with a call from the office manager. She asked me a few basic questions over the phone and then invited me to a group interview. The group interview consisted of approximately sixteen candidates and was conducted by the office manager, the director of recruiting and retention, and the chief marketing officer. My third interview was conducted by the office manager, director of recruiting and retention, and the accounting manager. This was a panel interview. My fourth interview was one-on-one with the president of Áegis." While not everyone we spoke with interviewed with the president, all of our correspondents were vetted by many levels of company hierarchs prior to receiving a job offer.

Money and Perks

Most entry-level job offers at Áegis aren't negotiable, employees tell us, but some found the company flexible on the start date. Our correspondents speak highly of Áegis' Enhanced Benefit Program; they also tell us that "the company offers a lot of soft benefits such as luncheons, group activities, etc." Those who work at corporate headquarters report that the hometown of Redmond is a major plus.

The Ropes

Orientation at Áegis, one worker reports, "begins on your first day of work. I met with everybody in the office separately and sat with [each of] them for a little while to learn about their roles in the company. This gave me a better feeling for the culture of Áegis and also the business itself. My orientation lasted for the first few days on the job." After that, "you sit down and dive right in." Most employees receive some specialized training early on to teach them how to deal with Áegis' clients; a chef writes, "I was new to Alzheimer's/dementia care and to Áegis itself, but the company took the time to train me on the aspects of care . . . so I felt comfortable and informed of what to expect. I also received training in CPR and first aid."

Day in the Life

Áegis hires first jobbers in almost all areas, from client care (in positions such as activities director, care manager, concierge, cook, and wellness nurse) to behind-the-scenes business management (in capacities such as bookkeeping, marketing, and office administration). As such, there is no typical day; most would agree that "as the company is growing, so is the challenge of keeping up with it." Nearly all the employees we spoke with feel they have ample contact with higher-ups in the company. One typical employee writes, "I have plenty of access to upper management. I feel as though I can approach any of them if I need some information. We have an all-staff meeting once a month; [this] allows everybody to find out what is going on in the other departments."

Peers

There is "a fairly high degree of camaraderie" among coworkers at Áegis; only a few people we spoke with distinguished between their relationships with fellow first jobbers and the company workforce at large. Everyone agrees, "the camaraderie is very strong, and it doesn't matter how long someone has been with the company. It feels [as if] we've all been here forever." Most employees enjoy getting together after-hours; one says, "Everybody is outgoing. I have met a couple of coworkers outside [of] the office for social occasions."

Moving on

Áegis has a very low employee turnover rate, a testament to the satisfaction level of its employees. One exuberant Áegis booster writes, "I don't hear anything but praise about the company. It's a really great place to be. It's challenging, busy, friendly, caring, and funny, and sometimes [it is] better to be at work than at home!"

AIR PRODUCTS
CAREER DEVELOPMENT PROGRAM (CDP)

"The advantage of the CDP program, and what attracted me to AP, was the fact that new hire graduates are given a chance to figure out where in the company they best fit and what jobs are best for them."

The Big Picture

Established in 1959, Air Products' Career Development Program is one of the longest-running entry-level programs profiled in this book. The deep roots of the program mean that there are always plenty of CDP graduates around to mentor the incoming class, and that's a real advantage for first jobbers here. Air Products supplies gases (oxygen, hydrogen, helium, etc.) and chemicals to a wide range of clients in the health care, technology, industrial, and energy markets.

LOCATION(S) WHERE ENTRY-LEVEL EMPLOYEES WORK

"Corporate headquarters is in the Lehigh Valley in Southeastern Pennsylvania. About 40 percent of our college new hires start at our headquarters." Others start at one of the company's many locations throughout the Mid-Atlantic, Southeast, and West Coast regions of the United States.

AVERAGE NUMBER OF APPLICATIONS EACH YEAR

Air Products receives 350–400 applications each year.

AVERAGE NUMBER HIRED PER YEAR

Air Products hires 34 entry-level employees per year.

ENTRY-LEVEL POSITION(S) AVAILABLE

There are numerous positions available, predominantly in engineering.

AVERAGE HOURS WORKED PER WEEK

Entry-level employees work 40 hours per week.

PERCENTAGE OF ENTRY-LEVEL HIRES STILL WITH THE COMPANY AFTER THREE, FIVE, AND TEN YEARS

Ninety-six percent of entry-level hires remain with Air Products after three years; 87 percent are still with the company after five years; and 67 percent stay on for ten years and beyond.

AVERAGE STARTING SALARY

Starting salaries are "competitive within the industry."

Getting Hired

All Air Products job seekers must submit applications via the company's website; while Air Products "does recruit on campus, all students we meet are directed to the website." Ideal candidates "demonstrate strong technical competencies, good teamwork skills, strong interpersonal skills, good leadership skills, and a willingness to be flexible in assignment content and geographic location." Those who don't make the cut, writes one successful hire, "are those who are just too one-dimensional. Air Products seeks well-rounded engineers with more than just strong technical skills. Strong interpersonal skills are also a must." The interview process is rigorous; one product coordinator reports, "Thirteen of us [prospective employees] traveled to Allentown for the same interview. The night before our interview, several Air Products employees met the interviewees at our hotel to take us out to dinner and get to know each other a bit better. We were told at dinner what to expect the next day in terms of our schedule. We were also told only two interviewees were going to be hired. The interview itself consisted of two technical interviews in the morning, a technical exam, an open-floor discussion among the interviewees about the exam question (which was monitored by the interviewers, who outnumbered the interviewees), two impromptu presentations about the exam-question discussion to two different interviewers, two nontechnical interviews, and finally an human resources debrief info session about Air Products. Although we were given meals and breaks between each section of the interview process, the stress of the very thorough interview may have weighed more on some interviewees than others." A number of the first jobbers we spoke with began their careers through college co-ops, then became full timers after graduation.

Money and Perks

All Air Products employees "are eligible for variable compensation. It is based on individual performance." Most first jobbers felt that their starting salaries were not negotiable, but most were also happy with their initial offer. Top perks include flexible work arrangements (called FWAs; one worker writes, "The company strives to be the best company to work for, and, therefore, offers this perk. As long as you complete your work and put in your forty hours, you are able to arrange your schedule as four days a week, ten hour days, or '9-80s,' which entail putting in eighty hours in nine days, with the tenth day off, etc."). First jobbers also love the work-related travel ("visiting customers is usually a good time"), relocation benefits, and "the onsite dry cleaner."

The Ropes

Entry-level hires at Air Products participate in the Career Development Program (participants are referred to as "CDPs, for Career Development Participants"), during which "each CDP rotates through three different assignments, with each assignment averaging approximately twelve months in length. The CDPs have input as to which assignments they prefer, so it is somewhat self-directed. This is a strength of the program; the CDPs begin their careers by taking three different developmental assignments in areas of interest to them."

Formal orientation is short and sweet, just a half-day introduction to the physical plant and reviews of benefits and company policies. One first jobber writes, "A new employee handbook was sent to my door a few weeks before I began work. A human resource representative contacted me to discuss the process and go over the forms and paperwork. When I began work, my supervisor and I went through the handbook. [We] discussed my benefits, such as retirement packages, and [my supervisor] directed me to the resources to manage my options. Later, training was conducted at corporate headquarters for new employee orientation." There's plenty of subsequent training "conducted by supervisors on the job," as well as "various safety classes (since we work at a chemical plant)."

Day in the Life

The rotational nature of the CDP means Air Products' first jobbers "perform many of the different engineering functions [including, but not limited to] process engineering, project engineering, product engineering, safety, environmental [projects], design, maintenance, production, etc." A product coordinator recounts his experiences as a CDP: "What was great . . . was the autonomy and experience it afforded me as an engineer. At my first assignment, I was put in charge of two high-pressure emulsion-production processes. Every day when I first got to work, I would check on the overnight production runs to ensure reactor efficiencies were at par. I would investigate and place controls on those [recurring] inefficiencies in the process, by either placing control changes, procedure changes, or process changes. I would also interact with the plant operators to get feedback on any process issues they may be facing in the plant to help streamline their jobs a bit better. After my first assignment, I moved into a similar one-year role as a process engineer at a plant location near Baton Rouge, Louisiana. After that second assignment was completed, I worked my way into the business area, where I have become a permanent employee and rolled out of the CDP program. The advantage of the CDP program, and what attracted me to AP, was the fact that new hire graduates are given a chance to figure out where in the company they best fit and what jobs are best for them."

Peers

"There is a lot of camaraderie with fellow employees" at Air Products because of "corporate-sponsored intramural sports leagues, clubs, etc." CDPs "get together for happy hours, [form] committees, and [partake in] community service days. Again, it's up to the individual to determine [his or her own] level of participation, but the opportunities are there. There is a common e-mail chain for all CDPs (and some recent CDPs) that circulates frequently, which tells where the next big social gathering will be on weekends and after work." Participants appreciate that "due to the size of the CDP program, there is instant camaraderie amongst all CDPs." And sometimes there's more than camaraderie; one first jobber reports, "I married another one of the CDPs!"

Moving on

Young hires who leave Air Products usually do so to "return to school for an advanced degree (typically in engineering or business)" or because "their spouse works in a different geographic location." Some "decide to change careers and do something different [from] engineering."

Best and Worst

"Our CDP program has turned out some of the best in the company. Our current CEO, as well as his two predecessors, all joined Air Products as CDPs. This program has been in place since 1959. We truly use this to develop the leaders of the company. Many of our managers, senior managers, and executives at Air Products joined the company through this program."

AMERICAN BIOPHYSICS CORPORATION
VARIOUS POSITIONS

"it's 'the best company in the world at what we do, and we're sitting on the verge of helping to create something truly groundbreaking'"

The Big Picture

If you hate mosquitoes—and besides frogs and bats, who doesn't?—and love the idea of a growing business, American Biophysics may be the right place for you. The producer of the Mosquito Magnet, a machine capable of capturing up to 1,500 of the pesky biters in one night, was the number one growth company on the 2003 Inc. 500 list. It was also named one of *Forbes* magazine's "Top 25 Hot Private Properties in 2004." This company plans to continue growing within this realm. According to its website, American Biophysics is "single-mindedly focused and dedicated to the business of biting insect control."

LOCATION(S) WHERE ENTRY-LEVEL EMPLOYEES WORK

Corporate headquarters are located in North Kingstown, Rhode Island.

AVERAGE NUMBER HIRED PER YEAR OVER THE LAST TEN YEARS

There are 108 employees, 25 of whom are entry-level employees. The company predicts a relatively substantial increase in the number of new hires.

ENTRY-LEVEL POSITION(S) AVAILABLE

There are anywhere from 15 to 20 entry-level positions available.

AVERAGE HOURS WORKED PER WEEK

Depending on the position, employees may work more than 40 hours per week.

PERCENTAGE OF ENTRY-LEVEL HIRES STILL WITH THE COMPANY AFTER THREE, FIVE, AND TEN YEARS

After two years, 90 percent of all entry-level hires remain with the company; after three years, 80 percent of all entry-level hires remain.

AVERAGE STARTING SALARY

The average starting salary ranges from $25,000 to $30,000.

BENEFITS OFFERED

The company offers Blue Cross/Blue Shield (20 percent employee contribution) and Delta Dental (20 percent employee contribution). Additional benefits include a 401(k) and 529 college savings plan.

Human Resources Manager
140 Frenchtown Road
North Kingstown, RI 02852
Tel: 401-884-3500, ext. 139
Fax: 401-884-6688
www.ambiocorp.com

Getting Hired

American Biophysics representatives tell us that they seek candidates who are "adaptable to ever-changing environ-ments, have an entrepreneurial spirit, are willing to make decisions, have a drive to succeed, and have excellent commu-nication skills." Currently the company does not advertise job openings on its website, but it does recruit at area campus-es. One of the company's recruiters says, "Applicants who stand out are [those] who have researched the company already, who seem confident and natural, [who don't give] canned answers to questions, and who have insightful, creative answers to our questions. We ask them how they handle pressure, ask them to describe a high-stress situation they feel they have handled well, and why, and then describe one they feel they didn't handle as well and what they would have done differ-ently and what they have learned. We also talk to them a lot to see how well they listen, which is very [crucial]." One suc-cessful hire says, "The interview process was very casual. Both people who interviewed me explained the history and the goals of the company. The human resources manager called me a few weeks later and told me I had the job."

Money and Perks

Because the company is quickly growing, new opportunities become regularly available for current employees. The company bases pay increases on "annual increases and changing roles." The benefits package is "evolving," and the com-pany is working to expand and add extras as it grows more profitable. According to some employees, the greatest perk is the excitement of working at a fast-growing company; it's "the best company in the world at what we do, and we're sitting on the verge of helping to create something truly groundbreaking," gushes one new entry-level hire.

The Ropes

As with most everything else at American Biophysics, orientation and training is a work in progress. According to company representatives, "We have some established training for our specialized products that involve hands-on experi-ences with our product. Training in regard to specific jobs is still being developed." Most of the employees we spoke with tell us that at first they "did not receive much training at all." One person says, "I was definitely thrown into the mix and left on my own to find my niche. How I dealt with that is what enabled me to advance in the company." Others add that they "receive constant training on company policies, procedures, and products, but none specifically on the job functions" and that, because the company is so small, "all employees have some knowledge of all operations."

Day in the Life

American Biophysics is still in the process of defining the jobs its new hires will fill. If the company continues to grow at its current rate, the experiences of new hires will be much like that of those already working at the company. A current employee explains, "My responsibilities varied from day to day. The company was moving so fast with so few employees that everyone had to pitch in." Because American Biophysics workers usually have several coals in the fire at any given time, "There is always a level of multitasking that needs to occur so you can get each of your projects completed on time and [within] budget." One of the great things about working at such a small company, entry-level employees agree, is the relatively easy access they have to everyone from the shipping room to the board room. One worker reports, "There is no isolation at American Biophysics. All departments have close contact [with one another]. The high-level executives know everyone's first name. They regularly interact with all employees on both a business and personal level."

Peers

There's "a mix of young and old workers" at American Biophysics, which "helps maintain a balance of youth and experience" and maintains a level of comfort in an otherwise hectic work environment. "We're all good friends, even when things get intense in the office," writes one employee. "Everyone respects [one another] even when there's a conflict. At the end of the day, all issues are forgotten." Workers "spend a lot of time together inside and outside of work. We all go out a few times a month after work."

Moving on

American Biophysics was founded in 1991, but its business has only moved into high gear since it introduced its first mosquito trap in 1998. As such, it doesn't have much of a history of employees who "move on," and only a few people could offer insights into where departed employees have gone. In fact, the vibe we get from them is that most people are happy to work here and bullish about their prospects of advancement within the company. Their few complaints concern poor communication. One first jobber says, "When a company is growing as fast as we are, some things slip through the cracks without all the appropriate people knowing about them. When the customer knows and you don't, it can be embarrassing. That's the main issue that comes up."

AMERICORPS
VARIOUS POSITIONS

"I have gained valuable skills that transfer into everyday life and my current positions. Finally, I have gained confidence in my abilities and myself."

The Big Picture

AmeriCorps representatives note, "This year [AmeriCorps will] engage 50,000 people in service to their communities and country. Every AmeriCorps member gains the personal satisfaction of making a difference by helping others. You can teach or mentor youth, build affordable housing, teach computer skills, clean parks and streams, run afterschool programs, and help communities respond to disasters. You can also put your college skills to work strengthening the capacity of charitable organizations by recruiting volunteers, expanding programs, providing training and technical assistance, and updating technology, thereby helping grantees to become more self-sustaining."

LOCATION(S) WHERE ENTRY-LEVEL EMPLOYEES WORK

AmeriCorps has offices in all 50 states; Washington, DC; Puerto Rico; and other U.S. territories.

AVERAGE NUMBER OF APPLICATIONS EACH YEAR

People apply directly to the nonprofit organizations that AmeriCorps members serve, and there isn't a centralized database of all applications; as a result, the exact number is unknown.

AVERAGE NUMBER HIRED PER YEAR OVER THE LAST TEN YEARS

AmeriCorps currently hires 50,000 people a year.

AVERAGE HOURS WORKED PER WEEK

Full-time members work 40 hours per week. A full-time member works 1,700 hours over 10 to 12 months. Some part-time members work 900 hours over the course of 10 to 12 months.

PERCENTAGE OF ENTRY-LEVEL HIRES STILL WITH THE COMPANY AFTER THREE, FIVE, AND TEN YEARS

"AmeriCorps members typically serve for a year. Some of them, however, continue for another year or accept positions as employees with the nonprofit organizations [at which] they've served."

AVERAGE STARTING SALARY

Members receive "a living allowance of about $9,300 a year, plus a $4,725 education award that can be used to pay back student loans or put toward future tuition. Each member receives the [education] award after completing a year of service."

BENEFITS OFFERED

Health care coverage is included in the living allowance. Additional benefits include forbearance on interest for student loans during the term of service.

CONTACT INFORMATION

To learn more or apply online, visit www.americorps.org or call 800-942-2677 or 800-833-3722.

Getting Hired

There is no surefire route to attaining an AmeriCorps position because "the hiring criteria are determined by the nonprofit organizations [that] select AmeriCorps members. The only general criteria [are] that you must be at least seventeen years old and a U.S. citizen, national, or legal permanent resident alien of the United States. For some programs, such as the AmeriCorps*National Civilian Community Corps (AmeriCorps*NCCC), members must be between eighteen and twenty-four years old, but for most [programs] there are no upper age limits." Openings available through AmeriCorps are listed on the website. Successful applicants recommend that interested candidates post their resumes online. One applicant writes, "I posted [my] resume and cover letter on the AmeriCorps web page. This was the better way to go since there was a much quicker response time than sending any application via mail."

Money and Perks

AmeriCorps representatives describe the living allowance that makes up its pay as "modest," so you know you won't be getting rich from this job. You will gain valuable experience, however, and you may also be eligible for other helpful perks such as student loan deferments, a grant toward paying off student loans (paid at the end of your term of service), health insurance, child care assistance, and money to relocate. For most, though, the greatest perk is the experience itself. As one AmeriCorps veteran tells us, "I really met some great people. I am still in contact with fellow members six years after we served together. I have gained valuable skills that transfer into everyday life and my current positions. Finally, I have gained confidence in my abilities and myself."

The Ropes

As with the hiring process, orientation for AmeriCorps jobs varies depending on the organization with which members are placed. A two-term AmeriCorps veteran reports, "Orientation was an intensive experience for the two AmeriCorps programs I participated in. The concept was to challenge the corps to learn about diversity, conflict, and other challenges they would be facing in the coming year. For one of my assignments, we actually went on a three-day retreat as part of the orientation process—which allowed for quick and deep bonding to occur." For many organizations, corps members receive training through various federal, state, and local agencies; the training sessions can focus on everything from intensely practical skills (i.e., how to fight a fire or how to build a house) to maddeningly bureaucratic chores (i.e., how to complete government forms).

Day in the Life

Because AmeriCorps workers undertake so many different projects for so many different organizations, there is no typical day. According to organization representatives, "Some typical assignments for AmeriCorps members are running afterschool programs, tutoring, developing and maintaining nature trails, addressing issues of homelessness, and responding to natural disasters." The work can certainly be gratifying, as the experiences of one graduate who worked at a domestic violence center illustrate: "I was responsible for answering the crisis hotline. I went to court with victims who needed help in obtaining restraining orders against their abusive partners. I did shelter intakes and talked with people who needed someone to talk to. I provided information and support to victims and survivors of domestic violence. I also did outreach events in the community to help spread awareness of the issues. Over time, I was given more and more things to do. I came up with projects that I wanted to do. I was really able to branch out and find my own niche. The experience I received was invaluable and has helped me in every position I have had since."

Peers

Peer relationships at AmeriCorps depend on the assignments members have. One member says, "We are spread out around the state, so there is no peer network." Conversely, an alum of AmeriCorps*NCCC reports, "The corps bond was very tight. I was a team leader, and this group was also very close-knit. This was my social circle, since I had moved to a new city to participate in the programs. To this day, I still maintain contact with many people with whom I served. Despite the fact that we are spread out all over the country, we commit to getting together at least once a year for a reunion." Another first jobber sums up the situation this way: "[During] the months you spend on projects, you are limited to interaction with your team, or if you are working at a site with other people, then [you interact with] coworkers. Some projects are team-based, and during other [projects], you work individually. Most after-work hours are spent privately or with your team if you choose to fraternize."

Moving on

AmeriCorps is a one-year program, and most people leave after their term is finished. Quite a few people, however, sign up for a second and even a third tour of duty. An organization representative notes, "One of the benefits of AmeriCorps is that it provides members with the opportunity to explore different career paths. Many members discover a love and talent for the service they have provided as members, including teaching and nonprofit management."

Attrition

About one in five people who start an AmeriCorps assignment don't make it through the year of service. Some members find themselves working on projects they deem trivial; other members find they can't handle the demanding workload and/or the low pay.

APPIAN CORPORATION
VARIOUS POSITIONS

"I think the common thread among Appianites (as we like to call ourselves) is the desire to engage and be engaged intellectually. This translates directly into the ways that we like to have fun (organized brainteaser contests are never hard to find on the cruise) and the fact that we are all driven to see this company succeed."

The Big Picture

A business-process management company founded in 1999, Appian Corporation breaks the mold in many ways. One employee explains, "What we do is somewhat unique, and it requires a fair amount of faith in the vision of the company's leaders to understand where we want to be in one, three, or ten years." Because Appian is both young and small, the company "likes to stay aggressive to compete with some of the competitive giants out there (the Microsofts, the Lockheed Martins, the Booz Allens, etc.)." As a result of its innovative philosophy, Appian is not, as one employee points out, "your typical consulting or software company."

LOCATION(S) WHERE ENTRY-LEVEL EMPLOYEES WORK

All positions are located in Vienna, Virginia.

AVERAGE NUMBER OF APPLICATIONS EACH YEAR

Appian receives about 10,000 applications each year.

AVERAGE NUMBER HIRED PER YEAR

Fifty entry-level employees are hired each year.

ENTRY-LEVEL POSITION(S) AVAILABLE

Entry-level employees may be hired as associate consultants, software engineers, quality engineers, and marketing associates.

AVERAGE HOURS WORKED PER WEEK

Entry-level hires work about 45 to 50 hours per week.

AVERAGE STARTING SALARY

Starting salaries vary based on applicants' majors and degrees, with additional compensation available in bonuses and revenue appreciation rights.

Getting Hired

Appian "recruits at five to ten schools per recruiting season in the United States and internationally. Recruiting oncampus includes attending university career fairs, [giving] company presentations, and [conducting] on-campus interviews. Schools that we regularly attend are: the University of Virginia, Duke, Dartmouth, the University of Pennsylvania, MIT, Harvard, Princeton, Yale, Cornell, Georgetown, the University of Texas, Tec de Monterrey, and IIT—Bombay. Students from other universities are encouraged to apply and may do so online." One first jobber who was recruited at Duke writes, "The first round of interviews was with two Appian employees who were alumni of my university. The interviews were mainly behavioral, with a few technical questions based on my academic focus, which was computer science. The second round—and admittedly the round that sold this company to me—was with two of the four founders of the company: the CEO and the CTO, respectively. Both of these interviews were challenging: the CEO's interview was centered around my experiences in college. For example, I described a particular project in one of my classes, and he changed a few of the parameters of the assignment and asked me to explain how these changes would [affect] the result. The CTO, [however], presented me with a technical case study, drew his conclusions, and asked me to challenge them. It was a fast-paced interview, and I realized very quickly in both interviews that these two founders, like myself, enjoyed being challenged, [and] challenging others to think in different ways and generally liked finding problems and solving them. The final round of interviews took place at the company's headquarters. [This] included an office tour, meeting most of the employees, two more interviews with senior employees, and a very nice night out on the town."

Money and Perks

Start date is negotiable at Appian, as is one's specific work assignment; location and salary generally are not, at least not for first jobbers. Employees "receive performance bonuses during their annual reviews," which are "based on the employee's individual performance throughout the year, as well as [the] company's performance."

The best perk, everyone agrees, is the annual corporate retreat, "which has traditionally been a seven-day cruise." One employee reports, "We use this opportunity to take stock of the state of our company and the market, to transfer knowledge gained on specific projects to the rest of the company, and to just have a good time. It's always an incredibly well-organized event that offers everyone the opportunity to get friendly with new faces and catch up with old ones we haven't seen since Appian Academy [the company's orientation program]."

The Ropes

Appian has an "extensive orientation process," a five-week long "Academy Program" during which new hires "hear from representatives from the different departments throughout the company about policies, procedures, and the role of each department. Employees also start to learn about our product and begin to work on projects that will ultimately result in a presentation for their peers and supervisors." One first jobber describes it as "a crash course on all things Appian featuring various units on specific technologies that Appian uses, Appian's products and history, how to consult (consulting etiquette), an understanding of the market in which Appian does business, and much more. During the academy, new employees have lectures, papers, projects, presentations, and yes, even tests! The purpose of the academy is to give all new employees a chance to bring whatever skills they have garnered in their college experiences and round them out with the skills that every Appian employee needs to succeed."

Day in the Life

First jobbers come aboard at Appian in a variety of functional areas. Once new hires complete their academy training, they take on consulting and technical assignments. No two jobs are the same—though nearly all the positions demand hard work, creativity, and the ability to work with others. A first jobber brought on as a software consultant writes, "My job consisted of gathering client requirements, developing prototype solutions, demonstrating them to the customer, and implementing (coding) and deploying them. A typical day early in my career at Appian would see me meeting with my manager to do a technical review of earlier work, spending a number of hours working on my current software task, then preparing for and meeting with the client to flesh out requirements for future enhancements to the system that Appian developed and delivered to the customer. Early on, these meetings were nearly always attended by my manager, and afterward, we would discuss our impressions of the client's needs to ensure that I took away from these meetings what I needed. As time went on, I would conduct these interactions with more and more autonomy, until my manager moved on to another project and I stayed on [this project], managing the team myself."

Peers

Appian is a magnet for young, smart, ambitious hires. One writes, "I think the common thread among Appianites (as we like to call ourselves) is the desire to engage and be engaged intellectually. This translates directly into the ways that we like to have fun (organized brainteaser contests are never hard to find on the cruise) and the fact that we are all driven to see this company succeed." Workers enjoy "a terrific camaraderie thanks to the common experience of the Appian Academy." One reports, "Not three months goes by that I don't try to organize dinner or a bar night with my academy mates to catch up on how work, Appian, and the rest of life is treating them."

Moving on

First jobbers leave Appian "to pursue another position or to return to school," according to the company. Very few leave before they've completed at least one year here; the average tenure is two to three years, though that figure should increase as the company ages (it was founded in 1999).

ASSOCIATED PRESS
VARIOUS POSITIONS

"Working at the AP means you'll always be in the middle of the action."

The Big Picture

The Associated Press (AP) is the framework for the world news industry; the organization maintains 242 bureaus around the globe and provides copy, photographs, graphics, audio, and video to more than 1,700 newspapers and 5,000 television and radio outlets. If you want your stories to be seen, there's no better place to work: AP news services reach a billion people every day.

LOCATION(S) WHERE ENTRY-LEVEL EMPLOYEES WORK

"Generally speaking, every major city has a bureau. We hire at all locations, if there are appropriate openings."

AVERAGE NUMBER OF APPLICATIONS EACH YEAR

The AP receives "hundreds" of applications per year.

AVERAGE NUMBER HIRED PER YEAR OVER THE LAST TEN YEARS

The number of people who the AP hires "depends on turnover and various economic forces."

ENTRY-LEVEL POSITION(S) AVAILABLE

Entry-level employees work as editorial assistants, temporary news people, and interns.

AVERAGE HOURS WORKED PER WEEK

Entry-level employees work full-time hours.

AVERAGE STARTING SALARY

"[Starting salaries] depend on location. Salaries are covered by a collective bargaining agreement."

BENEFITS OFFERED

The AP offers "health, dental, mental health/substance abuse, [and] life insurance."

CONTACT INFORMATION

E-mail the AP at apjobs@ap.org. Visit AP on the web at www.ap.org/apjobs

Getting Hired

The AP makes its hiring decisions locally; "the bureau managers generally review the applications," organization representatives tell us, and the three qualities they look for are "experience, experience, experience." The AP visits "a number of colleges, especially those with strong journalism/communications departments." The most important part of the application process, first jobbers tell us, is the AP test. One new hire explains that "among other things, it has exercises in spelling, grammar, AP style, and current events. There are hypothetical situations posed that require you to write a news story based on tidbits of information provided. The AP also expects its news staff to write for broadcast media, so there are exercises related to that as well." Passing "puts your name in the AP system as someone who [is] interested in working for the AP and has passed their test. After that, it's a matter of a position opening up. If they call you up for an interview, it's already a done deal; they've already formed an evaluation of you because they've seen your test." Many employees begin with temporary assignments; people who make a good impression have the inside track when a permanent position becomes available.

Money and Perks

Salary at the AP is entirely determined by its union contract. Available jobs usually require first jobbers to work in specific locations on specific shifts; only in rare cases are start time or location negotiable. First jobbers point out that the "AP does, however, have posts in every state and most countries, so sometimes people will take the test in one bureau, then wait for a position to open up somewhere else." Young employees love "being exposed to breaking news all over the world on the wire (it's an extremely exhilarating feeling)" and "the feeling of learning nonstop." One person says, "You have to [have] a very humble attitude. Sometimes a topic will be thrown [at] you that you know nothing about." Employees also say, "It's neat to see your copy in newspapers around the state and sometimes around the country, even if it isn't credited."

The Ropes

Each local AP bureau runs slightly different. At some bureaus, first jobbers are thrown into the job with little preparation or training; others receive an orientation and training that lasts several weeks. A first jobber at one end of the spectrum tells us, "I was sent out on a story on the very first day. I didn't even know how to use their internal computer system. You learn as you go. They're so short-staffed; when they need you, they need you." At the other end was the writer whose orientation "involved a couple of weeks of work on each part of the job—writing and reporting, dictating stories from the scene, writing broadcast copy, and working a supervisory shift that requires heavy editing." A former first jobber states, "Training [at most bureaus] is in the form of shadowing more experienced staff. For instance, I worked several broadcast shifts with the broadcast editor before I was left to man that desk on my own."

Day in the Life

Working at the AP means you'll always be in the middle of the action. One first jobber explains, "One of my first jobs was driving to the scene of an explosion in downtown St. Cloud, Minnesota. I collected information from people at the scene, law enforcement officials, and rescue workers, and then phoned in a story to the day supervisor. I also gathered information from energy companies about gas leaks. I phoned in a story to the broadcast desk, then updated both the newspaper and broadcast stories throughout the day." The sheer volume of work required is often overwhelming; many of the writers tell us they are expected to "write two or three stories on happenings of the day. There is also the expectation that you will write more extensive weekend stories a couple of times a month." Promotions usually entail more responsibility, higher-profile stories, the responsibility of coming up with original stories (rather than simply covering stories assigned by an editor), and more work. It's a news junkie's paradise.

Peers

AP peer networks vary from bureau to bureau. In the larger bureaus, "there is ample camaraderie." "I often socialize with my colleagues," explains one first jobber in just such a bureau, adding, "I constantly interact with my peers at work, and I probably spend two or three nights out with at least one other AP person." At some bureaus, social life is limited by the demands of work; "there isn't much on the social plane here, since we're all at work twenty-four hours, and if you're not on, someone else usually is," writes one newbie. At smaller bureaus, there may not be any other young hires; "there weren't any other entry-level people when I started," reports one staffer.

Moving on

AP first jobbers are generally future lifers in the news industry. People who leave often take jobs with newspapers or in broadcast news; however, many people stay with the organization and work their way up the ranks.

Attrition

Most AP writers know what they're getting into, so the attrition rate is low. The "pressure from editors," the "heavy workload," and the "tedium of some routine jobs, such as editing" are things that may drive others to leave this organization; but AP employees generally take these issues in stride and accept them as the cost of working at a world-class news outlet.

BALTIMORE CITY TEACHING RESIDENCY

TEACHER

> "All candidates should be prepared to teach wherever they are needed most."

The Big Picture

The Baltimore City Teaching Residency (BCTR) is "an initiative of the Baltimore City Public School System (BCPSS) that recruits, selects, and trains outstanding college graduates to become teachers in the schools that need them the most." Program hires, called residents, "become part of a cohort charged [with raising] student achievement." BCTR looks for "individuals interested in teaching in all subject areas, especially middle and high school math, science, and special education. Following an intensive and rigorous Training Institute, residents will enter the classroom [as teachers] while taking classes to obtain their teaching certification;" they also "have the option to earn their master's degree at The Johns Hopkins University or at the College of Notre Dame."

LOCATION(S) WHERE ENTRY-LEVEL EMPLOYEES WORK

All positions are located in Baltimore, Maryland.

AVERAGE NUMBER OF APPLICATIONS EACH YEAR

The Baltimore City Teaching Residency program receives 1,500 applications per year.

AVERAGE NUMBER HIRED PER YEAR

The program hires about 200 teachers each year.

ENTRY-LEVEL POSITION(S) AVAILABLE

Employees are hired as teachers/residents.

AVERAGE HOURS WORKED PER WEEK

Teachers work about 46 hours per week.

PERCENTAGE OF ENTRY-LEVEL HIRES STILL WITH THE COMPANY AFTER THREE, FIVE, AND TEN YEARS

Seventy percent of entry-level hires are still with the program after three years.

AVERAGE STARTING SALARY

Participants in the Baltimore City Teaching Residency receive the same starting salary as other first-year teachers in the Baltimore City Public School System. Depending on experience, relevant course work, and content area, starting salaries range from $41,226 to $49,340.

Getting Hired

BCTR recruits on eastern college campuses but "will consider applications from all institutions." The organization does not conduct on-campus interviews; all potential residents must apply online by completing an application and attaching a resume, a personal statement, and academic transcripts. Applicants are "notified two weeks from the application deadline of their status. If granted an interview, candidates will have the ability to select their interview date and time via an online scheduler." One successful hire reports that "the interviewers asked questions about [my] successes and challenges in past jobs, why I thought that I would be successful in this position, what I thought the challenges of the position would be, etc. I also had to teach a demonstration lesson." Following the interview, candidates are "notified of their status within two weeks. At this time, selected candidates are supplied with an enrollment package that contains additional information on the program and states the program enrollment deadline. To finalize the process, candidates must pass state teacher tests before entering the classroom as teachers." Successful applicants "span a wide range of ages and backgrounds and bring to the program a diverse set of talents and skills. Strong candidates are those who are committed to having a positive effect on student achievement, who display excellence in their previous endeavors, and who are dedicated to reaching and influencing students—especially those in under-resourced areas—on a daily basis." Placements in schools are determined "through a variety of processes including, but not limited to, interviews and placement fairs and coordination of interviews between individual schools and residents. All candidates should be prepared to teach wherever they are needed most."

Money and Perks

Salaries, raises, and benefits for Baltimore City teachers "are governed by the collective bargaining agreement in place between the district and the teachers union. The teacher salary scale is a step-based system in which employees increase a salary step each year they teach. Additionally, residents are compensated based on their highest-earned degree: bachelor's degree, master's degree, master's plus thirty credits, and PhD." Teachers here tell us that the best part of their job is "working with students every day. It's very stimulating."

The Ropes

All residents begin their work "with a paid Training Institute that is designed specifically for members of the BCTR. Residents will be exposed to seminars and workshops on standards, [the] foundations of teaching, and classroom management. During this training, residents will also participate in discussions and activities focused on the challenges and benefits of teaching in a diverse educational setting. The BCTR Training Institute consolidates a great deal of training time into only a few weeks;" as a result, "training is extremely demanding." During the training, "residents typically begin their days at 8:00 A.M. [teaching] in a summer school classroom, paired with an experienced teacher. For part of the morning, they may observe or teach; and they may work with small groups of students for the remainder of the session. In the afternoons, residents meet with an advisory group, led by excellent veteran teachers, for two- to three-hour sessions. These advisory groups are designed to build on residents' teaching experiences in the mornings and provide them with the key knowledge and skills necessary to begin teaching at the end of training. After this portion of the day ends, residents may have reading to do before the next day, preparation for work with their students, or graduate course work to attend [to]." Residents accepted into the winter program begin training in January; those accepted into the summer program begin training in late June or early July.

Day in the Life

Residents handle all the chores of a classroom teacher; in particular, they count among their duties the responsibility "to ensure that all students are achieving at the desired levels for their grade and skill levels and to complete any additional school requirements set by the principal or district (e.g., attending all staff meetings and participating on committees)." The school day lasts six-and-a-half hours; residents "on average work an additional two to three hours per day planning lessons, grading papers, or participating in afterschool activities."

Peers

"There is a high degree of camaraderie with first-year and new teachers at my school," writes one resident, observing that "most of the teachers I've encountered are smart and committed." Social life is hampered by the busy schedule residents keep, but they try to get together occasionally outside the confines of school.

Moving on

BCTR started up in 2002, so the program is relatively new. Consequently, relatively few of its hires have "moved on." Those who do typically move to other areas within education (in other districts, for example); a few leave education altogether.

Attrition

According to BCTR, "Individuals who leave the school system do so for a wide variety of personal and professional reasons." One teacher writes, those who are unhappy "usually criticize the administration. They tend to be negative types who don't really offer any solutions to problems." Over the past few years, between 12 and 15 percent of residents have left the program before completing two years.

Best and Worst

"There is not [a single] mold of a successful resident teacher," BCTR tells us. Great teachers have "diverse backgrounds, experiences, and skills [that] drive their success as classroom teachers." All of them share "a deep commitment to students and student achievement," the "ability to trouble-shoot, problem-solve, and develop innovative solutions rapidly," a "strong sense of responsibility for student outcomes," a "desire to become part of the school and neighborhood community," and a "commitment to working with parents and guardians." Less successful teachers include "individuals interested in 'easy work,'" such as those attracted by the "8:00 A.M. to 2:00 P.M. day with summers off."

BANK ONE
VARIOUS POSITIONS

"Individuals who are successful at Bank One tend to possess our core values [and] competencies: a customer focus; interpersonal effectiveness and teamwork; a drive for quality and results; ethics, integrity, and character; and courage."

The Big Picture

Bank One covers much of the financial universe, and it provides not only traditional savings and checking services, but also credit cards, insurance, financial planning, mutual funds, and annuities. The bank offers a variety of programs designed to integrate recent college graduates into each of its divisions.

LOCATION(S) WHERE ENTRY-LEVEL EMPLOYEES WORK

Bank One has locations in various cities in Arizona, Colorado, Delaware, Illinois, Indiana, Kentucky, Louisiana, Michigan, Ohio, Oklahoma, and Texas.

ENTRY-LEVEL POSITION(S) AVAILABLE

There are numerous entry-level positions available, including those that are part of the Bank One Scholar Program: Card Services' Business Associate Program and First Leader Program; Capital Markets Analyst Program; Finance, Accounting, and Audit Development Program; Chicago Sales Management Development Program; National Retail Management Development Program; Relationship Banker Development Program; National Enterprise Operations Management Development Program; and the Technology Development Program. Other opportunities may exist at any given time.

AVERAGE HOURS WORKED PER WEEK

Hours vary by position.

AVERAGE STARTING SALARY

Salaries also vary by position; they range from $25,000 to $50,000 for people with bachelor's degrees and from $51,000 to $85,000 for people with master's degrees, depending on the program.

Getting Hired

Bank One "actively recruits on campus at many schools in the Midwest and South (a copy of our recruiting schedule can be found on our website)" and also accepts online applications. An entry-level employee in the National Enterprise Operations Management Development Program describes the process: "I got the interview after turning in one of my standard resumes. I believe that my past work experience and GPA are what got me the interview. I was interviewed first by a Bank One finance manager on campus. After passing that first round, I was invited to the operations center for a tour and two more interviews, one with an operations manager and the other with a senior vice president and division manager. All of the interviews used a standard Bank One format consisting of behavioral questions like, 'Describe a time when . . . .'" Interviews for full-time jobs "typically occur in the fall of each year; internship interviews are conducted in the spring. Offers are typically extended in November and December for full-time positions and in March and April for internships."

Money and Perks

Entry-level salaries vary at Bank One by program: "Each program determines if and how bonuses will be distributed as well as how salaries will increase. Some individuals receive increases once they graduate from their specific programs; others receive merit increases at their annual performance reviews." Starting salaries are rarely negotiable, although they can be for candidates with well-developed skills (i.e., in technology areas). Respondents to our survey praise the long-term financial benefits of working for Bank One: "There are great 401(k) and pension plans. Also, we get fees waived or better rates on other financial products." One entry-level employee adds that "the best fringe benefit[s] for the short-term [are] the discounts. Bank One is partnered with several companies, from restaurants and cell phone companies to clothing stores and gyms." Other fringe benefits include "exposure to senior management of the company (their guidance was invaluable and very motivating)" and "four weeks of vacation!"

The Ropes

Everyone in Bank One's development programs starts off with "a week-long orientation, which includes an in-depth overview of Bank One as well as exposure to the heads of our lines of business. Each line of business continues from there with some form of orientation [and] training for their new hires during the individual's first 120 days of employment." One undergraduate hire reports, "The orientation process was the very best part of the program. They bring you in first to the corporate orientation, where you have an overview of the company and meet people from all different departments. The second day was the in-store orientation, where we were introduced to the program manager and were given our training schedules for the next 120 days. It made me feel very secure and eased my nerves about coming into a bank, knowing basically nothing about banking!" Training continues throughout the development programs and often includes substantial amounts of classroom learning.

Day in the Life

A typical day depends on the program in which a given entry-level employee participates. Bank One scholars work six-month rotations in various positions by day, then attend an MBA program in the evening. Card Services Business Associates Program is a "fast-track management program" that places trainees in one of the bank's many credit card-related areas. Capital markets analysts rotate through positions in the bank's Capital Markets departments, supplementing their training with formal classroom instruction. Development programs also entail rotations that expose participants to all the different specializations within their selected area. A participant in the Technology Development Program describes his work experience this way: "My job has been to take graphs of metrics [that] are reported manually each week and help automate them and make them viewable in a Web environment. To accomplish this task, I have spent a large [amount of] time learning the Java language and other technologies [that] I do not have much experience with. A typical day consists of learning new technologies, applying them to my metrics-reporting projects, and a daily meeting with the team on the project to go over our progress."

Peers

"There is a huge camaraderie within the members of our program," writes one program member. "I think the main reason is because for all of us, this is our first real introduction to the corporate world, so we have lots we would like to discuss, but more as friends than as coworkers." Another adds, "We spent a lot of time together in Chicago [during training], and that was a real bonding experience for all of us. A few times, we have gotten together after work, and most days I eat lunch with at least one or two people from the program."

Moving on

Most entry-level employees remain with Bank One. "I plan to stay for as long as I can continue to grow and feel satisfied with my job," one person puts it. Typically, they advance through the ranks of the area for which they received training. "I left after graduating from the six-month program when I was placed in a supervisory position," writes one such entry-level hire. Others move elsewhere within the bank; "I have moved through the program to [become] an assistant manager, a branch manager, and now I'm moving to a different program—the In-Lines—as a branch manager," explains one employee.

Attrition

According to Bank One representatives, fewer than 5 percent of first jobbers leave within twelve months. "Given that the majority of the new hires are recent college graduates with limited work experience, those that choose to leave the bank do so to pursue career opportunities outside of banking," writes a company representative. First jobbers add that some people leave because they "feel they were placed in a department that didn't utilize their skills, [feel] undervalued, or [feel] there was poor communication about [things] happening within the program."

Best and Worst

Bank One representatives tell us that "individuals who are successful at Bank One tend to possess our core values [and] competencies: a customer focus; interpersonal effectiveness and teamwork; a drive for quality and results; ethics, integrity, and character; and courage."

BASES
RESEARCH ANALYST

bases

"It is a pretty rewarding feeling to have clients look to you for multimillion dollar launch/no launch decisions. It is also gratifying to see a new product on the shelf and know that your insight went into its launch."

The Big Picture

"Researching new, innovative products" is the business of BASES; entry-level employees quickly find themselves immersed in the world of product development and marketing. The job, which "combines math, statistics, and analytical thinking," is a great fit for people "who love puzzles" and being on the cutting edge.

LOCATION(S) WHERE ENTRY-LEVEL EMPLOYEES WORK

BASES has offices in Westport, Connecticut; Chicago, Illinois; Covington, Kentucky (Cincinnati metropolitan area); Parsippany, New Jersey (New York metropolitan area); and a number of international offices.

AVERAGE NUMBER OF APPLICATIONS EACH YEAR

BASES receives thousands of applications each year.

AVERAGE NUMBER HIRED PER YEAR OVER THE LAST TEN YEARS

"In the last six years, we have averaged about 20 to 30 entry-level hires per year."

ENTRY-LEVEL POSITION(S) AVAILABLE

"The majority of our entry-level recruiting efforts are focused on the research analyst position. We do, however, fill other entry-level positions that occasionally become available."

AVERAGE HOURS WORKED PER WEEK

Employees typically work 40 to 50 hours per week, but the hours may vary given client needs.

PERCENTAGE OF ENTRY-LEVEL HIRES STILL WITH THE COMPANY AFTER THREE, FIVE, AND TEN YEARS

"BASES has very little turnover. The vast majority of our college hires stay with the company for years. Specific retention statistics are not available."

AVERAGE STARTING SALARY

"Competitive—salary varies depending on location."

Getting Hired

BASES recruits on select college campuses; students at campuses that BASES does not visit may apply online for jobs. Company representatives "review your resume and, if [they] feel that your experiences and qualifications may be a good fit [for] the position, contact you to schedule an interview. In addition to multiple interviews, you will also be asked to submit transcripts, as well as complete a seventy-five-minute analytical skills assessment." One entry-level employee says, "BASES values people who have diverse backgrounds and interests. During my interview process, I was not only asked about my academic and work experience, but also about my extracurricular activities." Another employee reports, "My first interview was with an analyst who had been at the company for [only] one year and had been hired right out of college. This surprised me, and at first, I thought that the company was not serious about hiring [me] since they sent a fairly new employee to interview me. However, I learned that this is often done, and it is representative of BASES culture (young, casual, everyone's ideas and thoughts are respected, etc.). Most of the questions I was asked required me to [discuss] a specific event or example from my life (behavioral-based questions). I was later invited to the office for several second-round interviews. The second round of interviews included more hypothetical questions specifically related to marketing research and consumer behavior." Company representatives tell us that "interviewers are interested in learning more about the candidate's background and experiences, career interests, analytical skills, communication skills, attention to detail, organizational skills, and work ethic, among other things."

Money and Perks

"BASES rewards employees based on their contributions and overall performance. All employees receive their first performance appraisal after six months of employment. Annual performance appraisals are accompanied by a salary increase." First jobbers tell us that "the job offer [is] not negotiable in terms of salary, office location, and duties," but that start time is sometimes flexible. First jobbers discuss perks, which include "the laid-back but highly driven atmosphere. Everyone is friendly but takes [the] work seriously. We deliver a superior product to our clients but enjoy ourselves while we're doing it!" Employees also enjoy "having insider information [about] new product launches. It is a pretty rewarding feeling to have clients look to you for multimillion dollar launch/no launch decisions. It is also gratifying to see a new product on the shelf and know that your insight went into its launch (plus, we get a lot of free new products)."

The Ropes

Orientation at BASES "is quite quick" and includes some "meet-and-greet" around the office and a day with a human resources representative "learning company policy and filling out paperwork." Training, however, is extensive and "lasts roughly six weeks. Training sessions have been led by almost everyone in the office, from relatively recent hires to senior-level managers. The first two weeks consist of full-day sessions, and the last three weeks consist of half-day training classes. The training sessions consist of presentations, case studies, and various exercises. At that point, we begin working with our managers on small projects, which is a great way to immediately apply the learning from the training. I really enjoyed this training model because it allowed us to get to know a large number of coworkers very quickly." In addition, "several formal job-specific training courses [are] conducted throughout the first few months of the new hire's employment, [and] other company specific and miscellaneous training opportunities are offered through the year."

Day in the Life

BASES research analysts hit the ground jogging and soon after reach full stride. One analyst says, "When I was first hired, my responsibilities mainly entailed data gathering and summarizing. However, as soon as training was over, I was given more extensive responsibilities. While my manager reviewed all of my work (from reports to e-mails), it was [ultimately] my work that was being sent to our clients. This was a great feeling: to have an entry-level job that really allowed you to think for yourself and contribute to the success of the company." Another analyst agrees and adds, "The responsibility curve at BASES is incredibly steep. I was put on my own project right away, which entails analyzing in-market and consumer data, checking marketing plan inputs, entering data into a complex model, drafting e-mails to clients, and writing toplines and lengthy (100-page) reports and presentations." First jobbers appreciate that "there is no typical day." One first jobber reports, "I am always working on something new. I am typically on one to four projects at a time. There is no set schedule to follow. I have a lot of independence as to how I spend my time."

Peers

"I feel like there is a definite BASES personality," writes one research analyst. "Nearly everyone I have met here is young, intelligent, and fun. No one tries to get ahead by stepping on other people's toes. Even though everyone is obviously trying to get ahead, no one is willing to do so at the expense of others. There is a definite team feeling at BASES." Another analyst adds, "I am constantly interacting with peers at the office. BASES encourages employees to bounce ideas off of one another. I would say I interact with my peers half (or more) of the hours I am at work." The camaraderie continues even after the computers are shut down for the day: "Socializing outside of the company with coworkers is big," explains one entry-level employee. "There is an organized off-site happy hour at least once a week and frequent weekend parties. There are also several company sports teams."

Moving on

Many new hires come to BASES expecting to stay for the long haul, and few are disappointed. Most first jobbers like the work and stick around as long as opportunities for growth and advancement exist. "The majority [of people who leave the firm after a few years do so to] return to school and obtain a master's degree. Others leave the company to start a family or pursue outside interests."

Attrition

Dropouts from the BASES entry-level job program are rare. Some who do leave "have voiced concerns about lack of managerial training—that people are promoted to management levels but not properly taught how to manage their direct reports. This leads to frustration among the newer hires." Others "complain about the workload or high expectations [from their managers]. However, the people with these types of criticisms are far less common than people who hold a positive view of their job[s] here at BASES."

BEARINGPOINT
VARIOUS POSITIONS

"Clients can be cranky and have unreasonable expectations, or they can be amazing friends for life."

The Big Picture

BearingPoint is a major consulting firm that provides "application services, technology solutions, and managed services to Global 2000 companies and government organizations." Clients include nearly half the Fortune 1000, all fourteen Cabinet-level departments of the U.S. Federal Government, the top thirteen global pharmaceutical companies, and many, many other heavy hitters.

LOCATION(S) WHERE ENTRY-LEVEL EMPLOYEES WORK

The BearingPoint headquarters are located in McLean, Virginia, but company officials note that BearingPoint has entry-level positions "in a number of its offices worldwide."

AVERAGE NUMBER OF APPLICATIONS EACH YEAR

BearingPoint receives about 40,000 applications each year.

AVERAGE NUMBER HIRED PER YEAR

BearingPoint hires approximately 500 entry-level employees each year; this number may vary given changes in corporate performance.

ENTRY-LEVEL POSITION(S) AVAILABLE

Entry-level employees are hired as management analysts, or in other entry-level positions.

AVERAGE HOURS WORKED PER WEEK

Entry-level employees work about 40 hours per week.

AVERAGE STARTING SALARY

Starting salaries are competitive with the industry standard.

BENEFITS OFFERED

"Our employees are offered an exceptional benefits package here at BearingPoint," reports a company official. Included in this package is "an employee-contributed health care plan, dental plan, prescription drug plan, disability insurance, health care for [the] employee's family, and health care for domestic partners." Other benefits include a 401(k) plan, stock options, maternity and paternity leave, subsidized child care, and health club discounts.

CONTACT INFORMATION

Visit www.bearingpoint.com, and click on the "Careers" tab.

Getting Hired

BearingPoint "advertises at selected colleges and universities," at which they also "conduct on-campus interviews," which are "followed by office visits." Many successful hires report that "my school has a strong working relationship with BearingPoint." Additionally, BearingPoint "collects resumes through career fairs, referrals, and networking." The firm seeks candidates who "exhibit our company's core values, possess strong leadership skills and integrity, are team players, have an interest for the consulting industry, are quick learners, can be flexible, exhibit an entrepreneurial spirit, and have a strong sense of customer commitment." "Good communications skills" are also a major asset.

One entry-level employee reports, "About a year and a half ago [the Public Services practice at] BearingPoint started a campus initiative in which they would hire people, but not to a specific project, and put them on the 'bench.' As you approached your start date, you would work with your resource manager to get set up on a project that had an open position that you were interested in. Through this campus initiative, they would have campus days at the McLean office with interview sessions. My interview session was in the afternoon, and [I] was brought in with about ten to fifteen other students. We interviewed with managers from the same industry sector, but as I said, you weren't interviewing necessarily for a position within their group, just a position within the company."

Money and Perks

"Start date is fairly flexible" at BearingPoint. Salary, however, "is competitive but pretty much nonnegotiable, and don't expect a signing bonus. The exception to this is those [who] come in with an MBA [or a] graduate degree or at the consultant level or above. Sometimes a relocation stipend is offered." Salary increases are based on performance reviews and productivity. First jobbers are eligible for bonuses, which "are given based on individual and company performance." Top perks include a personal laptop and "car benefits; we can buy cars [from certain dealerships and suppliers] at a company discount."

Employees may also take advantage of "performance-based bonuses, stock options, and a 401(k) plan," as well as "matching of employee contributions, maternity and paternity leave, employee referral program, health club discounts, subsidized child care, health and health-education programs, employee assistance program, telecommuting, flex time, and compressed work weeks, funding for attending professional conferences/trade shows, paid association memberships, a minimum of forty hours per year of on-site and off-site training, formal mentoring program, leaves of absence for education or specialized training, and an online-training system that offers over 10,000 courses (technical, operations, and strategic)."

The Ropes

"BearingPoint offers a new hire orientation called BearingPoint Beginnings, which is held each week in Northern Virginia," explains the firm, pointing out that "by bringing new hires together face-to-face and by giving them a high-touch, hands-on program, we help them assimilate more quickly into our company and culture. Through case studies, role-plays, and activities, participants learn about our vision and values, our business strategy and global operating model, and our financial management principles and tools. They also learn about our staffing and performance management processes, all of which are important to getting a great start with our company." One first jobber adds, "After about three months of working at BearingPoint, all consulting employees attended a three-day workshop where we learned about our company's financial system, marketing campaigns, and internal tools. In addition, we attend networking workshops." Beyond this, "there is little [other] formal training; it's all on the job, and you learn from other, more experienced management analysts and from your mistakes, as may be the case with most jobs—and life."

In addition, each new hire is assigned a peer advisor/performance manager. The peer advisor serves as a "guide, confidant, information resource, network resource, counselor, and advocate." New hires are also "assigned a specific managing director," who serves as a "team leader."

Day in the Life

We spoke with a number of management analysts at BearingPoint; all took the position immediately out of college. Here's how one describes a typical day: "At first, my main responsibility was to learn as much as I could about all facets of the BearingPoint systems that I would be working with. Learning and understanding this required a great deal of hands-on work and developing tracking tools to trace my pathways through the various tools and databases within the company and my group. A typical day would look like this: 9:00 A.M. to 10:00 A.M.—review e-mails from my boss; catch up on administrative tasks associated with on-boarding; take an online training course; 10:00 A.M. to 12:00 P.M.—receive training on systems in my boss's office; 12:00 P.M. to 1:00 P.M.—lunch; 1:00 P.M. to 5:00 P.M.—work through the systems I was trained on and reconcile what I learned with the spreadsheets I received; 5:00 P.M. to 6:00 P.M.—review documents that my boss sent me; compile a list of questions to ask my boss the following day; and begin to develop my own spreadsheets."

After gaining some experience and expertise, employees report taking on additional responsibilities and managing their projects with greater levels of independence.

Peers

First jobbers at BearingPoint are "constantly impressed by the resumes" of their peers, all of whom seem to have "attended impressive schools, engaged in many extracurricular activities, and worked in very interesting jobs for noteworthy companies before coming to BearingPoint. They are also energetic, driven, hard workers." Friendships are easily made here, though the after-hours scene is subdued. One newbie reports, "We have happy hours every once in a while, and they're always a good time. I wish we had more of them, and I think a fair amount of others do, too. I know those [who] work on projects in the intelligence community have frequent happy hours and are a fairly tight community, even with people they don't work on projects with."

Moving on

Top reasons for leaving BearingPoint, in descending order of frequency, are personal reasons, career advancement, a return to school, a move to an industry position (nonclient). For some, the consulting business just isn't a good fit; one management analyst notes, "Some people simply do not like the client-consultant relationship. Clients can be cranky and have unreasonable expectations, or they can be amazing friends for life. Some people do not like the ups and downs of that world. The good news is that I have seen my peers who feel this way easily and seamlessly placed in internal jobs in the company in fields like finance, accounting, and operations."

BOEING
VARIOUS POSITIONS

BOEING ®

"It is a challenge and a privilege to
work with so many brilliant minds."

The Big Picture

Boeing, maker of commercial airplanes, military aircraft, satellites, spacecraft, and missiles, is the largest U.S. exporter, and it conducts a pretty tidy business within the nation's borders, as well. There are a myriad of opportunities to work on groundbreaking projects and advance through the ranks for a go-getter with a flair for aeronautics or the aeronautic business. And they can be had in many far-flung locations, across the country and around the globe.

LOCATION(S) WHERE ENTRY-LEVEL EMPLOYEES WORK

"Most [of the] company locations have opportunities for entry-level work. Boeing operates in more than 70 countries and 38 states within the United States, with major operations in the Puget Sound area of Washington State; Southern California; Wichita, Kansas; and St. Louis, Missouri."

AVERAGE NUMBER OF APPLICATIONS EACH YEAR

Boeing receives "thousands" of applications every year.

AVERAGE NUMBER HIRED PER YEAR OVER THE LAST TEN YEARS

Boeing has more than 150,000 employees total. There are no figures for the number of new hires per year.

ENTRY-LEVEL POSITION(S) AVAILABLE

Entry-level hires work in engineering, information technology (IT), and business.

AVERAGE HOURS WORKED PER WEEK

"Forty hours is the typical work week for Boeing employees, with part-time work options also available. Boeing offers virtual work options, allowing employees to telecommute from their homes or use 'hoteling' or transit work spaces at company work sites."

AVERAGE STARTING SALARY

Engineering salaries start at $50,000; IT salaries start at $46,000; and business salaries start at $41,000.

Getting Hired

Although Boeing "does target schools and maintains an on-campus visit schedule based on curriculum and locations of schools," the company values all schools. "By having an online application process, every student is able to apply for open positions." The company seeks new hires who demonstrate the ability to work with a team and who possess "integrity, technical proficiency, and the ability to communicate effectively." The hiring process can drag on from start to finish. One electrical engineer writes, "A few weeks after submitting my application, Boeing gave me a phone interview. The interview was behavior-based ('Tell me about a time when . . .'). I'm sure that my having had a couple of these already and having brainstormed and practiced answering some of those questions helped." Boeing now holds "one-day events that allow job seekers to [have] pre-scheduled interviews with hiring managers. On-the-spot job offers and follow-on job offers are typical." The schedule for these events is posted on the company's website.

Money and Perks

The negotiability of Boeing positions varies widely from function to function; obviously, the more specialized your skills, the better your negotiating chances. Most first jobbers find that "location, activity, and salary are specified [in] the offer." One first jobber explains, "In my case, the first two [offers] were specific and seemed nonnegotiable. I did ask to negotiate the salary. They listened to my arguments, but didn't change it." A new hire in one of Boeing's rotational training programs reports that "the program is flexible in terms of the job you're hired into. You get to choose [what] department you start in and have a large degree of discretion in where you go over the two-year rotational period (mandatory rotations occur every four months)." Newbies love Boeing's flex-time arrangement, which "with proper approval (that is usually given), allows you to take a whole Friday off, and make up the hours during the rest of the two-week pay period. Or, you can work an extra hour one day and leave an hour early the next." They also appreciate "the Learning Together Program, known as one of the most generous corporate tuition reimbursement programs. It offers 100 percent paid tuition at accredited schools."

The Ropes

Boeing offers "a standard half-day schedule for orientation used by all company locations" that is "designed to congratulate and celebrate the success of the employee's newly obtained position at Boeing. In addition, it is an opportunity for Boeing to impart some very important values, responsibilities, and standards of conduct." In addition, "certain regions may add an afternoon session that is specific to their own region." Participants in the rotational training program have a longer formal orientation; a person in the Business Career Foundation Program writes, "We had a week-long orientation seminar that gave us an overview of the company and of the positions we would be rotating through." Other new hires complete the four-hour orientation, then jump right into their new jobs. Subsequent training is a mix of "on-the-job training as well as formal training," including some online instruction. How much of each an employee gets depends on his or her job. The more technical the position, the more likely it is to require specialized training classes.

Day in the Life

Entry-level employees work in just about every department in every location in which Boeing does business; as company representatives explain, "The responsibilities for newly hired employees vary; there is not one standard set of responsibilities." Much of the work at Boeing is project oriented, so new hires often jump in in media res; one engineer writes, "When I was first hired, there was a project that most of my coworkers were working hard to finish up. So, at first, I spent a lot of time doing the online training and learning the computer tools from coworkers. My first assignment was to draw up the wiring to install a new device, following the example of one that had already been done. Most of that time was spent using a 2-D drawing package on the computer, as well as using other tools to look up information I needed (guided, again, by my coworkers)." Mentoring plays a large part in the life of a new Boeing employee, as does "a program that is a network for new college hires. It allows college hires to network with others that are in the same circumstances." Those new hires participating in a rotational program tell us "the benefit of a rotational program is that each position only lasts for four months, which gives you a chance to figure out where you fit."

Peers

Because Boeing is such a big company, there are plenty of first jobbers. The company is even large enough to hire a number of students from the same school; one Texas A&M graduate writes, "Contact and camaraderie among the new hires from the same school [are] extremely good. There is a big after-hours social scene organized by different people from Texas A&M." Regardless of your alma mater, though, "there is definitely contact and camaraderie with other young workers. Not all of them are first jobbers, but several are still around [the same] age." Everyone we spoke with agrees that they "have a great group of supportive, intelligent, and driven peers. Friends are easy to make here." Another newbie writes, "It is a challenge and a privilege to work with so many brilliant minds."

Moving on

Most first jobbers stay at Boeing; one reports, "I've been told it's relatively easy to move around in the company." People who do leave, according to company representatives, go to work for "competitors in the aerospace industry and/or companies requiring technical professionals such as Lockheed, Raytheon, Northrop Grumman, BAE Systems, Honeywell, Microsoft, Rockwell, Sandia National Labs, Los Alamos National Labs, and Ball Aerospace."

Attrition

Boeing representatives report that some employees who leave the company do so because "the work was not what they expected." One electrical engineer concurs: "One or two of my peers have commented that this job doesn't seem to use our training." Company representatives also tell us that "money, level, and promotion ability" sometimes drive first jobbers to seek work elsewhere.

BOOZ ALLEN HAMILTON

Booz | Allen | Hamilton

JUNIOR-LEVEL CONSULTANT AND JUNIOR-LEVEL RESEARCHER

"I was surprised how quickly I was given responsibility and how much trust my team had in me even though I was very new."

The Big Picture

A large, international consulting firm based in the Washington, DC area, Booz Allen Hamilton hires recent grads as junior-level consultants and junior-level researchers, positions that afford unmatched access to "exciting project work, great client[s], and talented co-workers." An excellent place to start a career, Booz Allen Hamilton runs a top-notch professional education program, and "new employees benefit from mentoring and coaching opportunities that focus on their personal and professional goals, development, and growth." The company is willing to promote from within, and employees enthuse, "If you want to succeed and grow at BAH, nothing will hold you back."

LOCATIONS WHERE ENTRY-LEVEL EMPLOYEES WORK

The majority of the company's undergraduate hires join the firm in the Washington, DC metro area or at corporate headquarters in McLean, Virginia. Only about 10–20 percent of entry-level opportunities are located in offices outside the Washington, DC metro area.

AVERAGE NUMBER OF APPLICATIONS EACH YEAR

Booz Allen receives between 8,000 and 10,000 applications per year from undergrads and recent grads.

AVERAGE NUMBER HIRED PER YEAR OVER THE LAST TEN YEARS

The company hires an average of 150 entry-level employees per year.

ENTRY-LEVEL POSITIONS AVAILABLE

Entry-level employees at Booz Allen work as junior-level consultants and junior-level researchers.

AVERAGE HOURS WORKED PER WEEK

The number of hours worked by entry-level employees varies by team. Employees of all levels have the opportunity to work flexible schedules.

PERCENTAGE OF ENTRY-LEVEL HIRES STILL WITH THE COMPANY AFTER THREE, FIVE, AND TEN YEARS

According to company stats, "After three years, 72 percent of all entry-level employees remain with the company . . . after five years, 70 percent of all entry-level employees remain with the company."

Getting Hired

While they also accept applications via their website, Booz Allen Hamilton actively recruits on a number of college campuses, and many successful candidates have their first contact with the company through an informal interview at a career center or career fair. A prospective employee shares, "This first round of interview[ing] was mostly focused on my college experiences and (I believe) my personality and overall fit with Booz Allen. During the initial interview, I didn't speak too [much] in depth about my specific skill sets—it was a more relaxed interview in which I think I was just being assessed for my work ethic, personality, and drive." The second round of interviews is "more formal," and candidates are usually invited to a Booz Allen office to meet with a team looking to recruit a new member. Many candidates are also asked to participate in a mega-interview session at world headquarters in McLean, where "each candidate [has] between one and six interviews, and, after you finish your interviews, you [can] rank the teams you interviewed with in order of your preference." Later, the company matches desirable candidates with positions in their top-ranked departments. Current employees say you can expect lots of situational questions at second round interviews, as well as inquiries about "specific skill sets developed in college and how these skills would be useful to the team."

Money and Perks

Booz Allen offers competitive entry-level salaries to new hires, and "depending on your yearly evaluations, you have the ability to make rather nice leaps in your salaried amount." On the job, Booz Allen's excellent professional education program offers "fabulous online and off-site training" as well as "up to $5,000 per year in tuition reimbursement, so it is a very attractive place to work and get an MBA, for example." Booz Allen also displays a strong commitment to preserving the balance between work and personal life, offering employees the "opportunity to work from home and set your own hours depending on what is most convenient for you." An employee tells us, "A colleague that I sit next to leaves early twice a week so he can go to night classes for a Human Resources certification and that is perfectly fine."

The Ropes

The first day on the job, all new Booz Allen employees attend a half-day New Hire Orientation. At lunchtime, they head off to their branch office for a more personal introduction to the company. An employee remembers, "During this day-long introduction, we finished at around one in the afternoon and then we met our 'New Hire Buddy.' This individual was there to help with any immediate questions of concern and help us navigate the halls and get materials. My new hire buddy went around to each of the people he knew on my team and introduced me." On their second day, new hires join their group on projects and are encouraged to "watch, listen, and learn and ask as many questions as [they can]." Within the first few weeks, newbies are required to attend two more training sessions, which provide more information about the company and its policies as well as instruction in the consulting process. A new hire enthuses, "The session was very interactive with group projects and a final presentation. Both training sessions gave me the chance to network with other new employees and meet some really interesting and accomplished people." Once this formal introduction to the company is complete, Booz Allen prides itself on its professional education program, and that "there is always an opportunity to receive training on virtually any topic imaginable, either through an online course or through an off-site course taught by a Booz Allen instructor."

Day in the Life

During their first year with the company, most new hires "work in a team environment, have frequent interaction with clients, and own a discrete work stream for which they are responsible for driving." Recalls a former newbie, "I was surprised how quickly I was given responsibility and how much trust my team had in me even though I was very new." On a typical day, new hires could be involved in any aspect of a consulting project—visiting sites, meeting with team members or clients, or qualitatively and quantitatively analyzing data to support recommendations. A current entry-level employee shares, "Right now I'm doing a lot of data management—overseeing data collection efforts being done by the Air Force. I'm also analyzing data we receive and reporting the results back to the client on a regular basis."

Peers

Booz Allen is an exceptionally friendly workplace and employees describe their coworkers as being "very bright, energetic, and incredibly insightful." The transition from college to the real world is smoothed by the Junior Exempt Employee Forum (JEEF), which "is focused on helping new hires within Booz Allen." Through JEEF, "there are a lot of social events (such as happy hours) in addition to a lot of forums on important issues for young professionals." A newbie enthuses, "We have done a lot of fun activities since I've been here, including renting a crab boat on the Potomac River for three hours, having many happy hour events in the Rosslyn area, playing on a Booz Allen flag football team, enjoying a bowling competition . . . the list goes on. Booz Allen is a great place for young people—there are so many fun events going on all of the time!" While first-jobbers working at the smaller offices (rather than the larger branches in DC and McLean) might not have access to the same number of young comrades, the vibe is nonetheless sociable. An employee in Booz Allen's Richmond office attests, "We are of varying ages and some people have children, but we do make an effort to go out about once every two or three weeks and socialize and relax and be cool."

Moving on

After a few years of consulting with Booz Allen, a certain number of employees take their business expertise to positions with other companies. But Booz Allen takes attrition in stride. In fact, "Booz Allen has an active 'Come Back Kid' program that works with people who want to come back to the firm . . . [some] say that many of our best clients were once Booz Allen employees who have taken the expertise they gained serving many clients to one institution." However, as the company's reps point out, "Our people don't have to leave the firm to try something new. Booz Allen offers an internal transfer process through our Career Mobility Program. Staff can transfer between teams to pursue new opportunities and learn new skills."

BORDERS GROUP
COLLEGE GRADUATE TRAINING PROGRAM

BORDERS.
BOOKS MUSIC MOVIES CAFE

> "You automatically have a peer group spread throughout the company whom you can ask questions of and whom you continue to work with."

The Big Picture

The Borders Group, owner of both the Borders and Waldenbooks chains, has had "great success" with its College Graduate Training Program, which aims "to hire and develop college graduates to build a strong foundation of future leaders within [the] Borders Group." The program includes mentoring, cross-functional team projects, on-site training at stores and warehouse facilities, and seminars.

LOCATION(S) WHERE ENTRY-LEVEL EMPLOYEES WORK

The headquarters is located in Ann Arbor, Michigan.

AVERAGE NUMBER OF APPLICATIONS EACH YEAR

Borders Group receives more than 750 applications each year.

AVERAGE NUMBER HIRED PER YEAR

Borders Group hires six entry-level employees per year.

ENTRY-LEVEL POSITION(S) AVAILABLE

Entry-level employees enter the College Graduate Training Program, with placements in corporate finance, marketing, IT, and human resources.

AVERAGE HOURS WORKED PER WEEK

Entry-level employees work 40 to 45 hours per week.

PERCENTAGE OF ENTRY-LEVEL HIRES STILL WITH THE COMPANY AFTER THREE, FIVE, AND TEN YEARS

More than 80 percent of entry-level hires remain with the company after three years; and 80 percent stay on for five or more years.

BENEFITS OFFERED

Borders Group offers medical and dental insurance (the premiums for which are shared by the company and the employee). Additional benefits include basic life insurance, business travel insurance, short-term disability, a 401(k) program, store discounts and other corporate discounts, adoption assistance, and alternative work schedules.

Getting Hired

Borders Group recruits on campus and online. The company reviews the "academic performance, leadership traits, previous internships, analytical skills, results orientation, and flexibility" of all of its candidates. Preference is given to college graduates with relevant degrees (e.g., a bachelor's degree in computer science for IT applicants), a GPA of at least 3.0, and a record of campus involvement. Resumes are reviewed by human resources, and "the most qualified students are selected for our initial round of interviews [that are] conducted by a Borders Group human resources team member. Students selected for second-round interviews are brought on-site for additional human resources and functional team interviews. Roundtable discussions occur after that point to [review the qualifications of] all final candidates; all candidates are notified of their status shortly thereafter."

One successful applicant writes, "The interviews were very comfortable. The thing that stuck out most in my mind was that all three of the people I interviewed with mentioned career advancement to me. Considering I was just trying to get my first job, I was very excited that everyone would be so interested in what my second job could be. I also noticed that the entire company seemed very casual. I received a lot of smiles and nods from people in the halls who noticed that I stuck out in my full business suit."

Money and Perks

As is the case with many first jobs, base salary levels are predetermined by functional area at Borders Group. Annual raises "are based on performance evaluation," as are bonuses. The company explains: "The Performance Bonus Pool is a fund that is used to reward the highest-performing employees at the corporate office. These top performers are employees who continually go above and beyond expectations while delivering outstanding results. The Performance Bonus Pool is a tool to reward exceptional employees. It also reinforces our 'pay for performance' compensation philosophy."

Perks include "amazing employee discounts," "flexible work schedules that allow for four ten-hour days per week or nine nine-hour days with alternate Fridays off," and "at least one concert per quarter open to all employees at the home office."

The Ropes

The College Graduate Training Program commences with a one-day orientation, followed by a structured six-month plan that includes mentoring, diversity training, seminars, team projects, and on-site training at stores and warehouses. One trainee in finance reports, "The program gives you the opportunity to work on cross-functional projects, to visit and work in the stores and warehouse, and to learn about areas of the company [from] executives. In the finance area, it also allows you to go on a rotational program through three areas of finance, staying in each area for six months." Another trainee notes, "Each week, leaders and executives from the company talked with the College Grad group about their areas of the business, their key strategies and initiatives, and how they got to where they are."

Day in the Life

The College Training Program is rotational; details of rotations vary according to the new hire's specific job function. A human resources trainee tells us that "I spent the first three months supporting our Borders stores in recruitment. I then moved to the training department and learned to develop and facilitate training programs. I was also responsible for some project management in this role. After four months in training, I moved into corporate human resources, where I learned how to interview and select top talent, manage employee relations concerns, become a strategic partner to my client groups, and communicate with all levels of employees within the organization." An IT hire writes, "During a typical day, I'd receive requests to schedule [and] automate a process. I had to contact the requestor to collect requirements and determine if the requirements fit with the company standards for automation. I would take that information and summarize it into a document that my manager would approve before the request was fulfilled. After approval, I would create documentation of the new process." A trainee in promotions reports that "a typical day is pushing at least three different projects forward each day. On most days, I respond to questions and concerns from the field, work with vendors to solicit the best products, work with vendors to execute the details of our tests, and find ways to add incremental revenue to the bottom line by building awareness tactics or with promotions."

Peers

Meeting peers "is what the College Graduate Training Program is great for," writes one participant. "You automatically have a peer group spread throughout the company whom you can ask questions of and whom you continue to work with. In my different positions, I have had many business relationships with [my original] group. You also have someone to call on to relate subjects that you may not know much about. If I know I need to talk to the person in marketing that's responsible for X, I call one of the people in marketing [from] the program, and they tell me who to talk to." After work, "there is a significant amount of camaraderie" among new hires, "though as the years go on, you tend to split up into groups that continue to have more things in common (married/single, finance/merchandising, etc.)." The connections continue after the program ends; one grad reports, "We have actually created a group called 'Momentum' that people can join after the College Graduate Training Program is completed. This organization allows [us] to continue to get the exposure and access to the things that will help us in our careers." The group facilitates "access to working on special projects for the New Business Development area, roundtable discussions with executives and managers, volunteer opportunities with our Employee Foundation, etc."

Moving on

Borders Group informs us that "Our College [Graduate Training Program] has only been in effect for four full years (just starting out the fifth year as we speak). Of the forty participants in the program, 20 percent have left the company. All have had very positive things to say about Borders and their experience with us." Those who leave typically do so "to change industries or career focus (from retail to financial services, for example, or from marketing to education)." Some seek a change of venue, with many looking to move to a bigger city than Ann Arbor. Others go back to school; one such first jobber writes, "I [may] leave the company if I elect to pursue my MBA. However, I would like to secure my next position here at Borders before I would consider leaving. Borders has offered me challenging projects that many companies would not allow an entry-level employee to handle. I appreciate their merit-based advancement and enjoy the variety and challenging pace of a project management role here."

Attrition

Borders Group loses less than 3 percent of its college graduate hires within twelve months of initial employment.

BOSTON BEER COMPANY
SALES REPRESENTATIVE

"The higher you go with the company, the less you have someone holding your hand because BBC sets up such a solid way of teaching that you know how to conduct your job on your own."

The Big Picture

Recent grads have the opportunity to join Boston Beer Company as a part of its sales team, enjoying tremendous career opportunities, contact with local nightlife and culture, and the ability to "wake up in the morning with a smile on [their] face[s] and say, 'I love what I do for a living.'" In addition to perks like a car allowance and free cases of beer, Boston Beer employees love "the camaraderie among employees as well as their passion for the product they are selling."

LOCATIONS WHERE ENTRY-LEVEL EMPLOYEES WORK

Entry-level employees work in cities where there are major markets for Boston Beer, including but not limited to: Boston; New York; Philadelphia; Phoenix; Minneapolis; San Diego; Washington, DC; Atlanta; and Chicago.

AVERAGE NUMBER OF APPLICATIONS EACH YEAR

Boston Beer receives thousands of applications annually for entry-level positions.

AVERAGE NUMBER HIRED PER YEAR OVER THE LAST TEN YEARS

Since the inception of the entry-level sales representative program in 1999, Boston Beer has hired an average of 15 employees per year.

ENTRY-LEVEL POSITIONS AVAILABLE

Recent graduates are eligible to fill the position of sales representative.

AVERAGE HOURS WORKED PER WEEK

Sales representatives generally work between 45 and 50 hours a week, but it is not a typical 9-to-5 position. Employees frequently spend off-hours planning their daily schedules, and many sales reps work night and weekend events as part of the job.

PERCENTAGE OF ENTRY-LEVEL HIRES STILL WITH THE COMPANY AFTER THREE, FIVE, AND TEN YEARS

According to company data, "after three years, 70 percent of sales representatives are still with [the] company. After five years, 62 percent of sales representatives are still with the company."

Getting Hired

Seeking candidates who demonstrate, "strong judgment and problem solving skills, commitment to task, communication skills, leadership, [and] organizational skills," Boston Beer puts prospective employees to the test through their rigorous, "team-based hiring approach." In most cases, the process begins with a campus interview. After that, "candidates move to spending a day in the field with one of our sales people—they get to actually do the job for the day." Next, candidates have another campus interview, followed by an interview with a division manager, and finally, an interview with the national sales manager in Boston. According to survivors, the process is challenging, and candidates are routinely asked experience-based and situational questions. For example, one candidate tells us that in her final interview, the national sales manager "tested my confidence, asked about my organization, asked how I would handle difficult situations, and, at times, tried to make me squirm." Sound tough? An HR Rep explains the logic: "Since we are focusing on competencies in the candidates, we are looking for specific examples of a time in the past that they can use as evidence to answer the question."

Money and Perks

Entry-level sales representatives receive a decent salary with some potential for increase; however, employees warn, "If you are in this job for the money, you won't be happy." New hires stay bubbly with the predictable benefit of "free beer!" and reimbursement on Sam Adams–included bar tabs. In addition, sales reps "do get to travel quite a bit to Boston, Chicago, and Florida," and enjoy the "$500 car payment the company provides each month."

The Ropes

All new Boston Beer employees attend an intensive week-long orientation session, which provides, "a broad overview of the company, our people, our industry, the brewing process, and the selling process." A graduate tells us, "Orientation itself entailed a ton of learning! My head was spinning with all of the knowledge that I took back to San Diego the following week." Some head-spinning might also be attributed to company founder Jim Koch "doing a tasting of all the different styles of Samuel Adams," which traditionally kicks off orientation week. After orientation, new sales reps return to their region to begin a twelve-week training period. A sales rep details, "My boss had every day over those twelve weeks laid out for me, which involved watching my mentor sell, meeting with my boss regarding any questions or feelings I had, working with other employees on my sales team, and eventually learning how to make the transition to selling on my own." Excellent mentorship and direction is a hallmark of the program, and satisfied employees say supervisors are "understanding—they listened well and they challenged me to think in unique ways and really push myself to run with my ideas."

Day in the Life

While new sales reps are closely guided during their first few months in the program, they are afforded increasingly independent tasks over time. Explains a former sales rep, "I slowly received more responsibility and took over my own territory and even grew my own territory. The higher you go with the company, the less you have someone holding your hand because BBC sets up such a solid way of teaching that you know how to conduct your job on your own." Once on their own, sales reps "are responsible for planning [their] day, using sales numbers to find sales trends and opportunities" and are "expected to see at least eight accounts each day, selling in new distribution, becoming more visible, working on pricing, advertising, and programs within each account." A sales rep reports, "I would get into my market by 10:00 A.M. at the very latest, usually earlier. I would visit accounts all day long; I would sit down with decision makers . . . and [then] discuss how I could help them grow their business."

Peers

Naturals to the sales industry, Boston Beer employees are generally "extroverted people who love to interact with one another." Enthuses a newbie, "My peers were smart, laid-back, and, simply stated, good people. I could relate to them, and we all grew to depend on one another for support, advice, and motivation." While many sales reps live too far away from others to socialize on a regular basis, "there can be a big social scene if you are placed into a market where there are other account managers." However, even those who don't rendezvous every weekend say there is a great deal of camaraderie between first jobbers. "Everyone at Boston Beer is like family. Whether you see them weekly, monthly, or once a year, we communicate so often . . . it makes no difference," assures a sales rep.

Moving on

According to Boston Beer representatives, "Most people leave the company for personal or job-fit reasons. They may decide to go back to graduate school or find they are not able to relocate . . . in order to be promoted, or [find] that a career in sales is not the right fit for them." Indeed, there are great opportunities within the company, but employees agree that "being geographically flexible will give you a better chance of being promoted."

Attrition

Some tell us that money can be a contributing factor in a career change, as sales jobs in other industries, such as phar-maceuticals, often receive better compensation. For those who stay on, they say there are great rewards for good work. Shares a current employee, "I was only with the company for fourteen months when I received my first promotion, which also included a generous pay raise. I received my first pay raise after nine months, during the company's annual review process."

BP

VARIOUS POSITIONS

bp

Employees value the "career growth and potential for global travel," and "working for a company that seriously values the importance of diversity and inclusion."

The Big Picture

BP (originally British Petroleum) is a multinational energy company known for developing new ways to produce and supply oil and gas and for developing and investing in alternative fuels like hydrogen, solar, and wind. Its brands include BP, ARCO, Aral, Castrol, ampm, and Wild Bean Café. All new hires go into an early development program such as the much-praised Challenge Program, a three-year rotational program that provides learning opportunities and social support.

LOCATION(S) WHERE ENTRY-LEVEL EMPLOYEES WORK

BP has locations throughout the United States and the world. The largest offices are in "Alaska, California, Illinois, Ohio, and Texas."

AVERAGE NUMBER OF APPLICATIONS EACH YEAR

BP receives approximately 10,000 applications each year.

AVERAGE NUMBER HIRED PER YEAR OVER THE LAST TEN YEARS

Around 150 employees have been hired per year, on average.

ENTRY-LEVEL POSITIONS AVAILABLE

"BP has entry-level positions for engineers, geoscientists, and [those] with business degrees (i.e., accounting, economics, finance, human resources, land management, logistics, marketing, [and] procurement/supply chain management)." Other positions are "too numerous to list."

AVERAGE HOURS WORKED PER WEEK

Employees work a standard 40-hour week.

AVERAGE STARTING SALARY

The company states, "Average starting salaries range from $50,000 to $54,999." Some engineers and geophysicists report starting salaries over $60,000.

Getting Hired

Most new hires connect with BP through on-campus recruiting at about forty-four universities "and at the annual conventions of a number of professional societies—[e.g.,] National Society of Black Engineers, Society of Women Engineers, Society of Exploration Geophysicists, [and] National Society of Hispanic MBAs." At these interviews, BP "look[s] for employees who are intelligent, have some work experience [and] demonstrated leadership skills, are good communicators, and appear to be highly motivated." If the company is interested in you, expect a trip to Houston (and to your potential job site, if different), meals, a battery of interviews, and some serious wooing. One employee describes the trip: "I was met by a host who took me to dinner and then the Houston ballet . . . . The next day I had a series of three interviews." Another says, "Previous to the team interview, I was told how many applicants I was still competing with for the job as well as why they were interested in me. At the team interview, the tone was very friendly. There was only one technical question. Mostly, I was asked what kind of work I would be interested in doing for BP, [and] about personal hobbies and interests. After the last interview, I was told that I would be contacted in a week and was actually called three days later with the offer."

Money and Perks

"The start date and what kind of projects I worked on were negotiable, but the location and salary were not," reports one employee. Another adds, "The starting salary offers [are] so good in this industry . . . there's not much need for negotiation." In addition to the standard benefits and compensation package, employees value getting "every other Friday off." Other employees value the "career growth and potential for global travel," and "working for a company that seriously values the importance of diversity and inclusion."

The Ropes

Every new hire is part of a structured development program. BP's Exploration and Production segment, for example, offers the Challenge Program, which is "like an extended orientation" and includes "several training classes throughout the year for your chosen discipline—up to twenty-five days of training a year for the first three years." During the first year, employees also attend Induction, "a two-week training event held in various parts of the world, including Egypt, Trinidad, the UK, Vietnam, Indonesia, [and] Houston." A satisfied new hire reports, "Unfortunately, I went to Houston, but I still thoroughly enjoyed the program, [which] teach[es] you about the oil industry [and] reservoir, petroleum, and facilities engineering. You go on field trips to see various geological events. We had several projects [on which] we worked in teams and had to present our results at the end. It was also a good way to see how globally diverse BP is . . . 50 percent of the class is from the host country and 50 percent is from other countries." In addition, "after two years with the organization, university hires from around the world attend the Global Graduate Forum," a two-day company and career issues conference in London.

Day in the Life

On the whole, BP employees find their work challenging and stimulating. "A typical day might involve a few hours working on seismic interpretation," says a geophysicist. "During that time I might ask a colleague to help me with a specific problem or . . . for an opinion. If well operations [are] going on, I might sit in on a conference call with the rig to determine the progress of the well, and then update a plot or figure with the new data. I might also . . . attend a team meeting or a project meeting." Employees tend to enjoy considerable flexibility with projects. One employee reports: "I feel like my work is important, otherwise I would push for another project. With all it takes to run successful projects, time doesn't need to be wasted . . . if something needs to be done but is tedious and not meaningful, temporary hires are typically available and happy to fill in."

Peers

Newbies tend to share "a lot of camaraderie" since most "are from out of town, so they don't know a lot of people here—other new hires may be the only people that they have to hang out with." Because "BP is very good at hiring people with talent," it's not exactly pulling teeth to get colleagues to socialize. The Challenge Program coordinates many such opportunities, including "happy hours, general meetings," "lectures," "[a] holiday party, [and] intramural sports teams" for new hires.

Moving on

None of the staffers we spoke with had concrete plans to leave the company. "I am happily employed by BP and intend to stay until retirement," says one. Another adds, "The only reason I would leave [would be a] personal [one]."

Attrition

A company official reports that less than one percent of first jobbers leave during the first year.

Best and Worst

"Many university hires have moved up from entry-level jobs into our top management positions—including our current CEO, John Browne."

BRIGHTPOINT
VARIOUS POSITIONS

"The company is very good at [providing] on-the-job training. There is [always] the opportunity to learn from one of the many offered classes."

The Big Picture

Brightpoint "offers the most comprehensive selection of brands and products in the wireless industry," including a variety of telephones, PDAs, modems, and software. The company also sells logistics and subscriber services, channel development services, and advanced wireless services to corporate clients. Brightpoint's customers include such heavy hitters as Virgin Mobile USA, Cingular Wireless, and Motorola. First jobbers join the Brightpoint team in sales, customer service, operations, product testing, and accounting. Because Brightpoint is in the burgeoning wireless industry, "our business continues to grow." One first jobber reports "We have room for growth [at work], and I also have the ability to obtain a master's degree with 100 percent reimbursement. As a result, I believe my pay and responsibility within the company can only grow."

LOCATION(S) WHERE ENTRY-LEVEL EMPLOYEES WORK

Entry-level employees work in Plainfield, Indiana and Reno, Nevada.

AVERAGE NUMBER OF APPLICATIONS EACH YEAR

Brightpoint receives 1,200 applications for entry-level positions per year.

AVERAGE NUMBER HIRED PER YEAR

Brightpoint hires about 150 entry-level employees per year.

ENTRY-LEVEL POSITION(S) AVAILABLE

A variety of positions are open to entry-level employees at Brightpoint.

AVERAGE HOURS WORKED PER WEEK

Entry-level hires work 45 hours per week.

AVERAGE STARTING SALARY

Average starting salaries range; production assemblers, for example, earn $17,000; financial analysts earn $38,000–$40,000; and operation supervisors earn $40,000.

BENEFITS OFFERED

Employees receive a choice of medical plans and supplemental medical insurance as well as dental and vision coverage; Brightpoint also offers flexible spending accounts.

Additional benefits include short- and long-term disability; life, accidental death, and dismemberment insurance; an employee stock-purchase program; a 401(k) plan; tuition reimbursement; paid time off; holiday pay; an on-site cafeteria and on-site fitness center; and discounts on telephone accessories.

Getting Hired

All initial job applications to Brightpoint are made online. The Human Resources Department reviews all applications and then conducts a phone-screen interview with potential new hires. Those who sufficiently impress human resources have their files forwarded to hiring managers for review, who may contact them to schedule the first of a minimum of two face-to-face interviews. Reference checks, a background check, and a drug screen conclude the hiring process. The company "looks at technical skills; but in addition, we look at the soft skills necessary to position an employee for short-term and long-term success." Several of the first jobbers we spoke with here began their tenure with the company as temp workers or interns; once they had demonstrated their abilities, they were brought on as full-time employees.

Money and Perks

Salary, location, and job responsibilities are typically not negotiable for most Brightpoint first jobbers; start date is, however, "somewhat negotiable." Some entry-level hires, depending on their positions, "can be eligible for bonuses [that amount to] up to ten percent of their pay. These bonuses are based on company performance, department performance, and individual performance." New hires in sales earn a commission on top of their salaries. Prime fringe benefits here include "great discounts on electronics and accessories," "lots of travel to trade shows and company events," a "laid-back atmosphere" in the workplace, and the satisfaction of sharing in the "company's involvement with the community." Best of all, perhaps, is the fact that the company offers "many opportunities for growth."

The Ropes

Orientation at Brightpoint includes a detailed discussion, led by a company executive, of Brightpoint history and the responsibilities of the core divisions. "A great deal of time is spent going over the company policies and benefits," writes a company official. According to one newbie, the process "lasts about a day and a half;" it also includes lunch, a tour of the building, and an introduction to the fitness center. Subsequent training occurs on the job. An operations supervisor explains, "My training included instruction in how to process using the company's system and the standard operating procedures pertaining to the area in which I worked. I was trained by associates, team leads, and supervisors." A marketing coordinator adds, "I'm constantly learning how our internal processes work. I go through training with my immediate manager. I also have the opportunity to utilize Brightpoint University for any additional training needs [I may have]. An example of this would be Adobe Photoshop classes or time management skills training." One first jobber agrees, "The company is very good at [providing] on-the-job training. There is [always] the opportunity to learn from one of the many offered classes."

Day in the Life

Brightpoint hires first jobbers across a wide range of positions. Operations supervisors work in the distribution center, managing teams to ensure that orders are filled promptly. Project coordinators "manage and coordinate various sales and customer service projects and activities with the account managers." Staff accountants handle standard entry-level accounting duties by generating operational and financial reports. Financial analysts "develop, interpret, and implement complex financial and accounting concepts or techniques for financial planning and control" and "assist in determining operational cost evaluation of business performance." Product/test engineers "write, update, and maintain all customer files at Brightpoint while providing support (hardware, software, and troubleshooting) to all customers both internally and externally." The company also hires customer service representatives and production line workers at the entry level.

Peers

"Everyone is very friendly" at Brightpoint, and as a result, the work environment is "very comfortable." One first jobber writes, "Everyone here is very positive and upbeat. The company president is just as easy to get along with as those in entry-level positions." Workers "frequently go to lunch together," "participate in community service events," and enjoy an occasional night out as well.

BROOKSOURCE
CORPORATE RECRUITER

> "I know by putting myself out there, accepting challenges, and doing all that I can to prove my compassion for the company while striving for success, opportunities will be presented to me."

The Big Picture

A technical recruiting company based in the Midwest, Brooksource offers recent grads the opportunity to join their team as entry-level recruiters. While all new hires start in the same capacity, "there's a lot of flexibility with one's career path with Brooksource. It is definitely conducive to change, and adapts to each employee's strength(s)." Inspiring tremendous employee loyalty, this five-year-old firm suffers little attrition and is known for having a lively and sociable office environment that extends well past the workday. New employees are big fans of their jobs, the company, and their coworkers, and tell us that receiving an offer from Brooksource makes you "the luckiest person alive."

LOCATION(S) WHERE ENTRY-LEVEL EMPLOYEES WORK

Brooksource hires entry-level recruiters for each of their eight offices, which are located in Indianapolis, Indiana; Chicago, Illinois; Cincinnati, Ohio; Louisville, Kentucky; Columbus, Ohio; Nashville, Tennessee; Detroit, Michigan; and Philadelphia, Pennsylvania.

AVERAGE NUMBER OF APPLICATIONS EACH YEAR

Brooksource receives about 1,000 applications each year.

AVERAGE NUMBER HIRED PER YEAR OVER THE LAST TEN YEARS

The company hires between 20 and 25 new employees each year, though that number is rising.

ENTRY-LEVEL POSITION(S) AVAILABLE

All new hires enter the company as corporate recruiters, which "helps each new hire to learn the industry and the ins and outs of the company." Because "everything about Brooksource comes back to the recruiting foundation," even those who move on to new positions within the company say the recruiting experience was indispensable to their career.

AVERAGE HOURS WORKED PER WEEK

Corporate recruiters work between 45 and 50 hours per week.

AVERAGE STARTING SALARY

Depending on the local market, new employees earn roughly $30,000 per year plus commissions based on performance.

Getting Hired

Landing a job with Brooksource has much to do with your personality and character, as the firm looks for "genuine people [who] posses true leadership ability and outgoing personalities" and who "would be a good fit, personality-wise" within the company's distinct office culture. When reviewing applications, Brooksource tends to favor applicants who, during college, were "extremely involved on campus, whether with student government, the Greek community (fraternities/sororities), [or] volunteer programs, or were predominant leaders of certain groups or clubs." Interestingly enough, applicants need not be computer wizards: "Even though we're an IT company, you don't have to have a technical background in order to perform the job." Brooksource accepts applications through their website and attends career fairs on college campuses, inviting promising candidates to interview in person. Strong candidates are invited to a second interview and occasionally a third interview or day at the office. Due to the company's emphasis on a personal "fit," many report that Brooksource interviews aren't strictly formal but "more of a conversation." A recent hire recalls, "It was a very good interview process. Everyone who interviewed me made sure I was a fit [in terms of] my personal goals . . . as well as my personality. I was asked a good mixture of traditional interview questions along with questions [used] to gauge my interpersonal skills."

Money and Perks

While Brooksource employees believe the $30,000 base salary is a bit lower than what they might receive at a larger company, they are quick to point out that the stimulation and growth opportunities make up for the smaller paycheck. Besides, all employees—including new hires—have the opportunity to augment their earnings through a "commission structure based on performance." Motivated workers are tantalized by the possibility of a quick promotion and the vision of more money in their future. Explains a current recruiter, "As an account executive, there is no limit or ceiling as to how much money can be made. It's up to the individual and how hard they work." In addition to their paychecks, recruiters receive traditional sales perks such as commission for the people they place and reimbursement for miles traveled for work. Once a worker is promoted to an Account Executive position, he or she is also eligible for both a car and mobile phone allowance (this promotion typically takes place between eight and twelve months after an employee's start date). However, many tell us that the company's decidedly social atmosphere is the best perk of the bunch. A new recruit reports the best fringe benefit is "the office/company outings that are planned to help coworkers bond with one another outside of the office. So far, the Detroit office has been to two Detroit Tigers games and gone out after work for celebrations. As an entire company, we spent a weekend in St. Joe, Michigan, at the wineries, to thank employees for a job well done in the previous year and to promote interoffice relationships."

The Ropes

Every year, Brooksource operates four or five week-long training programs in Indianapolis, Indiana for new employees. Providing a general introduction to the IT industry and a crash course in recruiting techniques, the program proves indispensable to employees' performance and helps "new hires feel welcome" in the company. After their week-long boot camp, new recruiters are dropped directly onto the battlefield, where they learn the ins and outs of the industry through on-the-job experience. While more seasoned recruiters are always available to help, the Brooksource motto might be, in the words of one employee, "the best way to learn is to be thrown into the fire." Even so, another newbie assures us, "I hardly ever feel like I'm in over my head because I have been adequately trained as a recruiter and my peers are always available if I have questions." Fostering an independent yet supportive work atmosphere, "Brooksource gives you the opportunity to fail. But they're there to help you get up when it happens."

Day in the Life

Every Brooksource office begins the day with a "Five Star Meeting," during which the entire team reports their progress on current projects. When the meeting adjourns, the recruiting begins. On a typical day, new recruiters look for potential candidates to fill open positions, interview candidates in person and via telephone, and help facilitate the interview process with their clients. The minimum weekly expectations for a recruiter are "to complete at least 100 calls, which, in turn, should produce around 25 biographies on potential candidates for positions and at least 5 internal candidates brought in for technical positions for our clients." While these requirements are usually "a challenge to fulfill" at first, Brooksource employees enjoy being put to the test. Says one, "I know that, every day when I walk into work, I need to bring my 'A' game and be successful and put in 110 percent, or I'd feel like I cheated the company out of a day's pay." Employees embrace the fact that they are "getting some great experience" and feel that they "really contribute to any success that Brooksource has."

Peers

Brooksource employees express an endearing affection for their talented coworkers, describing them as "professional, intelligent, driven, successful, and friendly people." "Our company is comparable to a massive group of outgoing, type-A, successful, well-rounded individuals who have had major success in their high school and college careers," says one enthusiastic employee. Working together with just a tad of healthy competition, Brooksource employees find their niche and go with it. "I feel I am able to communicate with any member of the company, no matter what their position within the company, at any time," says a recent hire. Come 5:00 P.M., Brooksource is host to a "very large after-hours social scene." In fact, Brooksource employees are fond of describing their environment with the familiar "work hard, play hard" mantra, claiming that socializing and celebration are a big part of their corporate culture. Of the new hires that are recent transplants, many report that Brooksource has become a "home away from home," saying that Brooksource allows you to maintain "that college mentality, but transition into the real world."

Moving on

Founded in 2000, Brooksource is a fairly new company, and hasn't experienced much of an exodus in its half-decade of operation. As of this publishing, all of the company's original employees (those who were hired in 2000) remain in its ranks, and 80 percent of those who joined in later years have also stayed on board.

Attrition

Brooksource employees are characterized by a strong faith in and loyalty to their company. One employee explains, "I know by putting myself out there, accepting challenges, and doing all that I can to prove my compassion for the company while striving for success, opportunities will be presented to me." Those who move on usually do so for personal reasons, such the relocation of a spouse or a desire to relocate to a city where Brooksource does not have an office.

Best and Worst

Brooksource hopes that every new employee meets success within the company, and the company has structured their recruiting process in an effort to find and hire the best and most well-matched candidates. At Brooksource, "successful employee[s] are passionate about their job, their career, and about Brooksource." Given the high-energy and self-directed nature of the work, "unsuccessful employees are those who have no drive. They typically don't see the big picture and are looking for a predetermined career path."

CATERPILLAR
VARIOUS POSITIONS

"One of the best things about this program is the amount of exposure you get to leadership."

The Big Picture

Come work for the company that makes the big machines. According to the company's website, Caterpillar is "the leading manufacturer of construction and mining equipment, diesel and natural gas engines, and industrial gas turbines." Caterpillar is one of America's most successful industrial companies; employees enjoy a salary that they call "competitive" and a benefits package that they rate as "top-notch."

LOCATION(S) WHERE ENTRY-LEVEL EMPLOYEES WORK

"Caterpillar is a global company, with nearly 250 company facilities worldwide. While many of the entry-level new hires would begin their career at the company's Peoria, Illinois headquarters, Caterpillar has independent dealers and customers on every continent."

AVERAGE NUMBER OF APPLICATIONS EACH YEAR

"Caterpillar receives about 50,000 applications each year for all positions across the company. About one-third of those applications are from recent college graduates."

AVERAGE NUMBER HIRED PER YEAR OVER THE LAST TEN YEARS

"Over the last ten years, Caterpillar has hired about 1,000 people per year on the management payroll, which is where the majority of entry-level hiring takes place."

ENTRY-LEVEL POSITION(S) AVAILABLE

"Caterpillar hires entry-level employees in a variety of disciplines. The primary areas include engineering, information technology, manufacturing, marketing and communications, business, accounting, and finance."

AVERAGE HOURS WORKED PER WEEK

"The majority of positions within Caterpillar are full-time [and require] 40 hours per week minimum. Many jobs offer varying degrees of travel as a part of the position responsibility. Management employees are expected to manage their time and workload appropriately, often requiring time at work beyond the 40-hour minimum."

Getting Hired

Caterpillar recruits on campuses and also accepts applications through its website. Company representatives tell us that "the development of a diverse, global workforce within an environment that encourages innovation and rewards individual and team performance is critical to its future success. Caterpillar values diversity, not only in the race or gender of its employees, but also in their background, skills, and experience." First jobbers from Caterpillar's more than twenty different business units similarly describe the hiring process. Here's how one newbie in human resources recalls it: "The director of compensation and benefits, the director of succession management, the corporate [human relations] manager, and the director of human relations interviewed me. Each interview was one hour in length and was a structured behavior-based interview. The questions revolved around how I have responded in the past to given situations (i.e., 'Tell me about a time you had to convince a boss or coworker of your idea'). During my interview, the program coordinator gave me an overview of the program. She also took me to lunch. At the end of the day, I was given a drug test. The program coordinator contacted me approximately a week later with a job offer."

Money and Perks

"Salary increases are based on business conditions and strongly tied to job performance" at Caterpillar. "The highest performers are rewarded with the highest salary increases," company representatives report. First jobbers rave about the benefits package; one new hire tells us that "the entire package is excellent. If I were forced to pick one as the best, I would say the 401(k) plan. Caterpillar matches employee contributions to the 401(k) plan dollar-for-dollar up to the first 6 percent of gross salary. These contributions are immediately vested." Other new hires say the best perk is "working in a team environment. This allowed [us] to meet a large group of [our] people in a short time. Also, there were after-work sporting and social events that allowed everyone to get acquainted with [one another] outside of the work environment."

The Ropes

Orientation and training regimens at Caterpillar "vary by business unit or functional area." Many of the employees we spoke with describe a one-week orientation period; however, some (such as those in marketing) recount orientation periods that lasted over three months, and others describe being briefly introduced to their bosses before getting to work. For most positions, orientation and training are both thorough and rigorous, designed to ensure that new hires are familiar with both Caterpillar's corporate culture and the tasks for which they were hired; these processes typically involve classes and seminars, team-building exercises, plant tours, and equipment-specific training. New hires in manufacturing participate in a special three-year rotational development program, as do some beginners in human resources.

Day in the Life

Caterpillar is a huge company that hires entry-level employees for numerous jobs in most of its divisions. There is no typical day for all of these employees; they do, however, participate in a common corporate culture. Part of that culture involves close contact with upper management. As one new hire tells us, "One of the best things about this program is the amount of exposure you get to leadership. I've met with several vice presidents and upper-level managers." Another agrees: "It is sometimes scary [to think about] the extent to which I have interacted with high-level employees within the company. So far in my career, I have interacted with [many] vice presidents, and a group president and have given presentations to division managers. When averaged on a weekly basis, the time would be very minimal (not even an hour), but the time spent is very valuable." Another aspect is the emphasis on taking initiative. Supervisors, one entry-level worker reports, "are not afraid to let me take on as many challenges or responsibilities as I want (as long as I demonstrate that I'm capable of handling them). They do a great job of providing coaching and support as I take on tougher, more demanding responsibilities."

Peers

Caterpillar's emphasis on teamwork helps build strong relationships, both among entry-level workers and between entry-level workers and their bosses. One employee reports, "There is definitely camaraderie with our new hires. Part of my responsibility in my current position is to organize events for our new hires. These events have ranged from facility tours to bowling outings." After-hours socializing varies from division to division and from city to city. A manufacturing trainee says, "There is a large after-hours social scene at Caterpillar. I usually interact with my peers about ten to twenty hours a week at work, and after work I usually spend about eight hours a week interacting [with them]." A new hire in accounting tells a different story and says, "I do not live in the same city as most of my peers, so my social interaction with them outside of work is limited, but it [does exist]."

Moving on

Caterpillar doesn't lose many employees; over 90 percent of new hires remain with the company for at least three years. Company representatives brag that "the average length of service for full-time Caterpillar employees in Illinois is 18.7 years—nearly four times the manufacturing industry average of just five years. Since 1972, more than 17,000 current and retired employees have reached their thirty-year service anniversary." The few people who fly the coop usually do so "for personal reasons because they determine that the job isn't a good fit for them or because they identify another opportunity that they feel better meets their goals."

Best and Worst

"Four of the five group presidents started with Caterpillar soon after college. Their first jobs were in accounting, engineering, finance, and marketing. Today, their years of service with Caterpillar range from twenty-nine to thirty-six years, and each of these senior executives has administrative responsibilities for a group of business units."

CENTRA
VARIOUS POSITIONS

"Centra is very busy since it is growing. There are many interviews taking place and new hires coming on board, lots of equipment that has to be ordered on a daily basis, and many other tasks to complete."

The Big Picture

Centra provides software and support for real-time business-to-business collaboration via the Internet and corporate networks. The company conducts everything from one-on-one virtual classroom sessions to meetings with more than 500 executives from across the globe. Only a decade old, Centra could develop into a major growth company. If it does, today's first jobbers could be tomorrow's fat cats because—as they say on Wall Street—a rising tide lifts all boats.

LOCATION(S) WHERE ENTRY-LEVEL EMPLOYEES WORK

Most Centra employees work in Lexington, Massachusetts; some positions are available in other locations.

ENTRY-LEVEL POSITION(S) AVAILABLE

Various entry-level positions are available.

BENEFITS OFFERED

Centra offers its employees medical and dental insurance. Additional benefits include life and disability insurance, flexible spending accounts, a 401(k) plan, stock options, an employee stock purchase plan, a tuition reimbursement program, paid time off, holidays, vacation days, and sick days.

CONTACT INFORMATION

Visit the website at www.centra.com/corporate/jobs.

Getting Hired

Centra posts available positions on its website. One employee we spoke with found his job online; several others say they found their jobs through placement agencies. Some people were attracted by "the company, the people, and opportunities available at a small, fast-growing company." The hiring process is fairly standard; one employee explains, "I interviewed in two rounds; the first interview was with the hiring manager and human resources. The second interview was with the chief financial officer, to whom the department I would be working for reported. I was then called to confirm references and then called [with the] verbal offer by the hiring manager, which I accepted." Interviewers "ask very basic questions about computer skills. The interviews were very friendly. I think the interviewers were just trying to get a read on my long-term interests, my working style, and my work experience." Successful hires suggest you "express a willingness to learn and an interest in the industry."

Money and Perks

Centra first jobbers tell us that their "start date was somewhat negotiable," but "salary, what [we] did, and where [we] did it were not." Employees appreciate the company's extensive benefits package. They also praise the "informal work environment," which makes it easy to make friends. One newbie especially liked how he "was able to interact with all of the different departments and talk with people in various positions to determine areas of interest for [himself]. This was invaluable to [him]."

The Ropes

Most of the employees we spoke with started at jobs that didn't require much training. Since those we spoke with moved on to better positions relatively quickly, they didn't really mind. One writes, "I think the receptionist position [I held] was a perfect entry-level job. I learned a lot from this position, interacted with everyone in the company, and learned how the company worked." Another employee, who also began at a reception desk, agrees: "I viewed the position as a means to get to other positions in the company. My duties were very much day-to-day administration and not too difficult to learn or perform." Another new hire adds, "[That orientation and training is generally informal] because it's a young, small company. On my first day, I walked around and met everyone. By my second day, I was contacting customers and prospects." She also tells us that she had "no formal training, but [she] learned a lot from [her] coworkers."

Day in the Life

The core of Centra's business is facilitating e-Learning (college courses, training sessions, etc., conducted via the Internet) and virtual business meetings. Many first jobbers play a crucial role in these Web events as event managers; they "host" the event by coordinating logistics, training clients to use Centra software, and serving as moderators. Other new hires provide the type of support found in all businesses: clerical, human resources, sales, [and] customer service. While some consider this "mostly grunt work, it is important. Every company needs someone to manage those day-to-day tasks. Centra is very busy since it is growing. There are many interviews taking place and new hires coming on board, lots of equipment that has to be ordered on a daily basis, and many other tasks to complete."

Peers

As do many young companies, Centra has a large population of fresh-faced go-getters, many of them first jobbers, among its employees. These workers enjoy "a lot of contact with other first jobbers at the company."

Moving on

Centra does a good job of promoting from within, and many first jobbers find themselves quickly moving on to better jobs in the company. Two of our correspondents began as receptionists; today, one works in human resources, and the other has become a marketing specialist.

CH2M HILL
Various Positions

"CH2M HILL is an employee-owned company. Being able to purchase company stock is a nice perk. In essence, you work harder to see your investment grow more rapidly."

The Big Picture

Promoting itself as "a global leader in full-service engineering, construction, and operations," CH2M HILL gives recent college graduates the opportunity to work "on many of the industry's most exciting and important projects." Young engineers appreciate that the employee-owned CH2M HILL "is a large, stable company with plenty of opportunities . . . and offices all over the country and world." In order to ease new hires into the workflow, the company equips each rookie with an "integration plan" as soon as they arrive on the job. The integration plan, which varies according to each person's background, education, and position, "spells out who to meet with by when, and lists the individuals this person needs to become familiar with in order to do their job effectively." Very quickly, new hires become important members of a team charged with completing significant projects—to the company and the field.

Location(s) Where Entry-level Employees Work

CH2M HILL's headquarters are in Englewood, Colorado, but very few new employees actually work there. The company maintains many national and international sites, including "multiple office locations in various states."

Average Number Hired Per Year over the Last Ten Years

The company hires between 100 and 250 people each year.

Entry-level Position(s) Available

Newcomers can expect to fill one of four positions: staff engineer, staff scientist, staff consultant, or GIS/database analyst. In each position, employees may focus on specific areas such as transportation design, civil engineering, water resources, environmental engineering, geology, hydrogeology, chemistry, environmental science, and communications and information solutions.

Average Hours Worked Per Week

Entry-level employees work 50 hours per week.

Average Starting Salary

First-time engineers earn between $45,000 and $50,000 a year.

Getting Hired

CH2M HILL is a regular attendee at career fairs and recruitment events held by America's top engineering programs. In addition, the company posts all job openings on its website and invites applicants to submit materials electronically. After a resume is submitted, a recruiter reviews it and, if the candidate seems capable, passes it to a hiring manager for review. Candidates who seem like a good fit are then contacted for a phone interview with the recruiter. Qualified candidates are invited for a face-to-face interview with the hiring team. Each step along the way, applicants are eliminated and expectations rise. Those who land a job with CH2M HILL typically score well in six departments: "GPA, energy, enthusiasm, good communication skills, relevant course work, and leadership positions." On the flip side, applicants are likely to lose points by demonstrating a "lack of communication skills, irrelevant work/course experience, no ability to articulate longer-term goals, and any criminal history." While these pluses and minuses hold true across the board, hiring procedures often differ from site to site. One young engineer explains, "I was flown to Colorado to a specific (very large) project job site for an interview with several of the project's VPs. The interview was more of an informational overview of the project at hand, not so much your typical interview. . . . A year or so later, I transferred to another location for another position and had to go through interviews again. This time around it was much more structured, more technical, with questions such as, 'Why do you want to do this kind of work?' and 'How do you handle stressful situations?'" Whatever shape the interview takes, prospective employees should arm themselves with a clear sense of how they visualize fitting into the company. As the folks at CH2M HILL's headquarters tell us, "We need individuals who have some direction and know what kind of career path they want to pursue."

Money and Perks

In 2005, most new engineers at CH2M HILL earned between $45,000 and $50,000. Fluctuations among starting salaries are due to the typical factors: location, position, and experience. Strong "performance on projects" is the best way to escalate that salary. A second-year engineer tells us, "There are various ways to grow in terms of responsibility, and in turn, pay. I feel like there is much potential to stay here and continue learning and moving up." Another echoes, "There is great room to grow in terms of responsibility." But she adds, "I found that I had to be very proactive in asking for promotions. The trend is to promote people at similar times and give similar raises, despite differences in performance." Formally, performance reviews are conducted twice a year, and pay raises are given out annually. The best fringe benefit, one newbie tells us, stems from the fact that "CH2M HILL is an employee-owned company. Being able to purchase company stock is a nice perk. In essence, you work harder to see your investment grow more rapidly."

The Ropes

The "integration plan" mentioned earlier is just one of several tools in place to help fresh hires ease into their new positions. First jobbers are matched up with a "buddy," which translates into "a colleague who can answer everyday questions, like 'Where is the printer?'" A two-hour official orientation offers new employees an "overview of benefits, company history and structure, and an office tour." This welcome-to-our-world introduction to the company and workplace is followed by ongoing training for each individual. One project engineer explains, "On-the-job internal training was also a big part of the learning process. Most of this training was task-specific and delivered by senior managers or project team members." The higher ups at CH2M HILL believe strong orientation programs are crucial. To prove this point, one satisfied engineer explains that new hires are even "encouraged to form a group of 'associate staff' to come up with ideas to improve the orientation process and to provide a forum to discuss questions/issues."

Day in the Life

"A certain portion of any entry-level position is 'heavy lifting,'" admits an engineer now in his seventh year with CH2M HILL. "There is really no way around it. If it were all glamorous and fun it would not be called work." This said, new hires are often given indispensable roles in team-oriented projects. The seventh-year explains, "Most of the projects I supported as a new hire were made up of many individuals and were so large that they could only be completed through a team effort. To that end, if I did not complete my work component, it also meant that the team failed to achieve its end product." The company does its best to maintain a dynamic work environment that allows its rookies to get experience in both the office and the field. Here's how one employee, whose specialty is environmental engineering, describes those early days: "My responsibilities were to review and evaluate data, write reports, and work in the field. A typical day in the office included writing text, working with graphics and GIS staff to develop figures, working with administrative assistants to coordinate document production, reviewing data, and talking with my project manager about questions/issues. A typical day in the field included overseeing a subcontractor or working with one other CH2M HILL person to collect samples." One engineer sums up her new-employee experience by saying, "I felt I was given work with large responsibilities that mattered to the company."

Peers

"I feel I was surrounded by very smart people," recalls a former entry-level engineer, and his colleagues seem to agree. Other CH2M HILLers describe their entry-level peers as "friendly," which makes for a positive work environment in which first jobbers "share many outside interests and come to CH2M HILL with similar work ethics and skill sets." But "smart" plus "friendly" plus "similar" does not necessarily equal "incredibly social." At least not always. As one employee remembers, "There was limited after-hours socialization among new hires." When employees do get together after work, it's "driven mainly by mutual interest in activities outside of the office (e.g., playing music or biking)." Overall, CH2M HILL employs a good mix of personalities. As one seasoned employee says, "In general, engineers are pretty introverted and, while those folks do exist in the firm, the vast majority of my coworkers are pretty outgoing."

Moving on

Engineers who get their start with CH2M HILL most often leave to fill higher positions with competing firms or to join the public sector. Some employees seek positions with smaller firms, as well. On average, first jobbers stay with the company for two to three years.

Attrition

More than 90 percent of CH2M HILL's entry-level hires stay with the company for at least a year. What causes some young employees to leave CH2M HILL is often a disenchantment with the large corporate model. One young engineer admits she's heard coworkers criticize "the benefits, vacation time, raises, and lack of overhead budget" afforded by the company. Another says, "Raises and promotions are not that easy since we are a big company." Though people may leave to find a situation where advancement comes faster or easier, employees confirm that CH2M HILL gives its new hires a solid foundation in professional engineering. Says one employee, "From defense installations to manufacturing, my position has allowed inner access to many places, people, and operations that I would have otherwise never seen."

CHILDREN'S RIGHTS
PARALEGAL

"Because Children's Rights is primarily involved in litigation, work follows the litigation cycle. Some weeks are slow, whereas other weeks are incredibly hectic. I never feel that I cannot handle the workload, though."

The Big Picture

Some of the nation's child welfare programs are, tragically, underfunded and/or poorly managed. When such programs fail to execute their missions, children ultimately suffer. Formerly a project of the American Civil Liberties Union, Children's Rights became an independent organization in 1995. This small legal advocacy group combats the neglect and abuse of foster children with class action suits designed to force reform of failed child welfare systems. College graduates here serve a two-year tenure as paralegals; one explains: "Since Children's Rights is so small, paralegals are integral members of the litigation teams. We sit in on almost all important meetings. Paralegals work closely with the executive director and the other attorneys on a daily basis." The job is a great way to prep for a career in the law or social services and an even better way to serve a powerless constituency.

LOCATION(S) WHERE ENTRY-LEVEL EMPLOYEES WORK

All positions are located in New York, New York.

AVERAGE NUMBER OF APPLICATIONS EACH YEAR

Children's Rights receives 200 applications each year.

AVERAGE NUMBER HIRED PER YEAR

Children's Rights hires two or three paralegals each year.

ENTRY-LEVEL POSITION(S) AVAILABLE

Entry-levels hires are brought in as paralegals.

AVERAGE HOURS WORKED PER WEEK

Paralegals work 40 to 45 hours per week.

PERCENTAGE OF ENTRY-LEVEL HIRES STILL WITH THE COMPANY AFTER THREE, FIVE, AND TEN YEARS

Most paralegals stay for two years, then move on to graduate school.

AVERAGE STARTING SALARY

The starting salary for paralegals is $32,000.

Getting Hired

Children's Rights is "too small an organization to interview on campus." Instead, the organization posts job openings at such sites as Idealist.org. The applications come pouring in, [at a ratio of] about 200 for the two or three positions that open annually. The organization looks for evidence of "attention to detail, good editing skills, critical analysis capabilities, a solid work ethic, and the ability to juggle many tasks." Initial screening of applicants is done by current paralegals, whose choices are "then approved in a final interview by the paralegal supervisor, who is a senior lawyer in the office." One successful hire reports, "My first-round interview was with the four paralegals who were working at Children's Rights at the time. I had to do the interview over the phone, as I was far away from New York. The tone was quite friendly, though I was definitely asked questions that related to [what] I think about child welfare and the role of the law in advocating for children. We also talked a lot about my previous work experience, and I was given an opportunity to ask all the questions I had, as well. The second-round interview was in the New York office with a staff attorney who was also the paralegal supervisor; that interview was more formal. After I was offered the job, the then-paralegals gave me their contact information, including their cell phones, so that I could call them with any questions I had about the job. They were very helpful and generous with their time, and in the end, they definitely had me convinced that I should take the job."

Money and Perks

"Job location, tasks, and pay were all nonnegotiable," writes one Children's Rights paralegal, adding that "I was able to work out a mutually convenient start date." The starting salary makes living in expensive New York City difficult, but not impossible. Raises are awarded annually "and are generally in accordance with across-the-board raises throughout the organization," so the second year of the job is easier than the first. Overtime pay "is generally available." Paralegals brag about the "good vacation time" (they receive fifteen vacation days, four personal days, two floating holidays, and ten sick days per year) and the "good daily work schedule" but agree that the best perk of all is that "the work here positively [influences] the clients we serve."

The Ropes

Training of newcomers is handled by "the current paralegals, who train you on basic paralegal duties and case-specific duties. The attorneys on my cases also provided some training. Most of the training is on-the-job throughout the first few months of work." One paralegal writes, "I was paired up with an outgoing paralegal who oriented me to office logistics and trained me on the specifics of the cases I would be working on. I worked with her for about two weeks, though for part of that time I began performing tasks on my own with her supervision, and I was given time to read background materials to help me understand the nature of the work we do. I had lunches with the attorneys and paralegal on each of the case teams I was to be working on, during which I was taught the history of the cases and given the opportunity to get to know the people working on the cases. It was a generally informative and fun time."

Day in the Life

Paralegals at Children's Rights are assigned to work on specific ongoing cases, so "it's very difficult to explain a typical day here because the work varies tremendously depending on what cases you're assigned to and how active the litigation is on those cases. However, as best as I can describe it, a typical day begins with press monitoring; I check the websites of newspapers relevant to the cases I work on to find articles related to child welfare, child abuse, fatalities in foster care, etc. The rest of the day could include editing correspondence for attorneys and finalizing it to be sent out, reviewing discovery documents to find key information, reading over a monitoring report and culling out key areas of concern, answering intake phone calls from concerned foster parents or biological parents who have problems with their state's child welfare system, researching data related to the systems we're investigating, keeping track of contacts made with stakeholders in the jurisdictions where we're working, organizing and managing documents, sitting in on conference calls with local co-counsel or local advocates, or doing basically anything else for the attorneys you are there to support." Another first jobber adds, "Because Children's Rights is primarily involved in litigation, work follows the litigation cycle. Some weeks are slow, whereas other weeks are incredibly hectic. I never feel that I cannot handle the workload, though."

Peers

Children's Rights employs no more than five paralegals at any given time, so first jobbers here form a small contingent. Paralegals agree that their peers are "fantastic. We have all become close friends" who enjoy "a great deal of camaraderie. Happy hours occur on a weekly basis." The camaraderie extends beyond the bottom rung of the office hierarchy; one paralegal explains, "We hang out frequently outside of the office, and we all really enjoy [one another's] company. That includes the supervising attorneys. The office environment is generally laid back, even though we often work under lots of pressure."

Moving on

Paralegals at Children's Rights make a two-year commitment to the job. They "generally leave after two years and go on to graduate school as planned," with "many going to law school, but some pursuing degrees in social services (MSW or MPA)."

Best and Worst

Children's Rights has "had the good fortune to work with many exceptional paralegals who have moved on to graduate-level education at prestigious institutions, either in the law or in social services." The organization has had "very limited experience with unsuccessful hires. This has occurred when it was mutually determined that a new hire's skill set and interests did not dovetail well with those of the organization."

CHUBB
YEAR ONE AT CHUBB

"As a trainee, I most certainly felt that there was plenty of room to grow in terms of pay and responsibility within Chubb. Looking back over my most recent move with Chubb, I still believe that, in this organization, the sky is the limit."

The Big Picture

For recent grads looking to get their feet wet in the insurance industry, Chubb's first-year training program, Year One at Chubb, provides a comprehensive introduction to the industry and hands-on training in underwriting. Working under the supervision of coaches and mentors, new hires move quickly through the ranks, with "the authority to operate as a full underwriter approximately eleven months after beginning a full-time career with Chubb." Trainees enjoy the challenges of the industry and find the pace of the job stimulating. Jokes one, "There is no telling when you might have to put out many fires at once (pun intended)."

LOCATION(S) WHERE ENTRY-LEVEL EMPLOYEES WORK

Chubb has more than 50 locations in the United States; however, most new trainees are concentrated in certain offices. Finance, accounting, and actuarial trainees head to the Warren and Whitehouse, New Jersey offices, while underwriting and claim trainees work predominantly in the larger branch offices. Underwriting and claim trainees are often relocated to other branches as they move out of the trainee program and into permanent positions.

AVERAGE NUMBER OF APPLICATIONS EACH YEAR

Chubb receives between 50 and 150 resumes per open position.

AVERAGE NUMBER HIRED PER YEAR OVER THE LAST TEN YEARS

The company hires approximately 185 new trainees each year.

ENTRY-LEVEL POSITION(S) AVAILABLE

Trainee positions are available in the areas of finance, actuarial, accounting, claim, and underwriting (commercial, personal, and specialty insurance). All of these positions require several months of study and training, accompanied by on-the-job training and mentorship.

AVERAGE HOURS WORKED PER WEEK

Trainees work 40 hours per week.

AVERAGE STARTING SALARY

Entry-level salaries range from $42,000 to $46,000 per year.

Getting Hired

When initially screening applicants, "Chubb has a set of core competencies that we look for in all employees. These competencies are related to results-orientation, teamwork, communication, customer focus, leadership, and coaching/developing others." In addition to these intrinsic qualities, Chubb also looks for, "a strong interest in Chubb and the ability to relocate." Many entry-level employees were originally interns who made an impression and parlayed the experience into a permanent position. Those who do not have previous experience within the company usually approach Chubb's trainee application process with both interest and experience in the insurance industry. Says one lucky candidate, "I feel [what] helped me get an interview was that I had done a summer internship at a smaller insurance company in my hometown and then had worked [at] an insurance agency during the school year."

Money and Perks

Chubb salaries are generally nonnegotiable during the first year. The good news is that, following the completion of the training program, employees find there is lots of room for growth within the company. A former actuarial trainee affirms, "There are so many opportunities within the actuarial department, and I was pleasantly surprised when my year-end review came around. My salary has increased and [so has] my responsibility." Adds another, "Once I proved myself, it was reflected in my pay." Employees say Chubb is highly supportive of continuing education, paying for training courses and seminars to help job growth. In fact, an eighteen-year Chubb veteran is pleased to report, "Chubb paid for my MBA." The company has several add-ons to the base salary including "an annual incentive program . . . that enables all employees to earn cash payments based on company, business unit, and individual [performance]" and "a profit-sharing program that provides cash payments of up to 4 percent of base salary if certain business and financial measures are met." Employees also enjoy occasional business perks such as "entertaining and being entertained by our agents, including many lunches and an occasional ballgame or dinner."

The Ropes

Chubb's first-year training program, Year One at Chubb, offers a thorough, hands-on approach to the job and to the insurance industry at large. Typically, new employees begin their training with a week-long course at one of Chubb's larger branches. After arriving at their permanent location, new employees spend the first few months vigorously studying the insurance industry and taking industry-standard exams. The information, "for the most part, was self taught for the first few months, then you had a coach assigned to you who would act as your mentor," explains one underwriting trainee. While poring over insurance textbooks, new employees are gradually introduced to the job and office culture. Explains an entry-level employee, "My first three months was a good balance of self-learning, one-on-one with my coach, and hands-on experience in the market and in the office." After they have been brought up to speed on the industry, trainees begin "mostly informal, on-the-job training," in which they begin working on live cases under the supervision of senior employees. Over time, they are granted increasing responsibility on cases, making recommendations that are reviewed by senior underwriters. "The best part of the job is getting to make executive decisions, and reasoning out why you did it the way you did," says one trainee. After a little more than a year of employment, trainees are promoted to positions that require less supervision.

Day in the Life

Chubb trainees assure us that there is rarely a dull moment in the insurance industry. On any given day, trainees spend time "reading internal memos, underwriting accounts, meeting with the senior underwriter, and [speaking] with agents and other internal Chubb resources." A former trainee shares, "I didn't have time to get bored. If I wasn't taking a web-based course, I was either meeting with my coach, meeting with another underwriter from a different office, working on a submission to be reviewed by my coach, following up with department open items, or participating in other branch-related activities/committees." As time progresses and new hires become more seasoned employees, their responsibilities and assignments grow. "Once the company gave me authority (about nine months after I began working), it was my decision whether or not to put up $1 million of property insurance and what to charge for it. The company relied on me to make a good decision," shares a recent hire. While expectations are high, Chubb employees say senior management is supportive and doesn't breathe down their necks. A current employee says, "No one told me when to come or when to leave. To this day, no manager at Chubb has told me that I have to be in by 8:00 A.M. and that I could leave at 5:00 P.M. My work day has been totally up to me."

Peers

"Chubb attracts a diverse workforce" from across the United States, characterized by a strong work ethic and intelligence. New hires say they feel immediately comfortable within their training class, which feels like "an instant group of friends." However, trainees usually only see each other during their first week of orientation (though many keep in touch throughout the training period and the years to come) and are thereafter dispersed to varying office locations. While experiences vary from branch to branch, Chubb employees generally appreciate the supportive office environment, the emphasis on teamwork, and the fact that they have ample contact with senior underwriters and managers. While learning the ropes, mentors and bosses are extremely helpful and "always willing to make sure you have all the assistance you need to get your training underway." While the atmosphere is friendly at work, most of the Chubb branches are located in small or suburban environments, which means there is "not a big after-hours social scene."

Moving on

Most employees leave Chubb for personal reasons or to take a better opportunity with another company. Interestingly, of those that leave the company, less than half stay in the insurance industry.

Attrition

Annual turnover is about 20 percent and half of the claim and underwriting trainees hired over the past six years continue to work with Chubb. Of those who stay on, most say they are happy with the many opportunities afforded to them there. A loyal employee sums it up, "As a trainee, I most certainly felt that there was plenty of room to grow in terms of pay and responsibility within Chubb. Looking back over my most recent move with Chubb, I still believe that, in this organization, the sky is the limit."

CITIZEN SCHOOLS
TEACHING ASSOCIATES AND TEACHING FELLOWS

"Citizen Schools' Teaching Fellows "work primarily as front-line educators and community builders, leading hands-on activities for small and large groups [of] children, designing and teaching curriculum, leading peers in the planning and implementation of educational activities; recruiting students and volunteers; communicating with and engaging parents; and fostering partnerships with school faculty and community organizations."

The Big Picture

Citizen Schools offers afterschool programs that "deliver a creative and effective learning model that addresses community needs while building student skills through hands-on experiential learning activities," primarily in poor, urban settings. It's the kind of company that advertises its employment opportunities on websites like Idealist.org. In short, this is a job that you seek out if you're interested in challenging, rewarding work that has the potential to affect others' lives directly.

LOCATION(S) WHERE ENTRY-LEVEL EMPLOYEES WORK

Citizen Schools has programs in Tuscon, Arizona; Redwood City, California; San Jose, California; Boston, Massachusetts; Framingham, Massachusetts; Lowell, Massachusetts; Malden, Massachusetts; New Bedford, Massachusetts; Springfield, Massachusetts; Worcester, Massachusetts; New Brunswick, New Jersey; Baytown, Texas; and Houston, Texas.

AVERAGE NUMBER OF APPLICATIONS EACH YEAR

The company receives 300–400 applications per year.

AVERAGE NUMBER HIRED PER YEAR OVER THE LAST TEN YEARS

The Teaching Fellowship has grown from one teaching fellow in 1997 to sixty-three teaching fellows in eleven cities in 2006. The number of teaching associates has grown to eighty-eight nationwide.

Entry-level Position(s) Available

"We hire approximately 30 to 40 new teaching associates in the fall and an additional 10 to 20 in the spring. Every June we hire 25 to 30 AmeriCorps Teaching Fellows. The fellowship is a two-year position that includes earning a master's degree through Lesley University."

Average Hours Worked Per Week

Hours vary according to the position. Teaching associates work from 15 to 30 hours per week; program staff, (including teaching fellows), work from 40 to 50 hours per week (in addition to master's course work); headquarters staff work from 24 to 50 hours per week.

Percentage of Entry-level Hires Still with the Company After Three, Five, and Ten Years

After three years, about 80 percent of all entry-level hires remain with Citizen Schools.

Average Starting Salary

"Compensation varies by position and is commensurate with experience. Teaching assistants begin at $11.30 per hour; this wage increases with each year of employment. AmeriCorps Teaching Fellows earn a salary of $20,000 per year plus $4,725 in education awards."

Benefits Offered

"All full-time employees have the opportunity to enroll in [a] health care plan (currently HMO Blue, a provider of Blue Cross/Blue Shield). Citizen Schools pays 80 percent of the monthly premium, and the employee pays 20 percent. This amount is deducted from his or her paycheck on a pre-tax basis. Health insurance, like all benefits, is pro-rated for part-time FTE staff. Teaching associates are eligible to enroll in health insurance on entering their fifth semester with Citizen Schools; Teaching Fellows receive free health care. Citizen Schools offers both individual and family plans, which includes health insurance benefits for domestic partners." Furthermore, while working with Citizen Schools, "staff can concurrently receive a master's in education with a specialization in out-of-school time from Lesley University (assistance provided by Citizen Schools)." They have the "opportunity to enroll in a 403(b) retirement plan (currently with TIAA-CREF). Citizen Schools matches up to $500 annually after one full year of employment." Time off includes "15 vacation days, 9 sick days, 3 personal days, and 11 paid holidays per year. After 4 years of continuous employment, employees are eligible for a 20-day vacation splash." There is also an "opportunity to enroll in Section 125 flexible spending account (for nonreimbursed medical expenses) and dependent care account program. Long-term disability insurance [comes] at no cost to the employee." When junior comes along, staff members are eligible for "six weeks paid parental leave for primary caregivers [and] two weeks paid parental leave for secondary caregivers."

CONTACT INFORMATION

Teaching Fellows Program
Museum Wharf

308 Congress Street
Boston, MA 02210
Tel: 617-695-2300
Fax: 617-695-2367
www.citizenschools.org

Getting Hired

Citizen Schools scours its applicant pool for candidates who demonstrate "experience in education/working with kids; commitment to nonprofit/social service work in urban communities; flexibility and patience; excellent communication skills (written and verbal); enthusiasm; and entrepreneurial spirit. Bilingualism/multilingualism is a plus." All applicants fill out the online application available on the organization's website and submit a cover letter and resume with the application. One successful candidate writes, "I e-mailed my cover letter and resume and followed [up] with a call to the human resources specialist. The director of development called me back to arrange an interview. I then met with her, along with the manager of individual giving. The interview was casual, and they inquired about my goals, interests, and intent for the position. They stressed the importance of enthusiasm, flexibility, and dedication. The energy around the office was high, and I was impressed by the fact that employees seemed to be enjoying their jobs." Sample interview questions include "What about Citizen Schools most excites you? After reading and filling out the job application, what is your understanding of the impact we are trying to achieve? Tell me about your past work experience and how it relates to this position? What are your three greatest strengths and weaknesses for this job?"

Money and Perks

Teaching Associates in Boston earn $10.00 per hour during their first semester of work, but rates may vary; the annual stipend for Teaching Fellows is $21,800. According to organization representatives, "salary reviews occur on an annual basis. Annual increases typically are in the 2–5 percent range." The best perk, employees tell us, is "working with kids!" The organization points out that "the education award pays for the Teaching Fellows' master's."

The Ropes

"When an employee arrives on his or her first day, he or she already has a voice-mail account, an e-mail account, a network login, and a mailbox. All new employees meet with the human resources manager for an in-depth review of benefits and policies (typically one hour). New employees also receive technology training on computer systems, e-mail, voicemail, etc. New employees are also given an office tour by the office manager. This orientation usually takes about half a day." One new hire adds, "I got a thorough overview of the job and what my responsibilities were [before I started work], so I felt like I knew what I was getting into. Everyone was very accommodating to me [considering] the fact that I was both new to the organization and new to the workforce. I learned by asking questions, watching others, and using my best judgment. All of these things have helped me do my job well and improve many projects and processes with my own ideas."

Day in the Life

"There is no real typical day at the job" at Citizen Schools. As an organization representative explains, "Citizen Schools turns children into community heroes; children apprentice with lawyers, web designers, [and] architects and culminate their learning apprenticeships by arguing trials before federal judges, designing websites for their school, organizing public events, publishing newspapers, and much more." Citizen Schools' Teaching Fellows "work primarily as frontline educators and community builders, leading hands-on activities for small and large groups [of] children, designing and teaching curriculum, leading peers in the planning and implementation of educational activities; recruiting students and volunteers; communicating with and engaging parents; and fostering partnerships with school faculty and community organizations." They also recruit volunteer Citizen Teachers from the local community. Teaching Associates also handle a wide range of duties, including leading curriculum, designing and leading learning games, organizing sports activities, and directing hands-on learning experiences. They also confer with students' parents to keep them apprised of their progress.

Peers

"Citizen Schools attracts a wide variety of people. Most of them are very intelligent [and] friendly, and come with a unique array of past experiences," offers one employee with the organization. They're the type of folks who believe "that all communities are blessed with thousands of born teachers (old and young, professional and laborer, athlete and artist); [these are] people who would like to enrich their own lives and contribute to their community by sharing their skills with children." Many are young; one employee writes, "There is large camaraderie largely due to the young age of the Teaching Fellows. My peers are the coolest cats in town."

Moving on

Among those employees who use Citizen Schools as a springboard to land another job, "approximately 70 percent are involved in community-based education initiatives as program directors and teachers. Some are involved in graduate studies. Several graduates have become campus directors or start-up captains at our affiliate sites. Because of their excellent teaching, leading, and community-organizing skills, and Citizen Schools' strong reputation, Teaching Fellows are highly sought-after employees."

Attrition

Current employees warn that teaching for Citizen Schools is hard work. "I wish I had known about the amount of hours that would be needed after work," one employee tells us. The organization adds that "Teaching Associates often leave to find more full-time employment or because of scheduling conflicts. Other staff may leave due to new opportunities and/or better salary."

Best and Worst

According to organization representatives, the best new hire ever "began with Citizen Schools as a Teaching Associate, became a Teaching Fellow, and is currently a successful campus director." The worst new hire was "a recent college graduate who moved to Boston to become a teaching fellow and was overwhelmed by living in such a big city and not prepared to work with children nine to fourteen years old. She resigned after only six weeks. This shaped how we recruited for Teaching Fellows. All potential candidates now spend a day at a Citizen Schools campus as part of their interview process."

CITY YEAR
CORPS MEMBER

"To be honest, a full year of community service is not easy
but, in retrospect, it makes one feel like [one has] accomplished more in one
year than some people have in a lifetime."

The Big Picture

One of America's most far-reaching service-based organizations, City Year allows new college grads to "become part of a diverse workforce of talented young people [and] work in an exciting, fast-paced environment in which you can grow and become one of many great facilitators of hope and idealism." City Year's mission statement—which focuses on "citizen service, civic leadership, and social entrepreneurship"—serves as the guiding force for employees. Corps members are hired for ten-month stints and are placed in cities around the country. Yes, the pay is low and the work can be demanding, but those who have worked for City Year enthuse over the opportunities for personal growth. One City Year alum sums up her experience: "To be honest, a full year of community service is not easy but, in retrospect, it makes one feel like [one has] accomplished more in one year than some people have in a lifetime."

LOCATION(S) WHERE ENTRY-LEVEL EMPLOYEES WORK

City Year will have corps members at the following sites in 2007–2008: Boston, Massachusetts; Chicago, Illinois; Cleveland and Columbus, Ohio; Columbia, South Carolina; Detroit, Michigan.; Little Rock, Arkansas; Louisiana; New Hampshire; New York, New York; Philadelphia, Pennsylvania; Rhode Island; San Antonio, Texas; San Jose/Silicon Valley, California; Seattle/King County, Washington; and Washington, DC.

AVERAGE NUMBER OF APPLICATIONS EACH YEAR

City Year receives 8,800 inquiries each year.

AVERAGE NUMBER HIRED PER YEAR OVER THE LAST TEN YEARS

Though shifts in federal funding can alter the figures some years, City Year typically hires 1,100 corps members per year.

ENTRY-LEVEL POSITION(S) AVAILABLE

The "city year" is aligned with the academic calendar. Corps members report for work in late August/early September with a one-month training period before full-time service in schools and the community begins. There are some midyear positions with January start dates, but the majority are full-year positions—and graduation takes place in June for everyone.

Getting Hired

To land a position as a City Year corps member, an applicant must "be between the ages of seventeen and twenty-four" and "have served no more than two terms in another AmeriCorps, NCCC, or VISTA program." More importantly, an applicant must be in line with City Year's core values of service and leadership. As City Year administrators put it, "The most successful candidates are familiar with City Year, dedicated to the concept of citizen service, and prepared for the challenges and rewards of the year ahead. There are limited corps member positions, and the more that is done early in the process to indicate a true fit between the applicant and the City Year site, the better it is for both."

Those wishing to be considered should submit an application online or by mail. Applications consist of three essays, two letters of reference, and some basic personal information. Next comes a screening interview. Finally, there's a formal interview "regarding the four Cs: character, cooperation, commitment, and competence." One City Year alum says, "The application process was simple and straightforward . . . not even demanding a resume. I was interviewed by a City Year staff member, and the tone was very relaxed. They asked a lot of questions about my interest in serving for a year, commitments I have made, and experience I have had working with kids. They also probed . . . my experience with diversity issues. I was called about four hours after my interview and was offered a position." And what sorts of people don't get that call? Here again are the administrators: "Weaker applicants are those who show insufficient familiarity with the program to which they are applying. . . . Applicants who seem either unaware or uninterested in the particular rewards and challenges may not be ready to make the commitment necessary to succeed. Individuals who are either not ready for or not interested in being role models and leaders are ill-suited to a 'city year.'"

Money and Perks

Recent college grads do not sign up with City Year because they're looking to pull in a fat paycheck. "Corps members receive a modest living stipend, based on a site's cost of living and other factors," say City Year administrators. Because corps members are only hired for ten-month terms, there is no possibility for a raise; the stipends are determined before the ten months begin and remain the same throughout. The organization recognizes that getting by on such a tight budget can be difficult. To help new hires "learn to manage with limited income," City Year offers "training on personal finances." City Year also offers some nice perks. The one most corps members rave about is the "education award." City Year officials explain, "AmeriCorps, the federal national service initiative, offers corps members a $4,725 education award that can be applied toward existing student loans or future higher education tuition. Corps members can take advantage of this education award at any point during the seven years after successfully completing the 1,700 hours of service." Oh, and the "company-provided blackberry is a great fringe benefit" as well, says one alum, referring to the T-Mobile phone and service plan issued to each new member.

The Ropes

City Year's ten-month work period mirrors the academic year: The majority of the corps members start service in late August or early September. The first month on the job is actually a training month. As City Year administrators explain, "After a one-day registration involving completion of tax forms and other paperwork, corps members begin a one-month intensive training academy. The training provides an introduction to City Year culture, uniform, and history, [as well as] AmeriCorps regulations, and teaches skills related to leadership development, team-building with a diverse a group, managing service projects, and working with children and community leaders. As part of the training, corps members learn to be both followers and leaders in their teams, in their schools, and in their communities." New team members and experienced supervisors use this training period to "develop a specific agenda and goals for our year," says a former corps member. Something else occurs during that month: "memorizing and reciting mottos."

Day in the Life

Here's how one alum describes a typical day during his "city year": "My primary role was to assist in leading a team of my peers in providing service to a middle school in Northeast Philadelphia. We would start the day with calisthenics by City Hall and then travel out to the school. I had a schedule of classes that I worked with during the [school] day and afternoon. The team would provide after-school clubs for an hour and then do planning for the rest of the week after that time. The day usually went from 8:00 A.M. to 5:30 P.M." In fact, most corps members follow a similar schedule, devoting the bulk of their time to teaching, running after-school programs, conducting community meetings, engaging in service projects, producing newsletters, and always planning for the days ahead. The amount of work to be done is sometimes overwhelming. "I think the toughest part of City Year is realizing that you have to leave the office and take some personal time," says a CY first jobber. "There is so much work to get done . . . people often complain about working extra-long hours, when sometimes it's their own choice and they are not forced." Even if there is a little grumbling about those seemingly endless days, a former corps member assures us, "We are all proud of our work."

Peers

If you end up at City Year, the one thing you can count on is that most of your peers will be between the ages of seventeen and twenty-four. Other than that, "the corps is made up of a large and diverse crowd." Because so many corps members are still in their formative years, some are "immature and still learning about themselves." Even so, one City Year veteran asserts, "I can't say I have ever met someone at City Year [who] was not genuinely nice and well-intentioned. City Year has a lot of cool cats." And this is a good thing, because City Year employees tend to hang out together at work and away from work. Why? One CYer offers an explanation: "When you are a corps member, you tend to stick together—often because the pay is not top-notch and everyone understands the limits of your budget. It makes for an easy after-hours social scene."

Moving on

Following a "city year," corps members pursue a variety of paths, including graduate school (or college, if they haven't gone yet), further work with City Year (which can mean either a second term as a corps member or on staff), or gainful employment elsewhere. The leadership and organizational skills developed through City Year service prepare corps members for a wide range of professional pursuits.

Attrition

Most corps members leave because they have to—it is, after all, only a ten-month gig. About one-quarter of all first-time corps members stick with City Year in some capacity. The decision to leave City Year is usually based on a desire to "have a higher salary and [better] benefits." City Year reports that "the vast majority" of its corps members fulfill their 1,700-hour commitment.

Best and Worst

City Year administrators would be hard pressed to name the "best" employee they've had. "Some of City Year's most successful corps members," they say, now "advocate for social justice, lead foundations, work in schools, and create new opportunities for service. Other very successful corps members are those who incorporate an ethic of service and commitment to community in their work as doctors, lawyers, and business people. City Year alumni are also in government and on City Year staff." The worst employees? "There are some individuals for whom this is simply not the right fit, who do not complete the year of service and who often make that determination during the first month of training."

COLLEGE SUMMIT
VARIOUS POSITIONS

"College Summit is a very output- and results-driven place. In other words, it's not about how much time you put in, when you leave, and when you show up; it's about [the degree to which] you are on top of your stuff."

The Big Picture

"Low-income students who get A's enroll in college at the same rate as high-income students who get D's," notes the College Summit website. This nonprofit seeks to redress this inequity; to that end, it pursues its mission "to transform the college admissions process and increase the college enrollment rate of low-income students" by helping "low-income, academically mid-tier students" navigate the college admissions and financial aid processes to "ensure that the community harnesses the talent of all college-capable students." First jobbers serve in a wide variety of support roles at College Summit.

LOCATION(S) WHERE ENTRY-LEVEL EMPLOYEES WORK

College Summit's headquarters are in Washington, DC. The organization also has regional offices in Los Angeles, California; Denver, Colorado; St. Louis, Missouri; Charleston, West Virginia; New York, New York; San Francisco, California; Orangeburg, South Carolina; and an additional office in Washington, DC..

AVERAGE NUMBER OF APPLICATIONS EACH YEAR

College Summit receives about 1,000 applications per year.

AVERAGE NUMBER HIRED PER YEAR

Nine entry-level employees are hired by College Summit each year.

ENTRY-LEVEL POSITION(S) AVAILABLE

The entry-level positions available vary. "The general focus is on providing broad support to the department or manager, as well as contributing significantly to specific projects or initiatives."

AVERAGE HOURS WORKED PER WEEK

Entry-level employees work about 50 hours per week.

PERCENTAGE OF ENTRY-LEVEL HIRES STILL WITH THE COMPANY AFTER THREE, FIVE, AND TEN YEARS

After three years, 10 percent remain with the company; and after five years, 4 percent remain.

AVERAGE STARTING SALARY

The starting salary for entry-levels hires is $28,000.

BENEFITS OFFERED

Employees receive a fully-covered PPO health insurance plan, which encompasses medical, dental, vision, and prescription expenses. Additional benefits include a 401(k) program with a company match; paid sabbatical leave after five years of employment; fully-covered disability and life insurance; $1,000 per year in professional development funding; flexible spending accounts; and a generous vacation policy (ten personal days, five sick days, seven company holidays, and the full week between December 25 and January 1).

CONTACT INFORMATION

Visit College Summit online at www.collegesummit.org. To apply for a job, click on the "Employment" link or send an e-mail to jobs@collegesummit.org.

Getting Hired

Job openings at College Summit "are posted internally and on external recruitment websites, as well as [on] our own [website]." College Summit encourages applicants "to submit their materials via e-mail." The organization notes that because "our recruitment function is currently understaffed, our primary outreach is through websites such as Idealist.org, Teach for America's alumni network, and Net Impact. We do not yet target specific colleges, and [we] welcome applicants from any college." Model candidates evince enthusiasm for the organization's mission, have an entrepreneurial inclination, and demonstrate excellent communication and interpersonal skills. Applicants who meet these criteria "are invited to participate in a phone interview with the human resources department, [after which the pool] narrows down to final candidates to interview in person with the hiring manager and often other team members. In some cases, final candidates are asked to interview with other staff [members] as well; additionally, reference checks are performed as the final step in the hiring process."

One successful hire reports, "During the interview process, I spent an afternoon visiting College Summit in Washington. I was interviewed by many of the younger staffers and the founder and CEO of the organization. The interviews with the younger people were genuine and kind in nature. I was just struck by the humility of everyone, the like-mindedness of everyone (out of college, ambitious, [and] passionate about education). My interview with the CEO was very professional, rather short, but pointed nonetheless, centering on the principles that guide me. I was then offered the job a few weeks later."

Money and Perks

As at most nonprofits, there's little room for salary negotiation at College Summit, especially for entry-level hires. Raises are performance-based. When an employee demonstrates superior results, he or she is eligible for a raise or promotion. The organization also offers "additional professional development opportunities around time management and prioritizing tasks." Among the most appreciated perks are the "excellent health insurance," "a full week of vacation between Christmas and the New Year," and "the entrepreneurial environment of a fast-growing and successful nonprofit organization."

The Ropes

Orientation at College Summit "lasts about two days and is designed to welcome new employees to their teams and the organization and to give them the background information they need. A typical day would include a welcome breakfast with the office; a series of one-hour meetings to get new hires acclimated to their computers, office systems, and benefits; lunch with their supervisors; and then another series of meetings giving them background on College Summit's values, history, and program. All employees also receive a thorough introduction to the organization's growth plan." One first jobber writes, "The orientation process was great. There was a wonderful binder made for me, and I had a set of meetings organized for me during my first few weeks on the job. It was really nice, and I was impressed that people had been thinking of me in advance of my arrival."

Day in the Life

College Summit hires first jobbers for a wide range of positions. A development coordinator writes, "When I first started, some of my main responsibilities included grant management, fundraising data management, creating budgets and attachments for proposals, coordinating the annual appeal, supporting college sales and workshop set-up, supporting the deputy director, and drafting letters and other correspondences." A new sites coordinator explains that her first tasks involved "a lot of grant writing and research. I'd work on a draft of a proposal to a potential donor and do some preliminary research on other potential donors."

Peers

"My peers are some of the smartest, most idealistic, fun, talented, inspiring people I have ever met," writes a typical first jobber at College Summit, adding that "We are all like-minded and hang out together." Another agrees: "It's beyond friendship. It's like family." This is especially true for those who work in DC, where "we have hung out outside of work many, many times."

Moving on

Most first jobbers at College Summit remain with the organization for a period of one to two years, after which they typically find another job or move on to graduate school. Some leave because of the heavy workload; one young hire explains, "College Summit is a very output- and results-driven place. In other words, it's not about how much time you put in, when you leave, and when you show up; it's about [the degree to which] you are on top of your stuff. This [ethos] offers many perks, flexibility, and the feeling that you are an executive—but also can make work more consuming than one [may] plan."

Attrition

Less than 5 percent of College Summit first jobbers leave within twelve months of starting on at the organization. Relatively few remain for more than three years, though several have moved up into management-level positions. For most, however, this is a significant way station on the path to other career goals.

Best and Worst

Excellent first jobbers at College Summit are those "who have remained committed to the organization, who have pursued opportunities to grow within the organization, and [who] have advocated for themselves. Additionally, these are people who have stuck it out through jobs that may not have matched their interests until better opportunities opened up (or until they helped create those opportunities)."

Poor matches for the organization are those who expect to work directly with students; an organization representative explains, "Most of our positions involve working behind the scenes to move the organization forward in our effort to generate social change in low-income communities."

comScore
Analyst

"comScore seeks "energetic, enthusiastic, self-motivated, highly engaged individuals who are comfortable in an intellectually challenging, fast-paced environment where change is the norm."

The Big Picture

First jobbers tell us that comScore "is very unique and specializes in market research and consumer behavior." The company measures the Web activity, attitudes, and lifestyles of more than two million participating consumers who give comScore permission to "measure what matters across the entire spectrum of consumer surfing and buying behaviors." comScore uses this anonymous information to help hundreds of leading companies develop more effective marketing strategies. Good starting salaries and exposure "to a more innovative, technology-based aspect of research" are among the top allures of a comScore gig.

Location(s) Where Entry-level Employees Work

Entry-level employees who join as part of the firm's training program "begin work at comScore's headquarters in Reston, Virginia, but can ultimately work in any of the firm's offices, which are located in New York, New York; Chicago, Illinois; Seattle, Washington; San Francisco, California; Toronto, Canada; and the United Kingdom."

Average Number of Applications Each Year

comScore receives about 150 applications each year.

Average Number Hired Per Year

Seven employees were hired each in 2004 and 2005; comScore is looking to hire 24 entry-level employees in 2006.

Entry-level Position(s) Available

Entry-level employees start as customer data analysts, client service analysts, and specialized technology analysts.

Average Hours Worked Per Week

Entry-level employees work 45 to 50 hours per week.

Average Starting Salary

The average starting salary varies based on individual qualifications, but is competitive with the industry standard.

Getting Hired

comScore seeks "energetic, enthusiastic, self-motivated, highly engaged individuals who are comfortable in an intellectually challenging, fast-paced environment where change is the norm." The company recruits on college campuses and accepts applications online. Applicants who make the first cut "visit comScore's Reston office for day-long interviews with comScore employees from various levels of the organization." One applicant reports, "The interview was a two-day process. The night before the actual interviews, there was a three-hour reception at a restaurant. It was nice to informally meet some people in the company before being thrown into a day of interviews. The next morning started with breakfast at the office, followed by a short test. They also had us fill out a personality profile, which I assume is currently being used to best manage each new hire personally. I went through four forty-five-minute interviews. I was impressed by the fact that everyone in the company seemed to be involved in the interview process." Another applicant adds, "The tone of the interviews was very informal, relaxed, and conversational. They just wanted to find out who you were, what you liked, etc." The company typically notifies successful applicants within a few weeks of the interview. One successful applicant notes, "My education made me a perfect fit for comScore, [since I have] both people skills and an analytical mind."

Money and Perks

Most first jobbers we spoke with were satisfied with their starting salaries at comScore. The company points out that "employees are eligible for annual salary increases, which are based on performance," but that entry-level hires are not eligible for bonuses. First jobbers tell us that the potential to receive incentive stock option grants when the company has its IPO is a huge perk. They also appreciate the "free snacks and sodas provided in the kitchen," as well as the fact that "everyone has his or her own laptop with wireless internet access." The company also offers summer hours "to add more flexibility for work-life balance.

The Ropes

Some new hires at comScore experience a brief orientation (a "formal two-day boot camp," one first jobber called it), followed by supervised immersion in work supplemented by the occasional "training class in such areas as effective listening, negotiation skills, etc." Others participate in a more formal training program that "employs a three-month orientation process, beginning with an introduction to the company and its structure, followed by team-specific data analysis instruction. Candidates participate in an intensive series of meetings interspersed with work on live projects and simulations. Business- and management-skill workshops in conflict resolution, performance management, negotiating, and listening are [also] provided." One first jobber notes, "We've have had at least twenty-five different people train us, each filling us in on a different piece of what comScore does. This gives the new hires enough understanding of the company to think about what areas they would like to work in."

Day in the Life

Entry-level employees at comScore may work in one of a few positions. Client service analysts "provide analysis of data, client support, and support to the sales and client service teams in delivering customized analysis of consumer behavior." Custom data analysts "conduct data analysis, support internal clients, generate reports, and act as the conduit between the data warehouse and the sales and client service teams." Finally, technology specialists keep the whole system up and running. A client service analyst reports that "it is very difficult to describe a typical day because I still haven't had one. Every day [brings] something different. Basically, I am given pieces of projects to work on. This is meant to give me exposure to our clients and familiarize me with Excel, PowerPoint, our data collection, etc. It can be overwhelming at times." One custom data analyst reports, "Relatively quickly I started working directly with internal clients, from obtaining business requirements and translating them to delivering the project. I was pretty much on my own by the third month of my employment at comScore, but if I wanted, there were plenty of people to go [to] for help. It was up to me how much help I wanted to get." For technology specialists, "A typical day starts by fixing any errors that occurred over the previous night (the programs that a data stream engineer writes run each day, and they [have the potential to have] errors). After all errors are fixed, I work on coding more programs or researching the necessary information in order to code a new program. I also [assure the quality of] the data produced by the programs in order to ensure the program is working properly."

Peers

First jobbers at comScore are "very happy about the work environment," which "surrounds them with young people who are, for the most part, really fun." One notes, "There is camaraderie [among] the new hires. We sit together in the same area throughout training and work on some assignments together." Another agrees, "I rave to my friends that I am so lucky because I get to work with so many cool people in such a relaxed, yet intellectual, environment." Workers note that "Monthly happy hours are held at the corporate headquarters, [and] everyone is encouraged to come and socialize with employees of all job levels. There is little distinction between 'newbies' and those employees who have been at the company for a while; everyone is part of the comScore family."

Moving on

Because comScore's formal entry-level program is only two years old, there isn't much data on former trainees who move on. The company held onto half its first-year program participants; at the time of our survey, all the second-year participants were still with comScore.

Attrition

According to the company, people who leave the entry-level program do so "to pursue other opportunities," "to work [directly] for clients," or "to attend graduate school." For some, the company is "not a good culture fit." One employee notes that some leave because they are unhappy with "the pay-to-work ratio." Such sentiment, however, "did not cause employees to work less or provide less than superior work."

DC Teaching Fellows
TEACHER

"The job is difficult and demanding, but fortunately support is available in a variety of forms."

The Big Picture

Established in 2001, the DC Teaching Fellows (DCTF) program "recruits elementary to secondary teachers within the DC Public Schools. DCTF looks for candidates [in] a range of subject areas, including math, science, special education, English, and elementary education. Fellows will receive their Washington, DC teaching licensure while they teach in a high-need school within the district."

LOCATION(S) WHERE ENTRY-LEVEL EMPLOYEES WORK

The teaching positions are in high-need Washington, DC public schools.

AVERAGE NUMBER OF APPLICATIONS EACH YEAR

The DCTF program receives 1,400 applications each year.

AVERAGE NUMBER HIRED PER YEAR

The program hires 100 teachers per year.

ENTRY-LEVEL POSITION(S) AVAILABLE

Program hires become teachers.

AVERAGE HOURS WORKED PER WEEK

The DC Teaching Fellows program has a standard 35-hour work week, "plus before- and after-school planning, organizing, and tutoring."

PERCENTAGE OF ENTRY-LEVEL HIRES STILL WITH THE COMPANY AFTER THREE, FIVE, AND TEN YEARS

More than 67 percent of entry-level hires remain with the DC Teaching Fellows program after three years; and about two-thirds stay beyond five years.

AVERAGE STARTING SALARY

"The starting salary for these teaching positions is the same as that for all other first-year teachers in the DC Public Schools system; a first-year teacher can expect to make $38,434 annually. Teachers with a master's degree related to their teaching assignment receive $40,966 in annual pay."

Getting Hired

DC Teaching Fellows does "limited campus recruiting in the tri-state area," but the program "does not actively recruit on college campuses." DC Teaching Fellows is, however, "very much interested in college graduates who want to enter the field of teaching." All candidates must "complete and submit an online application, [submit] a resume and personal statement, and provide the program office with copies of college transcripts. Applicants who submit a complete application will be notified of their application status within two weeks. If granted an interview, candidates will have the ability to select their interview date and time via an online scheduler." During the interview, applicants must teach a brief lesson and answer questions that are "mainly centered on how we would react to hypothetical situations in the classroom." Afterward, candidates are "notified of their status within a designated time frame. At that time, selected candidates will be given an enrollment package."

Money and Perks

All compensation issues—salary, pay, and benefits—"are governed by the collective bargaining agreement in place between the district and the teachers union. Teachers receive [increased] compensation for each interval of fifteen education credits received with the proper university documentation." Top perks include the tuition reimbursement program, which is "unique to teacher candidates recruited by DC Teaching Fellows. Fellows are reimbursed for two years of university course work toward state licensure. In many cases, these two years of reimbursements will cover the entire cost of becoming a licensed teacher."

The Ropes

Because DCTF "is a fast-track program into teaching," all fellows "participate in a six-week training institute that starts in late June." This training "consists of two parts: classroom observation and teaching in the mornings and sessions [that focus] on designing instruction [plans], teaching strategies, managing student behavior, and understanding the diversity and culture in your school." This training regimen "is very intense but rewarding. Fellows typically begin their days at 8:00 A.M. in a summer school classroom [and are] paired with another fellow under the guidance of an experienced DCPS teacher. After the day ends—typically at 5:00 P.M.—fellows attend university classes held at the summer institute site."

Day in the Life

Daily life for a DC Teaching Fellow consists of fulfilling "the responsibilities of a classroom teacher." This involves teaching, planning lessons, grading student work, and sometimes attending staff meetings. The job is difficult and demanding, but fortunately support is available in a variety of forms. A program representative explains, "Throughout the summer training institute, we encourage the fellows to develop relationships with others in the program and to seek [one another] out for support, best practices, and insights over the course of the school year. Furthermore, the DC Teaching Fellows program staff employs a full-time professional development manager" who addresses "specific topics or the needs of fellows throughout the year [and makes] regular classroom visits. Additionally, fellows can contact the program office at any time for help with teaching or logistical issues."

Peers

Fellows in the DCTF program tell us that their peers are "smart and cool." There isn't much socializing after the bell rings; most teachers have too many other responsibilities (family, certification training, grading, lesson plans) to enjoy a booming extracurricular social life.

Moving on

DCTF reports that "fellows [who leave the program] largely stay within the field of teaching and education. They may become department and school leaders, seek out additional roles and responsibilities within their schools and the district, and may even apply to be school principals." The program has only been in existence since 2001, so information in this area is limited.

Attrition

DCTF loses about 10 percent of its first-job hires each year, most often because of "personal reasons" and "the challenges of their school placements."

Best and Worst

The most successful first-year fellow was a woman who "rationally and realistically faced every challenge she encountered as a secondary math teacher. After leaving a lucrative career in technology, she transferred her dedication and commitment to the students in her math classes. She was a diligent and creative lesson planner; she went above and beyond to foster positive relationships with her students; and she made significant efforts to involve parents in their children's education. [Her] most admirable traits were a mix of achievement and personal responsibility [that] she internalized and transferred to her students. She was and still is committed and dedicated to her students' achievement and personal growth."

Among the least successful was a teacher who "did not demonstrate flexibility or a realistic vision of teaching in a difficult school. Focusing on her students' achievement became secondary to classroom behavior, administrative problems, and parental struggles. In a nutshell, this teacher did not embody any [positivism] toward her students or her school."

DELOITTE TOUCHE TOMAHTSU
VARIOUS POSITIONS

"My responsibilities [from day one] were to have a good attitude, learn from every engagement I was assigned to, and ask questions. A lot of this job is on-site, learn-as-you-go training."

The Big Picture

Enter the expanding universe of professional services and advice at Deloitte Touche Tomahtsu, a firm that serves more than half the world's largest companies. Deloitte's services include everything from assurance to enterprise risk services to management solutions to tax services. Does this sound intriguing? Then maybe you're perfect for one of the nearly 2,000 entry-level jobs that open at Deloitte each year.

LOCATION(S) WHERE ENTRY-LEVEL EMPLOYEES WORK

"Deloitte hires entry-level candidates in nearly all of our 80 U.S. offices."

AVERAGE NUMBER OF APPLICATIONS EACH YEAR

"We review more than 10,000 resumes [and] applications each year."

AVERAGE NUMBER HIRED PER YEAR OVER THE LAST TEN YEARS

Deloitte hires 1,900 people per year.

ENTRY-LEVEL POSITION(S) AVAILABLE

"We hire a range of entry-level candidates [who have majored in] accounting, finance, information systems, computer science, business, marketing, economics, and others areas."

AVERAGE STARTING SALARY

Employees earn from $45,000 to $50,000, depending on the market.

BENEFITS OFFERED

Deloitte offers a comprehensive medical benefits plan for employees, their families, and domestic partners and includes a prescription drug plan, dental plan, and discount vision care. Additional benefits include a 401(k) plan, a flexible spending plan, a pre-tax transportation program, various forms of flexible work arrangements, parental leave, adoption assistance, adoption reimbursement, a child care resource and referral program, an elder care consultation and referral service, a mortgage assistance program, and paid time-off programs.

Getting Hired

Deloitte seeks candidates "who can provide evidence of excellent client-service skills; marketing, sales, and communication skills; management effectiveness (time management, project management, and people management); and leadership skills (team playing and driving results)." If that describes you, apply through your campus career center or online. "All resumes and applications are reviewed and selected for interview," firm representatives tell us. They use "a structured, behaviorally-based interview to hear real experiences that provide evidence of the skills/attributes that [they're] interviewing for." One successful hire in tax services describes the application process this way: "On my resume, I focused on experiences and knowledge that were specifically related to the job I was applying for. I was very truthful and genuine in my cover letter. I had a total of five interviews, and they were with partners and senior managers during first and second rounds. The tone of the interview depended on who I was interviewing with. They were all very friendly and asked questions to get to know who I was and why I wanted to be at the firm."

Money and Perks

Newcomers to Deloitte tell us that "the start date is definitely negotiable, and the office where you work is also, to some extent, but that typically requires another interview in that office." As for salary, everyone we spoke with agrees with the first jobber who states, "I do not think that if I asked for more, I would have gotten it." Company representatives note that "salary increases are based on performance, business growth, and marketplace." Full-time workers "generally start in August, September, and January." Most of our respondents say the best perks are "the great people who you work with" and "being able to work [with] so many clients from so many different industries."

The Ropes

A first jobber in tax services tells us that orientation at Deloitte "lasts, on the whole, about two weeks. We had [a] one-day new-hire orientation that covered benefits, a general overview of the firm, different support functions, etc. Then we went to a national training for four days. Although it was technically training, the new hires and I were all so new it was like an orientation into the firm as well as tax training. When we got back into the office, we had a week-long new-hire training that focused on more technical tax training as well as software training." Once orientation and initial training is done, newbies "are assigned 'buddies,' 'counselors,' and 'mentors.' These individuals are generally selected and developed for their roles—often based on their team-working skills and their involvement in recruiting generally. We consider the involvement of our client-service professionals as personal and professional development."

Day in the Life

After orientation and initial training, "New hires commence working on teams dealing directly with clients" at Deloitte, and "they fulfill these responsibilities through a fairly structured team-support approach." One entry-level worker explains, "A typical day involves coming in and checking our e-mails, then we start on our work. Sometimes we work on more than one project, so we have to balance our workload. The day involves our preparing the work papers and then getting them reviewed by our seniors. During this whole process there is also a lot of communication between the staff and the senior staff." Adds another, "My responsibilities [from day one] were to have a good attitude, learn from every engagement I was assigned to, and ask questions. A lot of this job is on-site, learn-as-you-go training." There's rarely down time; one newbie tells us, "I am almost never bored. When I am at work, I am always thinking and keeping myself busy, and the time flies by. Sometimes the amount of work can be a little overwhelming, but that makes the time go by faster."

Peers

There are many first jobbers; therefore, new hires describe an atmosphere that is "like a college class. We have a great camaraderie. We usually go out together for a while at least every Friday, and more often than not, we get together for something on the weekends." One worker says, "[Other new hires are] smart, nice, and hardworking. We also share a lot of similarities because I feel that every company has its own culture of people, and all of us were hired by Deloitte." Those in accounting tell us that they enjoy their peers' support and help in preparing for the CPA exam.

Moving on

Many entry-level employees come to Deloitte in the hopes of building a career. Those who use it as a way station often go on to business school, capitalizing on their experiences to build a more compelling business school application. Others "wind up working with clients they met through their work engagements; so in a sense, they continue to work with Deloitte."

Attrition

According to Deloitte representatives, "there's no overarching reason that stands out" for why some entry-level hires don't stick around long, "but generally when a person leaves that early in the process, it's because of a disparity between the job responsibilities and the person's goals or expectations." Some new hires, we're told, simply can't take the long hours required of them. "It isn't for everyone," concedes one audit associate.

DEMOCRATIC NATIONAL COMMITTEE
ADMINISTRATIVE ASSISTANT

DEMOCRATIC NATIONAL COMMITTEE

"Individuals who are [good at multitasking] and who are quick and creative thinkers are DNC material."

The Big Picture

The Democratic National Committee (DNC) coordinates the political party's presidential nominating convention; supports Democratic candidates for public office at the national, state, and local levels; and publicizes and promotes the positions of the Democratic party as a whole. Working here is a great way to break into politics and provides an equally stellar opportunity to move to Washington, DC, a fun town and a good place to start a career.

LOCATION(S) WHERE ENTRY-LEVEL EMPLOYEES WORK

First jobbers work in Washington, DC.

AVERAGE NUMBER OF APPLICATIONS EACH YEAR

The DNC receives 100 applications per year.

ENTRY-LEVEL POSITION(S) AVAILABLE

Entry-level hires work as administrative assistants to directors and offer administrative support.

AVERAGE HOURS WORKED PER WEEK

New hires work 50 hours per week.

PERCENTAGE OF ENTRY-LEVEL HIRES STILL WITH THE COMPANY AFTER THREE, FIVE, AND TEN YEARS

After three years, 5 percent of new hires remain with the DNC.

AVERAGE STARTING SALARY

New hires earn $30,000 per year.

BENEFITS OFFERED

The DNC offers its employees major medical, dental, and vision insurance. Additional benefits include life insurance, short-term disability, supplemental medical insurance, a 401(k) plan, and flexible spending accounts.

CONTACT INFORMATION

Democratic National Committee
430 South Capitol Street, Southeast
Washington, DC 20003
Tel: 202-863-8000
E-mail: Jewelle Hazel, Director of Human Resources, hazelj@dnc.org
www.dnc.org

Getting Hired

The DNC lists job openings on its website; internships, first jobbers tell us, provide an excellent gateway to subsequent employment. (According to DNC representatives, "Most of our entry-level hiring is done by word of mouth. We also hire prior DNC interns and people who have prior campaign experience.") Because interns are already known by human resources and other staffers, they usually avoid a prolonged vetting process (including resumes, letters of recommendation, etc.). All other applicants, however, must take the conventional route. Here's how one applicant describes it: "I sent my resume via e-mail, actually for another position at the DNC. However, my resume was noted and sent to the director of the Women's Vote Center, where I was eventually hired. When I heard that my resume was drawn from a pool of other resumes, it appeared that the DNC internally communicated; this impressed me. Since I was in Texas at the time, I interviewed via teleconference with the director. The questions were both [general] and specific, ranging from, 'Why do you want to work with the DNC Women's Vote Center?' to specific questions about my previous work experience." "Individuals who are [good at multitasking] and who are quick and creative thinkers are DNC material."

Money and Perks

The primary objective of most first jobbers is to acquire experience and gain a foothold in Democratic politics; accordingly, few people worry much about their starting salaries. "I didn't try to negotiate. I was perfectly happy with the start date and salary," writes one first jobber in the research department. One employee says, "The health benefits [we] receive [are] unbelievable. I am covered so completely that I have nothing to worry about." Other excellent perks include "working at the pulse of the DNC, so you get to interact with the entire staff. It's also a great way to make connections."

The Ropes

When candidates accept an offer, "a human resources package is mailed to them at least one week before the start date. This package includes their confirmation letter, benefits, and personnel information. On the first day a welcome package is awaiting the new employee, which includes information technology information, basic DNC information and policies, information on public transportation, and places to eat. Department directors conduct specific department orientation on the first day. Each department's orientation is different and based on how the department works. A human resources orientation is scheduled for several days after." While most DNC employees receive some formal training during their tenure, it is primarily "a learn-as-you go process. As I was working and questions arose, I asked them and had them answered by my colleagues."

Day in the Life

The first jobbers we spoke with at the DNC work on a wide range of assignments; for example, some assist senior strategists and organizers, others supervise and coordinate events for interns, and others perform basic clerical and administrative tasks. What all of them share in common is that they're very busy; one explains, "There is always something to do in our office. I always have a lot of work and long-term projects. While anyone can get bored during office work, I know that I have things I can be doing. If I find myself either overwhelmed or bored, a quick Internet read, such as a newspaper clips, can help with that. It's about pacing your day and allowing yourself to merge into the day and your work." They also get to mix and mingle with party bigwigs. As one newbie tells us, "Even as an intern, I was given the opportunity by my boss and other high-level people to sit in on meetings. I have the opportunity to work directly with them on a regular basis, depending on what we are working on and what kind of meeting is being held."

Peers

DNC staffers tell us that their peers "are extremely friendly. We often hang out at happy hours and events, and we have other outside contact. Sometimes it is just our department, and other times it's the entire staff." One first jobber notes, "One thing unites all of us, even if our personalities differ: [for example,] all of us [were] determined to win back the White House in 2004. From there, great, and even unexpected, relationships can form." The ubiquity of "mostly young, diverse individuals" on the staff means first jobbers have "people with whom one can talk with if [they feel] overwhelmed."

Moving on

"Since we are a campaign headquarters and a fundraising operation, employment with the DNC is very cyclical," officials tell us. "Most people move on after a particular campaign cycle to work for either candidates who have won a particular campaign or to work for other democratic organizations or nonprofit organizations to expand their campaign portfolio." Some leave to go back to school. The average tenure of a DNC first jobber is two years.

Attrition

Turnover rates are high at the DNC; approximately 50 percent of employees leave within a year of starting. Most people find work with an elected official or another political organization.

DOMINO'S PIZZA
PEOPLE PIPELINE PROGRAM

"With each rotation I complete, I am given more responsibility, larger-impact projects, and more visibility in the organization."

The Big Picture

The "People Pipeline," Domino's leadership training program, is "a cross-functional rotational program through three core assignments (store operations, distribution, and franchise services)" that is "designed to foster ongoing learning and development and prepare participants for future leadership positions within the company."

LOCATION(S) WHERE ENTRY-LEVEL EMPLOYEES WORK

HR officials note that "we have opportunities nationwide, but most are concentrated in Ann Arbor, MI."

AVERAGE NUMBER OF APPLICATIONS EACH YEAR

Domino's receives 400–500 applications each year; of those, 15 applicants are invited to complete the extensive application process.

AVERAGE NUMBER HIRED PER YEAR

At present, Domino's hires three entry-level employees each year; however, the company hopes to expand the program in coming years.

ENTRY-LEVEL POSITION(S) AVAILABLE

Entry-level hires participate in the People Pipeline Program for leadership development.

AVERAGE HOURS WORKED PER WEEK

Entry-level employees work 40–50 hours per week.

AVERAGE STARTING SALARY

Employees receive starting salaries of $30,000–$45,000, plus bonuses.

BENEFITS OFFERED

"On the first of the month following three months of service, team members are eligible for…medical, dental, and vision" coverage, for which "a small biweekly premium [is] paid by [the] team members [themselves]."

Additional benefits include generous short-term disability coverage; health care flex spending accounts; dependent care flex spending accounts; stock option awards; 401(k) plan; adoption assistance; paid time off; and bereavement leave.

Getting Hired

People Pipeline is an elite leadership training program, and the selection process is commensurately rigorous. The application starts when the applicant submits a resume. Human Resources contacts likely candidates for an initial interview, and those "who demonstrate they have the competence needed to do the job based on their answers to the interview questions . . . are asked to submit a formal application and complete an essay. Next, candidates interview with an advisory team . . . of senior team members from across the organization. At this point, all candidates' references and backgrounds are checked prior to completing the application process, which involves an interview with a group of executive vice presidents and concludes with the offer of employment." Explains one applicant who survived the ordeal, "The interview and application process was unlike any other company's. The interviews consisted of one-on-one interviews with the Leadership Team of Domino's Pizza (the executive vice presidents) and then a formal PowerPoint Presentation to the Leadership Team. Once you are successful in those steps, you move on to an interview with the CEO. It was a challenging process, but it reaffirmed the fact that Domino's would be willing to invest a lot of time and effort into my development process." The entire process, from initial contact to job offer, can take up to four months.

Money and Perks

Because People Pipeline fast-tracks participants up the corporate ladder, starting salary is not a matter of primary concern for most in the program. Even so, most find their pay more than adequate. Observes one Pipeliner, "Monetarily, the little extras like paid travel to each city we move to, paid housing in each city we are in (paid utilities, rent, etc.) are perks of this position. With no expenses going out, I basically put my entire paycheck in the bank every time!" Others tout the Team Achievement Dividend, which "rewards every team member for reaching our annual EBITDA target. As you know, EBITDA is an excellent measure of the profitability of a company and its controllable expenses. This bonus program has a 10-to-1 leverage element for exceeding the company's EBITDA target. This means that if we hit 101 percent of our annual EBITDA target, we get 110 percent of our annual bonus. We've never missed our target since the plan's inception, and have exceeded the goal every year but one." The job offers other perks, including "Domino's Days (extra days around each holiday which extend a three-day weekend to four days), and the holiday party, at which we receive huge picnic baskets filled with holiday-themed plate and silverware sets, baking goods, coupons, toys, and so much stuff."

The Ropes

All new hires at Domino's corporate headquarters start their tenure with the STAR Welcome program, "a day-long orientation in which we review various aspects of the company culture, review our benefit programs, go on a building tour and to meet key people from various departments, and learn how to make pizza in the test kitchen." The rest of the first week is spent at Pizza Prep School, "a four-day, 42-hour intense training program during which Domino's office members don uniforms, split into four-person teams, and immerse themselves into every detail of store culture. Team members learn about store operations and procedures during morning classroom sessions and work in the pizza theater in the afternoon to learn order taking, pizza making, oven tending, pizza routing, and store closing procedures. The training culminates with a written exam and a timed pizza-making test. Team members then have the opportunity to put their knowledge into action as they work a Friday night dinner rush in a store." Training continues throughout the People Pipeline program; notes one Pipeliner, "At the beginning of each assignment, there has been specific training and orientation provided by team leaders. There are also online training courses that we are responsible for taking."

Day in the Life

Domino's reports that "Leadership Development associates are integrated into new positions in a series of rotational assignments. . . . Typical position assignments are approximately six months in duration. The associate will complete four to five various position assignments while in the Leadership Development Program. . . . In addition to completing assignments, the associate is also provided with leadership and organizational training defined in a customized plan known as a learning map. Mentors are assigned to aid in the development of the associate. . . . Each Leadership Development associate graduates from the program once he or she has successfully completed all assignments and courses identified in the learning map, over [the course of] approximately 24 to 36 months." Writes one Pipeliner, "With each rotation I complete, I am given more responsibility, larger-impact projects, and more visibility in the organization. The contact with management is great. We present case studies to the Leadership Team, and they present synopses of their duties and departments to us. We also have outings with the Leadership Team, [among which was] a recent golf tournament at the CEO's country club."

Peers

The People Pipeline is a very small program (it had seven participants total as of this writing), and its rotational nature means that participants are not always in the same location. Occasionally there are opportunities for them to get to know one another; reports one, "A few of us have the chance to room together during some rotations, and we became really close. It was helpful moving to a new city with other people you know and being able to share our experiences with each other." Notes another, "Twice a year the seven of us in the program get together for a week-long training/team-building session." Pipeliners can make friends with other Domino's first jobbers, of course, "but this requires initiative on your part. There isn't a huge after-hours social scene; I would say that I probably go out for drinks or dinner with people from work approximately once a month."

Moving on

Graduate school and other career opportunities are the main reasons young workers leave the Domino's fold of their own accord.

Attrition

The company reports: "Domino's has worked tirelessly to provide a development program for recent graduates that [offers] both the training and support needed to be successful. We are proud that not a single person who has entered the Leadership Development program has left without successfully completing it." The program had been in operation for 18 months when we spoke with Domino's representatives.

Best and Worst

According to HR officials, the best entry-level hire fit this description: "Among all the exceptional people who work here, M. H. has been incredibly successful. Starting as an intern in 1988, M. H. established himself as a winner. Upon graduating from college, he came back to work full time as a corporate controller and worked his way up to VP of Financial Analysis. . . . When asked why he has been so successful at Domino's, M. H. answers modestly that he enjoys the work and the people."

DYNETECH
EVENT PLANNER AND ON-SITE COORDINATOR

"Dynetech seeks hires who demonstrate "'shine values,' which are: accountability, flexibility, entrepreneurialism, integrity, excellence, and open communication."

The Big Picture

Think of Dynetech as an "instant company"-maker. Say you have a great new product that you've been toting all over the country to sell at trade shows. Your overhead is high; your ability to reach potential customers is limited; and as a result, the growth of your business is constrained. That's where Dynetech comes in. The firm partners with its clients to provide consulting services, media and marketing strategies, software support, a direct-to-market sales campaign, and a number of other, similar services. Dynetech, in short, becomes the fully-staffed support company that clients need to spur "dynamic growth" in their businesses. First jobbers here assist clients by helping to plan training and sales events and then managing those events to make sure they run smoothly and successfully.

LOCATION(S) WHERE DYNETECH HIRES ENTRY-LEVEL WORK

Entry-level employees work in Orlando, Florida.

AVERAGE NUMBER OF APPLICATIONS EACH YEAR

Dynetech receives 80 applications each year.

AVERAGE NUMBER HIRED PER YEAR

Dynetech hires six entry-level employees each year.

ENTRY-LEVEL POSITION(S) AVAILABLE

Entry-level employees work as event planners and on-site coordinators.

AVERAGE HOURS WORKED PER WEEK

Entry-level employees work 40 hours per week.

AVERAGE STARTING SALARY

Salary depends on the position for which the recent grad is applying, his or her major at school, as well as participation in extracurricular activities, internships, part-time jobs, GPA, and other such factors.

BENEFITS OFFERED

Dynetech offers employer-paid medical and dental insurance. Other benefits include life insurance, a prescription plan, short- and long-term disability, and a company-matched 401(k) plan, which is fully vested after five years.

Getting Hired

Dynetech seeks hires who demonstrate "'shine values,' which are: accountability, flexibility, entrepreneurialism, integrity, excellence, and open communication." The firm recruits at numerous local school-based job fairs, especially in the central Florida region. The firm also posts job openings on its website. According to company officials, "The first step of the application process is for the organizational development department to review resumes. After reviewing the resumes, the organizational development department will select which applicants warrant an in-person interview and, if needed, pre-employment testing. The first interview is with organizational development, the second . . . with the hiring supervisor/manager, the third . . . with the Director, and the fourth . . . with the vice president." Interview questions "are tailored to the applicant." The firm advises that "applicants should research the company ahead of time on the internet" and "come prepared . . . with a portfolio with examples of their work (even if it's related school projects), letters of recommendation, etc. This demonstrates that the applicant is prepared and takes initiative. Also, during the interview, applicants should take their time, listen to the question, think about the question, and provide an articulate response with examples. Often, applicants are so nervous and want to tell you everything about themselves that they either just blurt out any response, or go off on a wild tangent without even answering the question. Silence during interviews is okay. It means that the applicant is actually thinking."

Money and Perks

For many first jobbers at Dynetech, starting salary is not negotiable. Employees note that "start date can be flexible, though." First jobbers we spoke with, however, reported satisfaction with the initial offer and did not try to negotiate a better deal. Raises "are given during annual reviews, which are completely performance-driven. Dynetech also offers promotional opportunities to associates. It's possible that an associate would receive a promotion during the year, at which point his/her salary would be readjusted to reflect the responsibilities of the new position."

Most beloved perks include the "great insurance program," "all the training opportunities," and a generous vacation plan. Writes one first jobber, "We get two weeks vacation [after one year of employment; newbies get one week], four paid personal days, and our birthday off. We also benefit from nine additional paid vacation days." Also, on-site coordinators collect their own frequent flier miles, "a great benefit considering how extensively they travel."

Dynetech also offers a myriad of training programs designed to facilitate personal and professional development among associates. Training programs include Management Training, Business Communication, and Associate Mentorship Certification.

Other perks of working at Dynetech include free parking ("a great perk when working in a major downtown area"), organized athletic teams, planned recreation with family participation, and workout facilities.

The Ropes

Employment at Dynetech starts with a week-long orientation; reports one first jobber, "The orientation includes getting assigned a mentor and a lunch date with your mentor as well as your boss." It also includes an introduction to Dynetech's "visions, goals, and values" as well as its "processes, procedures, products, and service lines." Toward the end of the week, new hires receive "departmental training with their manager and colleagues. Departmental training is unique to each department and is tailored to each position. Finally on Friday afternoon, new hires participate in the orientation wrap-up with the training and development department." Subsequent training is ongoing—"from the minute you report to work the first day until the present day. We learned about everything and everyone," writes one event planner.

Day in the Life

Recent college graduates often enter Dynetech as event planners or as on-site coordinators. The former are "in charge of planning each day of an event. . . . Event planners are assigned by DMA (Designated Market Area) and are responsible for researching the event city's demographics. . . . Once the research of the city is completed, contact is made to the best and most appropriate locations in which to hold the events that correspond with the demographic research the event planner has put together. Mostly hotel space is contracted but depending on the event, other locations, such as convention centers or large meeting spaces, could be used." According to one employee, "Event planners embody the following characteristics: they are extremely organized and detail-oriented, they have the ability to work in a constantly changing environment, and they are flexible when changes and/or challenges occur. They also have the ability to be extremely effective team players." Observes an event planner, "I normally have two or three campaigns that I am working on at a time." Once the event is planned, the on-site coordinator takes over. He or she attends the event and is "responsible for its successful execution"; this entails handling everything from corporate credit card authorizations to troubleshooting for clients and customers.

Peers

"There are a lot of younger people" at Dynetech," and so it's relatively easy for new hires to find friends and join a social scene. Writes one first jobber, "I've come to really appreciate the camaraderie and friendship I have here at Dynetech. This place is like my extended family." Explains another newbie, "Every Friday there is a happy hour crew heading out to the local bars, clubs, and restaurants. This is a company where we eat lunch together almost every day. We have parties and get-togethers on the weekends; we have a running program; we do charity drives together. . . . We're a pretty tight-knit group here with a lot of big ideas."

Moving on

On-site coordinators are most likely to leave Dynetech, we're told, because "they don't want to travel anymore and they are not interested in a position in the office." Event planners typically move on "when they want to plan larger-scale events and conferences" beyond what Dynetech offers.

Attrition

Our contact in Dynetech Organizational Development reports that the "turnover rate is very low. It is rare that a recent graduate comes on board and leaves during the first year. Out of all the recent grads we've hired, I can only recall one person who left Dynetech during their first year." Our contact also notes that "Dynetech has hired most of its associates (both experienced and entry-level) since 2001, so the average tenure company-wide is approximately three to four years (but this is only because we've grown from fifty associates to more than 500 associates during this time)."

There are several associates who have enjoyed careers of twenty-plus years at Dynetech. They started with Dynetech in the early phases of its existence and have since been promoted to senior-level managers, directors, and vice presidents. HR officials note that there are many career advancement opportunities at Dynetech for those "who wish to apply themselves."

EDWARD JONES
VARIOUS POSITIONS

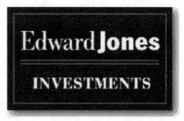

"I always have something exciting going on. I have felt overwhelmed a few times, but everything always works out great in the end."

The Big Picture

Repeatedly named in *Fortune* magazine's "100 Best Companies to Work For," Edward Jones is one of those rare companies that continued to grow rapidly during the recession. Edward Jones was also ranked number one in SmartMoney's annual full-service broker survey. It isn't just the growth-related job security that employees love, though; the *Fortune* ranking reflects worker satisfaction on a whole range of quality-of-life issues, including benefits, workplace culture, and advancement opportunities. Many new hires start in a rotational program—ideal for those who know they want a career in the world of finance but aren't sure what area best suits them.

LOCATION(S) WHERE ENTRY-LEVEL EMPLOYEES WORK

"Edward Jones is headquartered in St. Louis, Missouri; home offices [are] in Tempe, Arizona; Toronto headquarters [are] in Mississagua, Ontario; and United Kingdom headquarters [are] in Canary Wharf, UK; and [there are more than] 9,000 one-broker branch offices across the country, as well as [in] Canada and the United Kingdom."

ENTRY-LEVEL POSITION(S) AVAILABLE

New hires may work as investment representatives or hold positions in accounting, compliance and licensing, human resources, information systems, marketing, operations, products and sales, research, and training at a headquarters location.

AVERAGE HOURS WORKED PER WEEK

Employees work 40 or more hours per week.

BENEFITS OFFERED

Benefits vary according to the position.

CONTACT INFORMATION

Visit the website at www.edwardjonesopportunity.com/usa_home.html.

Getting Hired

Many first jobbers get their start at Edward Jones through the rotational development program, "a year-long rotational program through four different product and marketing areas of the firm. During the course of the year, [employees] were also required to become Series 7 licensed (Series 7 is an exam that qualifies an individual to trade in corporate securities). The program has recently changed to include areas beyond product and marketing." Many new hires find their way into the rotational program through internships they held while they were still in college; "the internships helped me get the initial interview," explains one trainee. The interview process, a first jobber reports, "is pretty unique. They have a three-interview minimum. The first one is just a sit-down, face-to-face interview; nothing complex. Then they do a phone interview/personality profile. What I liked was they knew what they were looking for, and I was able to answer the questions [honestly]. They were asking about my childhood, how I looked at things, that sort of thing. After that, if they think you're a good match, they extend an offer for a final interview."

Money and Perks

As far as working in the company's rotational program goes, one new hire says, "The salary is pretty much set. They were willing to negotiate the start date; they were really willing to work with me on that. [Rotations] were set when I got hired. However, I was told by my department leaders I would do better somewhere else and was able to move. A lot of people don't end up where they originally thought they would. The program is flexible in that way." Outside the rotational program, according to company representatives, hard-working, first-year investment representatives "can net an average income of $55,000." Since that takes long hours and above-average work, "the firm has developed a unique 'first year' compensation package: regular paychecks during training, salary support during the first twelve-selling months, and bonuses." First jobbers love "the fact that there's a lot of flexibility. If you need to go to an appointment, you just tell your leader. If [you] need to get something done, it's not like they're going to make you take away from vacation time or sick days." They also "like that it's a very big local company. Somewhere down the line, if [you] want to expand [your] horizons, [the company has] campuses in St. Louis, Tempe, Toronto, and London."

The Ropes

"Edward Jones does a terrific job with orientation," writes one first jobber who adds, "We had a week-long orientation in which they told us about the culture of the firm. We learned about the history of the firm, where they come from, what they do. Orientation sucks at most places, but everybody in the room was like, 'This is great. There's a great corporate culture here.'" For noninvestment representative positions, following orientation, "you go to the main campus where you start your job. You're told ahead of time who and where, so you know where to go. I sat down with my department leader, and she told me what was in store for me. Being part of the rotational program, I was encouraged to visit other departments." Ongoing training is a major component of the rotational program. Another first jobber explains, "I still get [trained] to this day, long after I started. During each of the three-month rotations, my first year I worked very closely with one or two associates in the department I was in and was trained by them. I also attended training sessions both internally and externally, ranging from diversity training to web content workshops. There are also a plethora of learning courses to sign up for on the learning site of our Intranet. They offer both independent study and class courses on the applications and software, presentation skills, leadership courses, etc."

Day in the Life

According to one trainee, most first jobbers' daily tasks "really depend on the department. You come in at the assigned time, maybe seven or eight. If I had a meeting, I'd go to that. If not, I'd work on old projects, try to get information on upcoming projects, and have meetings with other associates in the department to get ideas [from] them." Another trainee agrees, "My responsibilities changed, of course, with each rotation. Although looking back on it, I had some pretty important responsibilities for an entry-level training position. My responsibilities included working on ideas for a redesign of the public website entry page, designing fliers and posters, creating web pages, designing and implementing contests for the branches, setting up a Trade Show Booth program for our branches, designing the trade show booths, and many more projects. I don't really have an example of a typical day because each and every day is different." One new hire warns that "when you start a new rotation, it sometimes takes awhile to get going, and you can get a little bored, but from then on, you stay busy. I always have something exciting going on. I have felt overwhelmed a few times, but everything always works out great in the end."

Peers

First jobbers at Edward Jones "see one another a lot, especially with rotational associates, which is the number-one entry-level position." The company provides plenty of opportunities to socialize; one associate explains, "What's good about being a big company is they have tickets to every sporting event, every concert, any outing you want. We do an annual Founders' Day; we have baseball and softball tournaments. Our division took us to the Cardinals game. It's definitely a fun atmosphere." Another associate adds, "During our rotations, [all of us] had to work in groups on a competitive-strategies project together and present it to management. That was work, but a good experience to work with others." Associates usually remain close with their work group for the first year: "After a year, you're placed in your own department, and you've moved on to your other 'real' job, and you're kind of wanting to work as hard as you can to be beneficial to your department."

Moving on

Edward Jones is a great place to start a career, but it's not for everyone. One trainee writes, "It's just not a good fit for some. Maybe the rotations aren't what [some] thought they'd be. Maybe they thought they'd be earning more than they get here." People we spoke with agree that "there are more positives than negatives," but also explain that "sometimes people just don't like their actual job duties. It may not be what they really wanted to do or may not be related to what they studied in school, but it's the job they were offered." Some are turned off by the fact that "it's very challenging. If you're a slacker, it's not going to work for you. Also, it's a very conservative atmosphere. [People] wear suits every day. It's very structured." Some people who leave return to school for an MBA; others seek opportunities elsewhere in the world of banking and finance.

ELECTRONIC ARTS (EA)
VARIOUS POSITIONS

"No matter what the task, new hires are "expected to strive for the goals that their supervisor has set for them and learn as much about the project and skill sets needed for the task they are working on."

The Big Picture

For many, it's a dream come true: a job that pays you to develop and test games for PCs, PlayStation, Xbox, and Nintendo. Electronic Arts (EA) is a major producer of sports games, role-playing games, war games, driving and flight simulators, and all other manner of blissful diversions. It's kind of like the way you spent your free time in college, except that EA pays you for it.

LOCATION(S) WHERE ENTRY-LEVEL EMPOYEES WORK

EA has locations in Redwood City, California; Los Angeles, California; Orlando, Florida; Chicago, Illinois; Vancouver, Canada; Burnaby, Canada; Montreal, Canada.

AVERAGE NUMBER OF APPLICATIONS EACH YEAR

Approximately 82,000 applications are submitted to EA every year.

AVERAGE NUMBER HIRED PER YEAR OVER THE LAST TEN YEARS

EA has hired approximately 2,100 people per year over the last 10 years.

ENTRY-LEVEL POSITIONS AVAILABLE

New hires work as software engineers, technical artists, computer graphic artists, production assistants, marketing assistants, and financial analysts.

AVERAGE STARTING SALARY

"EA offers a competitive total compensation package." This includes base pay, a performance bonus, stock options, and the benefits outlined below.

BENEFITS OFFERED

"EA offers a choice of two medical programs through United Healthcare. One is a PPO, and the other is an EPO." For California employees, an "HMO is also available through Kaiser Permanente." Additional benefits include a 401(k) plan with matching program, an employee stock purchase plan, $100 toward a game console, and ten "EA points" per year for use toward games.

Getting Hired

EA posts available positions on their website, at which "an applicant can complete a profile and electronically attach a resume. The EA Recruiter system will automatically notify each applicant of an opening that matches his or her skill sets and interests via e-mail." The company visits "several campuses during the fall and spring seasons" (to find out which ones, visit the website). Many first jobbers we spoke with begin their tenure with the company as interns; internship opportunities are also posted on Jobs.EA.com. One former intern reports, "I was not interviewed for my full-time position, but when applying, I attached screenshots of my personal projects, and I believe this helped set me apart from the rest of the applicants."

Money and Perks

Entry-level workers at EA warn that little is negotiable in the job offer: "The position is quite popular given the number of gamers out there, so [the company] can be picky," explains one first jobber. Most newbies report that the "start date was flexible and accommodative," but that other aspects of the job were not. Key perks include "working in a field that is very much 'now' and the center of attention. [Getting] this kind of experience right out of school seemed almost impossible." Employees also enjoy "game rooms on-site to play the latest games, $100 toward the purchase of a gaming console, world-class facilities (state-of-the-art gym, cafeteria, indoor basketball court, sand volleyball courts, etc.), and free games!"

Other perks include an education reimbursement program (for which "regular full-time employees can receive up to $5,000 per year for education directly related to their position or career path") and invitations to special events ("such as private screenings of *Harry Potter*, *James Bond*, and *The Lord of the Rings* movies prior to general public viewing").

The Ropes

Orientation at EA takes a half-day and includes "completing the required paperwork [as well as getting] information on benefits, corporate culture, ergonomic equipment available, travel, and events." Subsequent training depends on the position. Newbies inform us that "Electronic Arts offers a variety of courses in all areas of game production. These are open to all employees." A designer we spoke with, for example, explains that he had "attended a couple of seminars/conferences. They were all related to design. One was a seminar on interface, and another was on Flash." A 3-D production artist reports, "I'd learned 3-D fundamentals from school, but most of what I do at work I learned during my Electronic Arts internship. Training was a steep and hectic process, but I'm really glad I came through." HR notes that "by offering training, the company not only ensures that employees are keeping abreast of the latest technologies and principles, but that they are also participating in education that will lead to their own personal development."

Day in the Life

There's much more to creating and selling games than you may imagine, and there are a myriad of tasks for first job-bers to perform at EA. One software engineer tells us that her typical day consists of "working with the game designers to figure out how they want the enemies to act, then working out how to implement that, and finally working with the artists to get any new animations that this behavior may require." An artist on the production team often spends the day "modeling props and environments for the game. I receive my task(s) in the morning, complete the task(s) by the after-noon, and receive critiques from [an] art director, then refine the model based on the feedback. Sometimes certain tasks may take up to three to four days." Other positions at EA may require an employee to "resolve player disputes, take report information about hacked accounts, report bugs, fix bugs that affect the general player base that are easily resolvable, action customers that use harassing language, fix doors; if they did not have us, the game world would be anarchy." No matter what the task, new hires are "expected to strive for the goals that their supervisor has set for them and learn as much about the project and skill sets needed for the task they are working on."

Peers

"Most people here are really smart and cool," say EA entry-level employees. "We also play a lot of video games!" One worker characterizes his colleagues as "a diverse group of people from all around the world. . . . I've gotten to work with people from all ages, walks of life, and several different cultures." EA "provides many opportunities for social and person-al interaction. This is not only for first jobbers, but [also for] anyone in the company. You can become great friends with producers and executives; no one is out of reach professionally or personally."

Moving on

Because "EA is very successful and constantly growing in every way," few first jobbers are anxious to move on." They like the security EA provides, as well as the excellent on-the-job training that they receive. People who leave, for the most part, move on to other gaming companies or return to school for an advanced degree.

EMC
VARIOUS POSITIONS

"Everyone has something to share and contribute.

The work culture is elite, competitive, and yet fun."

The Big Picture

EMC is one of the world's fastest growing, most profitable, and most highly valued information technology providers. A global corporation employing more than 30,000 individuals, EMC is uniquely focused on information and how to help organizations avoid the risks and reduce the costs of managing their information while fully exploiting the value of this asset for competitive advantage. It's a "vibrant, fast-paced" industry that places a premium on "creative ideas, innovative thinking, and unparalleled commitment" in its work force. The company offers a variety of entry-level opportunities, including several rotational training programs.

LOCATION(S) WHERE ENTRY-LEVEL EMPLOYEES WORK

Major facilities are located in Massachusetts; California; North Carolina; Toronto, Canada; and Cork, Ireland; 100+ sales offices and distributions partners; and 50 countries across the globe.

AVERAGE NUMBER OF APPLICATIONS EACH YEAR

EMC receives "5,000 applications per year for entry-level positions. The majority of the positions are college-level."

ENTRY-LEVEL POSITION(S) AVAILABLE

Entry-level hires typically work as software and hardware engineers, or enter into one of the following programs:

MLDP—Marketing Leadership Development Program
PERC—Program for Engineering Rotation in Clariion
FTP—Finance Training Program
HRLDP—HR Leadership Development Program

AVERAGE HOURS WORKED PER WEEK

Entry-level employees work 40 hours per week.

Getting Hired

EMC interviews on college campuses; first jobbers may also apply directly via the company's website. The company reports that "entry-level employees typically start at the end of the academic year." Interviews focus on behavioral questions that "allow the interviewer to get a sense of how someone will perform in a job and in various circumstances." One participant in the Marketing Leadership Development Program reports, "The tone of the interview was professional and direct. They asked me to describe academic and professional situations entailing decision-making processes, team projects, and work group collaboration. They inquired about how I would act in a given situation among these topics and scenarios." Most applicants endure several rounds of interviews before receiving a final offer. One who was interviewed three times writes, "The most impressive thing is how fast they moved. They had a quick debriefing and all three rounds were in quick succession. They made me a job offer on the same day of the third round. They demonstrated a 'sense of urgency,' which is big in the culture here." EMC points out that it "also hires a high percentage of co-op/interns as full-time employees."

Money and Perks

Some of the first jobbers we spoke with told us that their start dates were somewhat flexible, but that otherwise, their job offers were "not negotiable." For many here, the key issue is not salary but the opportunity to learn and advance. "The most attractive factor was that it was a structured program with classes and a curriculum. There were rotation opportunities, and it seemed like a very steep learning-curve experience," explains one first jobber. Another agrees, "The program's attributes fulfilled my notion of the ideal entry-level job." Some first jobbers travel frequently for EMC; their fringe benefits include "a monthly car allowance" and "lots of frequent flyer miles and hotel points." First jobbers also love the stock options.

The Ropes

All incoming employees at EMC receive an orientation that "covers a broad overview of the company, its organizations, recent financial results, and medical and 401(k) benefits. We were given an overview of the hierarchical structure of the company, a tour of the intranet and important links that we need to know about, and an introduction to the product line of the company. What was very clear at the end of this session was the sense of being a part of the company's vision and a feeling that we will be considered as important contributors to its success." Subsequently, first jobbers in rotational and training programs take classes that can last anywhere from a couple of weeks to a couple of months. An implementation specialist reports, "The training program was an intensive nine-week program in which we covered most of the EMC offerings in lecture, which was often followed by a lab section, during which we had the opportunity to get hands-on experience."

Day in the Life

EMC hires first jobbers to serve in a wide range of functions, and their daily responsibilities vary considerably. Many training programs here "entail a mentoring/shadowing phase during which we are assigned only to projects where there are other EMC employees on-site. This has provided a great opportunity to get important questions answered while gaining familiarity with the available software, tools, etc." Frequent rotations mean that trainees rarely remain in one role long enough to become bored.

Peers

EMC first jobbers see a lot of themselves in their peers, whom they describe as "intelligent, conscientious individuals" who "range from the highly experienced to people having diverse backgrounds but who have been in this industry for a while now to fresh graduates. Everyone has something to share and contribute. The work culture is elite, competitive, and yet fun." Many describe an enjoyable esprit de corps that forms during training classes but add that once in the field, they typically have regular contact with only one or two other first jobbers, and so "there's not much of an after-hours scene."

Moving on

EMC does a good job of holding onto first-time employees. Those who leave do so for various reasons. One worker explains, "I have heard some people complain that the office they are based out of doesn't have enough projects for them to be on, and so they have been stuck with more routine work. I have also, however, heard some people say they are working on so many projects that they are being overloaded, so I guess it really depends on what location you are being hired for. In general, though, I haven't heard of anyone with major complaints about EMC as a company." Many who leave return to school to earn an advanced degree.

ENTERPRISE RENT-A-CAR
MANAGEMENT TRAINEE

"No day at Enterprise is typical. The morning is usually about renting cars, midday is about marketing, and end-of-day is [about] next-day prep and training."

The Big Picture

Featuring an upbeat, fast-paced, and cheerful work environment, Enterprise Rent-A-Car offers a top-notch way to learn business skills and begin a career in management through its Management Training Program. Boasting a strong emphasis on customer service, Enterprise employees like the fact that their workplace is "always positive," and say they enjoy unparalleled opportunity to advance quickly in the company. In fact, Enterprise Rent-A-Car only promotes from within; at Enterprise, "from the newest employee all the way to the top, everyone started at the same position."

LOCATION(S) WHERE ENTRY-LEVEL EMPLOYEES WORK

There are positions for entry-level employees at nearly 7,000 branch locations across the United States, United Kingdom, Ireland, Canada, and Germany.

AVERAGE NUMBER OF APPLICATIONS EACH YEAR

Enterprise receives 240,000 applications each year.

AVERAGE NUMBER HIRED PER YEAR OVER THE LAST TEN YEARS

The company hires about 8,000 new college graduates every year.

ENTRY-LEVEL POSITION(S) AVAILABLE

Recent grads join the company as management trainees in the Enterprise Management Training Program.

AVERAGE HOURS WORKED PER WEEK

Management Trainees work 45 to 50 hours per week.

AVERAGE STARTING SALARY

In 2006, the average starting salary was $33,000.

BENEFITS OFFERED

Enterprise offers a choice of three medical plans, as well as dental, vision, and prescription drug coverage. Other benefits include a flexible spending account, a 401(k) plan with a company match, profit sharing, adoption assistance, and discounts on renting, leasing, and purchasing vehicles for employees and family members.

Getting Hired

Enterprise actively recruits at more than 1,000 college campuses nationwide, seeking entry-level candidates with "demonstrated leadership skills, sales and customer service ability, [a] strong work ethic, goal orientation, problem-solving [skills], good communication [skills], and flexibility." Because the Management Training Program provides future managers with lots of practical training to do the job, interviews are relaxed and focus on a candidate's character, history, and personality. A successful applicant recalls, "The interviews were very conversational. The recruiter asked me direct questions related to sales, customer service, and team building." A current branch manager adds that the interviewer had "a laid-back approach. They want to see how you respond to people and how you act in real life. They want to know how you will fit into customer-service and problem-solving situations." They also want to know "how you [have] handled hard situations in your life and how you have persevered." If you want to score a spot at Enterprise, keep the company's commitment to customer service in mind. "The more customer service–oriented experiences I had [for the interviewer], the better the interview, because ERAC is very customer-oriented," says a current employee.

Money and Perks

Enterprise promotes their management trainees rather quickly, thus the opportunity to step up your earnings (and your status) via promotion is ever present. Employees also enjoy additional perks like "marketing expense accounts, discounts on car rentals, and department store discounts." As they move up the ranks, trainees can look forward to even more perks, such as the ultimate status symbol: a company car.

The Ropes

"Because of the company's unique business model, employees at Enterprise have an opportunity essentially to run their own business," enjoying a great deal of autonomy within the structure of a larger company. To prepare future leaders for that opportunity, the company offers their "extensive training program, which many employees [refer to] as the 'virtual MBA.'" Employment with Enterprise Rent-A-Car begins with a four-day orientation that covers "customer service, sales, computer training, defensive driving, and the founding values and mission statement of Enterprise Rent-A-Car." After orientation, "trainees are sent to a branch location, where they develop skills in customer service, sales and marketing, accounting, and finance," and attend formal training sessions about once a month. New hires slowly work through every facet of running a rental car branch by watching and helping their mentors and managers. According to many, the superior quality of the management makes a job at Enterprise particularly appealing. A current employee attests, "The bosses I had as a new employee were great. They taught me so much and were very helpful."

Day in the Life

Management trainees work in a branch office, accruing more responsibility as they master new tasks. As "exceptional customer service" is the cornerstone of the company's business model, it's no surprise that everyone begins their employment at the service desk, working directly with clients. "When you are first hired, you are responsible for the actual renting of the vehicles. This entails reviewing customer documentation and the necessary details of the rental contract; showing the customer to the lot and ensuring that the vehicle will meet the customer's needs; and discussing protection packages that are available to the customer. Trainees say the environment is "very fast paced" and, as time progresses, new employees are brought into every aspect of branch management. Explains a current trainee, "No day at Enterprise is typical. The morning is usually about renting cars, midday is about marketing, and end-of-day is [about] next-day prep and training." New employees may also be charged with "some account-receivable and marketing responsibilities," maintaining current accounts, or building new clientele. By their first anniversary—sometimes even sooner—many management trainees have already been promoted to assistant manager positions.

Peers

Enterprise employees describe each other as "competitive, sales-oriented, friendly, and customer service–oriented." With a fairly young staff at many branch offices, "the social scene was and is available for those that do want to partake in it." In fact, one employee tells us, "I would say that the best fringe benefit would be all the great friendships that you will make. Enterprise Rent-A-Car is a large hirer out of college, which means there are a lot of other people just like you: fun, outgoing, and nice . . . all the same age."

Moving on

Enterprise representatives reveal that most management trainees leave the company "to take our business training to another company," or because they've "changed their career goals."

Attrition

While the company does not monitor the exact figures, they estimate that "after the first year, we retain about 51 percent" of management trainees. That may not sound too inspiring, but as an Enterprise representative explains, "It's a challenging program that may not end up being for everyone. However, those that stay with Enterprise and make it just one more step [to the assistant manager position], usually within or just after that first year, typically find long-term success at the company. The retention of entry-level employees with our company after five and ten years increases dramatically to well over 80 percent."

Best and Worst

Enterprise Rent-A-Car points to Pam Nicholson as the shining star of achievement within their organization. Ms. Nicholson "began her career at Enterprise Rent-A-Car in 1981 as a management trainee," right out of college. "Within nine months, Pam was promoted to assistant branch manager, and, within a year, accepted a position in the company's fast-growing Southern California group," eventually moving up to regional vice president in Southern California, followed by an increasing number of high-level posts. "Today, as COO, she oversees the activities of more than 64,000 employees, 711,000 rental cars, 168,000 fleet services vehicles, and nearly 7,000 branch offices in 5 countries. She is a corporate officer and one of the company's top operating employees."

GEICO
VARIOUS POSITIONS

"GEICO hires first-jobbers to serve a variety of functions, ranging from "selling insurance policies to investigating claims to special projects for upper management."

The Big Picture

GEICO's formal college recruiting program is relatively new (it started up in August 2003), but it has already delivered a lot of fresh faces to this sixty-eight-year old insurance giant. The company offers entry-level positions in nearly all its functional areas.

LOCATION(S) WHERE ENTRY-LEVEL EMPLOYEES WORK

Offices are located in Washington, DC (corporate headquarters); Buffalo, New York; Woodbury, New York; Fredericksburg, Virginia; Virginia Beach, Virginia; Macon, Georgia; Lakeland, Florida; Dallas, Texas; Tucson, Arizona; and San Diego, California

AVERAGE NUMBER OF APPLICATIONS EACH YEAR

GEICO receives about 22,000 applications each year.

AVERAGE NUMBER HIRED PER YEAR OVER THE LAST TEN YEARS

GEICO hires about 200–300 entry-level employees each year.

ENTRY-LEVEL POSITION(S) AVAILABLE

Positions are available as "actuarial associates, product management analysts, underwriting analysts, claims representatives, sales associates, customer service representatives, auto damage adjusters, and management-training programs in operations management and information technology. We have also hired recent graduates into our IT-project management office, marketing and HR departments, and our competitive analysis group."

AVERAGE HOURS WORKED PER WEEK

Entry-level hires work 40 to 45 hours per week.

AVERAGE STARTING SALARY

Starting salaries vary by position and typically range from $30,000 to the mid-$40,000s.

BENEFITS OFFERED

Medical, dental, flexible spending accounts are available. Additional benefits include life insurance, paid vacation and holidays, disability, long-term care, scholarships, tuition reimbursement, dependent care, business-casual dress, profit sharing, sports teams, on-site fitness facilities and cafeterias, commuter assistance, and a 401(k) plan.

Getting Hired

GEICO "strongly encourages students to do their research on the company prior to the interview," reporting that the best job interviews are distinguished by "the amount a student has researched and knows about the company. When their knowledge comes across as true interest in GEICO, this helps students shine." The company also seeks "strong communication and customer service skills, analytical and computer skills, well-rounded experiences, leadership potential, and work/internship experience." The interview process can be drawn out for applicants to the Emerging Leaders Management Development Program; one writes, "The process was long (one and a half months) but worth the time. There were four phases of interviews that ended in a meeting with very high ranking company officers." For other positions, the process is less formal—typically, a screening call from HR, followed by a behavioral-based interview with the hire's prospective supervisors. One hire writes, "I was asked about specific situations and how I reacted (i.e., 'Name a time in which you showed leadership skills/teamwork abilities/etc.'). I was given a tour of the facility and an overview of the different departments. I used the S.T.A.R. (situation, task, action, result) approach to answer. The interview concluded with a final employment offer."

Money and Perks

Starting salaries are rarely negotiable at GEICO. First jobbers have better luck negotiating their start date, but tell us that most other aspects of the job are off the table. GEICO reports that salary increases and promotions are based on performance, adding that the company "promoted nearly 1,700 of our entry-level employees in 2003. Promotion from within is serious business at GEICO." Employees tout the profit-sharing program; they also enjoy "the discount on car insurance, discounts with partner companies such as Microsoft and Dell, and the shorter workday than normal (we work for 7.75 hours and get .75 hours for lunch." Also, for some "the schedule is pretty flexible."

The Ropes

Formal orientation at GEICO begins with "a two- or three-day boot camp explaining benefits and GEICO in general, followed by a six-month certification period." The company notes that "different positions have to attend classes and/or complete rotations [that range] from days long to months long." Emerging Leader participants "rotate through all the areas: licensing, sales, service, and underwriting. All of the trainings are created and administered by different trainers (depending on their areas of expertise) in the training department." Those with more traditional positions "receive training on specific tasks on a need-to-know basis, informally (by asking questions). Usually this training is from a supervisor or other members of the department."

Day in the Life

GEICO hires first-jobbers to serve a variety of functions, ranging from "selling insurance policies to investigating claims to special projects for upper management." Among the first-jobbers we contacted were a programmer analyst, a cost-benefit analysis coordinator, a college-recruiting assistant, a business analyst, and two Emerging Leaders. Those in rotations "start with a one- to three-month training class, then work the phones. Eventually we get to shadow and interact with management."

Peers

First jobbers tell us that their peers "are all very intelligent, driven, team-based, professional, and hard-working individuals. Everyone brings their own uniqueness to the company." Some are "big on the bar scene, others are homebodies, but they are mostly great people in general." One new hire reports that she and her peers "frequently get together outside of work in several cliques. The HR department supports this with newsletters, a pizza party, and recruiting opportunities. Some groups of associates have social outings in the evenings, but it is rarely in large groups."

Moving on

The average overall tenure for all GEICO employees is thirteen years; the company does not currently have data for first jobbers. Those who leave do so to return to school or to pursue other career options. Those who plan to stay praise the "great exposure to business and leadership" and the "relaxed atmosphere and flexible schedules."

GENERAL ELECTRIC
CORPORATE LEADERSHIP DEVELOPMENT
PROGRAMS

In "entry-level positions at GE . . . specific technical skills are less important than a strong and consistent demonstration of the ability to learn, adapt, and excel."

The Big Picture

General Electric (GE) offers Corporate Leadership Development programs in many divisions. Typically they are "two-year rotational training programs [that] consist of formal classroom, digital, and on-the-job training" that prepare participants to continue their careers at GE when they end.

LOCATION(S) WHERE ENTRY-LEVEL EMPLOYEES WORK

GE has locations in more than 100 countries.

AVERAGE NUMBER OF APPLICATIONS EACH YEAR

The company receives about 50,000 applications per year in the United States alone.

AVERAGE NUMBER HIRED PER YEAR OVER THE LAST TEN YEARS

About 1,000 people are hired in the United States per year.

ENTRY-LEVEL POSITION(S) AVAILABLE

Entry-level positions are available in sales and marketing, engineering, finance, human resources, information management, and operations.

AVERAGE HOURS WORKED PER WEEK

The number of hours worked per week varies by position.

PERCENTAGE OF ENTRY-LEVEL HIRES STILL WITH THE COMPANY AFTER THREE, FIVE, AND TEN YEARS

After three years, about 80 percent of all entry-level employees remain with the company; after five years, 60 percent of all entry-level employees remain with the company; and after ten years, 50 percent of all entry-level employees remain with the company.

AVERAGE STARTING SALARY

The average starting salary ranges from $50,000 to $95,000 per year.

BENEFITS OFFERED

The company offers competitive, full medical coverage, and a generous tuition reimbursement program.

CONTACT INFORMATION

Submit resumes online at www.gecareers.com, or contact your career center to see if GE will be interviewing at your school.

Getting Hired

Applying for one of GE's Corporate Leadership Development Programs typically requires two interviews. The first, conducted on campus or over the telephone, is with a company representative and involves "many questions about working in teams, situations in which failure occurred, and how it was dealt with." Next, "candidates selected for on-site (second) interviews will be interviewing for a position with a specific GE business. Students are given the opportunity to choose up to three GE businesses they are interested in joining. We try our best to align student geographic and business preferences with internal business hiring needs; however, there is no guarantee that you will be offered a position at your preferred location," writes one company official. A former program participant who now organizes recruiting says, "I'd encourage candidates to be energetic and engaging. Ask a lot of questions! The goal of the process is to determine whether there is a fit between the candidate and the organization. Sometimes it is clear that a candidate has the technical and nontechnical skills to excel, but [it is] unclear whether the candidate is engaged with the environment and really wants the job. Asking questions about the work, organization, and program is the best way for both parties to accurately predict whether there is a fit." Another entry-level employee adds that in "entry-level positions at GE . . . specific technical skills are less important than a strong and consistent demonstration of the ability to learn, adapt, and excel."

Money and Perks

Participants in all GE development programs tell us that "the job offer is negotiable in terms of when you start, but nonnegotiable in terms of salary and placement." Many hasten to add that "the offer [GE makes] is highly competitive, so there's no need to negotiate the compensation." Pay increases come annually and are based on performance. One entry-level employee says, "Those raises are based [on] your on-the-job evaluations and your class grades, and they add up quickly during the two-year program." Perks include "discounts on products, ranging from GE appliances to gym memberships to Dell computers to automobiles." Program participants also love the educational package; as one student explains, "GE paid for my master's degree. It was a great opportunity; I got a master's degree at a top twenty-five engineering graduate school in about two-and-a-half years."

The Ropes

General Electric's Corporate Leadership Development Programs start with a brief orientation, usually half a day or one day long. One entry-level hire writes, "My orientation process was a three-hour long seminar-style event that entailed a presentation about The Big Picture of GE and how the research center [to which I was assigned] serves the business, overviews of how programs are funded, and how time accounting should be performed, procedures related to security and safety, and other rather unexciting, but necessary, topics." Orientation is only the beginning of a long and thorough training process, however. In fact, since first jobbers rotate through jobs throughout the two-year program, the training period never really ends. One engineer offers, "I received so much training it's hard to recall it all, so I'll give the highlights: two trips to [a] GE Corporate training facility at Crotonville [in Ossining, New York] for business leadership courses and jet engine teardown training [where] we disassembled and reassembled aircraft engines. In addition, Six Sigma green belt classes and training also were provided." Six Sigma is a management philosophy that holds sacrosanct the goal of constantly improving operational efficiency. Many employees also pursue master's degrees while working for GE; the company offers substantial support in this area (see "Money and Perks").

Day in the Life

GE is number five on the Fortune 500 list, and so it generates a great deal of revenue. Accordingly, the variety of tasks performed by entry-level employees is incredibly broad. According to company officials, "The average program member works about fifty hours per week. Additional time commitments may be required depending on job assignments. Course work, on average, will add another five to eight hours to your week." One program participant writes, "Responsibilities vary depending on the area of the first job assignment, but typically program members are directed [or] given work by a manager and given a mentor or engineer who provides help [and] advice in the area. As a program member progresses onto different assignments and gains more on-the-job engineering competency, the program member is typically given the same amount of work and responsibility as any other engineer in the area of work." Everyone in the program rotates positions within his or her business about every six to eight months; company officials tell us that "rotations outside your function or your GE business do exist, but [they] are an exception, rather than a rule, for all program participants. Assignments of these types are dependent on the GE business need and participant preferences and are also often based on merit."

Peers

"One attractive thing about a big program like this is that there is a continual stream of young, bright, and motivated folks coming in," notes one first jobber. The scope of the after-hours scene varies widely by division and location, program participants tell us, but all agree that there's "a tremendous amount of camaraderie" among people starting out at GE. One program participant explains, "You're in classes with twenty to thirty people [who are] your age every week, so it's kind of like being in college again. All of us made friends pretty quickly [and] went out after work [or] on weekends; and now, three years later [we] are still going out to happy hours and dinners together. We've all been to [one another's] weddings and have established a very close group of friends through this program."

Moving on

GE regards its Corporate Leadership Development programs as stepping stones to careers with the company. Its website states, "GE's Leadership Programs prepare graduates for positions with significant levels of responsibility and challenging off-program assignments. Some graduates join the GE audit staff. Others enter positions in one of the GE businesses. Cross-functional assignments are also a possibility. If someone successfully completes one of our leadership programs, other advanced educational degrees or certifications are not required to succeed at GE. Training and experiences gained while in a program may accelerate an individual's career growth in much the same way an advanced degree [may] at another corporation. Inevitably, some program graduates feel the need to seek further education. In these instances, GE's support, whether it is in the form of tuition reimbursement, leave of absence, executive MBA, etc., is considered on a case by case basis and differs according to the GE business."

Attrition

People who leave GE site the lack of "work/life balance" as their reason, and report that this is something that GE as a whole struggles with. Most jobs require pretty long hours, especially during programs where you have to work until late at night on homework every week. There's not much time for friends or spouses outside of work. Also, "the traveling aspect of the program turns a lot of people off, even after they take the job knowing they [may] move every six months. Above all else, [employees] say the lack of [geographic] stability is the number one criticism."

GOLDMAN SACHS
FINANCIAL ANALYST

"With the right mentors and teachers on my desk—people who love to teach—I sprinted up a steep learning curve."

The Big Picture

A premier investment banking, securities, and investment management firm, Goldman Sachs offers entry-level jobs that appeal to college grads ready to challenge themselves in a fast-paced work environment. Employees in Goldman Sachs's New Analyst Program quickly adjust to the intensity of their jobs. While they are technically entry-level employees, "new analysts are integral members of their team, often dealing with clients, contributing directly to their success." As such, they are expected to perform key functions within the company even as they learn the ropes.

LOCATION(S) WHERE ENTRY-LEVEL EMPLOYEES WORK

Entry-level positions are available at Goldman Sachs headquarters in New York City and 45 regional offices worldwide.

AVERAGE NUMBER OF APPLICATIONS EACH YEAR

Goldman Sachs receives over 10,000 applications per year.

AVERAGE NUMBER HIRED PER YEAR OVER THE LAST TEN YEARS

The company hires between 1,000 and 1,500 new financial analysts globally each year.

ENTRY-LEVEL POSITIONS AVAILABLE

All entry-level financial analysts participate in the New Analyst Training Program at Goldman Sachs, which aims to provide new hires with the "skills and knowledge necessary to become an integral member of our business teams." In the U.S., most new analysts start during the summer.

AVERAGE STARTING SALARY

On average, new financial analysts make $55,000 per year.

BENEFITS OFFERED

Goldman Sachs employees receive medical and dental benefits, tuition reimbursement for continuing education degree programs, 15 paid vacation days per year, a 401(k) plan, charitable gift matches, and relocation-expense compensation. Depending on office location, they also enjoy either an on-site gym or discounts to local fitness centers.

CONTACT INFORMATION

All application materials must be submitted via the company website at www.gs.com/careers.

Getting Hired

Students fortunate enough to be chosen for a summer internship at Goldman Sachs often find the experience paves the way for a full-time job offer after graduation. Other successful applicants enter without experience in the company; however, they possess some related experience or, at the very least, a strong interest in finance. A successful candidate reports, "I believe my various summer internships in finance, including a summer on the floor of the American Stock Exchange [and] a summer working for a boutique hedge fund, significantly helped me get the first-round interview." All applications submitted online are "reviewed and considered for employment, regardless of school." But you might have an advantage, depending on where you've earned your degree. "We currently target thirty-five to forty undergraduate institutions in the U.S. Our top five undergraduate hiring schools for the 2006 summer analyst program were: University of Pennsylvania, Harvard, New York University, Cornell, and Princeton. Other top hiring schools were Columbia, Stanford, Georgetown, MIT, and University of Michigan." So what are they looking for on school visits, and in general? Goldman Sachs seeks candidates with a "passion for excellence; belief in the power of the group (teamwork); integrity; leadership; a desire to be challenged; and the drive to make your mark on the world." Many employees feel that the point of "the recruiting process [is] to find someone that is not only intelligent, but will be a good fit within the culture of the firm." In fact, many report that their interviews were surprisingly low-key and focused more on the candidate's personal qualities than on their background or math skills. But don't relax just yet. Candidates warn that "a prospect can expect, on average, eight interviews" before receiving an offer.

Money and Perks

With a solid base salary for new employees and ample opportunity for growth within the company, most Goldman newbies happily accept their hard-earned offers of employment. While it is understood that "starting packages are pretty standard across Wall Street and within a particular firm," Goldman Sachs recruits know their earnings will only increase with their years at the company. In addition to the fair pay, employees appreciate perks like discounts and free memberships to local attractions and museums.

The Ropes

The Financial Analyst Training Program is certainly challenging, and new employees at Goldman Sachs should be prepared for a year of high-intensity training. As their employment with the company kicks off, new analysts participate in an orientation program and "interact with new members of [their] division's analyst class from various office locations." After that, it's into the trenches with a ten-week crash course in business and finance. A survivor depicts the experience: "I studied business, and the training took us through about four semesters in six weeks. It was intense. We covered economics, accounting, and every aspect of the financial markets in every part of the world. We trained from 8:00 A.M. to 5:00 P.M. every day, in classrooms of about twenty to twenty-five with teachers from a consulting firm." After training, novices are sent to work in their assigned group, where they are required to learn the job even as they perform it. An employee affirms, "The real training started three months after I arrived at Goldman and started working. Working on real deals . . . is what fortifies information in the mind." While it's obviously challenging, professional education is a "constant" at Goldman Sachs through Goldman Sachs University and "almost all Goldman Sachs employees are involved in . . . formal mentorship programs—either as a mentor, mentee, or both in some cases." A new employee recounts, "I definitely have felt in over my head, especially when I started. But with the right mentors and teachers on my desk—people who love to teach—I sprinted up a steep learning curve."

Day in the Life

After they have completed the introductory training course, new analysts spend a few weeks getting acquainted with their group. A new employee remembers, "I would help to assist in setting up meetings, listen into conference calls, attend meetings. Most of my job was just observing before I was really able to do much on my own." However, new analysts are quickly thrown into the fire, where they are expected to perform key functions and fulfill important responsibilities after a very short period of time with the company. According to a trainee, "I always thought that I would be in the robot function of just completing projects for my boss, but my opinion is asked on deals and on pitches to clients. There are times that I speak directly to clients because I am the contact and it is my responsibility to understand the client and the market so that information is correct." Explains another, "Goldman Sachs is a place that will give you a tremendous amount of responsibility at a young age if you demonstrate the capability." With so much responsibility, first-year employees (as well as second- and third-year employees) can look forward to very long workdays and lunch "always eaten at [one's] desk." The upshot is a dynamic daily routine and loads of excitement. One new hire shares his daily task list: "I arrive in the morning, print out the morning notes for everybody to read, read as much as I can about the market, and then get jamming on my project list, occasionally getting interrupted by fire drills for live trades or other tasks that need to get done 'now.'"

Peers

As Goldman Sachs combs top college campuses for America's best and brightest grads, it reasons to follow that, "everyone is extremely bright and talented at the firm." They are also extremely ambitious. Reports one analyst, "People are self-driven to not just meet expectations, but to rather exceed expectations." Even so, the culture is exceedingly friendly, and an individual in this talented group "will always go out of his or her way to help a fellow peer." "I depended on my peers heavily to help me do my day-to-day work," insists a new employee. Social relationships are a part of life at Goldman Sachs. During the first training session, "everyone is encouraged to branch out and meet people from different groups." The attitude seems to be: "We all have to work together, so we might as well hang out together. It makes more sense to know someone that you have to work with and understand them."

Moving on

Some analysts leave Goldman Sachs to pursue an MBA. Others change positions within the firm to expand their skills in a new business or division. Internal mobility at Goldman Sachs is very popular.

Attrition

While the company's abundant opportunities keep many employees hanging around for years, employees who decide to pursue jobs elsewhere are confident in the name-brand experiences they take along with them. However, most Goldman Sachs employees prefer to stick it out until it's time to go back to school and earn a graduate degree. Says one, "I feel the sky is the limit. The job is very entrepreneurial and you make your own success here."

GOOGLE
VARIOUS POSITIONS

"I have already had two promotions in terms of job responsibility, and two raises within a year, and I think that that is achievable for anyone who is willing to work hard and show their initiative."

The Big Picture

Not many new companies grow so big that their name becomes a verb, but Google's has. And if you don't believe us, google it and see for yourself. Besides presenting a really cool product, Google is also a place where go-getters can rise through the ranks relatively quickly. No wonder the company receives thousands of job applications every day.

LOCATION(S) WHERE ENTRY-LEVEL EMPLOYEES WORK

Google has locations "in Mountain View [California], New York [New York], Santa Monica [California], and most of our 20-plus sales offices."

AVERAGE NUMBER OF APPLICATIONS EACH YEAR

Google receives "thousands per day."

ENTRY-LEVEL POSITION(S) AVAILABLE

Positions are available as AdWords representatives, legal assistants, and administrative associates.

AVERAGE HOURS WORKED PER WEEK

Entry-level hires work 40 hours per week.

AVERAGE STARTING SALARY (BY POSITION)

AdWords representatives earn $30,000–$40,000 per year. Legal assistants earn $40,000–$50,000 per year. Administrative assistants earn $40,000–$50,000 per year.

BENEFITS OFFERED

"Employees receive several HMO and PPO medical plans, plus vision and dental. They receive coverage beginning on the date of hire. We pride ourselves on providing extremely generous employee benefits," writes a company official. These include three weeks of vacation for the first three years of employment, increasing in subsequent years; eleven paid holidays per year; free healthy lunch and dinner buffets, Monday through Friday; on-site doctor, dental, dry cleaning, oil change, and more services; on-site gym; subsidized yoga and Pilates classes; subsidized on-site massages; and maternity coverage and parental leave.

Getting Hired

Many first jobbers start at Google as contract workers: They are brought on as temps without benefits. A typical hire explains: "Initially, I was a temporary employee for a stipulated twelve-week period. During the twelve-week time, I would be evaluated as well as have an opportunity to evaluate the position, and a mutual decision about conversion to full-time employment would be made sometime after week eight. Once I became a full-time employee, the salary and contract I committed to were based on multiple factors. These factors included my educational background, relevant work experience, performance within the first twelve weeks, as well as my potential growth within Google." Google tells us it seeks "smart, flexible" hires with "interesting experience, unique accomplishments, a passion to learn, and creativity. We are not inclined toward inflexibility, overly process[-based] orientation." In interviews, the company "tries to learn what makes [candidates] passionate, how they think, and how they approach problems. The best interview is when a candidate, no matter at what level, has researched the position and our products. He/she has a passion for the job and the responsibilities, and the clear ability to succeed in the role and develop beyond it." The company "actively seeks employee referrals, so having a friend in the company helps."

Money and Perks

"The job is not negotiable other than in terms of start time," most first jobbers at Google report, and that's fine: They agree with the respondent who told us that "I was happy with what they offered me, so I signed my offer letter without trying to negotiate. I cared much more about finding a place I wanted to work than about salary—otherwise, I would have joined an I-banking firm or something." Google notes that "entry-level employees are eligible for the same bonuses as other full-time Googlers, which are based on individual, team, and company performance" and that "for some employees, there may be promotion opportunities at six-month intervals. The goal is to keep our employees challenged and engaged with new opportunities." Perks are numerous and beloved; they include "a great, free shuttle service that runs from two locations in San Francisco down to Google's offices in Mountain View, which will save you years of life in commuting stress, as well as lots of money in gas, insurance, and maintenance!" Also, "all of our meals are provided to us free of cost. I save a significant amount of money on food and definitely factor this fringe benefit into my overall compensation package."

The Ropes

For many new hires at Google, "the contractor program is like an extended orientation. It lasts eight weeks, giving you the opportunity to learn the function of your job and the skills you need to succeed." Formal orientation occurs after employees land permanent positions; it takes place on Monday, lasts half a day, and includes "brief introductions of all new employees, a review of Google's history and culture, and an overview of policies and benefits. Orientation concludes with a tour of the building and lunch with the new hires' mentors." AdWord representatives and coordinators "get a 'buddy bag' on their first day with a toy and some Google goodies, and they meet a buddy from their new team. The buddy is their guide for the first week at Google and beyond this time, as needed." Google's internal website "contains myriad information" that helps newbies learn their various responsibilities.

Day in the Life

AdWords representatives spend their days checking ad content, quality, and relevance, as well as screening ad submissions based on fixed guidelines. They also work on the advertisers' keyword lists, provide customer service and support, and train new hires. Administrative assistants "perform a host of administrative duties, including scheduling, interacting with visitors, attending meetings, and keeping a steady flow of office communication. One consistency in most days is to communicate on behalf of my manager and team to individuals from different departments within our office. The job has the potential to be entirely different from one day to the next, which is nice." Legal assistants "do legal research, correspond with outside parties, write reports, etc." They "also continue to do some administrative work, which is fine—after eight years (high school and college) of nothing but reading and writing, I don't mind doing some filing. And since I'm going off to law school in the relatively near future, I welcome the opportunity to take a little mental break now and then."

Peers

Google first-jobbers tell us that they are "continually impressed workers. They are an incredible and diverse group of individuals with a wealth of talent and enthusiasm for what they do." Most are bright, young, ambitious, and friendly, and the company capitalizes on that, "placing a strong value on socializing and maintaining a sense of fun within the company's corporate culture. This breeds a great sense of contentment amongst employees. Work becomes less of [a] mundane duty, but rather a membership into a special large extended family that coworkers feel privileged to be part of." Workers enjoy "happy hours, TGIF, and offsite gatherings regularly. There is much contact and camaraderie. This is a very social place to work."

Moving on

Google's turnover rate is extremely low. Those few who leave generally do so to pursue advanced degrees, to pursue new job opportunities, or to relocate out of the area. Most stick around because they "feel like there is a lot of room to grow here at Google." One first jobber reports, "I have already had two promotions in terms of job responsibility, and two raises within a year, and I think that that is achievable for anyone who is willing to work hard and show their initiative."

GREEN CORPS
FIELD ORGANIZER

"It's incredible to have such a tight network of such talented, motivated, creative people who are out there making a difference day in and day out."

The Big Picture

"Hey, you titmice, let's have a little more chirping, okay? Frogs, don't all bunch up in one spot—spread out! And who in blue blazes cut the grass so short?" No, that's not what Green Corps field organizers do, but wouldn't it be cool if it was? What they do is just about as cool: They coordinate with local activists to affect Green environmental goals. Working with this organization is a great introduction to the world of ecoactivism.

LOCATION(S) WHERE ENTRY-LEVEL EMPLOYEES WORK

"Nationwide—placements are temporary (usually two to three months), and entry-level employees move to a couple of locations throughout the year."

AVERAGE NUMBER OF APPLICATIONS EACH YEAR

Green Corps receives 800 applications each year.

AVERAGE NUMBER HIRED PER YEAR OVER THE LAST TEN YEARS

The organization hires 24 people per year.

ENTRY-LEVEL POSITION(S) AVAILABLE

New hires work as field organizers.

AVERAGE HOURS WORKED PER WEEK

Hours are "highly variable based on campaign schedule[s]." When big events approach, field organizers work "approximately 60 to 70 hours [but] less during other times."

PERCENTAGE OF ENTRY-LEVEL HIRES STILL WITH THE COMPANY AFTER THREE, FIVE, AND TEN YEARS

"The program is a year-long training program, so all employees leave for other organizations after one year."

AVERAGE STARTING SALARY

New hires earn $23,750 during their year-long program.

BENEFITS OFFERED

Field organizers get health insurance. Additional benefits include a loan repayment program, paid vacation, holidays, sick days, and job-placement assistance.

Getting Hired

Green Corps interviews "on as many college campuses as possible and conducts first-round phone interviews for all other qualified applicants." A successful applicant describes the process this way: "Green Corps has a three step application/interview process. First, there's a short, written application, at which point you provide your resume. It was helpful that my resume showed that I had been active on campus. Second, I interviewed on campus with the assistant director of the program. What made my first interview work was that I made a personal connection with the person interviewing me. I told stories that got her attention, made her laugh, and showed her that I was smart and motivated. On that basis I was invited to the interview weekend. Third, Green Corps takes the best candidates from the round of first interviews and invites them to group interview weekends. There are about five around the country during the hiring season, and they have about forty to fifty candidates per weekend. Over the two days, Green Corps runs you through a couple of skills sessions and another individual interview and evaluates overall chemistry and social skills. Even those who don't get hired generally agree that it's inspiring to meet so many smart, committed people like them."

Money and Perks

For Green Corps field organizers, "the salary and length of employment are fixed. Because Green Corps is a fellowship program, it runs thirteen months, and all of the thirty or so fellows [who] are hired each year work from the beginning of August until the end of the following August, when Green Corps staff helps them find more permanent positions in the environmental or social-change fields." The best perks include "a loan repayment program (for student loans), full staff-subsidized vacation in Aspen, Colorado, in December, spending time organizing in communities around the country, and a great outplacement service. Because Green Corps has such a great reputation in the environmental field, other organizations end up competing with one another for the chance to hire Green Corps organizers."

The Ropes

All field organizers start at the beginning of August with a four-week orientation in Boston. The training is run "by Green Corps staff, alumni, and veteran leaders from across the environmental field. That's where you learn how to write a press release, run a meeting, recruit and develop volunteers, organize an event, build a coalition, etc." One corps member adds, "Green Corps is very much based around building a team among the organizers and on learning by doing, so we jumped right into classroom training the day after we arrived. There were different social events every night where all of the fellows could hang out—the people in each Green Corps class remain close friends, and a lot of times people become close friends with other Green Corps alumni who weren't in their class." Organizers then set off on two-month campaigns in the field, after which they "meet for a week to debrief the previous campaign, get some additional training, and prepare for the next project."

Day in the Life

Perhaps the most appealing—and intimidating—aspect of Green Corps' program is the amount of responsibility first jobbers take on. One newbie explains: "Basically Green Corps organizers are the directors of their campaigns in the cities where they work—so they don't have a boss overseeing them on the site, and they recruit and train everyone they work with. On my first campaign, I was responsible for signing on dozens of organizations to a coalition letter, holding media events, meeting with reporters, and recruiting and training citizen volunteers. On a typical day, I'd come into the office at 8:30 A.M. or 9:00 A.M. and make a detailed plan for my day. I'd spend the next two hours calling potential coalition groups and talking to them about the campaign. At noon, I'd take a break for lunch and meet with one of my student interns about her plan for the week and what she was going to accomplish for the campaign. In the afternoon, I would nail down the logistics of a press conference in the coming week, including the site and permit, and prep the speakers for the event. I would talk to existing coalition partners about turning out members to the press event. In the evening, I would spend a couple of hours [on the] phone [with] banking volunteers to [get them to] turn out for the press event."

Peers

Because "most Green Corps organizers are in their campaign cities without any other Green Corps organizers there," the organization lacks the regular after-hours social scene present at many entry-level jobs. Even so, the peer network is a potent one. One organizer explains: "One of the biggest perks about the job is that you are in a class with an incredible group of Green Corps organizers. You bond with them during the classroom training in Boston. Then you keep in touch via phone and e-mail during the campaigns. When you get back together between each campaign for the follow-up trainings, it's like a mini-reunion. And then after the year is over, these people become your friends, colleagues, and support system. It's incredible to have such a tight network of such talented, motivated, creative people who are out there making a difference day in and day out."

Moving on

According to Green Corps, about 85 percent of its program graduates continue in "the social change and environmental field." Others travel, study abroad, or head to graduate school. Some of the graduates we spoke with now work for the Sierra Club, the Campaign to Ban Landmines, and Physicians for Human Rights.

Attrition

Green Corps isn't for everyone. Those who don't make it through the program usually cite "being overwhelmed, having too much responsibility, [and] working hard when their friends [who] care less about their jobs leave at five" and get paid much more. As one Corps graduate puts it, "The same things that are great about the job also make it tough."

Best and Worst

"For more than a decade, the oil and gas industry has lobbied to exploit the pristine Arctic National Wildlife Refuge. Now the industry is pushing to include drilling as part of the federal budget. Green Corps organizer Josh Buswell-Charkow needed to rally pro-Arctic groups and leaders in Minnesota to convince Senator Norm Coleman to protect the Arctic. Using skills learned from our classroom training, Josh recruited volunteers, and in just ten days, generated more than 8,000 phone calls and 300 letters to Senator Coleman's office. Hours before Senator Coleman made his final decision, Josh organized a press conference outside his St. Paul office. The press conference was covered in more than thirty newspapers and media outlets across the state and country. In the end, Senator Coleman voted no on drilling in the Arctic—helping to deliver a very narrow fifty-two to forty-eight victory. With the House set to vote on the budget this fall, the fight to protect the Arctic is far from over. And the Alaska Coalition has one again asked Green Corps to serve as their field team. In the 2005–2006 year, eleven Green Corps organizers [worked] across the country to raise media attention to protect the Arctic. The Green Corps organizers helped mobilize more than 5,000 Arctic supporters to travel to Washington, DC for Arctic Refuge Action Day."

HABITAT FOR HUMANITY INTERNATIONAL
INTERNSHIPS AND EXTERNSHIPS

"You won't get rich monetarily working for Habitat for Humanity International—but you are likely to find the experience soul enriching."

The Big Picture

Habitat for Humanity International describes itself as "a nonprofit, ecumenical Christian housing ministry" that "seeks to eliminate poverty housing and homelessness from the world and to make decent shelter a matter of conscience and action." The organization "invites people of all backgrounds, races, and religions to build houses together in partnership with families in need." Over the years, Habitat has succeeded in building more than 200,000 homes across the globe. The pay isn't great, and the work is hard, but few organizations offer the potential to experience satisfaction from having accomplished important work.

LOCATION(S) WHERE ENTRY-LEVEL EMPLOYEES WORK

The headquarters are located in Americus, Georgia; the organization has field offices across the United States.

AVERAGE NUMBER OF APPLICATIONS EACH YEAR

About 2,400 applicants seek out positions at Habitat for Humanity International each year.

AVERAGE NUMBER HIRED PER YEAR

Habitat for Humanity International hires about 100 people each year.

ENTRY-LEVEL POSITION(S) AVAILABLE

"Habitat for Humanity International has both internship and externship opportunities, which are particularly helpful to both current students and recent college graduates acquiring on-the-job skills and experience."

AVERAGE HOURS WORKED PER WEEK

Entry-level hires work about 40 hours per week.

PERCENTAGE OF ENTRY-LEVEL HIRES STILL WITH THE COMPANY AFTER THREE, FIVE, AND TEN YEARS

Forty percent of entry-level hires remain with Habitat after three years.

AVERAGE STARTING SALARY

Entry-level hires earn $25,000 a year.

Getting Hired

Habitat for Humanity International does not recruit on college campuses; rather, it posts openings on its website and encourages prospective employees to apply online. Hiring is determined annually in accordance with the organization's budget and areas of need. The organization seeks those who have "a true commitment to the mission of Habitat for Humanity—people with the heart and faith to eliminate poverty housing worldwide." One successful hire notes, "I was convinced to apply because Habitat's Christian values appealed to me, and I saw the potential for meaningful work." Screening involves "asking candidates what their goals are, what they know about Habitat for Humanity, and how they learned of the open position." According to one first jobber here, "My resume and application were reviewed by the Human Resources Department. [I was then called] for an interview a few weeks after I sent my information. The interview was fairly casual; it worked in my favor that I had the qualifications they were looking for in education and experience and was willing to come as a volunteer (i.e., live on a small stipend) and live in the housing they provided. As best I can remember, the interviewer asked the expected questions about why I wanted to work for Habitat and my experiences working on my college newspaper. Also, she was able to answer my questions about the office environment and arranged for another employee in the department to call me later to answer my questions about living in volunteer housing." According to the organization, top interview performances show that "the candidate has done homework on Habitat for Humanity and is thoroughly versed in the organization's work, structure, and philosophy." The worst interview ever? "A candidate who thought that Habitat was an organization geared toward helping animals."

Money and Perks

You won't get rich monetarily working for Habitat for Humanity International—but you are likely to find the experience soul enriching. There's not a lot of wiggle room to negotiate about your position, either; first jobbers we spoke with described their offers as pretty much take-it-or-leave-it affairs. A few even came on as volunteers; their positions morphed into "real" jobs over time; or they worked as volunteers until a paying job opened up. There can be "some flexibility in terms of when you start," but "position description determines the salary, department, and job duties." Merit-based increases "are considered after one full year of employment, during the annual performance review. Salary or wage increases are based [on] performance." Workers agree that "the best fringe benefit of working for Habitat is the satisfaction that the organization's work changes people's lives for the better, in a permanent and sustainable way." One first jobber writes: "I'm not working to further someone else's bottom line; rather, our work makes an impact on communities all over the world."

The Ropes

Habitat for Humanity International hires on a rolling schedule and holds orientation sessions every Monday for new hires. Orientation is a one-day affair that "involves general information, benefits counseling, online training, and technology training." One first jobber writes, "During orientation, we learned about the phone system, e-mail software, benefits (time off, insurance, etc.), the history of the organization, and functions of different departments." Subsequent training is handled by one's supervisor.

Day in the Life

Entry-level hires at Habitat for Humanity International serve in all types of roles. They perform typical entry-level tasks and are carefully supervised. One newbie in editorial writes, "My responsibilities were to check facts, edit articles for length, write short articles on assigned topics, and generally be helpful to my boss, the editor. I used the Internet to fulfill a lot of research and fact-checking assignments and [made] many phone calls to complete articles." A first jobber in information systems notes, "My main responsibilities were data entry and backup. I would receive a batch of donation pieces, and I would enter the names, address info, donation amounts, or any other partner information that was made available for our partners into the database. I would [then] save the changes and pass [it] to the next person, who would manually total all the donation amounts and compare [it] to my total, for reconciliation purposes." First jobbers tell us that "there is room to grow for people in certain, but not all, positions" and that "pay probably won't grow very much because we are a nonprofit ministry." That said, "the potential to develop your skills to a higher level are very good."

Peers

Habitat for Humanity International is home to "a healthy-sized group of people in their mid to late twenties who have come to Habitat early in their careers; and they are a fascinating, diverse group of people! Habitat's work tends to attract people with similar values but very different skills and life experiences, so getting to know them has been wonderful." Around the home office in Americus, "There is a social scene, but as one would expect in a small, Southern town, it's very casual and low-key. Front-porch sitting is still a major pastime in Americus!" First jobbers enjoy the "many opportunities to meet and greet newcomers. There are potlucks and other events that welcome newcomers to our organization." Employees also appreciate the "very open environment" within the organization.

Moving on

Those who leave Habitat for Humanity International, we're told, do so most often because of "family/spouse relocation" or "a new job in a different location." One first jobber writes, "The most common criticism I hear is from people who feel a bit overwhelmed by the rate of change in the organization. The last year, especially, has seen a lot of staff turnover and policy changes, and it can be difficult not to fear that your position will be the next casualty." Another agrees: "Lately [there] has been stress created by turnovers and the [possibility] that we may relocate."

HEWLETT-PACKARD COMPANY
VARIOUS POSITIONS

invent

"Every so often I fall on my face and make a mistake, but if I get up and recover quickly I am congratulated, not scolded."

The Big Picture

Hewlett-Packard Company (HP) is a manufacturer of computers; but the company also provides much more, such as "technology solutions for consumers, businesses, and institutions across the globe; IT infrastructure; global services; and imaging and printing for consumers, enterprises, and small and medium businesses." In its literature, HP emphasizes the importance of a comfortable, positive work environment.

LOCATION(S) WHERE ENTRY-LEVEL EMPLOYEES WORK

Entry-level employees work in Cupertino, California; Palo Alto, California; Roseville, California; San Diego, California; Mountain View, California; Colorado Springs, Colorado; Fort Collins, Colorado; Atlanta, Georgia; Boise, Idaho; Marlborough, Massachusetts; Corvallis, Oregon; Austin, Texas; Houston, Texas; Richardson, Texas; Vancouver, Washington; Indianapolis, Indiana; and Omaha, Nebraska.

AVERAGE NUMBER OF APPLICATIONS EACH YEAR

"HP receives more than 250,000 external applications each year for all levels of positions in the Americas."

AVERAGE NUMBER HIRED PER YEAR OVER THE LAST TEN YEARS

"On average, the number of entry-level employees hired in the United States each year over the past ten years is 600."

ENTRY-LEVEL POSITION(S) AVAILABLE

Entry-level hires work as computer engineers, computer scientists, electrical engineers, management information systems analysts, sales representatives, supply chain management analysts, chemical engineers, chemists, materials scientists, and physicists, among other positions.

AVERAGE HOURS WORKED PER WEEK

New hires work 40 hours per week.

Getting Hired

HP "focuses its proactive campus recruiting efforts and long-term relationships on HP partner schools;" but students at other schools are encouraged to apply via the company website. Company officials tell us that they most highly value a prospective employee's ability to work in a team, to take initiative when required, and to write and communicate effectively. Many jobs require technical expertise; one employee notes that during the interview process, "they asked a lot of C++ questions, so if someone didn't nail those, I suppose [he or she] probably wouldn't get the job." The interview process proceeds in several stages; one employee recalls, "Originally I did a phone interview with the recruiter, then a phone interview with the hiring manager. I was then flown in for a round of interviews with several people currently working in the group. The phone interviews were about gauging interest and job/education background. The on-site interviews [focused on] job and education experience, along with [my] technical abilities." HR officials note that "the best interview performances are typically done by those candidates who have spent a significant amount of time researching the company prior to their interviews. It is essential that candidates distinguish themselves from their peers by learning as much as possible. They [may] then leverage that information by showing the interviewer how their background can benefit the company." Successful interviewees also "listen well to the interviewer, engage in an active two-way conversation, and give examples of results they've achieved." Many newbies also report that working as an intern during college presents a great way to get your foot in the door.

Money and Perks

According to the company, "HP has an annual review date and increase process, at which time consideration is given to increasing an employee's salary based on market comparisons, performance, and time in position." HP also has a "bonus program that is available to all employees;" bonuses are "based on meeting company performance goals."

New hires report that their starting date can be "totally flexible" and that there's occasionally some latitude in their choice of location; the company representatives similarly report that "there is a lot of flexibility offered to employees [regarding] work-life options, [as] arranged between manager and employee." Employees' favorite perks include "discounts associated with a large company [as well as] local discounts (percent off, reduced price tickets, etc.), free books, and tons of online technical material, [and] the work-life balance: Your personal life is valued very, very highly here."

The Ropes

New HP hires begin their tenures with the You + HP program, in which they "learn about the company strategy, culture, metrics, and organizational structure. They are also given individual [orientations] by their managers and mentors (if assigned);" these guides teach newbies "about working at HP and [serve as] someone to go to for questions." The amount and kind of training workers receive varies from one department to another. A software/firmware developer tells us that he "spent a month working with the group that tests the firmware that [his] group develops" before doing any work on his own. A marketing manager, however, reports having received "no training. It took me a long time to figure things out." Mentor relationships are not uncommon and often serve as a new hire's informal training; one first jobber writes, "I learned about some of the software processes by reading documentation or books. The majority of what I learned was guided by a team leader [who] was designated as my mentor."

Day in the Life

As already mentioned, HP offers a wide range of positions to first jobbers. They're responsible for designing and developing software, hardware, computer systems, and components; coordinating manufacturing and product development processes; managing the supply chain; and conducting research and development in chemistry, physics, and material sciences. For many employees, a typical day consists of "research, attending meetings, talking with partners, and thinking (on [their] own)." One developer says, "Some days I work alone; others I work with other people from my group." Over time, workers "get more and more freedom in making decisions." An atmosphere of positive reinforcement encourages workers to take initiative. "Every so often I fall on my face and make a mistake, but if I get up and recover quickly I am congratulated, not scolded," explains one newbie.

Peers

Most first jobbers wind up in offices with much more experienced employees. "There are no other first jobbers in the department," writes a typical survey respondent; adds another, "This is one of the biggest weaknesses of working at Hewlett-Packard. I don't know any other first jobbers at this time. I hang out with guys on the team sometimes, but a lot of them are married, so they don't want to do the same things I do." Even so, newbies describe their coworkers as "very smart, hardworking, and willing to teach."

Moving on

HP reports a "low attrition rate of 2 percent in 2003;" people who leave head to various technology companies, with others heading back to school (an increasingly popular option during the down period the job market has experienced in recent years). Other people have left due to issues in the computer industry; workers have growing concerns that outsourcing and sluggish computer sales may ultimately erase jobs at HP. The company is confident, though: "HP is a global company," says an HP representative, "[and] at the end of the 2003 fiscal year, all [HP's] businesses posted strong revenue and record unit shipments, and all [the] businesses were profitable."

HILL-ROM
VARIOUS POSITIONS

"I never felt like I was performing grunt work," says one employee of his time in an entry-level job at Hill-Rom. "On a scale of one to ten, with 'ten' being the most important, I would rate the importance of my work . . . during my entry level position as a 'nine'."

The Big Picture

Founded in 1929 with the mission to "bring the home into the hospital," Hill-Rom is a major international provider of patient care products. Catering to the special needs of long-term care, acute care, and home-care patients, Hill-Rom designs and manufactures patient care beds, stretchers, therapeutic surfaces and devices, patient flow systems, and nurse communication systems. Offering entry-level positions throughout the organization, in both business and product development, Hill-Rom's most successful employees share the company's commitment to improving the health care environment. On their website, the company claims, "Working at Hill-Rom is the opportunity to put your sincere and heartfelt passion for making a difference to work."

LOCATION(S) WHERE ENTRY-LEVEL EMPLOYEES WORK

Entry-level positions are available in Charleston, South Carolina; St. Paul, Minnesota; Acton, Massachusetts; and Cary, North Carolina; as well as the company's headquarters in Batesville, Indiana, where more than 2,000 people are employed.

ENTRY-LEVEL POSITIONS AVAILABLE

Entry-level employees may enter Hill-Rom as a credit analyst, financial analyst, accountant, mechanical engineer, electrical engineer, biomedical engineer, manufacturing supervisor, HR representative, or IT support specialist.

AVERAGE HOURS WORKED PER WEEK

Entry-level hires work between 40 and 45 hours per week.

AVERAGE STARTING SALARY

Depending on their position, entry-level employees earn between $35,000 and $47,000 per year.

BENEFITS OFFERED

The company's comprehensive benefits package includes health and life insurance, retirement plans, holidays off, paid vacation (after one year), and tuition assistance. They also offer flexible spending accounts and a 401(k) plan with a 4-percent contribution by the company even if the employee decides not to make contributions.

Getting Hired

Hill-Rom operates a summer internship program, and successful participants are often offered a full-time job with the company upon graduating from college. Other job seekers can search for open positions via the company's website. Representatives from the company say that they do not recruit from any specific colleges, and are open to interviewing qualified candidates regardless of the school from which they have earned their degree. When sifting through thousands of resumes, the company is primarily interested in applicants who are honest and ethical, have demonstrated intelligence through their GPA and test scores, and are "driven and somewhat competitive." In many cases, recent grads are considered for several positions simultaneously. While this may boost a Hill-Rom hopeful's chances of scoring a spot on the team, it also means more interviews. A financial analyst explains the first two phases of the hiring process: "I had a phone interview with the HR Director followed by three one-hour interviews for three different jobs." Hill-Rom reps say the ideal interviewee is "well-prepared but doesn't sound rehearsed." They also look for "great body language—good eye contact, good posture, active listening." Individuals should also be comfortable "speaking up in groups." Those looking to be hired by this company should focus on projecting "good energy" and being "articulate" and "very straightforward about the various choices made throughout his/her education and career." All the same, don't stress too much beforehand. Hill-Rom is a self-professed "warm and friendly" workplace, and at interviews the tone tends to be "very relaxed and informal."

Money and Perks

In addition to a solid entry-level salary, the "health insurance, dental plan, and eye plan are excellent benefits within the company." A new employee says he appreciates the "401(k) plan that I am already invested in." Merit raises are given to employees once a year at Hill-Rom, based on individual performance. Employees may also receive promotions, which warrant an out-of-cycle salary increase. Employees mention travel opportunities and a "yearly opportunity for bonuses" as other on-the-job perks. The bonus is based on company and individual performance, and, although it is not guaranteed, ranges from 6 to 12 percent (of base salary) for entry level employees.

The Ropes

All new Hill-Rom employees participate in a day-long orientation session during which they are introduced to the company through "training and safety videos, tours of the manufacturing plants, tours of the product museum" as well as some job-specific technology training. After that, training takes place on the job, within each new employee's department. A Hill-Rom HR rep explains, "The hiring manager will be responsible for putting together a thirty-day orientation plan to make sure that the employee is well acclimated to the company through one-on-one meetings, group meetings, and other pertinent education." A financial analyst confirms, "The training that I did receive came from a variety of people. I was trained by one of the training specialists, my boss, and also by one of my peers. The training was on the different programs that I will be using while working at Hill-Rom." Many Hill-Rom newbies praise the special efforts made by their managers. A new financial analyst commends her boss, describing him as "extremely patient and willing to show or teach me anything." An electrical engineer echoes, "My manager during my entry-level position was previously an electrical engineer. He spent a lot time teaching me methods and concepts to help further my understanding of the engineering subjects required for the position and of the general company processes."

Day in the Life

"I never felt like I was performing grunt work," says one employee of his time in an entry-level job at Hill-Rom. "On a scale of one to ten, with 'ten' being the most important, I would rate the importance of my work . . . during my entry level position as a 'nine'." First jobbers are given significant responsibilities and hands-on experience. A new electrical engineer "was immediately placed at the same professional level as the rest of [his] colleagues and was tasked with the same responsibilities." In his case, "responsibilities included electrical hardware design, embedded software design, requirements gathering and management, interviewing end users of our products, documentation creation, and small amounts of project management." In such a demanding and fast-growing marketplace, work at Hill-Rom can be stimulating due to its changing nature. An engineer enthuses: "I never really had a 'typical' day, as my responsibilities changed weekly." "There were always new and exciting projects, travel, and experiences related to the development of concept products," adds another. True to its entrepreneurial roots, Hill-Rom continues to support an atmosphere of innovation. An electrical engineer tells us, "I was also given the freedom to work on 'pet projects' when I had downtime on my assigned projects, which allowed me to further grow and mature and [to] provide exciting new opportunities for myself and the company."

Peers

An engineer is happy to share, "My peers were exactly like me. They all took pride in their work, loved to design products, and loved to travel and meet with our end users to discuss future products and revisions to current products." Outside of work, however, contact is sparse and sporadic. New employees report that "the company will have the first jobbers get together every couple of weeks if there is new training that needs to be done" for the projects at hand. Outside these work-related opportunities, however, "there is not much contact with the other first jobbers," and "there is not a big after-hours social scene since not everyone lives close to work."

Moving on

According to Hill-Rom's HR department, "Individuals leave the company typically for the following reasons: commuting, personal reasons, [and] career opportunities that they feel are a better fit to their interests if they are not available at Hill-Rom."

Best and Worst

Hill-Rom reps single out their "most successful entry-level employee" as a person "who began as a co-op in our manufacturing facility during the time he was in college. After graduation, he joined Hill-Rom full time and has since held various positions of increasing responsibility, and was most recently promoted to the Executive Director of North America Manufacturing position."

HYATT HOTELS CORPORATION
CORPORATE MANAGEMENT TRAINEE

> "I have the ability to grow personally and professionally all while traveling the world from hotel to hotel, and making more money as I advance."

The Big Picture

Hyatt's corporate management training (CMT) program is designed "to effectively recruit and train individuals to be future leaders in all areas of Hyatt management." These areas include accounting, catering, culinary, engineering/facilities, human resources, operations, and sales. The program readies new employees (almost exclusively recent college grads) to take that big step into the tiers of hotel management by requiring them to "rotate" among different departments prior to engaging in a concentration. First jobbers rave about the opportunity to see new places and fresh faces—all while earning a living. Says one, "I have the ability to grow personally and professionally all while traveling the world from hotel to hotel, and making more money as I advance."

LOCATION(S) WHERE ENTRY-LEVEL EMPLOYEES WORK

Hyatt operates more than 215 hotels worldwide, and all U.S. and Canadian hotels are an option for those entering the CMT program.

AVERAGE NUMBER OF APPLICATIONS EACH YEAR

Hyatt receives more than 4,000 applications for the CMT program each year.

AVERAGE NUMBER HIRED PER YEAR OVER THE LAST TEN YEARS

The company brings 160 new employees into its CMT program annually.

ENTRY-LEVEL POSITION(S) AVAILABLE

For those aspiring to enter the realm of hospitality management, the position of corporate management trainee (CMT) is stage one of Hyatt's fast track.

AVERAGE HOURS WORKED PER WEEK

CMTs are expected to put in 47.5 hours per week.

AVERAGE STARTING SALARY

Average starting salaries range from $33,000 to $41,000.

BENEFITS OFFERED

Hyatt offers medical, dental, vision, and prescription drug coverage. Additional benefits include a 401(k) retirement plan, life insurance, an employee assistance program, tuition reimbursement, and plenty of complimentary or discounted hotel rooms.

CONTACT INFO

All applications must be submitted to at www.careers.hyatt.com.

Getting Hired

Hyatt "strives to find candidates who are energetic or enthusiastic, have a good sense of service, [have] industry experience, and are flexible and professional." The company "visits 48 [schools with] hospitality-related programs" semiannually. Students at these schools "have the opportunity to see a presentation, network with recruiters, and interview on campus. This does not eliminate students from other institutions because anyone can apply for the CMT program and we offer [positions] to many of them." The Hyatt website keeps a running tally of all available opportunities. One CMT says that, whatever the job, "the qualities Hyatt is looking for [are] drive" as well as proof the applicant "will want to work for them." Typically, Hyatt presents on campus and students get two face-to-face interviews. If a student is not interviewing on campus, they go to the closest hotel. A CMT in sales recalls, "They asked about my experiences working and how I handled confrontational situations in the workplace. They also asked questions to see if I was truly interested in working for hotels, and if I was passionate. The tone was very friendly and relaxed. I was never nervous, and I felt comfortable throughout the entire process." The key to a good interview is to walk in with a strong understanding of what Hyatt is all about and why you fit well with that company. All CMT candidates are asked about their GPA, experience, and flexibility. The company says the "best interview is when a student shows genuine interest in the company and the opportunities available by engaging in meaningful conversation with questions." As one CMT explains, his classmates who did not receive job offers from Hyatt "just interviewed with everyone blindly and hoped to 'get lucky' and get a job on the fly without any effort."

Money and Perks

To help relocating newbies make the transition, Hyatt is kind enough to cover the cost of household goods and chip in $1,000 and up to two weeks of hotel accommodations upon arrival. Once they get situated, "CMTs receive feedback after each department rotation, a program midpoint evaluation, and program completion evaluation." These evaluations can have an impact on pay raises. Company officials say, "Depending on the length of the program, some [CMTs] receive incremental increases. All CMTs who successfully complete the program get a minimum [raise] of 10 percent when finished." Despite the raise at the end of the training period, not all employees are thrilled with Hyatt's rate of pay. One says, However, one employee notes, "I can learn so much more from them [than from other employers in the industry], which was why I tactically made the move to Hyatt." And experience isn't the only perk. A CMT points out that he also gets "discounted/free room nights for myself and family, 15 percent mobile phone discount, car/cinema discounts, etc."

The Ropes

Hyatt's "on-boarding process begins with Corporate College Relations," which makes "personal offers" and provides "an offer packet. Upon acceptance, the placement hotel contacts [the new hires] immediately to begin orientation of the hotel and geographic area. Once they arrive, a formal orientation takes place during their first few days of employment. All CMTs spend the first week with Human Resources, which aids in ensuring a comfortable start." Following that stint is when the real training begins. Hyatt bigwigs explain, "The trainee is put through a rotation of all departments at the property. They are really there to assist, learn, and understand what the department does. This component is extremely popular and allows the CMTs to form relationships with associates outside their area of concentration. The trainee spends the final training period in their area of concentration. Upon completion, they are placed into their first management role with Hyatt." CMTers speak highly of this training process. One alum of the program says, "During my rotation, I dressed as a line employee (where applicable) and performed the same duties right alongside. I was able to get a better grasp of how the whole hotel works as a unit to achieve a common goal."

Day in the Life

The shape of each day is determined, initially, by where a CMT is in the rotation process; later, the CMT's area of concentration becomes the determining factor. Wherever trainees are in the process, their sole goal is "to learn each department and how it relates to the 'overall' picture of the hotel in its entirety." This means that each day a new hire must "look, listen, watch, learn, be proactive instead of reactive, and ask questions." It also means that CMTs try their hands at all the nitty-gritty tasks that keep a hotel afloat, like heading to the laundry room to pick up "linens, towels, duvet covers, bed runners, and sham pillows to be stocked in the closets on their assigned floors" and "switching the balcony chairs from the old ones to the new." They also lead property tours, conduct guest satisfaction surveys, work with the budget books, brainstorm strategies for limiting overtime hours, and develop the motivational and leadership skills required of managers. A CMT who is four months into his training remarks, "I believe that a major purpose of my training is a transformation in my thought process from a worker into a leader."

Peers

"Everyone is great," promises a newbie, adding that there exists "a lot of diversity in the workforce." Another new hire comments, "Most are older but I get along with them great. I have made a lot of friends." At Hyatt, a strong sense of community pervades. For instance, "managers are encouraged to sit with and get to know their line-level employees." One front desker who has worked for the company for over a year says, "My friends and [the] people that I hang out with range from line-level to upper management."

Moving on

First jobbers most frequently leave Hyatt to move closer to home, to work for a company that has an opening in a geographical location they desire, or because a competitor offered them a higher paycheck.

Attrition

Less than 10 percent of Hyatt's new hires leave the company before the end of their first year. Sure, the training period can have its ups and downs—"There were certain departments that moved slower than others," confesses a former CMT—but most new hires understand that it's a means to an end. And that end is a managerial position in one of the world's most prestigious hotel and resort chains. As one CMT in the sales programs says, "What keeps me going is that I know I am a quick learner and I plan to be a great sales manager in the near future."

Best and Worst

"There are many Hyatt executives who began their Hyatt career as a management trainee," assure company administrators. Higher ups that have risen from the CMT program include "Mr. Chuck Floyd, Executive VP & Chief Operating Officer; Mr. Doug Patrick, Vice President of Human Resources; Julie Cocker, General Manager; and Pete Sears, Senior Vice President of Field Operations, just to name a few." But all success stories have their counterpoints in unsuccess stories: "The least successful . . . are those who give up on a career opportunity with Hyatt. Hyatt has high expectations and high rewards, but [the latter] don't come without ambition and motivation to take the challenge."

INTERNATIONAL RESCUE COMMITTEE
VARIOUS POSITIONS

"Being in the field allows you to be close to beneficiaries and see the impact of your work."

The Big Picture

The International Rescue Committee is a large, nongovernmental organization dedicated to helping political refugees successfully relocate to the United States. Grateful employees say they love having "contact with people working with very relevant issues" and appreciate "learning more about the world through firsthand accounts of people who are trying to make a difference." Boasting a "fantastic reputation in the NGO world," the IRC provides entry-level employees with a range of opportunities in administration, fieldwork, and fundraising, most of which begin on the volunteer level. Says one volunteer who has been with the organization for two years, "While Doctors Without Borders may be more famous, and Save the Children has a flashier name, IRC is known for the high, steady quality of its work. Overheads are kept low, and a big commitment is made to empowering national staff and even assisting them in becoming expatriate staff themselves."

LOCATION(S) WHERE ENTRY-LEVEL EMPLOYEES WORK

The IRC's headquarters are in New York City; however, entry-level employees may be hired at any of the organization's many national and international offices.

AVERGAE NUMBER OF APPLICATIONS EACH YEAR

The IRC receives 5,700 applications for entry-level positions annually. This includes both domestic and international applicants.

AVERAGE NUMBER HIRED PER YEAR OVER THE LAST TEN YEARS

The organization hires about 170 people each year, both domestically and internationally.

ENTRY-LEVEL POSITION(S) AVAILABLE

The International Rescue Committee fills a variety of entry-level positions in various locations throughout the United States. Most national employees are hired as volunteers, administrative assistants, administrators, or specialists. Internationally, the company fills the positions of volunteers, interns, and officers in numerous developing countries. While potentially entry-level, positions in foreign countries usually require previous international experience.

AVERAGE HOURS WORKED PER WEEK

Employees in the U.S. work 37.5 hours per week; international employees work 40 hours per week.

Getting Hired

Evaluating their current needs internationally and nationally, the IRC chooses candidates for a range of volunteer and paid positions. Sought-after qualities depend on the type of program to which the candidate is applying and whether the program is domestic or international. Many full-time employees enter through an internship or volunteer job. A program manager in West Africa attests, "Once I had the internship, it was much easier to get considered for an overseas position." Likewise, many overseas employees begin with very simple office jobs in the New York office and work their way into more exciting positions both here and abroad. A current staff member says, "I was hopeful that this entry-level job would be the foot in the door for an overseas assignment. It was." While there isn't any specific formula, IRC recruiters say they look for candidates who display "previous international experience, strong writing skills, excellent interpersonal and communication skills, the ability to work productively in a team environment and independently, flexibility, and a sense of humor." Domestic candidates should also possess "strong administrative skills and attention to detail." Not surprisingly, IRC interviews usually focus on a candidate's previous experience in nongovernment organizations (NGOs) or volunteer work, as well as his or her knowledge of and interest in the organization.

Money and Perks

IRC employees aren't in it for the money. (In fact, according to those who do the hiring, "interviewees who show more interest in the salary and benefits than the position or specifics of the job are not considered the best candidates.") Though eligible for yearly salary increases, the IRC has an unfortunate "reputation of not paying quite as well as other NGOs or UN agencies." Instead, new hires say they appreciate their job for giving them "access to interesting talks at organizations like the UN," as well as "opportunities for travel." International volunteers, interns, and employees receive transportation and housing costs in their host country.

The Ropes

All international interns meet for an orientation in New York City before flying off to their assigned location, where they receive further training on-site. Staff working at the New York City headquarters or in U.S.-based resettlement offices typically have a short orientation followed by training within their departments. In most cases, the majority of the orientation and training takes place on the job. An administrator from headquarters explains, "I don't recall receiving any formal training in the three years in my position. However, I met with my boss every morning who helped prioritize my workload and gave me suggestions as to how to complete projects. I found this daily mentoring to be invaluable and it helped me learn how to manage my time. There were also other more experienced admin staff who were very generous in giving me their time and guidance on departmental projects." The feeling is widespread across the organization: "Working on a day-to-day basis with the vice president was the best part about this job. I learned so much from him both professionally and personally, such as how to manage my time, make and follow through on work plans, and . . . give [my] absolute focus to each person or task at hand . . . . He made me a better person as well as a better employee."

Day in the Life

A day as an IRC employee can vary greatly depending on who and where you are, and what you are doing. A headquarters staff member says his entry-level position was "basically data entry, photocopying, and filing; tasks that hardly required a college degree and sophisticated critical thinking skills." On the other end of the spectrum, a new employee in Africa shares this tale: "My boss sent me off to a refugee camp for my first time by myself in the middle of a threatened strike against IRC because of a water shortage (with a security briefing, of course). It was exciting to be sent off alone so soon after arriving in country, and it demonstrated the fact that they were taking me seriously and expecting a degree of independence, which made me very happy." While their daily functions vary, IRC employees carry a great deal of pride for the work they do. A field employee shares, "Being in the field allows you to be close to beneficiaries and see the impact of your work"; office workers tells us that, while it can be occasionally boring, "the job I was doing was important in that somebody absolutely had to do it."

Peers

IRC employees describe their coworkers as "very smart, interesting, driven." A former office staff member tells us, "I really, really liked my fellow administrators. They were all smart and cool (unlike myself), which made our mundane tasks all the more ironic. I felt we had a kind of unspoken fellowship between us." Needless to say, most IRC staff develop a similar sense of purpose and philanthropy, which drives their work. After their time with IRC, employees often find that "the best part was being around people that have an international curiosity about the world, the things happening in it, and how to make a change." At the New York office, employees say their peers are friendly, though there isn't much contact with their coworkers outside the office. "In HQ, I didn't find that much of a social scene, but it was New York so people had their own lives," is how one staffer explains it. "Overseas, you spend every minute . . . with your colleagues," fostering a strong and intense bond between peers. In that case, "You have to make a special effort to really widen your circle and not get trapped into going from home to office and back and never interacting with the local community and with the national staff."

Moving on

On average, IRC employees stay with the company for about two years before leaving to pursue other opportunities. Domestically, most staff leave to pursue higher education or other professional opportunities. International employees often leave to work in a more stable environment or to take a break from overseas work.

Attrition

Some office-based staffers leave the IRC in search of more interesting jobs. Explains a former New York City employee, "Some highly educated entry-level staffers were overqualified for their position and this sometimes brought on feelings of resentment when doing menial tasks that were part of the job, such as making photocopies." In addition, poor pay is among the reasons that IRC staff look for new positions. However, "The IRC has recently made a commitment to improving staff retention, so hopefully people worth keeping will begin to receive higher pay or more training opportunities or more flexibility from post to post." Those who have stuck around say it's worth the wait, as they rise in rank and responsibility within the organization. A former volunteer tells us, "My responsibilities and pay increased each year, and I have since obtained an overseas job with the organization. Many people at IRC have been there for more than five years and many of them started as volunteers, like myself."

J.E.T. Programme
Coordinator for International Relations, Assistant Language Teacher, and Sports Exchange Advisor

"The J.E.T. Programme is a one-year deal, though J.E.T.'s have the option to renew their contracts twice and extend their stays to three years."

The Big Picture

J.E.T.'s—that's what participants in the Japanese Exchange and Teaching Programme are called—spend a year (or more) in Japan, primarily teaching English, though the programme also offers some other community service jobs. The J.E.T. Programme offers a great way to visit Japan and immerse yourself in Japanese culture while doing worthwhile work.

Location(s) Where Entry-level Employees Work

The J.E.T. Programme has many locations across Japan.

Average Number Hired Per Year over the Last Ten Years

Approximately 2,500 people are hired per year.

Entry-level Position(s) Available

New hires work as assistant language teachers, coordinators for international relations, and sports exchange advisors.

Average Hours Worked Per Week

New hires work 35 hours every week.

Percentage of Entry-level Hires Still with Company After Three, Five, and Ten Years

Not applicable. "The programme is for one year with the possibility of extending twice."

Average Starting Salary

New hires earn 3.6 million per year (calm down; that's yen, not dollars!). Exchange rates fluctuate daily; you may use an online currency converter to see how much this amounts to in U.S. dollars.

Benefits Offered

New hires receive Japanese national insurance and accident and medical insurance.

Contact Information

Visit the website at www.jetprogramme.org.

Getting Hired

The application process is "run by Japanese embassies and consulates in forty countries and differs slightly accordingly." Applications may be downloaded at Japan's Ministry of Foreign Affairs home page; the application is standard and asks for education and employment background information, a statement of purpose essay, academic transcripts, and letters of reference. After reviewing applications, the Japanese government contacts likely candidates to schedule interviews. One new hire writes, "I was interviewed by three people: a former J.E.T. employee, a university professor, and a Japanese consulate representative. It was a formal interview; all questions had been prepared by the interviewers and written down beforehand. Each interviewer asked three to four, mostly situational, questions. Some examples are: 'Since you are a vegetarian, what would you do if the principal at your school invited you over for dinner and offered you meat?' [and] 'Boys can be curious about female bodies. What would you say if one of your students asked for your bust-waist-hip measurements?'" Another adds, "I was intimidated when being interviewed by three people, but it wasn't bad. The interviewers were friendly. The application process is long, and you don't find out where you are placed until after you accept the position, which could be a drawback for some."

Money and Perks

J.E.T.'s think you should know that "the terms of [their] contract are government policy and in no way flexible," so don't bother trying to wrangle a few extra yen during the interview. J.E.T.'s mostly think they get a fair deal. One writes, "I was supplied an apartment; was helped getting set up with a bank account and phone, etc.; and was paid well." They also appreciate the fact that "J.E.T. is affiliated with both the Japanese and United States governments, so you know it isn't a back-door, monkey bars company." For the teachers, the best fringe benefit—besides the free trip to and from Japan—is the work schedule, which includes many vacation days.

The Ropes

New J.E.T.'s start out with "a couple of orientation sessions at the Japanese embassy in DC," then continue in Tokyo once they arrive. One J.E.T. writes, "The [Tokyo] orientation was a grueling three days in an overpriced hotel. It was a series of meetings and seminars relating to the J.E.T. Programme and teaching ideas." Another new J.E.T. adds, "They told us things like 'Don't stick your chopsticks in your rice' and 'Never put sugar in green tea.' Yes, their orientation programs need some help. I know that most J.E.T.'s (including me) were disappointed that we didn't get more practical information or teacher training." Afterward, "most training was on-the-job, learning the boundaries of what was and wasn't expected of me."

Day in the Life

The vast majority of J.E.T.'s serve as assistant language teachers. Here's how one describes her typical day in Japan: "Arrive at 8:20 A.M. Sit through a five-minute morning meeting in Japanese. Drink green tea. Begin reading my teaching materials or the textbooks to make a lesson plan. (I typically had two to three classes, fifty minutes each, a day.) Read a book or the newspaper. Eat lunch in the teachers' room. Go to the convenience store to buy chocolate. Continue making a lesson plan for the week. Talk to students in the hall. Drink more green tea. Leave by 4:00 P.M." Another J.E.T. agrees that the workload is often surprisingly light: "Typically, I taught anywhere from one to three fifty-minute classes per day (out of an eight-hour work day). The rest of the time I [planned lessons], e-mailed, read, wrote, studied Japanese, spaced out, and observed. Teaching consisted of reading a one-page passage out of the textbook that my kids would repeat and then write in their notebooks. About every two weeks, I would plan a game or speaking activity." Despite occasional bouts of boredom, most J.E.T.'s describe their experience as a valuable one. As one notes, "I worked with some incredible teachers and some mediocre ones. The best ones helped me with my Japanese-language studies and answered questions I had about Japanese culture. I learned both what I wanted to aim for in my teaching career and what I wanted to avoid in terms of style of teaching."

Peers

Peer relationships in J.E.T. depend largely on the assignment. As one newbie tells us, "I was the only J.E.T. in my town, so it was pretty much up to me to meet other J.E.T.'s and make plans with them. There were other towns that had, like, thirteen J.E.T.'s, and some of these people hung out exclusively with other J.E.T.'s at western-type bars, clubs, and restaurants. I tried to [balance hanging out] with other J.E.T.'s and [with] Japanese people." Another J.E.T. offers, "I made friends, but the other J.E.T.'s were all across the board. I definitely met some great people; I even met my boyfriend through the J.E.T. Without fellow J.E.T.'s, life in Japan can get lonely;" as one teacher explains, "I felt isolated. There was the language barrier, as well as the fact that an outsider, especially a foreigner, is not really welcome into the larger group or expected to do real work or take on real responsibilities."

Moving on

The J.E.T. Programme is a one-year deal, though J.E.T.'s have the option to renew their contracts twice and extend their stays to three years. Most of them return home to attend graduate school or seek teaching jobs in the United States. One recalls, "I left after one year. I had a great time and would recommend the [programme] to anyone, but it was time for me to go. I felt that I had a good experience and staying any longer would have dragged it out to the point that it [would become] unpleasant."

Attrition

Homesickness and loneliness are the chief causes of attrition, but there's a huge disincentive to leaving the programme early: Participants are then responsible for their airfare home, plus other related expenses (rent and fees on a participant's apartment in Japan, for one) that quickly add up to a small fortune. If they fail to complete the contract for any but the most dire reasons (i.e., a death in the immediate family), they must pay all of these costs.

John Wiley & Sons, Inc.
Various Positions

"Wiley often promotes within the company, so I feel confident about my future advancement as long as I continue to do quality work."

The Big Picture

John Wiley & Sons, Inc., "an independent, global publisher of print and electronic media products," offers the "perfect" opportunity for "transitioning into the publishing field." One workforce freshman says that from the start "Wiley seemed like an excellent organization to work for." At Wiley, new hires learn about the publishing industry from the ground up. An editorial assistant says that during her seven months at Wiley she's been trained by "acquisition editors, a project manager, two developmental editors, a production editor, other editorial assistants, assistant editors, accounts payable personnel, and others." In other words, she's getting a thorough education in the ins and outs of the biz. She adds, "Honestly, there has yet to be a 'typical' day. Each day is very dynamic, fast-paced, and filled with constant changes."

Location(s) Where Entry-level Employees Work

New hires work in Hoboken, New Jersey; Indianapolis, Indiana; or San Francisco, California.

Average Number of Applications Each Year

In recent years, the average number of entry-level applications received was 228.

Average Number Hired Per Year over the Last Ten Years

Wiley hires 57 entry-level assistants each year.

Entry-level Position(s) Available

The company's entry-level positions include editorial assistant, marketing assistant, production assistant, and sales assistant. Positions in related fields are sometimes available as well.

Average Hours Worked Per Week

Newbies log 35 hours each week.

Average Starting Salary

New colleagues average $30,600 per year.

Getting Hired

Wiley recruits at a number of universities and regularly attends college career fairs. In addition, the company posts job openings on its website, Wiley.com, PublishersLunch.com, and on general and industry-specific career sites such as Monster.com, Bookjobs.com, and Mediabistro.com. Wiley also "has a referral-bonus program for its colleagues—they get either $500 or $1,000 for referring someone to the company, provided that they stay on for three months." The candidates that Wiley tends to hire are those with a "solid academic foundation coupled with internship and/or exposure to an office environment; demonstrated intellectual curiosity and an interest in the publishing industry; excellent written and verbal communication skills, organizational skills, and ability to multitask; [and] PC skills [and] attention to detail." They're "team-oriented, but also able to work independently." To get the ball rolling, applicants should submit a resume. Candidates who meet expectations for positions are often contacted for a preliminary interview. If there is continued mutual interest, the candidate is invited in for a formal interview, at which time an application is completed. Applicants may be asked to complete exercises relevant to the open position. Applicants are then interviewed by a member of the Human Resources department, hiring managers, other management staff and/or colleagues within the department." In most cases, at least two lengthy, face-to-face interviews will take place. One editorial assistant promises that the interview process is a good experience: "The tone of the interviews was both professional and very friendly, leading me to instantly feel comfortable with each person."

Money and Perks

Most new hires bring home a similar paycheck—around $30,000—and that paycheck can stretch pretty thin in a city with a high cost of living. But first jobbers don't complain, because they've landed themselves in a position with plenty of upward mobility. Colleague performance is normally reviewed after the first six months, and once a year after that. Colleagues are "generally eligible for merit increases that coincide with performance reviews. . . . Successful entry-level colleagues are eligible to receive four merit increases in their first three years of employment." Nonexempt colleagues are eligible to participate in the Success Sharing Incentive Plan. (Payout is contingent on the company and the respective business group's meeting annual financial goals and on individual job performance.) Wiley colleagues also receive a wide range of discounts and freebies, including no-cost admission to many cultural events, cheap tickets to the movies, free on-site cholesterol and blood pressure screenings and flu shots, and a fitness center at all three locations. The best perk? Many young colleagues say it's the workplace itself. "The relaxed work environment was hands-down the best part of my entry-level job," says one. "There was no pressure to dress a certain way, and I was allowed to set my own hours every day, as long as I worked a total of seven hours each day."

The Ropes

"The official orientation was a day long," says an editorial assistant. But training is a different story. At Wiley, training is an ongoing process that continues, formally and informally, throughout the first year of employment. Company officials explain that "during the first three months, the orientation process is comprised of four programs: Orientation for New Colleagues conducted by Human Resources, point-of-hire orientation conducted by the new colleague's manager(s), Corporate Orientation conducted by our president and CEO and senior vice president of Human Resources, and a benefits orientation conducted by Human Resources." To supplement these events, "managers are provided with tools to assist them in effectively training and integrating new colleagues to Wiley and their department/area during their first year." All in all, Wiley offers a very supportive environment for newbies. Says one, "When I had questions about something, I knew I could go to any of the editors for help. A few of my team's production editors had started out in the same boat I was—as the team assistant. So they were extra helpful in helping me adjust to the new systems and programs I was asked to use."

Day in the Life

A typical day on the job all depends on the position, the departmental workload, and the time of year. A production assistant admits, "I had so much downtime during my first year with the company that I became very bored at work." But that's not the case company-wide. "Bored? Heck, no!" says an editorial assistant. "We're constantly overwhelmed with work." A diplomatic editorial assistant steps in to say, "I am comfortable with my workload." One thing that assistants in all four areas—editorial, marketing, production, and sales—have in common is that their primary job is to "support" colleagues who are higher up in the chain of command. For instance, an editorial assistant "provides general editorial and administrative support to editors and publishers," which includes editing documents, maintaining databases, responding to e-mails, assisting with contracts, and serving as a liaison between authors and editors. Early on, new hires come to see themselves as an integral part of a team. An enterprising entry-level says, "My job responsibilities did not actually take that much time once I'd mastered them. . . . To fill [the] time, I created and updated documentation for the team, volunteered to help others with their books, [and] brainstormed ways to make our team function better." From the beginning, says a production wiz, "I felt that my job did have an impact on the company."

Peers

Wiley's publishing-world neophytes are thrilled to know that the company had the good sense to hire people as cool as, well, themselves. One rookie raves, "There's contact and camaraderie with other recent hires, as well as with more established employees. People frequently spend time together outside of work (including on a company softball team). I recently visited Napa for a wine tour with two friends from here. It was just the best weekend I'd had in a long time." She adds, "My peers are amazing and I'm thrilled with the friends I've made, and am continuing to make."

Moving on

The four primary reasons first jobbers leave Wiley are to take better opportunities (in terms of content or pay) elsewhere, to return to school, to relocate, or to switch industries altogether.

Attrition

Over the last five calendar years, 17.3 percent of new hires left the company before completing a year of service. Colleagues suggest that "the constantly overwhelming workload" of some positions and the "low pay" for newbies might have something to do with it. On average, however, first jobbers stay with the company for more than two years before moving on. Those who have stuck around say that patience is the key. One explains, "My assistant position was almost treated as an apprenticeship, where I could ease into editing by learning the book production process step-by-step. . . . Wiley often promotes within the company, so I feel confident about my future advancement as long as I continue to do quality work."

Best and Worst

Wiley's prize for the best entry-level employee goes to a woman who "began her career in 1980 as a production aide (modern job-title equivalent: production assistant)." With time and hard work, "she was promoted through the editorial career track to her current position of Senior Vice President within our Professional/Trade business. In 2005, this colleague was inducted into Wiley's 25-Year Club, demonstrating her commitment and loyalty to both publishing and the company." The prize for worst entry-level employee goes not to an individual, but rather to a type of person. According to Wiley officials, it would be someone "who provided a lack of focus, lack of interest in the industry, and an inability to collaborate. Someone who was not team-oriented, lacked verbal and written communication skills, lacked initiative, and whose expectations did not meet ours."

JOHNS HOPKINS UNIVERSITY APPLIED PHYSICS LABORATORY
VARIOUS POSITIONS

"What is wonderful about APL's structure is the different paths available. You can climb up the typical management chain or proceed up the technical route. You can go into research or business areas. You can even stay in your current position and do great work and get recognized with seniority and raises."

The Big Picture

Located on a verdant college campus and offering a range of entry-level positions to applied scientists and engineers working in research and space science, Johns Hopkins University Applied Physics Lab (JHU/APL) features a "nice mixture of academia, industry, and government." With challenging research projects and unparalleled opportunities to pursue advanced degrees while working at the lab, job satisfaction at JHU/APL is extremely high. New employees say they are easily welcomed into the professional community, and prevailing sentiment is that JHU/APL is a "great place filled with many opportunities to expand your career and education."

LOCATION(S) WHERE ENTRY-LEVEL EMPLOYEES WORK

Johns Hopkins University Applied Physics Laboratory is located on the Johns Hopkins University campus in Laurel, Maryland.

AVERAGE NUMBER OF APPLICATIONS EACH YEAR

The lab receives about 2,500 applications per year.

AVERAGE NUMBER HIRED PER YEAR OVER THE LAST TEN YEARS

JHU/APL hires between 50 and 60 entry-level employees each year.

ENTRY-LEVEL POSITION(S) AVAILABLE

There are various research positions available at JHU/APL for new graduates with bachelor's degrees, master's degrees, and PhDs in aerospace, applied mathematics and physics, electrical engineering, and mechanical engineering.

AVERAGE HOURS WORKED PER WEEK

Lab employees work 40 hours per week.

AVERAGE STARTING SALARY

Exact numbers are not available but employees tell us their offers are "very generous."

Getting Hired

APL recruits on top college campuses across the country, looking for bright new physicists and engineers to join their team of applied scientists. Many successful applicants have their first encounter with the lab at a career fair and are subsequently invited to interview at the lab. Strong undergraduate performance and or graduate work in applied sciences are the first and most important elements of any application. The lab also requires Department of Defense security clearance, for which U.S. citizenship is a requirement. There are, however, more personal factors that come into play before hopefuls receive an offer from JHU/APL. One candidate explains, "I felt that I was being 'tested' on two different levels. Technically, they wanted to ensure I had the skills required. I believe that coming from a known university with a decent GPA, it was automatically assumed I was somewhat competent. Then there were the standard questions about classes and research. On another level, they wanted to see if I was a good 'fit' for APL." Echoes another, "Although I was asked about my previous work experience, in most cases very little time was spent drilling me with technical questions. Most of the questions were behavioral and geared towards trying to figure out if I would make a good fit within the group."

Money and Perks

The lab offers generous salaries to successful candidates, as well as 100-percent tuition reimbursement for employees who wish to pursue a part-time advanced degree at the university. "What really drew me in . . . was APL's continuing education program. Not only could one pursue his or her MS, but also [a] PhD! Most companies have MS programs, but I [had] never heard of a PhD program." While it probably isn't the sexiest answer, employees also cite the retirement plan as one of the lab's greatest perks; "the lab matches 2:1 for up to 4 percent of my contribution into my retirement plan. Additionally, they give 2.5 percent for free after the first year."

The Ropes

Following a short orientation session, most new hires are sent directly to their department, where they receive personalized professional training depending on the candidate and the project. A new hire explains, "Almost all training is 'on the job' and comes directly from my boss and coworkers." Another remembers that "there was no formal training. Instead, whoever was in charge of each task given to me would sit down and work with me for a few days." New employees are often working on a project for which they were not entirely prepared by their previous education, and therefore, often spend a good deal of time in self-directed study. Says one, "My initial responsibilities were to get acquainted with some general theory to be able to start working on one of my projects. For the first three to four weeks my average day involved doing lots of reading ([approximately] three to four hours a day) and some experimentation on the side." In the meantime, new employees must complete lab orientation courses that provide an introduction to the lab and its many functions. One new physicist explains the general process: "I began working almost immediately while attending the New Staff Orientation Program (NSOP) for my department every two weeks for about nine months. During NSOP we listen[ed] to presentations about the department's work and socialized with other new hires over lunch. Once NSOP was complete, I attended a week-long Professional Staff Orientation Program (PSOP), where I learned about the work of the entire lab and took tours of the facilities."

Day in the Life

Most new hires are surprised to learn the breadth of their activities at JHU/APL. A lab employee could be involved in a "variety of responsibilities ranging from hands-on laboratory work to computer data analysis to writing reports and papers." A current employee attests to his experience: "A large amount of this work has been down in a lab, processing and analyzing data and algorithms, but more recently I have been called upon to assist with the writing of internal lab proposals to get funding and have also assisted in the publication of some of our work in the open literature." Multitasking is part of the job, and employees say they are usually working on several things simultaneously. On top of that, many lab employees are concurrently pursuing an advanced degree at Johns Hopkins. Shares one such student, "Between working on my master's part-time and working full-time, it's easy to feel a little overwhelmed, but that's what keeps me going." As they move from novices to more seasoned employees, new hires are pleased to see a steady increase in their level of responsibility and professional opportunities. In response to these trends, one newcomer shares, "I think the pay will continue to grow steadily along with the responsibility. I can see that both of these have gone up quite a bit since starting a year ago."

Peers

JHU/APL employees describe their coworkers in terms such as "brilliant" and "the smartest people I have ever known." In addition, employees tell us that the vibe between staff members is friendly and supportive. In fact, one tells us that "the camaraderie with first jobbers is great. It is relaxing to know that you have coworker[s] who can relate to what you are facing." Adds another, "Within my own research group, I have a good relationship with all my team members." While most new employees report that they have "made quite a few friends," on the staff, many say that the social scene is confined to lunch breaks, and doesn't include much after-hours socializing.

Moving on

With so many options within the company, JHU/APL employees say there is little reason to look for a job at another company. Explains one, "What is wonderful about APL's structure is the different paths available. You can climb up the typical management chain or proceed up the technical route. You can go into research or business areas. You can even stay in your current position and do great work and get recognized with seniority and raises." For that reason, most employees who leave do so for personal reasons. Says a conflicted soul, "If I could, I would work for APL until I retired. However, my wife and I miss our families in North Carolina and will likely move back home when we're ready to start a family of our own."

Attrition

JHU/APL doesn't suffer much attrition—voluntary turnover of professional staff is less than 4 percent. In fact, they suffer from a very different problem. "One of the major complaints I hear is that it is very hard to get rid of people here," admits an employee.

KPMG
AUDIT ASSOCIATE, TAX ASSOCIATE, AND ADVISORY ASSOCIATE

KPMG "provides knowledge from many different facets [of the business world], and I feel like I just signed up to go to school for a few more years, but this time I am getting paid for it."

The Big Picture

One of the "the Big Four accounting firms," KPMG delivers "audit, tax, and advisory services" to an international client base. Fresh college grads relish the chance to sign on at KPMG because it offers "a good chance to learn about the business world and the inner workings of large, diverse companies."

LOCATION(S) WHERE ENTRY-LEVEL EMPLOYEES WORK

KPMG has 80 U.S. offices in locations including: New York, New York; Chicago, Illinois; Los Angeles, California; Atlanta, Georgia; Dallas, Texas; and Washington, DC.

AVERAGE NUMBER OF APPLICATIONS EACH YEAR

Every year, KPMG receives more than 10,000 applications for its entry-level openings.

AVERAGE NUMBER HIRED PER YEAR OVER THE LAST FIVE YEARS

The annual number of entry-level hires is around 2,200.

ENTRY-LEVEL POSITION(S) AVAILABLE

The company hires entry-level employees in its audit, tax, and advisory divisions. According to KPMG officials, "These associate positions begin with a national training program lasting up to two weeks. Associates then return to their local office where they are assigned to client engagement teams." In all three areas of specialization, employees "work as a part of a team to provide various services to our clients."

AVERAGE HOURS WORKED PER WEEK

On average, new hires put in 50 hours each week.

AVERAGE STARTING SALARY

Company officials say that starting salaries vary "by degree, practice, and geographic location, [but are] competitive within our profession." Among the first jobbers we spoke with, first-time salaries ranged from $48,000 to $55,000.

Getting Hired

By no means is it the only way to go, but, according to our respondents, the clearest path to the front door at KPMG is through one of its sought-after internships. "I decided to go after a winter internship instead of the more coveted summer internship," explains one newbie, noting that the more coveted summer opportunities are often snagged by MBA students. He continues, "I went to every recruiting event and really made a point to get to know a few of the main recruiters. I would make sure to e-mail the people I talked to and thank them for their time and advice. I truly believe that every single person applying (besides the MBA students) all look the same on paper or on a resume [so] I wanted to make sure that I . . . would be remembered by the interviewers and recruiters. I think that helped me the most in attaining my spot in the company." As this experience reflects, the candidates most likely to be hired are those who begin the application process long before they graduate from college. In fact, another first jobber remembers that his "application process and job interview took over a year." (Not everyone, we should note, reports such a drawn-out process; "relatively uncomplicated" is how one newbie describes her experience.) The company seeks applicants "with effective communication, leadership, and time-management skills." To test a candidate's mettle, hiring officers use "a behavior-based interviewing methodology." For a list of sample questions—as well as a wealth of other advice about applying to the company—go to KPMGcampus.com and click on "Interview Process."

Money and Perks

First jobbers describe the salary as "fair" and say that "there is a lot of room for growth in terms of responsibility and pay." Beyond the paycheck, KPMG employment comes with plenty of perks. The greatest fringe benefit, a newbie says, is "vacation, by far! Twenty-five days to start with is pretty much unheard of, even in the Big Four." One recent college grad adds, "There are a lot of social events that are just to celebrate you and your work for the firm." Still, some suggest that the greatest perk is in the boost working at KPMG gives to their resume. According to one young associate, it's simply a case of "job prestige."

The Ropes

An audit associate at the company's Chicago branch explains that his four-day orientation entailed "an introduction to the firm, distribution of materials and laptops, and a lot of administrative activities. We were also allocated time to take required tests that included self-study materials and a final exam. We were introduced to many of the firm's partners and other employees and had time to meet all of the other new hires." Additionally, rookies nationwide convene for a week-long training program. (In 2006, this was held in Orlando, Florida.) Reflecting on the experience, a recent hire tells us, "We were instructed by an accounting professor from Texas A&M University and a woman who has been a member of the audit practice for four years. Our training was very interactive and hands-on, and not only did we learn a lot, but we had a lot of fun!" KPMG's training program is a major draw for entry-level employees; says one, "KPMG has the only national training program of all of the Big Four accounting firms, and I felt that it was a major advantage to be able to interact with peers from all over the U.S."

Day in the Life

The "very fast paced" environment at KPMG provides newcomers with a wealth of "pretty interesting" tasks to tackle on a daily basis. "Feeling overwhelmed is not uncommon," admits one associate, while another adds, "There is a steep learning curve" in this profession. The KPMG website warns newcomers to expect long hours: "We won't mince words—experience tells us you should expect a significant workload in your first year, including evenings and some weekends." Typically, "a first-year associate's responsibilities revolve around supporting other members of [his or her] team as needed." Each job and each client comes with its own list of demands. "Updating work papers; organizing and comprising lists, binders, and activities; and writing memos" are among the duties a second-week associate handles. Another employee mentions "performing specific audit procedures, documenting the procedures performed, and [completing] other work as needed to support the audit team." Sure, it can get hectic at times, but these first jobbers say it's well worth it. According to one, a position at KPMG "provides knowledge from many different facets [of the business world], and I feel like I just signed up to go to school for a few more years, but this time I am getting paid for it."

Peers

During the 2006 "new-hire national training in Orlando," KPMG freshmen "hung out and basically lived with each other the entire time," says an associate. "Many friendships and relationships were started while I was out there." And these friendships didn't end when training was over. KPMG is praised for hosting regular social events that "allow for interaction between employees of the company and between your peers." One newbie raves, "My peers are the biggest perk to the job. Not too many jobs allow you to work with so many people your age." New hires describe each other as "hard workers, goal-oriented, fun, smart, cool, and generally great people," which perhaps explains why "there are always after-hours activities going on."

Attrition

Less than 5 percent of first jobbers leave KPMG before the first year is out. This high rate of retention reflects the fact that "there are great advantages, career-wise, for professionals to reach the manager level at the firm"—and climbing the ladder at KPMG, like anywhere else, takes time. While employees praise the opportunities "for promotion and pay increase" within the company, others note that a strong track record at KPMG can result in an offer "to make a considerably higher salary somewhere else." First jobbers also observe that "the hours and commitment required by this job" lead to departures. But, adds an associate, "Most people in the firm don't mind the hours because they realize that a job must be done and they are more focused on maintaining the reputation and integrity of the firm."

Best and Worst

KPMG's "Best Entry-Level Employee Ever" award goes to Timothy P. Flynn, who "joined KPMG as an audit associate after graduating from college" and "currently serves as chairman and CEO of KPMG LLP." And the worst? Well, let's just say that individual is no longer with the company.

LifeScan
Associate Marketing Manager and Associate Financial Analyst

"Your Partner in Quality Patient Care and Service"

"LifeScan first jobbers handle the nitty-gritty tasks of keeping LifeScan afloat: developing budgets, assisting with sales campaigns, and collaborating on advertising campaigns to expand the company's presence around the world."

The Big Picture

LifeScan, a Johnson & Johnson company, produces diabetes-monitoring equipment for home use. According to the company's website, new hires can "explore [their] entrepreneurial drive in a small-company environment that encourages personal and professional growth. At the same time, [they] discover the stability and resources of an international health care company developing life-enhancing technology."

Location(s) Where Entry-level Employees Work

Entry-level employees work in Milpitas, California.

Average Number of Applications Each Year

Lifescan receives 60 applications per year.

Average Number Hired over the Last Ten Years

The company hires 11 people per year.

Entry-level Position(s) Available

Entry-level hires work as associate marketing managers and associate financial analysts.

Average Hours Worked Per Week

New hires work 40 hours per week.

Average Starting Salary

Undergraduates earn from $66,000 to $89,000, while employees who have their MBAs earn from $77,000 to $103,000.

Benefits Offered

On the health care front, the company offers medical, dental, and vision insurance. Additional benefits include life insurance, tuition reimbursement, a 401(k) plan, on-site company store (headquarters), and on-site workout facility (headquarters).

Getting Hired

LifeScan accepts applications on its website; company officials add, "We have our core schools that we recruit from, but we also accept students from other colleges and universities." The company's recruiters seek "customer market focus, interdependent partnership, mastering complexity, and creativity" in potential hires. One successful applicant describes the vetting process this way: "I was interviewed by different levels of people: the associate marketing managers, marketing managers, and directors. The interview was a mixture of behavioral and case questions. Some questions focused specifically on the competencies required for the position. After two or three weeks, I received an offer from the company. LifeScan hosted an event in January for people who received an offer. The purpose of the event was to convince us to accept the job." Applicants with prior experience in marketing and/or financial analysis have a leg up.

Money and Perks

Starting date is negotiable at LifeScan, first jobbers tell us. Job description and salary are not, though some first jobbers are able to negotiate their signing bonuses; company representatives say, "Salaries are determined based [on] the economy and internal equity." Top perks include "access to an on-site company store, where Johnson & Johnson products are sold at an employee discount, [and] a free on-site health club facility."

The Ropes

LifeScan newbies begin their jobs with their eyes wide open, they tell us. "I knew about the job before I started. The team leader for recruiting communicated a general description of the job to me. Around June, I discovered the area that I was going to be working in. I also received a call from my manager a week before I started my position. I didn't need to know more beforehand." Orientation "is very generic [and limited to] company goals and regulatory requirements. It lasts one to two days, depending on your position." Subsequent training varies according to function; some first jobbers continue with formal training "given by various marketing managers, finance, operations, etc.," while others simply learn through "on-the-job training by our manager."

Day in the Life

LifeScan first jobbers handle the nitty-gritty tasks of keeping LifeScan afloat: developing budgets, assisting with sales campaigns, and collaborating on advertising campaigns to expand the company's presence around the world. The company expects much from its employees, as "the organization is very lean." "There's no time to be bored, and sometimes it's pretty overwhelming, depending on the timing within the month," one new hire tells us. People who show promise are quickly handed "even more responsibility to cover more areas." Fortunately, "impressive lower-level managers" are there to offer guidance and support. Although the bare-bones staffing means that [all] workers [have] at least as much work as [they] can handle—this, employees admit, is often stressful—the upside of the situation is that low-level staffers have relatively good access to higher-ups. One first jobber writes, "I feel that I have exposure to senior management. I sit in on a meeting once a month with senior management—vice president of marketing, vice president of marketing and sales, directors of various areas of marketing. Also, the associate marketing managers have lunch with the vice president of marketing."

Peers

"There is a lot of contact" among LifeScan first jobbers, especially among the assistant marketing managers, who tell us they frequently enjoy "AMM Happy Hours." "We interact every day of the week at work and probably go out together after work once or twice a month," explains one newbie. Friendships are easily forged among the workforce at LifeScan.

Moving on

"There is no one particular reason" that first jobbers leave LifeScan, company officials report, listing "better opportunities, more money [offered elsewhere], going back to school, and relocation" as the most common reasons. The first jobbers we spoke with report that some coworkers bristle under the heavy workload required of them; it's enough to make some people move on. Even so, most people we spoke with are highly satisfied both with their jobs and their prospects for advancement.

LOCKHEED MARTIN
LEADERSHIP DEVELOPMENT PROGRAMS

"[I enjoy] moving every six months. It was so great to have the opportunity to live in four cool cities in two years."

The Big Picture

Lockheed Martin, an advanced technology company that does the lion's share of its business with the Defense Department, offers Leadership Development Programs (LDP) in communications, engineering, finance, human resources, information systems, and operations. All of these programs incorporate job rotations, technical training, and leadership development conferences to fast-track college graduates into management positions with the company.

LOCATION(S) WHERE ENTRY-LEVEL EMPLOYEES WORK

Lockheed has locations in nearly every state in the United States.

AVERAGE NUMBER OF APPLICATIONS EACH YEAR

Lockheed Martin receives 1.2 million applications for positions in the entire company; specific numbers for Leadership Development Programs are not available.

AVERAGE NUMBER HIRED PER YEAR OVER THE LAST TEN YEARS

"In the past six years, we've hired an average of 2,200 [people] per year."

ENTRY-LEVEL POSITION(S) AVAILABLE

There were approximately 2,800 available positions in 2003.

AVERAGE HOURS WORKED PER WEEK

New hires work 40 hours per week.

PERCENTAGE OF ENTRY-LEVEL HIRES STILL WITH THE COMPANY AFTER THREE, FIVE, AND TEN YEARS

The percentage of employees who remain with the company after three, five, and ten years are 84 percent, 76 percent, and 66 percent, respectively.

BENEFITS OFFERED

The company offers health, dental, and vision insurance. Additional benefits include a retirement plan.

CONTACT INFORMATION

E-mail: jobs.lmc@lmco.com

Getting Hired

Lockheed recruits on select campuses; the company accepts applications from all college students through its website. In examining candidates, Lockheed "focuses on senior projects, work experience, and skills that are job related." Interviews are "extremely friendly and somewhat casual/candid." That doesn't mean candidates don't get a good going over; most of the first jobbers we spoke with tell us they were interviewed numerous times before the company reached a decision. One writes, "Five managers, in fifteen- to thirty-minute increments, interviewed me. A few asked technical questions. They told me about their positions/departments and life within Lockheed, [i.e.] it is family friendly. Another thing that was discussed was the typical 'how do you work in groups?' type questions."

Money and Perks

The salaries of LDP participants are "based on certain variables, such as education level (bachelor's or master's) and previous work experience. Within that framework, salary is written in stone." First jobbers praise the company's tuition reimbursement program, telling us "it's 100 percent, and it's easy to get your reimbursement for tuition and books." They also like that employees "accrue vacation days, and if you don't have enough, you can actually debit them and make them up later." One participant says, "[I enjoy] moving every six months. It was so great to have the opportunity to live in four cool cities in two years. The company [relocated] me each time."

The Ropes

Lockheed's Leadership Development Program runs two to three years (depending on the department), with participants rotating jobs every six months. In each rotation, "You start off slow (I took a few days to read any manuals and Lockheed documents I could find, and I asked my manager if there was anything he might recommend to shorten my learning curve), try to follow the format of what was done previously (when available), and ask lots of questions!" Some training is conducted in person by managers, but much of it occurs online; one LDP explains, "You can always take free online training classes from a list of several hundred at different levels (and they don't have to be job-applicable!), or your department sponsors you for further training at one of our many computer labs or external computer classes." All LDP participants must attend Leadership Development Conferences, which stress teamwork, problem-solving strategies, communication skills, and familiarity with Lockheed's corporate culture, values, and goals.

Day in the Life

An LDP participant's typical day depends on his or her program and placement, of course. One participant in finance explains, "My typical day has changed drastically with each rotation. In the Financial Analysis Department, I worked on financial models dealing with sensitivity and impact. I reported to both the director and vice president of financial planning. I updated charts and aided in financial statements management. In the tax department, I worked on federal tax packages for our three biggest sites (spending the day on the phone with our sites to make sure that everything [was] accounted for properly and using the previous year as my model). In billing and collections, I checked my computer for invoices that are declared billable, [spoke] with government payment offices to clear up any discrepanc[ies] with contract payment reconciliation issues, and deal[t] with our contract administrators to make sure that the billings [were] correctly done."

Peers

"LDP participants tend to group together at each site, both formally and informally," program participants tell us. "At some sites we had an LDP council where we planned community service activities as well as happy hours, etc. At other sites, it was more informal gatherings. At each site my group of friends was made up of LDP participants; there is a real sense of camaraderie between us since all of us were in the same situation." There is "a big after-hour[s] social scene, with a relatively large group [who] goes out a few times a week" at most sites. These first jobbers have a lot in common with one another, we're told; one writes, "It's easy to make friends. LDP participants tend to have outgoing personalities since all of us were chosen in part because of our leadership ability."

Moving on

Leadership trainees at Lockheed generally enjoy the "great exposure and diverse assignments that they have" at the company, and most plan to stay at Lockheed for a long time. A few people complain about the difficulty of finding suitable rotations, and some others feel that salary and relocation packages could be more generous. Those who are unhappy at the company sometimes return to school to study business, technology, or science.

L'ORÉAL
VARIOUS POSITIONS

"It's the largest beauty retailer in the world.

It's a network of seventeen brands now, so

there's plenty of room for you to move around. Different brands have differ-

ent roles. They're supportive of you finding your career path here."

The Big Picture

L'Oréal's Management Development Program is a rotational training program with a focus on marketing. At first, hires "spend time working in the field, literally getting hands-on experience working with products in stores and working with customers." Later they are assigned to a marketing team in which "they are considered a full member of the team. They are expected to propose ideas just as any more senior person would. Responsibilities can include anything related to brand management: market research, media and promotions, budgeting and forecasting, and interacting with manufacturing and research and development." L'Oreal has similar rotational programs for finance, supply chain, IT, R&D, manufacturing, and human resources.

LOCATION(S) WHERE ENTRY-LEVEL EMPLOYEES WORK

Entry-level employees work in New York (marketing), New Jersey (finance, IT, logistics, manufacturing, and research and development), and many other locations (sales).

AVERAGE NUMBER OF APPLICATIONS EACH YEAR

L'Oréal receives approximately 450,000 applications for all positions; about 1,000 applicants try for the Management Development Program.

AVERAGE NUMBER HIRED PER YEAR

L'Oréal expected to hire 60 first jobbers for its undergraduate Management Development Program in 2006.

ENTRY-LEVEL POSITION(S) AVAILABLE

While L'Oréal's only structured entry-level program is the Management Development Program, it also has opportunities in marketing, sales, finance, IT, logistics, manufacturing, and research and development.

AVERAGE HOURS WORKED PER WEEK

Entry-level hires work 35-plus hours per week.

AVERAGE STARTING SALARY

Management Development Program participants earn starting salaries of $50,000.

Getting Hired

L'Oréal seeks "flexible, energetic individuals who are business-minded and are interested in a dynamic, innovative industry" for its Management Development Program and warns that "people who aren't comfortable in a fast-paced, highly flexible, and team-based environment will have a more difficult time at L'Oréal." It also states that internships are the favored entryway to the Management Development Program. While the company "focuses on certain top schools with both strong liberal arts and business programs" in recruiting, it considers all applicants and points out that "given the planned expansion of our program, we expect the list of schools where we have a visible presence (via corporate presentations, classroom presentations, sponsorship of student-run activities, etc.) to increase." Company officials also note, "Students who attend schools that L'Oréal does not visit may apply online at LorealUSA.com/careers. Applicants submit resumes and cover letters, which are vetted to select candidates for a round of on-campus interviews. One successful hire explains, "The general tone of the interview was pretty conversational. When I left, I got the sense [that] she wanted to know me. She wanted to see if I had a passion for the industry." Those who clear this hurdle "are invited back to the New York office for a day of interviews with line management [that] includes several networking sessions and opportunities to learn more about the company (pre-evening reception, luncheon with marketers)." Another adds, "Anyone they invite to a [second-round] interview is technically qualified, so it's all about fit."

Money and Perks

First jobbers tell us that their first L'Oréal salary is generally not negotiable. Starting location is on the table for some, though others report that their entire job offer was presented as a package deal. Most here agree that the best perk is the program itself; one hire explains, "Other companies didn't have a specific brand-based training program for undergraduates. That was really attractive for me that they invested so much in new employees." Other favorite benefits include summer hours on Fridays between Memorial Day and Labor Day (the work day ends at 1:30 P.M.), healthclub reimbursement, and "cool products." One first jobber reports, "I never have to buy Christmas presents ever again!" There's also lots of "invites to events. We're very image based."

The Ropes

L'Oréal explains that "the way the program is designed, some would consider [it] in its entirety to be somewhat of an orientation and integration program. We want our new hires to become accustomed to our culture and our work, and that doesn't happen overnight. When a new hire joins, they will attend a week-long corporate orientation program [that] gives an overall picture of the company. After this, the new hire will gain hands-on experience through fieldwork and special marketing projects. We believe in learning by doing, as understanding markets, strategy, cross-functional relationships, and clients are essential to success." The rotational nature of the program means that first jobbers are often in the process of training in a new product or function. One trainee explains, "In each rotation, I was assigned to work with a manager or above, usually a director. Most times [it] was a long-term project, but [I also did] day-to-day work. I'd experience what that area does, as well as do a marketing analysis. We also take classes; the management development center offers classes on category knowledge as well as leadership, finance skills, and presentation skills. There's a whole center that manages that."

Day in the Life

Participants in the Management Development Program begin the program with "rotations in field sales." One explains, "I was living outside of Nashville, Tennessee, where I was given the responsibility to service stores. I was supposed to make sure promotionals were up, do international market research, and do day-to-day management research. I also worked on analysis of market franchises, finance, cost of consumer goods, and inventory analysis. It was always interesting, fast-paced, and always new and exciting." After rotations, trainees are assigned to marketing teams, where they take on considerable responsibility. One writes, "I've been given my own projects. Coming from not knowing anything to managing my own projects has been a great learning curve. It's been hands-on throughout, but in the beginning, it was just learning and absorbing." Another reports, "I have a good mix of short-term responsibilities and long-term responsibilities. It gives me a good scope of where business is going."

Peers

Management Development trainees are spread throughout L'Oréal, so they don't form a natural social community; they are more likely to interact with coworkers in the division to which they're assigned than with [one another]. To counter this, says L'Oréal, "the company recently has been putting together quarterly networking events to facilitate community building." One trainee writes, "Each department does a good job of creating events. I've gone to receptions and happy hours, and this is a great opportunity to network" and meet other first jobbers. Trainees also report that "it's easy to make friends here. There's a really great camaraderie. Everyone is bright and creative, and each [person] brings something new to the table. Nobody has the same background."

Moving on

Management trainees at L'Oréal see "plenty of room to grow in terms of pay and responsibility," describing the opportunity as "one of the most important things about this company." One first jobber explains, "It's the largest beauty retailer in the world. It's a network of seventeen brands now, so there's plenty of room for you to move around. Different brands have different roles. They're supportive of you finding your career path here." What's a boon for some can be frustrating for others; "everybody's experience [in this program] is different. People anticipate this super-structured program, but the first few weeks into the program, you realize the beauty of it is making it what you want. For some people, this [may] not be what they're looking for. Some people need more guidance."

Attrition

L'Oréal's Management Development Program has only been up and running for a few years. Attrition has been minimal since the program's inception.

Best and Worst

The company writes, "If you look at many of our top managers worldwide, many began their career at L'Oréal as entry-level employees. In fact, our last two global CEOs were recruited on campus."

LYONDELL
ENGINEER DEVELOPMENT PROGRAM

"A typical day in the life of a new-hire production engineer is devoted primarily to learning the unit to which you've been assigned. The more you learn, the more responsibility you take on."

The Big Picture

Lyondell is a huge chemical and polymer producer; its products provide the building blocks, literally, for automobiles, houses, clothing, food packaging, home furnishings, and many other consumer goods. Through its Engineer Development Program, Lyondell brings aboard freshly-minted chemical, electrical, mechanical, and safety engineers. The five-year program is rotational, with engineers switching jobs every eighteen to twenty-four months.

LOCATION(S) WHERE ENTRY-LEVEL EMPLOYEES WORK

Company headquarters are in Houston, Texas; the company also has operations on five continents. According to an HR official, "Entry-level engineers often work at U.S. manufacturing facilities located in Texas, Louisiana, Iowa, Illinois, Ohio, Pennsylvania, and Maryland."

AVERAGE NUMBER HIRED PER YEAR

Lyondell hires 26 entry-level employees each year.

ENTRY-LEVEL POSITION(S) AVAILABLE

"Lyondell seeks chemical, mechanical, electrical, and safety engineers to fill various entry-level full-time roles in maintenance-, reliability-, process-, project-, safety- and production-engineering capacities."

AVERAGE HOURS WORKED PER WEEK

New hires work 40 hours per week.

PERCENTAGE OF ENTRY-LEVEL HIRES STILL WITH THE COMPANY AFTER THREE, FIVE, AND TEN YEARS

Eighty-eight percent of entry-level hires remain with the company after three years, and 75 percent stay on past the five-year mark.

AVERAGE STARTING SALARY

Lyondell offers employees worldwide a "total compensation package that includes premium pay and benefits."

Getting Hired

Lyondell "actively recruits [new hires] from thirteen colleges," including Clemson, Georgia Tech, Purdue, University of Texas, Texas A & M, and Rice; the company notes that "students from other schools can express interest in working at Lyondell by visiting the college recruiting section of our website." Lyondell seeks out "results-oriented team players" who "thrive on change, communicate effectively, take prudent business risks, challenge [one another] to improve, treat [one another] with respect, and operate safely and responsibly with a focus on integrity." Interviews, according to one successful hire, "are a two-part process. For me, the first part was an on-campus interview with one of the senior engineers. I recall how impressed I was with the company sending other engineers to interview new-hire engineers. Previous companies that I had interviewed with often sent people from their HR department who had very little technical knowledge and were not able to identify with me or my interests at all. The interview was a behavioral interview that focused more on soft skills than [on] technical knowledge. The interview was very relaxed and felt like a conversation the majority of the time. I found out later that evening that I would be invited back for an on-site interview. I remember being very impressed with the quick response and high level of personal attention I was getting. About a month later, I was on a plant visit for the second round of interviews. At the plant, I interviewed with an HR representative, one of the plant superintendents, and a plant manager. In addition, I had lunch with two other engineers who worked at different plants. All of my interviews were behaviorally-based. Later that week, I had dinner with another Rice graduate who worked at the company. The following day, I received a phone call from the HR representative at the plant notifying me of my offer."

Money and Perks

"Salary is not negotiable" for starting engineers at Lyondell because the company "pays all employees of the same grade level the same salary, with a multiplier included paying those who have been at that level for a while more than those who just reached that level." "Dialog," Lyondell's term for "face-to-face, purposeful, and results-oriented discussions focused on enhancing performance and achieving business results," takes the place of traditional performance reviews. It "encourages continuous feedback among employees, supervisors, colleagues, and peers." Entry-level employees are eligible for a promotion as soon as six months after hire. Raises are also given "if the market reference for a position increases." Stellar perks include the flexible work schedule, which allows a nine-day, eighty-hour work week (in which employees work eighty hours in nine days and then receive the tenth day off), and 6 percent stock matching program.

The Ropes

Work at Lyondell begins with "a two-day orientation involving corporate philosophy, policies, and benefits. At the plant, there is a written process [that outlines] types of training and topics to be addressed in the first day, week, month, year, etc. This process details training through the first five years of experience." This is followed by "a two-week course [that provides further instruction] about Lyondell's engineer development program and operational excellence, and Lyondell's process for driving continuous improvement in our operations." Subsequent training "is typically informal" and is conducted "one-on-one with peers."

Day in the Life

Young engineers start their Lyondell careers in the Engineer Development Program, which spreads eighteen-to-twenty-four month rotational assignments over each new hire's first five years with the company. Engineers here love how quickly the program integrates them into essential and challenging functions. One production engineer writes, "We were given unit responsibilities almost immediately. Granted, you rely heavily on the specialist, the operators, and other engineers until you've learned the unit to the extent that you can make decisions about operations, etc. A typical day in the life of a new-hire production engineer is devoted primarily to learning the unit to which you've been assigned. The more you learn, the more responsibility you take on." A process engineer adds, "When I was hired, there was a multimillion dollar project going on that was going to replace the existing control system with a newer-generation one. I became an integral part of that project team when one of the principal engineers working on the project left the company. The project was completed very successfully."

Peers

Engineers at the Lyondell's home office in Houston report a huge social network of first jobbers. One writes, "There is a lot of socializing among the new hires at the company. We often go out after work and on the weekends. Many of us live in the same area and have all come from a variety of places. There [are also many] co-ops and interns who participate in the after-hours social scene." Employees also praise the company for hiring "some of the most talented people [just] out of school. They are intelligent, hard working, and team oriented. These are very impressive people and great friends." Away from the home office, though, the ranks of young hires are somewhat thinner; one newbie explains, "Because I'm located away from [headquarters] in Houston, there is only one other young engineer I talk to regularly. But when I go to Houston for training, I meet with all the other young engineers I've met in the company (through training), and we have lunch or dinner."

Moving on

Lyondell is a company at which employees hope to stay for a long time; retirement is the number one reason folks stop working here, according to the company. "Continued education" and "personal reasons" are numbers two and three on the list. One first jobber reports that "less happy workers sometimes complain about the workload. We do have a lot of responsibility and a lot of work. Lyondell intentionally operates lean, [and that's] great for those of us who enjoy challenges and responsibility. This is certainly not a job for someone who is looking to slack off, though. The level of responsibility and demands in this job require strong prioritization skills and careful communication with supervisors."

Attrition

A negligible number of first jobbers fail to complete their first year at Lyondell, the company informs us, adding that "71 percent of entry-level employees stay with the company for at least six years."

Best and Worst

"Dan Smith, President and Chief Executive Officer of Lyondell, is the company's most successful entry-level employee," writes our correspondent in HR, daring you to try to top this example: "Smith began working for Atlantic Richfield Co. (ARCO) as a co-op while attending Lamar University. Following his graduation in 1968, he was hired as a full-time engineer. By 1994, Smith was president of Lyondell, and he rose to CEO two years later."

MARLABS
HR ASSOCIATES, RECRUITERS, IT CONSULTANTS

"Throughout an employee's tenure here, Marlabs provides "multiple vehicles for the continuing education and training of our consulting staff."

The Big Picture

Marlabs, a full-service provider that offers "outsourced application development, managed services, and professional services" works with clients in the health care, pharmaceutical, life sciences, technology, and financial industries and also addresses a number of retail and manufacturing concerns. Founded in 1996, Marlabs now employs more than 400 people, the majority of whom hold graduate degrees. The company is growing fast and is building a reputation for being a place where go-getters can advance fairly quickly through the ranks. In 2005, Marlabs was named one of the "Fifty Best Places to Work in New Jersey" by NJBIZ (in partnership with the New Jersey State Chamber of Commerce).

LOCATION(S) WHERE ENTRY-LEVEL EMPLOYEES WORK

Marlabs has offices in Edison, New Jersey (sales and marketing); Cheyenne, Wyoming (regional office, development and training); Allentown, Pennsylvania (development and training headquarters); Austin, Texas (data center); Bangalore, India (global development center); and other sites.

AVERAGE NUMBER OF APPLICATIONS EACH YEAR

Marlabs receives 700 applications per year.

AVERAGE NUMBER HIRED PER YEAR

Marlabs hires about 125–150 entry-level employees each year.

ENTRY-LEVEL POSITION(S) AVAILABLE

Marlabs hires entry-level employees as human resources associates, recruiters, and IT consultants.

AVERAGE HOURS WORKED PER WEEK

New hires work 40 hours per week.

PERCENTAGE OF ENTRY-LEVEL HIRES STILL WITH THE COMPANY AFTER THREE, FIVE, AND TEN YEARS

Ninety-nine percent of entry-level hires remain with the company after five years. The average tenure of a Marlabs first jobber is, according to an HR official, seven to eight years.

AVERAGE STARTING SALARY (BY POSITION)

HR associates earn $25,000 per year; recruiters earn $40,000 per year; and IT consultants earn $50,000+ per year.

Getting Hired

Marlabs posts job openings on its website; and it cross-posts those listings at other major job websites. Applicants may apply via e-mail and are encouraged to indicate the desired position in the header of the message and then attach their resumes and cover letters. Successful candidates are those who are "trustworthy, flexible, and hard-working" and who "do their homework before they come in for their interviews. Great interviewees arrive having studied our website and [know] all about Marlabs and the position they are applying for." Poor candidates "are not at all prepared, know nothing about Marlabs, are not personable, and cannot answer our questions even though they appear on paper to have the appropriate background." One successful hire in HR reports "I had no background in HR whatsoever. I had two interviews. One was with my immediate boss, and the second was with his boss. During the interview, they were asking about my experience and why they should accept me for the job position. I had no experience, so I just told them that I really would like to work here. They liked the fact that I didn't have any experience. They wanted to be able to teach me what [to do]. Also, we talked about my schooling. I graduated high school and only have attended some college classes. We talked about starting college again and what I wanted to go for. I really wanted the job. The environment here is great; [there are many] wonderful, friendly people who are very professional, yet also very caring."

Money and Perks

Marlabs, according to its website, "offers challenging assignments, competitive salaries, and career opportunities including promotions within the organization. Marlabs provides a positive appraisal process and an open-door policy. A strong benefits package and positive work environment foster a positive attitude toward Marlabs and give employees the stability they require while performing assignments." Employees are evaluated once a year or when they earn a new assignment—"whichever comes first." Raises are merit-based. Asked to name the best fringe benefit of working here, one Marlabs employee reported that "We celebrate every employee's birthday with a cake and pizza."

The Ropes

New hires at Marlabs "receive training in a lot of areas." One human resources first jobber writes, "I was trained in the legal aspect, finance aspect, and HR aspect. I was taught about formatting resumes, posting resumes, payroll, contracts and agreements, medical and dental insurance, general liability and workers' compensation insurance, filing for visas, employment verification letters, etc." Throughout an employee's tenure here, Marlabs provides "multiple vehicles for the continuing education and training of our consulting staff. We offer training courses conducted by various professional institutes in addition to our tuition reimbursement program." Marlabs uses Learning Tree International, DevelopMentor, Oracle, and Microsoft training systems.

Day in the Life

Marlabs hires first jobbers in three areas. HR associates "handle all human resources activities with regard to legal, finance, contracts, bonuses, and payroll." One first jobber in this position writes, "My responsibilities were to e-mail consultants for updated information, send birthday cards/e-greetings, collect timesheets, keep records of payroll changes, prepare new hire packages, etc. A normal day would consist of sending and replying back to dozens of e-mails. I get all types of e-mails about timesheets, payroll issues, client changes, updates, etc. I answer tons of phone calls, and in between, get contracts signed and sent back to clients. That is a typical day." Recruiters do exactly what their job title indicates; they help Marlabs find top engineers and technicians in their fields. IT consultants study the IT systems of clients and make suggestions about how to improve their efficacy.

Peers

With a majority of its workforce holding graduate degrees, it's safe to say that Marlabs employees are "extremely smart. They have so much knowledge about things I don't even know," writes one first jobber, adding, "I learn things from them every day I am with the company." Employees also praise the friendly, unpretentious work environment that Marlabs provides.

Attrition

Relatively few new hires—1 percent, according to our sources in Marlabs HR—leave before a year is out. Those who leave do so because they "find permanent positions in another company" or for personal reasons, such as relocation.

MERCK
VARIOUS POSITIONS

"Working at Merck Research is like trying to take a drink of water from a fire hydrant—you need to soak up as much as you can!"

The Big Picture

Big pharmaceuticals is big business, and Merck is one of the biggest pharmaceuticals there is. This is a place where you can parlay a degree in the sciences or engineering into a fulfilling and lucrative career. There are also plenty of opportunities to sell drugs—legal ones, that is.

LOCATION(S) WHERE ENTRY-LEVEL EMPLOYEES WORK

Engineering and science positions are available in New Jersey, Pennsylvania, Massachusetts, North Carolina, Virginia, and Washington state; sales positions are available nationwide.

AVERAGE NUMBER HIRED PER YEAR OVER THE LAST TEN YEARS

Merck hires 350 entry-level employees per year.

AVERAGE HOURS WORKED PER WEEK

New hires work 40 hours per week.

BENEFITS OFFERED

"Health care benefits include medical, vision, dental, health, and dependent care accounts; short- and long-term disability; life insurance; long-term care; and financial planning benefits. Additional benefits include a 401(k) plan, a pension plan, [a] mentoring program, paid vacation/holidays, and [a] flexible work arrangement. On-site services include cafeteria, coffee bar, health services, fitness center, dry cleaning, credit union, gift and sundries store, mailing services, and child care."

CONTACT INFORMATION

Visit the website at www.merck.com/careers.

Getting Hired

Merck targets schools that "meet its hiring requirements based [on its] business needs (i.e., science, engineering, information technology, etc.)," but through its website the company accepts applications from all college graduates. Many of the first jobbers we spoke with had a previous relationship or experience with Merck: Some people had previously served summer internships, and others made connections through their college professors. One newbie we spoke with who didn't take either of these routes presented a strong background in her chosen field. Here's how she puts it: "Marketing of vaccines has a public health emphasis, so my joint degree in business and public health made me a perfect fit (for the available job). To prepare, I visited Merck's website and learned all about their products. I made sure to understand how I was differentiated compared to other candidates based on my public health background, and I communicated that in my resume and interviews. The interviews were very conversational. There were a few case questions [behavior based] and many questions requesting that I give examples from past experience."

Money and Perks

Starting salary at Merck is somewhat negotiable, depending on the skills and background a new hire brings to the company. Advanced academic work and previous work experience in the field should provide some leverage in these negotiations. In addition to base salary, new hires are eligible for financial rewards such as incentive (bonus) pay and future-oriented offerings such as stock options. Other perks include educational assistance programs which provide financial support for higher education as well as matching gift programs for employee giving. The start date, all our survey respondents agree, is highly negotiable. The coolest fringe benefit, according to newbies, is the flex-time arrangement: "They don't care when you do it, as long as the work is getting done; I could decide not to work every Wednesday if I wanted to. It comes [down to the fact] that they completely trust everyone to perform and deliver."

The Ropes

Merck's new hires waste little time getting to work. One reports, "The orientation was very quick. I had an administrative orientation on the first day, but was then immediately introduced to my supervisor and the research group. Within one week I was running experiments." Afterward, training occurs primarily on the job. One scientist explains, "I got basic safety training from our safety officer and then received training on laboratory techniques from a colleague at my level. This colleague was referred to as 'my buddy'. The buddy-system was very effective; initially we did all [the] experiments together to ensure that my techniques met Merck standards. My supervisor also provided some basic analysis training." In some areas, formal training sessions are also part of the indoctrination process.

Day in the Life

Merck is a huge company; while primarily engaged in research, the company requires a substantial support network to handle human resources, payroll, sales, and other essential functions. For employees in the glamorous research field, every day is an adventure: "Given the proprietary nature of our job, it's difficult for me to provide an example [of what I do]. However, my responsibility includes developing a portion of a manufacturing process that would be used in producing an HIV vaccine. The work was challenging, and I did not necessarily work under another engineer—it was my primary responsibility, and I was expected to drive the development. Working at Merck Research is like trying to take a drink of water from a fire hydrant—you need to soak up as much as you can!" Employees in the less glamorous areas—we spoke with one person in payroll—also find their work challenging and fulfilling; our respondent says, "A former compensation analyst was transitioning into a new role approximately three months after I came on board. I slowly became a point of contact for people in the division concerning compensation-related matters. I was also given more projects with more complexity and became more challenged in my analytical and leadership abilities. My manager began to give me increased autonomy, meaning he would give me a project and expect me to deliver with minimal supervision."

Peers

Many Merck entry-level employees tell us that the company supports "a large social scene because so many of [the new hires] are so young. There is a large group of people [who] are less than thirty years old. There is a great sense of camaraderie, and these people have evolved into true friends. [They] routinely hang out together; [they] feel like [they are] back in school, and all of [them] are in the same lab." One first jobber writes, "Many of us were new to the area where we work; therefore we tended to socialize after work to help one another become acclimated. The great thing is that I got to meet people who like to do a variety of things and are very open-minded to my suggestions and those of others."

Moving on

Though Merck does not have an official first-job program, it offers rotational plans for new college and business school grads in human resources, information services (IT systems), manufacturing, and sales and marketing. People who come on board do so expecting to start and build careers at Merck or with a related business.

Best and Worst

When asked about the best example of an entry-level hire, company representatives said, "Roy Vagelos was an intern and became our chief executive officer."

Miami Teaching Fellows
Teaching Fellow

"Teaching is a profession that does not enable anyone to be bored during any period of time. Every second of every workday is filled with opportunities to [have an] impact [on] students' lives, [both] in and out of the classroom."

The Big Picture

The Miami Teaching Fellows is "a program created specifically to bring in a cohort of high-quality new teachers, or fellows, every year." The program "helps address [the] persistent teacher shortages [that] districts face, especially in critical-need subject areas like math, science, and special education." Teaching fellows "receive their Florida state certificate as they teach," by completing course work in addition to fulfilling their teaching duties. The job requires nine months of very hard work, but the vacations are long and the personal rewards enormous.

Location(s) Where Entry-level Employees Work

Teaching positions are located in Miami, Florida.

Average Number of Applications Each Year

The program receives about 1,045 applications each year.

Average Number Hired Per Year

The program hires 50–100 Fellows each year.

Entry-level Position(s) Available

Those hired achieve the title of Teaching Fellow.

Average Hours Worked Per Week

Employees work about 40 to 50 hours per week.

Average Starting Salary

The starting salary for fellows is the same as that for all beginning teachers in the Miami-Dade County Public Schools. The minimum base salary is $34,200. Bonuses are granted to those working at certain sites, those holding an education-related master's degree, and those who teach math, science, and special education.

Getting Hired

Recruiters for the Miami Teaching Fellows program "want people with little or no teaching experience who are driven to succeed. We want people who have excelled as students and who want to do something that matters." Successful candidates are "committed to having a positive effect on student achievement; display excellence in their previous endeavors; and are dedicated to challenging, reaching, and influencing students—especially those in under-resourced areas—on a daily basis." Unsuccessful candidates "lack commitment, flexibility, or respect for the students and local communities in which fellows work." The application process is demanding. Applicants must submit an application, a personal statement, and academic transcripts. Those who impress recruiters are invited to interview. Here's how the interviews work, according to one current Fellow: "The first part of the interview was a five-minute teaching sample. They let us know ahead of time what to expect, and they were very honest about everything. Communication before and after was very good. After sharing my teaching sample in front of the other nine candidates (very nerve-wracking!), we had a group discussion, a small-group discussion, and a personal interview. A woman from Teach For America interviewed me. She mostly asked situational questions and asked me to rate myself on the teaching sample. It was not a hard interview; but the whole day [had been] stressful, so by the time I got there, I was tired! It was very professional. The interviewer wrote the whole time, but made sure to look up and smile a lot, [and that] seriously helped." After these interviews, candidates are notified of their status within two weeks. To finalize the process, "candidates must pass state teacher tests before entering the classroom as teachers."

Money and Perks

Teaching Fellows' salaries are set by the Miami-Dade County Public School system and are nonnegotiable. Most other aspects of the job are similarly inflexible; as one Fellow points out, "We have to be at work for the training, then teach summer school, and then be ready by August, so we can start school!" There is room to negotiate the school to which one is assigned, as "each Fellow has the opportunity to interview with just about any school in the district with teaching vacancies and choose the most appropriate placement." The best perks, Fellows agree, are the "winter, spring, and summer vacations!" Some say "the hours are great," though they admit that "we put in a lot of outside hours!" The free medical coverage is also considered a huge plus.

The Ropes

The Miami Teaching Fellows program puts new hires on the fast-track to teaching with a "six-week training [program] that starts in early June." The training consists of two parts: morning classroom teaching and observation during summer school, and veteran teacher-led afternoon sessions that focus on instruction design, effective teaching strategies, student behavior management, and diversity and culture awareness. One fellow explains, "At first, we sat in training classes for eight hours and learned how to teach" by reviewing "classroom scenarios, classroom management, laws in education (federal and state), student/teacher praxis, and pedagogy and formulation of curricula." After two weeks, "We started working part-time in summer school classes." One fellow writes, "It was a pretty okay experience, [though] I wish we could have worked more in the classrooms and [spent] less time taking notes."

Day in the Life

"Teaching is a profession that does not enable anyone to be bored during any period of time," observes one Miami Teaching Fellow. "Every second of every workday is filled with opportunities to [have an] impact [on] students' lives, [both] in and out of the classroom. Teachers [must attend] meetings with their colleagues, administrators, parents, and students; plan lessons; decorate classrooms; hold detentions; [and participate in] reading, training, etc." Quite a few program participants work with the learning-disabled; one writes, "I am responsible for seventeen learning-disabled students, and I teach them reading and math. I do reading for two-and-a-half hours and math in small groups for an hour each. I am still learning how to fulfill all of my obligations and how to get things done for my students so that they can learn. It's a struggle every day!" Be prepared for there to be "times when the job feels overwhelming." One Fellow cautions, "Because I was so new to everything, it took me double the time to write lesson plans, learn transitions, and deal with classroom management." Fortunately, "After a month or two in the classroom, it fell into place and was easier and quicker. Experience comes with time."

Peers

Fellows are scattered throughout the Miami-Dade school system, so program participants don't see [one another] on a daily basis. They do participate in "happy hour meetings, cocktail parties, and barbecues and other social gatherings." These "allow Fellows the opportunity to exchange ideas and interact in different settings." One Fellow writes, "The camaraderie goes much further beyond happy hours. We meet to have parties at houses, go to the beach together, and go to malls and movies. We're a bunch of like-minded adults switching professions or right out of college who understand each another."

Moving on

The program is too new for there to be much data on where former fellows go. Program managers report that "the expectation is that the individuals who become teachers through this program will be in the classroom for years to come."

Attrition

"Those who leave the Miami Teaching Fellows Program to date have cited personal reasons (moving from the city) as well as challenges at their school placement," program managers tell us.

Best and Worst

According to program managers, successful teachers tend to enjoy spending time in the classroom and seek to assign their students meaningful, growth-inducing tasks that will foster their development.

MINDBRIDGE
VARIOUS POSITIONS

"Mindbridge is great for self-starters who want a lot of responsibly immediately."

The Big Picture

Mindbridge sells IntraSmart, an "intranet software suite" that "helps companies share information and knowledge" and leads to "improved collaboration resulting in the kind of teamwork that is necessary to dramatically increase productivity." The company works with organizations that range from nonprofits to government agencies and from hospitals to midsize and large corporations, and it is currently developing a more economical product for small businesses. And it's also hiring; Mindbridge "is currently undergoing a period of rapid growth" that has it "looking for talented and enthusiastic people." Entry-level jobs are available in sales, web development, and graphic design.

LOCATION(S) WHERE ENTRY-LEVEL EMPLOYEES WORK

The company's headquarters are located in Norristown, Pennsylvania (near Philadelphia).

AVERAGE NUMBER OF APPLICATIONS EACH YEAR

Mindbridge receives 500–750 applications each year.

AVERAGE NUMBER HIRED PER YEAR

Mindbridge hires 55 entry-level employees per year.

ENTRY-LEVEL POSITION(S) AVAILABLE

Entry-level employees work as graphics designers, sales assistants, web developers, and sales engineers.

AVERAGE HOURS WORKED PER WEEK

Entry-level hires work 50 hours per week.

PERCENTAGE OF ENTRY-LEVEL HIRES STILL WITH THE COMPANY AFTER THREE, FIVE, AND TEN YEARS

Seventy percent are still with Mindbridge after three years; 60 percent remain after five years; and half of the entry-level hires stay with the company for ten or more years.

BENEFITS OFFERED

Mindbridge offers medical and dental benefits that vest immediately. Additional benefits include life insurance and stock options, both of which are also available immediately.

CONTACT INFORMATION

Applicants should send resumes and cover letters to hr@mindbridge.com.

Getting Hired

HR holds in-person interviews at their Norristown, Pennsylvania office every Tuesday and Wednesday between 10:00 A.M. and 12:00 P.M. These are open interviews; slots are allocated on a first come, first serve basis. According to employees, Mindbridge "does not discriminate based on where you went to school or even if you went to school," the company tells us, noting that "we have hired PhDs, and we have hired people who have not graduated [from] high school." As a general rule, Mindbridge "looks for smart people" but "tries to avoid prima donnas." Available positions are posted at the company's website. First jobbers here often enter the company via internships or co-ops and then parlay these experiences into post-graduation jobs. One such hire explains, "I wanted to work at Mindbridge badly, but I did not have the skill set they wanted, so I took an internship and they trained me on the job. I appreciate how this company gave me a shot when other companies passed on me."

Interviews focus on practical matters. An HR rep writes, "We always ask technical people how many computers they own or have owned. We get them to talk about the make and model, what they did with the computers, and what programs they ran on them. We want people who are intellectually curious; these questions break the ice and start a dialog. People who have a lot of computers or have had them in the past generally do very well here." Want to be the best interview ever at Mindbridge? According to HR, you'll have to top the guy who "came in with a piece of code that we actually used in one of our products." Avoid the mistake made by the "worst interview performance" ever here, during which "the applicant physically struck an HR person."

Money and Perks

Full-time positions at Mindbridge offer "competitive salary and a benefits package that includes stock ownership plans, a stock option plan, medical insurance, free parking, and snacks and beverages." Full-time employees are also eligible "to share a percentage of revenue for products that they have worked on." Contract jobs offer fewer benefits, though even contract workers enjoy "free ice cream, water, and beer at all times," as well as "free lunch on Fridays" and "some sort of afternoon activity on Fridays that is free to all employees." One first jobber writes, "Summers are fun because it's not as hectic here. And we have casual Fridays, which is nice."

The Ropes

Fresh hires at Mindbridge are "thrown to the wolves to sink or swim," according to one first jobber. Indeed, an HR official reports that newbies "are usually put on some type of project immediately." One graphics designer writes, "I learned more in my first six months on the job than I did during four years as an undergraduate." Another new hire adds, "Mindbridge is great for self-starters who want a lot of responsibly immediately."

Day in the Life

First jobbers at Mindbridge work in a variety of positions. Graphics designers "design web-based graphics for IntraSmart," a job that requires "a strong graphics art and web design background and an ability to work effectively with team members." One young designer notes, "There's a lot of grunt work, but everyone does it, from management all the way down to entry-level. At the end of the day, no one is above doing what has to be done." Newbies in sales and marketing are needed for a wide range of jobs, including telemarketing and web design. Technical hires work on developing web applications and Middleware components; their chores require knowledge of HTML, Java, JavaScript, and SQL, as well as good communications skills and the ability to work well with others. They also require a lot of determination; one technician notes, "This place is a pressure cooker. It is Darwinism at its best and worst."

Peers

Like many other modern tech companies, Mindbridge is the type of place that attracts "really smart people" who are "somewhat cool." There is "a lot of camaraderie among the first jobbers," as well as "a big after-hours social scene."

Moving on

Mindbridge is not for everyone. Some who leave here "go on to start their own businesses or go to a larger company." An HR representative reports, "We actually help place some of them at other companies, if they request that we do so."

Attrition

First jobbers typically last about five years at Mindbridge. About one in ten doesn't stay on past the demanding first year.

MONITOR GROUP
CONSULTANT

"Monitor is very much a meritocratic culture where success is driven by performance, not seniority. I feel an amazing potential for growth and genuinely think I have had a steep trajectory at Monitor to date."

The Big Picture

Soon after picking up their undergraduate diplomas, the Monitor Group's new hires have the chance to become integral players at a collective of consulting firms "dedicated to providing products and services which fundamentally enhance the competitiveness" of its clients. Young employees have the opportunity to interact with colleagues at all levels of the company, as well as the clients that the company serves. These interactions prepare Monitor's first jobbers to move up the company ladder or to test themselves with other firms in the industry. One rookie admits, "I sometimes do feel overwhelmed with the responsibility I am entrusted with so early on in my career." Responsibility, however, is earned at Monitor. "When you first start, your module leader provides lots of guidance on research, slide design, and work flow. After you start to prove yourself on a case team, you're given more and more responsibility and begin to take ownership over specific aspects of the work."

LOCATION(S) WHERE ENTRY-LEVEL EMPLOYEES WORK

New hires work in Cambridge, Massachusetts; New York, New York; Chicago, Illinois; Los Angeles and San Francisco, California. International opportunities are available as well.

AVERAGE NUMBER OF APPLICATIONS EACH YEAR

The Monitor Group receives up to 4,000 applications each year.

AVERAGE NUMBER HIRED PER YEAR OVER THE LAST TEN YEARS

Traditionally, the Monitor Group brings in 40 to 50 fresh college graduates each year.

ENTRY-LEVEL POSITION(S) AVAILABLE

Entry-level workers serve as consultants, working on "various client-facing and internal case teams."

AVERAGE HOURS WORKED PER WEEK

Different projects require different time investments. This said, new hires work an average of 60 hours per week.

PERCENTAGE OF ENTRY-LEVEL HIRES STILL WITH THE COMPANY AFTER THREE, FIVE, AND TEN YEARS

Though Monitor does not keep official data on the average length of employee tenure, it does note that "many undergrads stay longer than two to three years because they gain the opportunity to try different types of consulting domains or focus on areas that are of greater interest."

AVERAGE STARTING SALARY

Beginners can expect a salary ranging from the mid-$50,000s to the low $60,000s. New hires also receive signing bonuses and moving expenses.

BENEFITS OFFERED

All employees receive full medical, dental, and vision coverage, as well as a 401(k) plan and a generous allotment of paid vacation days.

CONTACT INFORMATION

For further information or contact details, visit www.Monitor.com.

Getting Hired

"Monitor recruits at a number of top colleges across the country, holding interviews on campus," company officials explain. "For those schools where we do not have an active presence, candidates are encouraged to apply through our website and will need to visit a Monitor office for their first-round interview. Standards for off-campus selection are as selective as those for our on-campus efforts." While "there is no single determining factor when screening applicants," Monitor is seeking "incredibly well-rounded candidates, with strong academic performance and positions of leadership in work and extracurricular activities. Strong analytical skills and comfort with numbers, as well as an agile and creative mind, are critical components to a successful candidate, as are interactive skills and a demonstrated work ethic. Our recruiting process is also designed to determine the level of fit between Monitor's core values and the candidate. Monitor's core values include openness to learning, integrity, and passion." The hiring process involves several rounds of interviews, beginning with "an hour-long first round interview, the bulk of which entails a case interview, with some time spent discussing the candidate's background." Rounds two and three each entail "a group case exercise, a scenario role-play exercise, and a feedback conversation on the day's performance, with the hope that all candidates interviewing with Monitor will have an opportunity to learn from their experience." One newbie warns, "The case interviews can be tough. Of all the interviews I had while going through recruiting, Monitor's was by far the most difficult, even among other consulting firms." He says that those who fare best in the case interviews are those who can "get through a lot of information and make sound recommendations very quickly."

Money and Perks

It's true that Monitor's employees are expected to work long hours right off the bat, but they are well paid for their efforts. On top of a healthy salary, "a new hire's compensation package for their first year of work typically includes a signing bonus, moving assistance . . . and a performance-driven year-end bonus." In addition, "employees are eligible for raises on an annual basis, determined by their historical and anticipated performance." As a second-year employee says, "Monitor is very much a meritocratic culture where success is driven by performance, not seniority. I feel an amazing potential for growth and genuinely think I have had a steep trajectory at Monitor to date." Other perks that please employees include the fact that the "week between Christmas and New Year's the company shuts down." And, of course, the "free soda and other drinks in the kitchen."

The Ropes

Monitor is determined not to leave its new hires adrift in the vast sea of corporate consulting—this wouldn't serve the needs of the employee or the company. Thus, training is taken quite seriously. Each fresh hire "is given a professional development advisor who is responsible for helping the entering consultant think about [his or her] career and its progression over time. They serve as an advocate for the consultant as well as a confidante." These advisors tend to be individuals with numerous years in the firm. There's also a standard orientation that brings all of North America's new hires to Cambridge, Massachusetts, for a week-long introduction to Monitor. As one new consultant describes, "It entails a series of modules about the firm, its strategy, our roles and other more 'tradecraft' (PowerPoint, Excel, brainstorming) sessions." Also, "at some point in their first eighteen months on the job" each newbie will complete a more job-specific, week-long training session. A third-year worker says that he "found this skills-based training to be very relevant to [his] day-to-day work, and a great way to get to better know the individuals in the marketing group."

Day in the Life

"What interested me about consulting is that you never exactly know what you're going to be doing," explains a first jobber. "That was true then and it is true now. The nature of what you do every day can be so different based on the project you're working on." According to the official company line, newly minted consultants can expect to "interact with case teams and clients at multiple levels; design qualitative and quantitative research tools; understand the client's market and customer base using online and offline tools (industry reports, annual reports, etc.); synthesize findings; manage and oversee outsourcing of the research process; analyze and model market data sets; [and] assist with the creation of presentations." Heavy workloads and unbendable deadlines are par for the course, and this sometimes causes the uninitiated (and even the veterans) to feel overwhelmed. One consultant admits, "There have undoubtedly been days and weeks where I worked far more hours than I might have liked or expected and times when I was not sure how I was going to meet the deadline I had in front of me. Despite this, I have found that there has never been a time when I was alone in this—where my team wasn't working just as hard, or where I felt I had nowhere to turn."

Peers

"Bright, down-to-earth, and fun to work with"—this is how one first jobber describes his colleagues. Another adds, "I have been consistently amazed by how intelligent, helpful, and collegial the individuals Monitor hires are, and feel very lucky to work in such a stimulating environment." Considering all the hours that these young consultants spend in the office, this sense of respect and camaraderie is a good thing. New hires frequently take these friendships outside of the office, too. "Our first-year class hangs out together pretty frequently," reports one. In essence, Monitor offers "a work-hard, play-hard environment." One employee sums up her feelings about her coworkers this way: "I really no longer call my work friends my 'work friends.' At this point they are just my friends, and people I feel very fortunate to have met."

Moving on

Employees depart Monitor for a range of reasons: to pursue additional schooling (particularly to earn an MBA), to pursue an area of business outside of Monitor's scope, to find a job with saner hours, or to take advantage of better compensation offered by a competitor.

Attrition

Employees express frustration over "the two-case model. As consultants at Monitor we are staffed on two cases at a time. The cases are supposed to be a fifty-fifty allocation, but inevitably one ends up taking up most of your time and it leads to very long working hours." The long hours can certainly take their toll. But as a consultant points out, "The amount of time we spend working . . . is more the industry than Monitor."

Best and Worst

Reflecting on Monitor's most successful entry-level employees over the years, company officials say, "If success is defined through impact on the company over time, many of our senior partners began in the 1980s and 1990s as entry-level consultants." And an example of a not-so-successful first jobber? "Shortly into his career a consultant [he] was let go for cheating on expenses." Enough said.

MONSTER
VARIOUS POSITIONS

monster
today's the day™

"Monster makes you feel at home and gives
you ample opportunities in different forums to learn what you need to do to
be successful."

The Big Picture

What distinguishes Monster from the rest? According to the company's website, it's a combination of "incredible vision, endless energy, unlimited creativity, steady profitability, and the simple fact that we believe life is way too short not to enjoy what you do today and every day." Monster's new hires assure us that the company's PR folks have it right. A first jobber says, "I loved the fact that Monster was an up-and-coming company that had a lot of young people and the good possibility of promotions within the company." The higher ups, too, get glowing reviews from the newbies: "I have had nothing but the best management here at Monster," says one. "I know this sounds cheesy, but I feel this is a huge part of why I am so happy with my job. So much of it is the people you work with and for."

LOCATION(S) WHERE ENTRY-LEVEL EMPLOYEES WORK

Entry-level employees work out of Tempe, Arizona; Maynard, Massachusetts; Indianapolis, Indiana; Milwaukee, Wisconsin.; Chicago, Illinois; Cincinnati, Ohio; Los Angeles and San Francisco, California.

ENTRY-LEVEL POSITION(S) AVAILABLE

While Monster hires entry-level employees to fill a variety of positions, the jobs most frequently available include associate internet recruitment consultants, accountants, business development representatives, client service associates, customer service representatives, and technology professionals. Each position comes with its own set of responsibilities; this said, all new hires have the chance to learn about the company's services, products, and values—oh, and its ability to balance work and fun.

AVERAGE HOURS WORKED PER WEEK

Recent college grads typically log 40 hours a week.

AVERAGE STARTING SALARY

Monster does not report an average starting salary. Among the new hires we spoke with, starting salaries were typically around $30,000 (excluding bonuses and other incentives).

BENEFITS OFFERED

The company offers all full-time employees medical, dental, and vision coverage. Additional benefits include life insurance, disability plans, flexible spending accounts, auto/homeowner insurance, a 401(k) savings plan, 21 days paid time off, paid maternity/paternity time off, paid bereavement leave, tuition reimbursement, and adoption assistance.

Getting Hired

Monster officials say that "students from any school can apply to our entry-level roles" by going to Monster.com and following the "Work at Monster" link at the bottom of the page. If an applicant's materials seem appropriate, the next step is a telephone screening, followed by a series of in-person meetings. The company also interviews "at colleges local to respective hiring offices, offering face-to-face meetings with hiring manager(s)." Wherever the interviews occur, applicants should expect a process that is "fairly laid-back" and "informal." A second-year employee at the company's Maynard, Massachusetts, headquarters describes her second (and final) interview like this: "I was taken to the Monster Den, which gave me a feeling of comfort due to colorful surroundings and people walking through and having lunch or playing pool or ping pong. The interview was more about my personal goals, how hard I was willing to work, and then an emphasis on what I had done throughout college, including work and intern experience." Another way to get a foot in the Monster door is to land an internship at the company. A designer with Monster recalls, "A friend of mine was hired by Monster as a designer out of college and encouraged me to apply as an intern. I did, and was granted the internship for a year, while still in college. After graduation, I re-interviewed and was hired full-time."

Money and Perks

"I have quadrupled my income since I began working here full-time in customer service," says an employee who's been with the company for more than two years. This experience is echoed by other first jobbers who promise that "there is always room to grow and advance within the company!" Advancement aside, Monster newbies say a plethora of perks keep them smiling. For instance, employee "prizes" include "a car or trip to all places around the world." Bonuses, tuition reimbursement, and employee discounts also make the list. Merit-based raises are handed out annually.

The Ropes

"The orientation process was perfect," a first jobber tells us. "Monster makes you feel at home and gives you ample opportunities in different forums to learn what you need to do to be successful. Whether it was through listening to other reps, 'lunch and learns' with executives, or formal training in classrooms where you receive prizes for answering questions right, it was fun and [the company] made it very easy to learn." One employee sums up her experience by saying simply, "The training was very impressive."

Day in the Life

Daily duties depend on the job. One employee admits, "I was often bored because a lot of my job was data-entry," while a colleague asserts, "My management did a great job with keeping me challenged." Often, entry-level workers spend a healthy part of the day on the telephone, talking to confused customers, prospective businesses, and others who utilize of Monster's services. Though new hires are not necessarily thrilled about "telemarketing"—which is what many entry-level positions here amount to—they promise that, "for the money you are making in an entry-level position, with the knowledge and motivation that you will eventually advance to a better role, you continue to work hard." And the company always has a cadre of trainers and coaches nearby, who are prepared to lend a helping hand if a new hire can't answer a customer's question. Says one very satisfied first jobber, "You never had to worry that you were by yourself as help was right behind you."

Peers

"The people [have] always been a major selling point of coming to the company and staying," beams a Monster employee. "I have [felt] and still do feel like the luckiest employee on earth!" A fellow Monsterite adds, "Everyone has such a great personality and there are so many people to learn from." At many company locations, this flood of on-the-job respect translates into plenty of after-work hanging out. As one internet recruitment consultant describes, "Everyone is friends with everyone and there are always social after-hours at local bars where everyone meets up."

Moving on

First jobbers typically leave Monster to take more suitable or lucrative opportunities with other companies. Employees often move on to other positions or locations within the company.

Attrition

If Monster employees can make it through those early days of entry-level phone work, data entry, etc., they enjoy terrific opportunities to climb the company's ladder quickly. This is exactly why so many people stick around. A first jobber, now in her sixth year, explains, "I started with the company in an entry-level position and moved up in level three times—but had the ability to change and challenge myself again about five times. My income has increased every year. . . . I am now making three to four times as much as I did with my first role. Everyday I am given new responsibilities here, which keeps it exciting."

Best and Worst

Monster officials say that their best entry-level hires have risen "from entry-level to managerial roles; most of these individuals moved through various parts of the company. There are several people that were here at the very beginning of Monster and have moved through the ranks. People who do well usually take charge of their career and make things happen." The Monster brass also recall an employee who "left on the first day of work during orientation. She showed up a week earlier than scheduled but it wasn't a problem. We put her in that week's orientation class just to begin things early. Halfway through the day, she decided to leave. She said she was very embarrassed. This anecdote highlights that those who can't roll with the punches may not do so well here."

NATIONAL CANCER INSTITUTE
VARIOUS POSITIONS

"Not only does my work matter to me and to my boss but it matters to the general public who is dependent on us to apply our knowledge in looking for a cure for cancer."

The Big Picture

An organization within the National Institutes of Health (NIH), the National Cancer Institute (NCI), conducts basic, clinical, and epidemiological cancer-related research. It also provides funding to academic institutions, cancer centers, and other organizations that conduct cancer research, treat patients, and provide educational materials to health providers and patients. NCI offers entry-level positions in a wide variety of areas, from lab work to administration. Satisfied employees feel their work has a "daily impact on people and the world," and they appreciate the "opportunity to develop and be [at the] frontiers of drug development in the oncology setting." Working with expert doctors and researchers, entry-level employees gain valuable, real-world experience in their positions.

LOCATION(S) WHERE ENTRY-LEVEL EMPLOYEES WORK

The National Cancer Institute operates out of three principal locations: Bethesda, Rockville, and Frederick, Maryland.

AVERAGE NUMBER OF APPLICATIONS EACH YEAR

Depending on the job description, NCI may receive anywhere from 5 to 50 applications for an entry-level position.

AVERAGE NUMBER HIRE PER YEAR OVER THE LAST TEN YEARS

Each year, on average, NCI hires 100 full-time federal employees, 250 summer interns, 100 one-year interns, and 400 postdoctoral fellows.

ENTRY-LEVEL POSITION(S) AVAILABLE

In addition to full-time administrative, clinical, and nursing positions, the National Cancer Institute operates several fellowship and internship programs designed to provide hands-on research experience to recent graduates planning to pursue an advanced degree in medicine or science. NCI also runs a summer internship program.

AVERAGE HOURS WORKED PER WEEK

On average, entry-level employees work 40 hours per week.

AVERAGE STARTING SALARY

Full-time entry-level employees with a BA or BS earn $30,000 to $40,000 annually; full-time entry-level employees with a doctorate earn $43,000 to $64,000 annually. Interns earn $25,000 to $35,000 annually.

Getting Hired

While eligibility for employment depends on the position you are applying for, there are several key qualities that NCI seeks in every applicant. These include a "commitment to the mission," the "ability to work as a team member," and a high level of motivation. Hiring managers also say they generally prefer candidates who "demonstrate quiet confidence [and] knowledge without conceit." As NCI is a branch of NIH, applicants warn that, "The application process for a government job can be quite daunting," requiring lots of paperwork and supporting documents. However, they reassure us that, once one makes it through the initial screening, interviews are relaxed and friendly. Thinking back on her experience, a new research fellow recalls, "The interview was really about their research, and just conversation. They were trying to get a good feeling of my personality to see if I would fit into the lab."

Money and Perks

"The National Cancer Institute has a salary table that includes . . . salary for the appropriate years of experience." However, the organization conducts salary and performance reviews twice a year. Not surprisingly, NCI offers excellent medical benefits. Employees in certain departments also have the ability to telecommute part of the time, or to work flexible hours. It's the small things that count, and employees also appreciate the free parking and the above-average cafeteria which serves Starbucks coffee.

The Ropes

Orientation begins before you set foot on the National Cancer Institute campus, as "every new employee is sent a huge packet of information that is to be completed as much as possible before you get to orientation." On their first day, new hires attend a short NIH orientation, followed by a short NCI orientation. After that, training is department-specific. For NCI fellows, on-the-job training and mentorships are major components of the program. A fellow tells us, "My boss was an excellent mentor and boss. I learned a lot from my mentor and my other colleagues. . . . The training that I received was from [a] laboratory technician who has more than fifteen years of experience in research." However, education and training is fundamental across NCI—not just within their educational programs. A research nurse specialist reports a particularly positive mentorship experience: "The second orientation was a hands-on mentor to help me learn my role as a research nurse. This mentor was also a research nurse assigned to work on my team. She was the rock I needed to learn my job as best as I could—I couldn't have done it without her." A contract specialist likewise attests to her high level of job-related education: "I received extensive training within and outside the organization. The training spanned the spectrum of training specific to my particular job as well as training related to the organization as a whole." As part of their education, "the junior staff are highly encouraged to attend high-level meetings to get exposure [to] and experience regarding the entire institute."

Day in the Life

On any given day, throughout the National Cancer Institute you'll find entry-level staff answering calls, staining slides, making rounds with inpatients, or participating in any number of important tasks within the organization. Each new employee—even those who have the same job title—spends their time differently. Many tell us that "each working day was different" in this dynamic environment. A health science analyst shares, "My duties vary depending on the project. I have chaired meetings, joined various work groups and ad-hoc committees, I have been a liaison between contract employees and our office." In contrast, from a research fellow, "An example of my typical day was running at least two SDS-polyacrylamide gels for Western Blotting, plating cells in ninety-six well plates, and helping the technician with other laboratory work." In addition to their work opportunities, fellows benefit from "the opportunity to conduct cancer research at the NCI with top-notch scientists, meeting new people from different countries, and the opportunity to present my research work at national conferences." Across the board, employees feel their work is making a significant contribution to the organization and to the greater good. Job satisfaction is high: "Not only does my work matter to me and to my boss but it matters to the general public who is dependent on us to apply our knowledge in looking for a cure for cancer."

Peers

"My peers are very intelligent and are always available if you need their guidance and or assistance," says a typical NCI employee. Indeed, it's easy to feel comfortable in this friendly, collaborative environment, where "the hospitality of the NIH workers is a 'ten' on a scale of one to ten." A contract specialist recalls her first day: "I was impressed with the warm welcome . . . [I] walked into a completely furnished office with supplies placed on to[p] of the desk and some of the best homemade cookies I have ever tasted." Staff enjoy "a great deal of camaraderie within the office" and try to keep the workplace cheerful through little gestures, like bringing "treats for staff meetings." Many employees also say they get together for happy hours and parties during their free time. A recent graduate of the fellowship program remembers, "My peers were very smart and helpful. I made a lot of friends in Maryland [among] not only post baccalaureate students . . . but also [the] postdocs, principal investigators, secretaries, and so on."

Moving on

While the exact numbers aren't available, NCI assures us that they have a very high retention rate, with a large percentage of staff making long careers at the facility. In some cases—such as positions in the fellowship program—a job at NCI can become "a stepping stone into medical school or a PhD program."

Attrition

Entry-level employees usually leave NCI to pursue an MD or an advanced degree. While many employees choose to stay on board for long careers, they may also take advantage of the opportunities to switch departments or change focus afforded by such a large organization. A current employee tells us, "I think there is plenty of room to grow at NIH. I think if you are a motivated person and want to grow and learn, you are in the right place. You can certainly [meet] goals to achieve and grow as much as you wish to."

Best and Worst

At NCI, success has a lot to do with the heart and soul you bring to your work. NCI says their best employees are "individuals who have a desire to work in public service and have a passion for the mission of the National Cancer Institute, [which is] to eliminate suffering and death due to cancer." On the other hand, those who aren't team players tend to suffer in this large, government-controlled environment. "NCI is not the best employer for individuals looking to make lots of money quick or be the one individual in the spotlight. While each person is given the opportunity to contribute fully and is recognized for excellence, there are few individual spotlight moments on the road to curing cancer."

NATIONAL PUBLIC RADIO
PRODUCTION ASSISTANT, EDITORIAL ASSISTANT, RESEARCH ASSISTANT, DEVELOPMENT ASSISTANT, AND ADMINISTRATIVE ASSISTANT

"There's always something going on in the office . . . Things are busy, but never overwhelming."

The Big Picture

If you've "always been interested in news media" and you're eager to work for "an internationally acclaimed producer and distributor of noncommercial news, talk, and entertainment programming," then look no further than National Public Radio (or, as it's often called, NPR). At NPR, there are newbies involved in nearly every aspect of the operation, including show production, segment editing, industry- and project-specific research, and fundraising. First jobbers say NPR offers them two great benefits: a strong professional foothold and an ongoing learning experience. A rookie research assistant heaps praise upon his more senior colleagues who "have been supportive in my development and have made me feel important even though I am the youngest in the division. From the first day, I felt like part of the team. [They] have been instrumental in my learning process." It's no wonder one new hire exclaims, "People love working for NPR—[they] are proud of it, as am I."

LOCATION(S) WHERE ENTRY-LEVEL EMPLOYEES WORK

Positions are primarily in Washington, DC. On occasion, new hires are placed in Culver City, California.

AVERAGE NUMBER OF APPLICATIONS EACH YEAR

Around 2,000 entry-level applications arrive annually.

AVERAGE NUMBER HIRED PER YEAR OVER THE LAST TEN YEARS

NPR fills about 26 entry-level positions each year.

ENTRY-LEVEL POSITION(S) AVAILABLE

First jobbers at NPR join the organization as production assistants, editorial assistants, research assistants, development assistants, and administrative assistants. As NPR officials tell us, production and editorial assistants "conduct research and assist editors, producers, and reporters," as well as perform an array of pre-production and programming tasks. Research assistants use the phone, the Web, and the mail to gather information for NPR's "carriage monthly surveys," which includes processing and interpreting data from surveys and outside sources. Development assistants provide "general administrative support" for NPR's fundraising efforts. And administrative assistants lend "administrative and computer support and coordination for departmental projects."

Getting Hired

NPR visits "a variety of colleges" for on-campus interviewing, but makes clear that "students from any campus who wish to be considered for an open position are welcome to submit their application materials to NPR." The organization is keen on up-and-comers who possess "strong communications, . . . organizational, . . . writing, and research skills; [are] team orientated; and work well in a fast-paced environment." The application process is a multilayered affair, initiated by simply submitting a resume and cover letter by post, e-mail, or fax. If the resume and cover letter do their job, several rounds of interviews come next. Here's how a development assistant describes her experience: "I had three rounds of interviews. One preliminary interview in the office, one phone interview with the manager of Major Gifts West, and [another] in the office, this time with the director of development. I was then called with a preliminary offer . . . it was about another two weeks until I received the official offer." Want to be well prepared? A research assistant recalls the following string of questions from his interviews:

- "Why do you want to work here?"

- "What are your strengths/weaknesses?"

- "Discuss a time where you were given little direction in a task and how you executed that plan."

- "How do you handle criticism?"

- "What are you hoping to gain from this position?"

- "What professional/academic accomplishment are you most proud of?"

Money and Perks

Starting salaries all depend on the job (see the "Stats" section above for details). Production and editorial assistants land on the high end of the scale, while administrative assistants occupy the low end. Each employee's performance is officially reviewed "once a year," and these reviews contribute to the "performance rating" that determines pay raises. Typically, increases in pay occur annually. The best fringe benefit? It's too hard to settle on just one, according to a newbie. So he offers us a list of his favorites: "Free evening/holiday/weekend parking at the underground parking lot right in downtown DC. Location right in the heart of DC next to the Verizon Center, shops, restaurants, and bars. Discounts at local businesses if I show my ID badge. Free access to the gym. Ultra-modern business furniture and lounge area. Access to studios. Kick-ass business cards."

The Ropes

"The orientation process was comprehensive and interesting," says a first jobber. "It spanned the three-month probationary period and entailed attending seminars covering HR benefits, facility services, IT services, company policies/procedures, harassment prevention training, and a company overview." A colleague with a different opinion on the matter describes orientation as a series of "long and boring sessions about benefits, time sheets, etc., but nothing practical that could be put to use on a daily basis." As for job-specific training, one assistant claims that this is dished out on "a need-to-know basis." The bulk of a new hire's training comes from supervisors and veteran colleagues. NPR also has a mentoring program in place. As NPR officials explain, "Mentoring matches are based on the content that the mentee is interested in, the experience of the potential mentors, [and] opportunities to connect people across divisions and establish working relationships that will help with cross-functional synergies. [We] also take into consideration time/availability, management styles, and interest of the employee to be matched with a particular mentor (and interest of the mentor to be matched with a particular employee)."

Day in the Life

What does a typical day for a newbie at NPR entail? "Everything!" says a frosh in the fundraising office. "Scheduling mass mailings, event coordination, travel, drafting correspondence. There is no typical day—except having more to get done than you can possibly do!" A fellow first jobber agrees that life at NPR can get a little hectic: "There's always something going on in the office. Sometimes I feel overwhelmed, but the atmosphere is always laid-back and never demanding. Things are busy, but never overwhelming." The specific tasks of a rookie depend on the area of concentration; this being said, all assistants serve as support staff to more senior colleagues in the department. Often, gathering and organizing information is a big part of the job. Yes, the tasks can get a little tedious at times. But, says a research assistant, "The work I help produce is very important to the company. I have seen the importance of the work my division generates and it is used by literally every other division" within NPR.

Peers

"You meet other newbies in the orientation process," says an assistant in his fifth month, "and there's a big social network amongst the newer workers. But we also welcome the seasoned veteran—we're not exclusive." One thing that young and old alike have in common is that "everyone is really passionate about NPR and there is always an interesting story to talk about." But while the obligations of home life often call away the older workers at the end of the day, "happy hours are frequent among the younger workers!" According to a rookie research assistant, the newbie crew is made up of people who "all have different interests, but are all genuine, deep-thinking people who are always curious to learn." And this makes them enjoyable to be around inside of the office as well as out.

Moving on

When first jobbers leave NPR, it's often to enroll in grad school or accept a competitive job offer with higher pay or better opportunities to move upward in their chosen area of concentration.

Attrition

On average, 13 percent of recent college graduates stay with NPR for less than 12 months. Some people grumble that "the lines of communication are not always open between the different departments in the company," which can make the workday frustrating. Others simply don't have the patience for the desk-bound grunt work that comes with the entry-level territory. As a one-year employee confesses, "[I] plan on leaving in three months to do something more adventurous. I am not happy sitting at a desk all day." Others are more than happy to endure a little new-hire drudgery, though. Why? As one explains, "I feel like there are many routes of upward mobilization within the division and within the company."

NETWORK APPLIANCE
VARIOUS POSITIONS

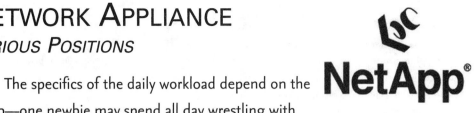

The specifics of the daily workload depend on the job—one newbie may spend all day wrestling with code and "the bug-tracking system," while another may devote his or her hours to "configuring hosts and filers" and "pulling wires and installing software."

The Big Picture

Network Appliance (or NetApp), is a leading provider of "storage solutions that deliver simplified data management, flexible and scalable storage infrastructure, comprehensive data protection, and reliable data access." The company attracts college graduates with degrees in engineering, computer science, and the like, offering them the chance to work with NetApp's vast network of professionals to provide "simple solutions to complex business problems."

LOCATION(S) WHERE ENTRY-LEVEL EMPLOYEES WORK

New college grads are eligible for positions in Sunnyvale or Redwood City, California; Research Triangle Park, North Carolina; Waltham, Massachusetts; and Pittsburgh, Pennsylvania. International placements are also available in Bangalore, India.

AVERAGE NUMBER OF APPLICATIONS EACH YEAR

Approximately 4,000 entry-level applications arrive at NetApp each year.

AVERAGE NUMBER HIRED PER YEAR OVER THE LAST FIVE YEARS

In 2007, NetApp expects to hire more than 100 new graduates.

ENTRY-LEVEL POSITION(S) AVAILABLE

The many areas in which recent grads can find openings at NetApp include "software, IT, finance, [and] marketing." Newbies often find their way into these openings by taking part in the Summer Intern Program, which "is specifically targeted at college students and recent college graduates." Company officials say, "The goal of this program is to fill our pipeline with new-graduate job candidates."

AVERAGE HOURS WORKED PER WEEK

New hires spend in excess of 40 hours per week on the job.

AVERAGE STARTING SALARY

According to NetApp, in 2006 "the average (50th percentile, or midpoint) starting salary for an individual with an Engineering BS [was] $75,000."

Getting Hired

Each year, NetApp recruits from a handful of universities: Berkeley, Brown, California State Polytechnic Institute, Carnegie Mellon, Clemson, Harvard, MIT, North Carolina State, Northeastern, San Jose State, and Stanford. This being said, the company also welcomes applications submitted through its website. NetApp officials offer a long list of qualities they look for in new hires; among them are integrity, trustworthiness, strong communication skills, self-motivation, intelligence, leadership capabilities, and a willingness to learn. The "typical interview process involves six to eight interviews," and these interviews can stretch over a long period of time—especially when candidates are first contacted while they're still in college. One first jobber says, "I initially interviewed six months prior to graduation. I spent a day interviewing about eight people overall. . . . The interviews were mostly standard—discussing school projects and such—but a couple were technical quizzes and design conceptualization/comprehension. I was told I'd hear back soon, but I didn't." In fact, it was four months before he was invited back for his next round of interviews. Though the interview process may seem grueling, those who have been through it say the interviews themselves are "pretty casual" and warn against going into them too uptight. A brand-new member of the technical staff notes that the applicants who didn't make the cut "were smart people who just had bad interviews because they were nervous." It's worth noting that many of the young NetApp employees we spoke with first joined the company through the Summer Intern Program; this, they say, worked well, because they "already knew what the position was about . . . prior to becoming full time."

Money and Perks

"I did not try to negotiate my salary," says a new hire. Why would he? First jobbers at NetApp start their careers with a healthy sum of money flowing to their bank accounts, and there's a good chance they'll see even more of the green stuff going forward. One young techie, who's only been on the job for five weeks, points out, "The average salary for a software engineer at NetApp (as published by Fortune magazine in 2006) is about $128,000, so that puts $48,000 between me and average." NetApp employees are given annual merit-based increases to their salary. When asked about perks, one rookie points to "the employee stock purchase plan that allows [him] to purchase stocks at a 15-percent discount," as well as the fact that NetApp matches "up to $3,000 on a $5,000 contribution to [his] 401(k)." Others beam about "flex work hours" (e.g., "total autonomy in setting my schedule"). But, says a first jobber, "the best perk we brag about is beer on Fridays."

The Ropes

The "new player" festivities are broken into several components. An employee in his second year explains, "The first part of orientation was the 'new hire orientation.' It was basically just a class where they went over company policies, legal issues, payroll issues, benefits, etc." A colleague also notes, "For most of my first week, I was instructed to read the 'Hitchhiker's Guide,' which is NetApp's everything-you-need-to-know document. I learned mostly about using NetApp's source-version control system and bug tracking system but also about company policy pertaining to things from conduct to coding standards." And these resources are only the beginning. Soon after new employees settle in, they participate in a one-day event called T.O.A.S.T. (or Training On All Special Things), where they "get to hear about company goals and directions. Top executives (including the CEO and President) come and talk about their views on the direction of the company and field questions from the new hires." One first jobber tells us, "This experience was extraordinary." During this same time, rookie engineers also participate in a training program called "Engineering 101, which is a three-day class that covers NetApp's technologies and provides an introduction to the source-code architecture at NetApp." And if all this isn't enough, "NetApp provides new engineering hires with a buddy, an experienced peer who helps with acclimation and clues them in on the miscellany they should 'just know.' The buddy system works well."

Day in the Life

A freshman engineer says that, in the early going, her primary responsibilities were "to learn as much as [she] could to come up to speed with the rest of the group." As this is accomplished, new hires ease into the day-to-day tasks of an entry-level employee. "Some of it is grunt work," admits a tech staffer who's been with NetApp for six months. But, he adds, "Some of it is really cool." The specifics of the daily workload depend on the job—one newbie may spend all day wrestling with code and "the bug-tracking system," while another may devote his or her hours to "configuring hosts and filers" and "pulling wires and installing software." Downtime comes with the territory. One employee explains, "Transition[s] in-between projects are often big voids." A concurring colleague admits, "Sometimes I get bored because I don't have anything to do. I feel like I have to pester people a lot to get them to give me more work." On the other hand, when a project picks up steam, the days can become overwhelming. "From time to time I was of course in over my head," a first jobber tells us. "That's how I learned to swim."

Peers

"Everyone loves NetApp," exclaims a junior employee—and this has a lot to do with the people. "Anyone in the company can ask anyone else in the company any question that they need answered and not only not have to be worried about people thinking their question is stupid but also expect to receive either a very thoughtful answer or good directions to where that answer can be found." This sense of openness and camaraderie extends beyond the workplace. One engineer notes an "after-hours social scene" each Friday "where people get together and have a great time getting to know each other." All employees—not just new hires—participate in this weekly tradition.

Moving on

The company reports that if first jobbers leave NetApp, they typically accept positions with competing companies in the industry.

Attrition

New hires seem generally content, noting that there's room to grow both in terms of pay and responsibility. On the rare occasion when newbies gripe, it's usually due to boredom or the feeling that they're mired in "grunt work." Still, most plan to stay with the company for the foreseeable future. They say that "there are many projects and groups that need leadership," and many of these ambitious young employees have leadership on their minds.

THE NEW TEACHER PROJECT

The New Teacher Project

OPERATIONS AND COMMUNICATIONS ASSOCIATES

TNTP seeks "strong, critical thinkers who are committed to the organization's mission of ensuring that all students are taught by excellent teachers [who are] achievement-oriented, productive, [and] sensitive to others."

The Big Picture

The New Teacher Project (TNTP) is "a national nonprofit organization that partners with school districts, states, and other educational entities to develop programs that recruit, select, and train exceptional individuals to become teachers for high-need public schools." It's a great place for people who want to "make a difference." One first jobber explains, "I had left my previous position in entry-level market research because there was no sense of purpose or employee interest, and I also did not feel as though I had much in common with many of my coworkers. When I found the position with TNTP, however, I knew almost instantly that it was an ideal match. I found my coworkers to be driven, intelligent, and genuinely concerned with the work at hand. Also, the organization worked directly to help people, not just help profits and track numbers."

LOCATION(S) WHERE ENTRY-LEVEL EMPLOYEES WORK

"Our entry-level employees work at various locations, depending on where we have programs and openings. Sites include major metropolitan areas such as New York, New York; Chicago, Illinois; Washington, DC; Philadelphia, Pennsylvania; Baltimore, Maryland; Miami, Florida; Memphis, Tennessee; New Orleans, Louisiana; Houston, Texas; and Oakland, California." Additional sites may be found "in states with large rural populations, such as Louisiana and Virginia."

AVERAGE NUMBER OF APPLICATIONS EACH YEAR

TNTP receives 2,000 applications a year.

AVERAGE NUMBER HIRED PER YEAR

TNTP hires ten entry-level workers a year.

ENTRY-LEVEL POSITION(S) AVAILABLE

TNTP usually hires operations and communications associates, "and sometimes other positions, as well."

AVERAGE HOURS WORKED PER WEEK

Entry-level workers usually work 45 hours per week.

AVERAGE STARTING SALARY

In 2006, the average starting salary was $34,000.

BENEFITS OFFERED

TNTP has "a strong medical benefits package that vests on an employee's first day. Medical insurance is fully paid; dental and vision coverage requires a small contribution from the employee." Additional benefits include a 403(b) tax-free retirement plan, flexible spending accounts for health care and dependent care, paid disability, paid vacation, and personal time off."

CONTACT INFORMATION

The New Teacher Project
304 Park Avenue South, 11th Floor
New York, NY 10010
E-mail: jobs@tntp.org
Visit www.tntp.org

Getting Hired

The New Teacher Project recruits on college campuses; the specific campuses vary annually "depending on the cities [in which] we have programs and openings." Openings are also posted on the organization's website. TNTP seeks "strong, critical thinkers who are committed to the organization's mission of ensuring that all students are taught by excellent teachers [who are] achievement-oriented, productive, [and] sensitive to others." Communication skills are also considered very important. Interviews here "can be intense. We ask in-depth questions about each candidate's background experiences—including times [he or she has] been challenged or disappointed, not just what [he or she has] achieved, and questions with hypothetical scenarios about situations [that may arise] on the job."

All applications begin with the submission of a resume and detailed cover letter; this is followed by a short project related to the work that we do and three interviews. One successful hire reports, "I was given about four days to complete the project, which asked me to analyze a set of data and make recommendations based on my findings. Afterward, I was invited for a second-round in-person interview with the director of selection and one of her supervisors. We spent a lot of time discussing the exercise I completed."

Money and Perks

The negotiability of salaries, start dates, and other work-related details vary by position. The organization does lots of contract work; and this often allows for little flexibility in the terms of employment. Raises are awarded annually; while "entry-level employees are generally not eligible for a bonus," occasionally "there are exceptions." TNTP first jobbers love that "the culture here is very results-oriented and flexible, with lots of autonomy for workers. They trust you to do things in the style that makes sense for you, as long as you achieve the desired results in a timely and high-quality manner. Newbies also appreciate that because it is "a nonprofit company, TNTP is very responsive to not having typical work weeks. While some days might be very busy, when it is slow, people are very willing to let you go home early. Also, we get an amazing number of vacation days!"

The Ropes

Formal orientation at TNTP "occurs over the course of a few weeks [and] generally includes an overview and history of the organization, an overview of benefits and policies, an in-depth overview of the particular program and the employee's job responsibilities, and, as [may be] relevant, an overview of resources available within TNTP to help staff in their new roles (e.g., manuals, contact information for staff with similar roles in similar TNTP programs, etc.)." Training is "ongoing and informal, more a schedule of somewhat informal meetings with managers" and a "learn-as-you-go process." In an effort to facilitate the transition of entry-level staff into their new positions and ensure they succeed, TNTP is currently refining its employee orientation process and expanding its professional development opportunities.

Day in the Life

TNTP hires first jobbers for two key positions: operations associates and communications associates. Operations associates are "responsible for program logistics and materials, entering and maintaining program data, [and] coordinating special program events," while communications associates are "responsible for delivery of accurate, timely, and courteous recruitment and/or program messages by phone, e-mail, and in-person [contact] with candidates, accepted teachers, and teachers already in the classroom." One communications associate reports, "I am primarily focused on dealing with public interest in the program: e-mails, phone calls, public information sessions in the evenings, and creating a database to track all of this. On a typical day I arrive at 9:00 A.M. or earlier and begin by responding to any program e-mails or calls from the day before. This continues throughout the day, but my primary focus eventually switches to sending and tracking correspondence to candidates at different stages of the application process. After lunch, I generally have some candidate screenings to complete, and then I work on building the database needed to house information on selected candidates and [on] completing data requests. Finally, at least once a week, I need to spend an evening assisting or presenting at an information session [at which] the public can get a rundown of the program and ask questions."

Peers

"The New Teacher Project does not have a 'cohort' of people that comes in every year." As a result, explains one newbie, "there is not much first-job camaraderie here. However, everyone gets along great and tends to socialize with [one another] without the boundary of 'this is my boss/employee.'"

The organization is also a magnet for extremely bright individuals; one first jobber writes, "It can definitely be a bit daunting at times, since everyone was clearly an honors student in the past. However, everyone cares about working together." One employee sums up, "Each person in my organization could be working for a corporation, making a ton of money, but instead [we] choose to work toward this cause. I love going in to work every day!"

Moving on

Those who leave The New Teacher Project generally do so to attend graduate school or to "gain different experiences elsewhere." There is a sense among some here that "there is not much room for growth, and sometimes there is not much interaction between different contracts," both of which present situations that may thwart ambitious careerists in their efforts to advance. Over the past few years, however, the fast pace of The New Teacher Project's growth has increased opportunities for upward movement for its staff. Whenever possible, the organization prioritizes the promotion of existing employees to fill new positions as they arise. The average tenure of a first jobber in an entry-level position here is two years.

Attrition

About 10 percent of college-grad hires leave The New Teacher Project within twelve months of arriving. Some complain about the "uncertainty" arising from contract-based programs. "Due to the fact that we are often working with the delayed budgets and number projections common in the education world," writes an entry-level employee, "we often have to pull together quickly once our goals are set."

Best and Worst

Among the most successful first jobbers at The New Teacher Project is a woman who "began working as an intern on one of our contracts right after graduation from college. It was clear from the beginning that she was a quick learner and a hard worker and was really inspired by our goals and mission. She took every opportunity to help out when she could. As a result, we offered her an operations associate position in November of that year. In that position, we saw that she consistently produced high-quality work and was highly accountable for meeting her goals and the contract's goals. One year later, she was promoted to recruiter in our largest contract, and less than a year after that, she was promoted to director of placement, [a position in which she was charged with] coordinating a placement process for approximately 2,000 newly-recruited teachers each year."

NEW YORK CARES
VARIOUS POSITIONS

"The folks who are most successful are passionate about [New York Cares'] mission," and believe in "the impact that volunteers can have on the lives of New Yorkers. They are team players and go-getters."

NEW
YORK
CARES
www.nycares.org

The Big Picture

New York Cares is a hydra-headed nonprofit that deploys about 33,000 occasional and regular volunteers to schools and other nonprofits. Its innovation is allowing volunteers to choose, from a full menu of short- and long-term community-service project, those which are convenient to their schedules and compatible with their interests. Projects relate to AIDS, homelessness, education, the environment, and many other causes. The organization's four major philanthropic events—New York Cares Day, Hands-On New York Day, Winter Wishes for Kids & Families, and the Coat Drive—appear on the calendars of many prominent New Yorkers. Says one former staffer, "Entry-level employees do the bread-and-butter work that makes New York Cares such a well-known and loved institution throughout New York City."

LOCATION(S) WHERE ENTRY-LEVEL EMPLOYEES WORK

The New York Cares office is located on West 29th Street in Manhattan (New York, New York).

AVERAGE NUMBER OF APPLICATIONS EACH YEAR

New York Cares receives approximately 300 to 400 applications annually.

AVERAGE NUMBER HIRED PER YEAR OVER THE LAST TEN YEARS

The organization hires six or seven entry-level employees each year.

ENTRY-LEVEL POSITIONS AVAILABLE

New hires start as annual events managers, program managers, and corporate relations managers and assistants. "In addition . . . each year New York Cares brings on an additional [three] staff member[s] through the Americorps program. For many, this is also an entry-level position."

AVERAGE HOURS WORKED PER WEEK

Staff work a standard 40-hour week "plus some nights and weekends."

PERCENTAGE OF ENTRY-LEVEL HIRES STILL WITH THE COMPANY AFTER THREE, FIVE, AND TEN YEARS

According to company officials, the average tenure of first jobbers is "two to three years."

Getting Hired

"New York Cares looks for people who are passionate about New York Cares's mission and who are excited about the possibility of working at New York Cares. We seek people with diverse backgrounds and work/life experiences, and people who are team players and hard-working. New York Cares posts its open jobs on its own website and on such industry-wide websites such as Idealist.org. . . . Candidates [should] send their resume and cover letter via fax or e-mail." Many new hires are either former New York Cares interns or volunteers, or have worked with affiliated organizations. Whether an applicant is experienced or not, "it's a must to have researched the organization ahead of time!" Interview questions may require answers about how the workings of the organization fit an applicant's strengths and goals.

Money and Perks

New employees report annual starting salaries in the low $30,000s. New hires "are formally reviewed after their three-month probationary period, at six months, and at twelve months. After one year, employees are reviewed annually [and] receive raises at their annual review." Factors that determine salary increases include "performance evaluations, progress towards goals, contribution to the organization . . . and the organization's finances." Just as salaries vary, so do perceived perks. "There is a lot of room to grow in terms of responsibility, but not in terms of pay or job title," says one woman. Another employee disagrees: "The 7-percent raise that employees are eligible for each year is substantial. Growth in responsibility within one's position . . . is absolutely possible—assuming that employees make the effort!" Says one staffer, "The hours were much more flexible than I expected, and, while I definitely averaged over forty-five hours a week, it did not feel that way as I was spending the time . . . on my terms." Folks also appreciate summer Fridays (when the office closes early), "free food," and the "fun" environment. During one recent benefit, for instance, staff guest-bartended at a West Village pub. "New York Cares is well known for [its] ability to throw an incredible party."

The Ropes

"Most of the training at New York Cares happens on the job," reports an organization official. "Preliminary orientation lasts a day or two and consists primarily of meeting with various staff members, including the finance and operations officer, office coordinator, and other members of the [new employee's] department to understand office procedures and job specifics." The overall length of orientation depends on a new hire's boss, with some new staffers describing longer processes—e.g., "a two-week boot camp" with tutorials and "meetings with the directors of each of the other 10 departments"—than others.

Day in the Life

An ordinary day might begin with "a departmental or full-staff meeting," since "New York Cares loves to make sure all teams are communicating and brainstorming together!" After that, the daily schedule varies considerably by department. "Program managers work directly with agencies to design meaningful volunteer projects," so typical tasks include "making numerous phone calls, reviewing agency applications, going over numbers and statistics . . . and meeting with outside contacts to further explore the nature of developing partnerships." The "annual events staff run [the] coat drive . . . holiday gift exchange for needy children, and two citywide volunteering events in the public schools and parks." "Corporate relations managers" manage said relations, "mainly through enlisting [companies'] support for [the organization's] annual events and other service projects." As in many nonprofits, this can be a touchy subject with members of other departments, who sometimes object to the "the necessity to bend over backwards to accommodate the needs of our sponsors and corporate partners."

Peers

Employees see each other as "smart, funny, motivated, proactive, inspiring, and diverse," and socialize outside the office to various degrees. "The after-hours social scene is not huge," says one staffer, "but definitely exists, [and is] spurred by the later hours in the busy seasons and the amount of collaborative work."

Moving on

"Movement within the company is always promoted," says one respondent, "so if someone wants to apply for a position in another department, they're often encouraged. This does happen a lot at our organization and it's a great way to keep great workers from getting burnt out and leaving." For those who do leave, the most common destination is graduate school, with programs in business, public administration, social work, and medicine being the most popular choices. Says a former employee now enrolled in medical school, "I cried when I announced my resignation! I miss the organization, the position, and [the] amazing coworkers and volunteers every single day." Many employees also relocate to other organizations and other cities.

Attrition

Employees frequently leave to "return to school," "move on to more senior positions," "move from New York," or "have children."

Best and Worst

"Many of our entry-level employees succeed. The folks who are most successful are passionate about our mission," and believe in "the impact that volunteers can have on the lives of New Yorkers. They are team players and go-getters."

NYC TEACHING FELLOWS
TEACHER

"My job has not changed, but I have. I started the school year clueless as to how to reach and teach the children. I believe I have grown as an individual and as a teacher through this experience."

The Big Picture

If you like the idea of "leaving corporate America" for the opportunity to make a difference and help shape the lives of young people, the NYC Teaching Fellows program may be just the thing for you. While you are in front of one classroom you are a student in another as you earn your master's degree in education.

LOCATION(S) WHERE ENTRY-LEVEL EMPLOYEES WORK

All teaching positions are located in New York, New York.

AVERAGE NUMBER OF APPLICATIONS EACH YEAR

The NYC Teaching Fellows Program receives 18,000–20,000 applications each year.

AVERAGE NUMBER HIRED PER YEAR OVER THE LAST TEN YEARS

The organization hires about 2,000 people each year.

ENTRY-LEVEL POSITION(S) AVAILABLE

New hires work as New York City public school teachers.

AVERAGE HOURS WORKED PER WEEK

Fellows work at least 40 hours per week.

AVERAGE STARTING SALARY

Teachers with only a bachelor's degrees earn $42,512; teachers with additional course work can earn higher salaries.

BENEFITS OFFERED

Teachers have a choice of health insurance plans, including medical, dental, prescription, optical, and hearing. Additional benefits include a subsidized master's degree, disability insurance, mortgage programs, special discounts, a pension plan, TransitChecks, and flexible spending accounts.

CONTACT INFORMATION

Apply at www.nycteachingfellows.org.

Getting Hired

Teaching Fellows tell us that the program has "a reputation for being very selective. The process of applying is more rigorous than graduate school applications." Applications are accepted online; they require essays that "require thoughtful answers outside of the typical 'I want to be a teacher because I love children.'" Those who make the first cut are called for a half-day interview. One Fellow reports, "The interview started in a group format. I had to prepare a five-minute lesson (which, by the way, is not much time at all!). All of us were nervous, and the best thing I can recommend to anyone going through the process is to make friends with the other interviewees before the process begins. This puts everyone at ease, and, more likely than not, these are not the people you will be competing with, since there are many subjects areas for which qualified teachers are sought." The next part of the process is a one-on-one interview, which "consists of pre-written questions. The questions are read, and then the responses are written down word for word. The questions are mostly what-if situations: 'If you were teaching and blank happened, what would you do?' The woman who interviewed me was helpful, kind, and patient. She made me feel comfortable. She explained that later that evening she would meet with another group to review the results of the interviews and then make her recommendations. . . . I was told that I would have an answer within the month. I was accepted into the program five weeks later."

Money and Perks

Teaching Fellows belong to the teachers' union, so their salaries are determined by the union contract. Because of the program's prescribed training program, starting dates are also nonnegotiable. Regarding specific teaching positions, "we were given an opportunity to state our preferred borough and region, but the point of the program is to assist schools and children [with] the greatest need; the needs of the program come first. The desired subject [and] grade level was also needs-based, but we were given a chance to state our preference." Union membership ensures a solid benefits package. Teaching Fellows also earn a subsidized master's degree in education; in 2005, teachers were required to cover $4,000 in master's-related expenses over two years, with the city picking up the rest of the tab. Other fringe benefits of the job include "great vacations." One teacher writes, "I hate it when people say the best part about being a teacher is the summers off! This is the most demanding and difficult job I have ever held. If we didn't have vacations, I would burn out within a year. Besides, the next two summers of my life will be spent in graduate school classes!"

The Ropes

Pre-service training, which is a full-time commitment, is required of all Fellows. Referred to by many as "boot camp," it is "consuming, exhausting, and demanding" but ultimately "a very positive experience." Here's how one Fellow describes it: "You get both academic classes and the 'straight dope' from actual New York City teachers called 'Fellow advisors' who give you the lowdown on what to expect in the classroom. My Fellow advisor was cool, and I was very impressed with that aspect of the program. Halfway through the summer, we were placed in a school in our district to assist another teacher teaching summer school. We assistant taught in the mornings, then went to grad school in the afternoons." Although teachers are usually required to hold a degree in their area of specialization, New York makes an exception for math and science teachers (because they are in such short supply). Immersion training, in addition to the above-mentioned training, is required of prospective math and science teachers who do not qualify to teach under the standard guidelines.

Day in the Life

Teaching is a demanding job, and the Fellows we spoke with describe filled-to-bursting work days. According to one Fellow, "My days typically started at 5:30 A.M. at home doing planning and correcting papers and homework. At school by 7:30 A.M. Teach until 3:00 P.M. or 4:00 P.M., depending on the day. Three days a week at college until 7:00 P.M. Home by 8:30 P.M. Planning, paperwork, studying, etc. until 10:00 P.M." Lather, rinse, repeat—no wonder teachers are so effusive about their summer vacations! There are also after-school faculty meetings, professional development sessions, and occasional teacher-parent meetings. It's a grind for sure, albeit a fulfilling one for the right individual. The job doesn't evolve over time, but the teachers do; one explains, "My job has not changed, but I have. I started the school year clueless as to how to reach and teach the children. I believe I have grown as an individual and as a teacher through this experience, and not," she adds pointedly, "through my college courses."

Peers

Between teaching, grading assignments, and studying for a master's degree, most Fellows have precious little time to hang with peers. "There was more camaraderie with my NYC Teaching Fellows classmates this summer," explains one teacher. "I find it difficult to maintain an active social life while teaching and attending graduate school simultaneously. I keep close phone contact with several classmates, and we have a mass e-mail system set up for our group, which we use regularly." Most understandably admire their peers, since they know exactly how heavy a load they are shouldering. One writes, "I like most of my fellow Fellows and genuinely admire many. They are mostly committed and intelligent people."

Moving on

The program is designed to generate career teachers; the master's degree in education is a huge incentive to remain in the school system, since it translates roughly into a 10 percent pay hike. Thus, many of those who complete the program continue to teach in the New York City school system. Other people move elsewhere in the state and continue teaching. A few teachers, however, get burned out by the demands of the job and seek employment outside the education world.

Attrition

Teachers who leave the program early receive no tuition compensation for their master's work, so the incentives to tough it out, regardless of how difficult it may be, are great. Even people who complain most bitterly about incompetent administrators, unreasonable demands and standards, the challenges of teaching in the city school system, and the superfluity of some graduate courses in education tell us they planned to remain in the program to the end. Retention beyond the first two years is also very high. More than 80 percent of those who complete two years of teaching return for a third.

THE NEW YORK TIMES
COLUMNIST ASSISTANT/EDITORIAL ASSISTANT

"In addition to administrative duties "such as answering the phone, opening the mail, [and] arranging logistics of travel and media engagements," assistants serve "as another set of eyes and ears for [the columnist]."

The Big Picture

The public image of the newspaper columnist is that of the solitary scribe, but in fact they're not solitary at all—they have assistants to keep them company! Their assistants also fulfill a wide range of duties, including interviewing experts, checking facts, and—if their relationship with their mentors grows strong enough—offering feedback and criticism for their columns.

LOCATION(S) WHERE ENTRY-LEVEL EMPLOYEES WORK

Entry-level employees work in New York, New York.

ENTRY-LEVEL POSITION(S) AVAILABLE

Entry-level hires work as columnists or editorial assistants.

AVERAGE STARTING SALARY (BY POSITION)

Starting salaries range from $40,000 to $45,000.

Getting Hired

"It's been a word-of-mouth position," say all the *New York Times* researcher/assistants we spoke to; everyone we contacted either knew his or her predecessor or knew someone who helped him or her find another position at the paper, then luckily snatched the assistant's job. As a result, the application process is much less formal than at most other jobs. One writes, "My resume was unformatted, just a summary job history, very informal. This is where knowing people and being recommended goes further than anything you'd imagine. When I got this job, my first job was to reject all the applicants. There were great resumes—people applying right out of college, people who had lots of experience. It's hard; people [are lucky to get] these columnist jobs." Even so, the interview process can be grueling. One assistant [says], "My initial interview was with my predecessor, who informally described the responsibilities of the job. In the second interview, [the columnist] and my predecessor further described the work involved, then engaged me in a discussion of the current events and potential topics for [the columnist]'s next column. The final interview was something of a death match between me and two other candidates: Each of us was called upon to meet separately with [the columnist] and offer more developed ideas for his next column."

Money and Perks

Union rules strictly limit the negotiability of many jobs at the New York Times, editorial assistantships among them. First jobbers are occasionally able to negotiate start time and may even win some small concessions on salary; most, however, are more interested in the experience than the pay, so they don't push too hard on their initial terms of employment. Once here they find that "there are a lot of perks, which is one reason it's hard to leave the Times. I've written for other publications, and I've called and called and they're not interested because you need a contact there. Not so here." There's also "a lot of free stuff that comes in: books, tickets to premieres, CDs, that sort of thing." Finally, "there's a lot of respect that comes from calling from the New York Times, even if you're not a big person, and that's nice. I used to work in a nonprofit, and I didn't get any of that then."

The Ropes

Training at the Times begins with orientation, "a couple of hours around a table. They basically gave us a handbook and a little union talk." And that's about it for formal training mechanisms here. Lucky assistants learn from their predecessors and their peers. Unlucky ones replace fired predecessors and have only their peers to fall back on. They also generally lose access to their predecessor's files. One such ill-fated assistant wrote, "I had to start without even a Rolodex, which was hard. But I used common sense, figured out who to call to get info and check things, that sort of thing. It would have been nice to have a Rolodex of experts on gun control and bulimia in Zanzibar because it's hard to find them on your own, even for the quicky stuff." Overall, though, "it's not a hard job to learn. Any questions I had, I could ask other assistants. This is a friendly place, and there's always somebody there to help you."

Day in the Life

Editorial assistants do everything their bosses don't have time to do. One explains, "It would be difficult for [the columnist] to do as much as he does without an assistant. These guys, they do a lot of public stuff. They go on television shows, they work on books, and they get so much feedback because they're the opinion people here. They have a lot of stuff to deal with that a reporter doesn't, and they wouldn't be able to put out a column every week without an assistant." In addition to administrative duties "such as answering the phone, opening the mail, [and] arranging logistics of travel and media engagements," assistants serve "as another set of eyes and ears for [the columnist]. That means reading newspapers, magazines, online sources and the occasional book; watching/listening to cable and network news, entertainment TV, radio, and the occasional film; and generally keeping abreast of the news of politics and culture. A typical day begins with reading newspapers and checking several regular websites for string on subjects relevant to the column. I'll gather a number of news stories, transcripts of speeches or news shows, and organize them into files based on subjects of immediate and ongoing interest. I'll field several calls from publicists pitching stories, news program producers requesting interviews, and friends and colleagues."

Peers

"Everyone here is smart and talented" is the unsurprising consensus among assistants at the venerable Gray Lady. One writes, "First when I got here, I felt like the only non–Ivy Leaguer. That's true to a certain extent, but it's not really like that. There's a mix of people." While there's not a big after-hours scene, "there are efforts among young staffers to connect with one another, including a writers' group that organizes lunches/talks with senior reporters and editors." Also, "one of the guys on the editorial board decided to give us a once-a-week writing class. He used to teach at Harvard. That's amazing. Oh, and we have a softball team. That's a great way to meet nonwriting people."

NEWELL RUBBERMAID
SALES AND FIELD MARKETING
REPRESENTATIVE

NewellRubbermaid™

A new hire's responsibilities are "to execute merchandising initiatives at the store level that were dictated by account managers, build relationships with store employees, train employees on the features and benefits of our products, utilize the sales process to gain additional merchandising space, and share successes with the team to nationalize any sales successes."

The Big Picture

Designed to groom entry-level employees for leadership within the Newell Rubbermaid organization, the Sales and Field Marketing Program offers almost "unlimited opportunity to quickly move up in the company." Participants benefit from over a month of intensive training, followed by one to three years of merchandizing and marketing experience in an assigned region. New hires say what the program "teaches you is job and leadership skills," and that it is highly agreeable, thanks to the "the independence, the pay and the company car."

LOCATION(S) WHERE ENTRY-LEVEL EMPLOYEES WORK

Sales and field marketing representatives are located in and around major cities throughout the United States.

AVERAGE NUMBER OF APPLICATIONS EACH YEAR

Newell Rubbermaid receives 10,000 applications annually.

AVERAGE NUMBER HIRED PER YEAR OVER THE LAST TEN YEARS

There are usually about 250 entry-level openings with the company every year.

ENTRY-LEVEL POSITION(S) AVAILABLE

Newell Rubbermaid hires students straight out of college to work in the Sales and Field Marketing Program.

AVERAGE HOURS WORKED PER WEEK

Number of hours worked varies by location and assignment.

PERCENTAGE OF ENTRY-LEVEL HIRES STILL WITH THE COMPANY AFTER THREE, FIVE, AND TEN YEARS

Approximately 75 percent of all entry-level hires remain with Newell Rubbermaid after three years.

Getting Hired

If you haven't gone to a mock interview at your campus career services center yet, you might want to set one up before applying to Newell Rubbermaid. The company's "relatively rigorous hiring process" involves several rounds of interviews with recruiters, managers, and executives, and candidates are often asked questions designed to test their quick thinking and problem-solving skills on the spot. A successful candidate shares this example: "One person gave me the situation of setting a display in a store, knowing I had to get another one done, but also knowing I didn't have time to do both. What would I do to accomplish the goal of getting both displays set?" Another candidate reveals that, in her third round of interviews, "one interviewer even asked me to sell a pen to him." In addition to behavior-based questions, the company looks for candidates who were highly involved in their campus communities. According to company representatives, "The biggest quality Newell Rubbermaid looks for is demonstrated leadership. We need leaders at all levels in our organization, and we want to recruit only those applicants who have shown that they are leaders." After meeting Newell Rubbermaid reps on campus, one successful candidate says, "I believe that I was asked for an interview due to my leadership positions, problem solving skills, and GPA."

Money and Perks

Since the job requires a lot of local travel (sometimes up to two hours a day), "many sales and marketing new hires also receive a company-branded vehicle." An employee admits, "The best fringe benefit was the company car. You don't realize how much insurance/gas/car payment[s] actually cost until you have to pay for [them] yourself." Another adds, "There were three wonderful fringe benefits: a company car that you did not have to pay for (no monthly car notes!), flexible working hours, and the employee purchase website [through] which you could purchase Newell Rubbermaid product[s] for a fraction of their cost at retail." The responsible types also mention the company's generous 401(k) plan, for which "the company will match 100 percent of the first 3 percent that you put in and 50 percent of the next 2 percent, and you are vested immediately."

The Ropes

Before beginning their specific assignments, Newell Rubbermaid trainees from various divisions and locations meet in Atlanta for a one-week orientation to the company. A new hire details, "We learned about each of the NWL divisions through company presentations and product show times. There was interactive learning through skits, demonstrations, and quizzes." The orientation also focuses on team building and collaboration, making the experience "extremely energetic" and a lot of fun. After orientation, new employees are given their official assignments and sent to another training session, during which they learn the specifics of their job. A current employee gives us the rundown: "The Lowe's account spent two weeks training on product knowledge (directly from the product divisions we would be dealing with) and general account knowledge (from our district managers and from a visit to Lowe's corporate offices) in Charlotte, North Carolina. Once those two weeks were over, my district team (compris[ing] eight individuals) met up for a few days in a central part of the Midwest where we learned hands-on the Lowe's account together with our manager." From then on, young team members are basically on their own, though they continue to receive supervision and training from their regional manager. A current employee reports, "My boss visited me every two weeks and trained me more each visit."

Day in the Life

The life of a new sales and field marketing representative is fairly solitary and autonomous. Assigned to a region that includes ten to fifteen stores operated by a national retailer, new reps are charged with increasing sales on Newell Rubbermaid products in their area. Explains a newbie, "My territory included ten stores in the Dallas area. I was responsible for the store-level service of our product lines, the training of the store staff [on] our products, and the execution of event marketing activities." While regions, target products, and accounts vary, a new hire's responsibilities are "to execute merchandising initiatives at the store level that were dictated by account managers, build relationships with store employees, train employees on the features and benefits of our products, utilize the sales process to gain additional merchandising space, and share successes with the team to nationalize any sales successes." While operating on a local level, sales and marketing newbies feel they are contributing the company's overall success. Says one, "I felt that my work was part of [the] greater work that was going on nationally. One hundred reps calling on, selling to, merchandising in, and training [at] Lowe's did make a big impact. Our sales for categories like Shur-Line and Rubbermaid went through the roof, due to cross-merchandising."

Peers

The Sales and Field Marketing Program tends to attract a lot of "type-A" personalities, but the similarities between its participants do not end there. As most staffers join the program directly out of college, they are generally around the same age and share similar life experiences. Exclaims one, "One of my favorite parts of Newell Rubbermaid is the people . . . they hire great people!" Unfortunately, the job is largely independent and staffers are necessarily placed in different regions. A new hire laments, "There was no one else that worked for Newell Rubbermaid close to where I lived, so most of my interaction was through phone calls, e-mails, and an audix system." Echoes another, "There usually isn't anyone else from your team in the same market."

Moving on

Company reps say they don't keep track of where employees go after leaving Newell Rubbermaid. However, they notice a fair share have taken positions in pharmaceutical sales.

Attrition

"By far the most common reason people resign from our entry-level program is because of location." A Newell Rubbermaid rep explains, "We ask these individuals to be very flexible in their first few years of employment, as when they get promoted they will most likely be asked to move. In many cases, they are not able to leave the city they are in for personal reasons, and instead resign from Newell Rubbermaid."

Best and Worst

Great entry-level hires "are defined as such by their results. Great hires have a huge impact." Bad representatives are either developed or "coached out of the organization."

NEWS AMERICA MARKETING
ACCOUNT COORDINATOR

NEWS AMERICA
MARKETING.
A NEWS CORPORATION COMPANY

The position "requires a person to be extremely detail-oriented. Also, there is a lot of back and forth with the client to be sure that programs are meeting the client's needs."

The Big Picture

A marketing-services company that sells online, in-store, and home-delivered media packages to its clients, News America Marketing runs an intensive Sales Development Program for entry-level employees. "Because [its] sales positions are filled only by internal candidates," News America Marketing offers novice staffers incredible growth opportunities and the potential to make an entire career with the company. In their first year, "account coordinators work on teams that sell advertising and promotion solutions to major packaged-goods clients," learning valuable sales techniques on the job and through formal training sessions.

LOCATION(S) WHERE ENTRY-LEVEL EMPLOYEES WORK

New employees work at New America's New York, New York headquarters, or in one of the sales offices in Boston, Massachusetts; East Brunswick, New Jersey; Pittsburgh, Pennsylvania; Atlanta, Georgia; Chicago, Illinois; Minneapolis, Minnesota; Cincinnati, Ohio; Los Angeles and San Francisco, California; Denver, Colorado; and Dallas, Texas.

AVERAGE NUMBER OF APPLICATIONS EACH YEAR

News America Marketing receives around 2,000 applications per year.

AVERAGE NUMBER HIRED PER YEAR OVER THE LAST TEN YEARS

There are generally openings for about 100 new account coordinators across the country.

ENTRY-LEVEL POSITION(S) AVAILABLE

News Marketing America hires recent grads to fill the position of account coordinator, the first step in the company's Sales Development Program.

AVERAGE HOURS WORKED PER WEEK

New account coordinators average about 50 hours per week, though some work much more.

PERCENTAGE OF ENTRY-LEVEL HIRES STILL WITH THE COMPANY AFTER THREE, FIVE, AND TEN YEARS

Eighty percent of New America's Sales Development employees remain with the company past the account director position, a promotion that typically occurs at two years of employment. Once employees make it to the account director position, they usually remain with the company another five to seven years.

Getting Hired

News America is "constantly recruiting for talent," combing college campuses for promising young professionals. Even so, getting a job at this top marketing company is no walk in the park. After weeding through thousands of applications and conducting campus interviews, News America invites promising candidates to spend three days in New York. There, candidates must try to remain charming and confident through "consecutive interviews from 8:00 A.M. until 5:00 P.M. with executives." A survivor admits, "I will not lie. It was a very grueling process." According to the company, there are certain qualities that make a candidate stand out at News America, such as "demonstrated excellent communication skills, a strong work ethic, time management skills, leadership skills, [the] ability to work in a team, and, most importantly, a desire and ability to sell." However, the most important factors would be the candidate's intrinsic work ethic and character. A representative from the company explains, "We have a simple hiring philosophy: hire for attitude and train for skills. Our CEO has instructed the HR department to 'hire nice people.' We feel that we can teach the rest." Therefore, it's not surprising that the interview process, while taxing, has a conversational quality and often focuses on the candidate's interests and background.

Money and Perks

Entry-level salaries at News America are nonnegotiable but account coordinators have the chance to earn an extra $2,000 through performance-based target bonuses, available to all new employees. Through the company's many corporate partners, employees benefit from "discounts and special rates in industries such as health and beauty, fitness, retail, entertainment, finance, and technology." The company also hosts holiday parties and summer outings, for which employees might be invited to "attend a baseball game, go on boat rides, or spend a day at a sports and entertainment complex."

The Ropes

The "very extensive training program at News America Marketing" begins at the branch office, where veteran employees go out of their way to welcome and initiate new hires. On his first day, one employee was impressed to discover "a welcome letter on my desk next to [my] first set of business cards." Another newbie says her boss, "introduced me to other people in the office, took me out to lunch, and connected me with other 'seasoned' account coordinators who would be helping me with the day-to-day order processing." Generally, new account coordinators "participate in on-the-job training for the first three-to-eight weeks before attending their first formal training session." During this initial period, "other account coordinators (ACs) train you individually on the job responsibilities." Roughly a month later, ACs go to New York for a week of training by executives and sales support departments, during which they learn "the day-to-day details, such as using [New America's] systems, working with other internal departments, [and] order processing." Six months after their start date, employees attend another formal training, this time "a more strategic session involving higher-level thinking (consultative selling, print, and production)." In addition to the formal training programs, "News America Marketing has a mentor program which gives you an opportunity to have a relationship with a high-level manager outside of your own team." A former trainee in his second year with the company reports, "My mentor and I still speak on a regular basis."

Day in the Life

"My responsibilities when I was first hired were very limited. This job requires a lot of learning and what you will be taught is not something you learned in college," recalls a former account coordinator. However, responsibilities rapidly expand at News America, and "within a month of being with the organization, my responsibility consisted of processing orders worth approximately $300,000 to the organization." Most first-year account coordinators perform the same function, primarily: "to make sure orders were executed properly without mistakes." Veterans tell us that the position "requires a person to be extremely detail-oriented. Also, there is a lot of back-and-forth with the client to be sure that programs are meeting the client's needs." On top of that, account coordinators are "responsible for preparation of sales meetings for your account director, as well as all executionary details of programs." The sheer number of responsibilities can be overwhelming. A new staffer confides, "I can never focus on one task at a time because there is always something of greater importance to interrupt my work." Another adds, "Sometimes it seems like there are not enough hours in the day to get it all done. I typically work from 8:30 A.M. to 7:00 or 8:00 P.M. and sometimes on the weekend." However, employees assure us that their efforts will be answered with promotions, increased responsibilities, and, of course, more money. A former entry-level staffer exclaims, "I have been with the organization for a little over two years and I manage two account coordinators and $11 million in business for the organization. I have also increased my salary by $14,000 a year and my target bonus by $10,000 a year."

Peers

"ACs always start around the same time, and this group goes through various trainings together. There is a definite bond that is formed with this group and this carries through outside of the office," explains a News America newcomer. In fact, many feel "the social environment is the biggest benefit" of their new career. "The organization is very young and there are a good deal of social events to participate in." An LA-based account coordinator tells us, "The people are wonderful! Everyone is very motivated, smart, and friendly. I am friends with everyone I have met. One of my current roommates even works at the company." For recent grads, a current employee says working at News America "made the transition from college life to the working world very [easily]. I came in with fifteen other 'fresh graduates' that I could relate to." There are even extracurricular activities! For example, an AC reports, "I am in a NYC Urban Professional Basketball League with two employees of News America."

Moving on

Most employees leave News America to pursue careers in marketing fields such as research, marketing services, and brand management. Others leave to pursue graduate degrees.

Attrition

About 30 percent of new account coordinators leave the company within the first fifteen months of employment. According to News America reps, "The most common reason for leaving is that [the employee] has determined that a career in sales is not for [him or her]; secondarily, some leave due to the pace of the work environment; others leave because they don't enjoy having direct contact with the clients."

Best and Worst

At News America Marketing there are so many examples of successful entry-level employees, it's hard to pick just one. "Currently, all three of our Executive Vice Presidents for Sales are former entry-level employees who went through our Sales Development Program," all of whom "reached this level within ten years of their start with the company." In fact, "Most of our current senior sales managers went through the Sales Development Program, beginning as Account Coordinators." Reps tell us that employees who are overwhelmed by attention to detail and the challenging workload are generally unsuccessful.

NORTHROP GRUMMAN CORPORATION
VARIOUS POSITIONS

NORTHROP GRUMMAN

At Northrop Grumman, the workload ebbs and flows, and each day differs depending on the project, the customer needs, and the ideas that pop into an employee's head. A satisfied newbie beams, "My job is always changing, and I am always learning."

The Big Picture

According to Hoover's, Northrop Grumman is now "the world's number-one shipbuilder and the number-three defense contractor (behind Lockheed Martin and Boeing)," which means that new hires at the company get the chance to work on big-time projects. One newbie says, "From what I have observed and experienced, Northrop Grumman encourages and makes great efforts to retain and grow young employees into strong leaders and managers." Indeed, first jobbers frequently cite the opportunity to "move up the ladder quickly" as one of Northrop Grumman's best features. Another perk is that rookie employers quickly find themselves working on projects that are—let's say—on the down-low. "Since most of the work is sensitive, I was not allowed to know much about the job until I arrived on the first day," says an intelligence analyst. She adds, "I was assured when the manager told me that if I didn't like it, there were numerous other jobs open to me within the company."

LOCATION(S) WHERE ENTRY-LEVEL EMPLOYEES WORK

Northrop Grumman has locations in each state.

AVERAGE NUMBER OF APPLICATIONS EACH YEAR

Northrop Grumman receives thousands of applications each year.

AVERAGE NUMBER HIRED PER YEAR OVER THE LAST FIVE YEARS

For the past five years, the company has hired around 1,500 entry-level workers annually. It expects this number to rise to 2,000 in coming years.

ENTRY-LEVEL POSITION(S) AVAILABLE

Northrop Grumman has "various programs throughout the company, including leadership, business, and engineering programs. Additionally, Northrop Grumman hires entry-level employees for specific engineering and business opportunities."

AVERAGE HOURS WORKED PER WEEK

Rookies should anticipate working 40 to 50 hours a week.

Getting Hired

"Northrop Grumman is strategically aligned with a group of universities [that] have programs, research opportunities, etc., that best fit our hiring needs and best align with our business objectives," say Northrop Grumman officials. Nevertheless, they add, "we visit many schools and hire top students from various universities." Interested undergrads at institutions NGC doesn't visit at all "can apply by going online and visiting our college site at Careers.NorthropGrumman.com." Landing a job at Northrop Grumman is no easy task. An employee in her second year notes that many managers in her division "will not consider hiring someone unless they are referred by another NG employee; have past government/military experience; and, above all, have a U.S. Government security clearance." One young gun notes that she kept her "resume short and to the point and only highlighted pertinent qualifications," which impressed the Northrop Grumman hiring squad. The interview process seems to vary, depending on the department to which a candidate is applying. Often, a successful interview with an on-campus recruiter will "lead to an invitation to a 'college center' or on-site interview," explains a newbie who went to a center in Baltimore. "At the college center, 50 to 100 students are brought to one location to interview with three managers, tour the Baltimore site, meet recent hires for casual discussions and Q&A, and get a feel for life in Baltimore."

Money and Perks

At minimum, Northrop Grumman "employees go through an annual salary review. Raises are based on merit and market comparisons." Not everyone agrees that these raises come frequently (or generously) enough. A young optimal engineer says that, while there's room to grow in terms of responsibility, "growth in terms of pay is a different matter. I feel like the growth that takes place [comes in] small incremental steps." On the topic of pay raises, a second-year engineer offers this advice: "Strategic career management is necessary for those who have ambitious career goals. There are many resources for this type of planning, however; so any employee who values status and monetary reward[s] certainly has many routes available through which to attain his or her goals." One of the biggest perks at Northrop Grumman is that graduate classes "taken in pursuit of departmentally-approved degrees are paid in advance by the corporation. Employee[s] never [have] to pay tuition—even temporarily—unless they fail to make the grade required for reimbursement."

The Ropes

At Northrop Grumman, "no formal mentor program is in place, but we have many mentor/protégé relationships which occur naturally. We have found this to be beneficial, since the new hires typically select someone with whom they feel comfortable." Beginners have no complaints about this method. The early days on the job often involve rotations that allow rooks to get a strong sense of how to move forward. One first jobber explains, "In each of my rotations, I learned several different job functions, and received on-the-job training from a wide range of entry- and mid-level engineers, as well as constant mentoring from senior engineers and managers." There's also a standard orientation that covers "basic security procedures, time-charging, benefits, facility and computer accesses, and a business overview." Ultimately, though, newbies acclimate to Northrop Grumman through observation and participation, which convinces "the managers [to] rely on you more and more."

Day in the Life

Northrop Grumman says that all entry-level "positions are challenging and detail-oriented." They're also team-oriented, which allows new hires to collaborate with and get to know many of their colleagues. One mechanical engineer says that a typical day on her first project "consisted of meeting with different engineers to discuss their design requirements, approaches, and results on legacy programs; discussing with my mentor how these designs and results related to the current project; working with 3D CAD modeling software to design test fixturing; and spending time in the product qualification labs overseeing the tests and operators and recording data." In other words, there's a lot to be done, and this keeps new hires on their toes. "I am never bored," says one. She quickly adds, "At times I feel slightly overwhelmed, but nothing a couple of deep breaths can't handle." An engineer in his third year agrees: "Earlier, I would say I felt overwhelmed and in over my head. I think it just takes some time getting used to the type of work that's done in the industry." At Northrop Grumman, the workload ebbs and flows, and each day differs depending on the project, the customer's needs, and the ideas that pop into an employee's head. A satisfied newbie beams, "My job is always changing, and I am always learning."

Peers

When Northrop Grumman's newcomers talk about other young employees, they throw around adjectives like "smart," "intelligent," "fun-loving," and "hard-working." One newbie admits that "not everyone is 'cool,' but with the large number of young employees, it is not hard to make friends and have fun at work, whatever your social preferences." A second-year analyst notes, "Most entry-level employees join the Society of Young Professionals. . . . They love the atmosphere. They are always meeting during the lunch hours and after work. The people involved tend to be young, single, and searching." There's also "an organization that deals with . . . coordinating activities aimed at . . . newly hired employees." And, on a less formal basis, there's a "pretty active after-hours social scene."

Moving on

Often, young employees will leave their positions to take up new responsibilities in another sector or group within Northrop Grumman. Other reasons for moving on include finding better pay or projects with a competing company, enrolling in grad school, relocating to a more affordable area, or switching industries altogether.

Attrition

More than 95 percent of Northrop Grumman's fresh-from-college hires stay with the company for at least one year. Many newbies are compelled to stick around because they've "heard stories of new hires that move up the ladder quickly," and they hope to be one of them. But rookies also report that they sometimes have difficulty connecting with the company as a whole. One explains, "The majority of the younger employees seem to agree that they have a strong loyalty to their first-level managers, and to their peers and teammates, but that there is a disconnect with the larger corporation. It seems the experience of each employee in his or her group is often projected to the company as a whole, and not everyone works with the most dynamic, supportive, open team/group. Also, the merit plan that is used to determine and administer raises is theoretically consistent, but some employees feel the plan is dysfunctional, and does not adequately measure and reward 'performance.'"

NOVA GROUP
ENGLISH LANGUAGE INSTRUCTOR

"It's a very satisfying feeling, when a student passes a test or gets accepted to a foreign university, knowing that you have helped improve their communication skills."

The Big Picture

"Nova is one of the big three English-language schools in Japan," annually hiring a slew of recent grads to teach conversational English in over 800 locations across the country. While Nova offers ample growth opportunities for employees who choose to make a career with them, most teachers choose to spend just one or two years in Japan, enjoying the opportunity to "live in an amazing country and work there, making a very comfortable entry-level salary."

LOCATION(S) WHERE ENTRY-LEVEL EMPLOYEES WORK

Teachers work at more than 800 branch locations across Japan.

AVERAGE NUMBER OF APPLICATIONS EACH YEAR

Nova Group receives more than 10,000 applications each year.

AVERAGE NUMBER HIRED PER YEAR OVER THE LAST TEN YEARS

Nova Group hires well over 2,000 new employees each year. Roughly 1,000 of these new hires hail from the United States.

ENTRY-LEVEL POSITION(S) AVAILABLE

All new employees enter the company as a language instructor, teaching conversational English to Japanese students.

AVERAGE HOURS WORKED PER WEEK

New hires teach eight 40-minute classes per day, usually averaging about 29.5 worked hours per week.

PERCENTAGE OF ENTRY-LEVEL HIRES STILL WITH THE COMPANY AFTER THREE, FIVE, AND TEN YEARS

Because the job is international, the majority of employees only stay with the company for three years.

AVERAGE STARTING SALARY

First-year teachers receive ¥2.7 to 3 million per year (U.S. conversion depends on current exchange rate).

Getting Hired

After submitting an application to the company, qualified candidates are invited to attend a group information session about Nova, followed by a personal interview. Students with a bachelor's degree from any accredited four-year college or university are eligible for the program, though Nova Group says they specifically look for "well-rounded, flexible, enthusiastic, energetic, and adaptable individuals." Teaching experience is not required, nor is Japanese language ability; however, eagerness and ability to live abroad are important factors in a hiring decision. A current employee reveals, "The interview seemed like a question session more focused on how I might handle life in Japan, asking questions about my travel history or any adversity I have faced in my life."

Money and Perks

In addition to paying a solid, entry-level salary to their instructors, Nova helps new hires make travel arrangements and set up life in Japan. They even offer shared, semi-furnished, low-rent apartments to Nova employees. Obviously, "being in Japan" is a major perk of a job at Nova, as are local travel opportunities. Additionally, employees appreciate the company's flexible scheduling and the fact that "Nova gives you paid vacation time as well so there are chances to travel all around Asia."

The Ropes

For many new hires, a position with Nova is the first time they will work as teachers, as well as their first opportunity to live abroad. A few days after arriving in Japan, Nova employees go through a short orientation session, designed to acquaint new hires with the company, as well as the local culture. A former Nova instructor tells us, "The orientation was very detailed—there was an orientation to talk about the particulars of living in Japan, the job itself, getting yourself acquainted with Nova, etc. They helped us set up cell phones and answered any questions about living in Japan. This was vital." After that, new hires complete a three-day training program—essentially a crash course in teaching techniques and Nova's curriculum and materials. By the second day, new instructors are already testing out their teaching skills in real Nova classrooms. While trainees tell us that their orientation was comprehensive, they also say it is "a bit difficult to remember the vast amount of information being thrown at us at once."

Day in the Life

On a typical day, Nova instructors prepare for and teach eight forty-minute classes to students of varying ages and abilities. While the company has developed its own series of textbooks, instructors are expected to choose and tailor lesson plans based on student need. An employee elaborates, "I was given a schedule of what classes I had to teach and I had to go in and prepare a basic lesson plan—something that involved teaching a new verb tense or using vocabulary, and come up with ways to implement the lesson through conversation." Instructors are also encouraged to add their own touches, like "thinking of role-plays to help the students practice what they just learned." One of the most challenging aspects of the job is becoming accustomed to varying "types of personalities that an instructor must handle in the classrooms." A former instructor elaborates: "There were generally one to four students in a class at a time, and their abilities were varied. Some students were extreme beginners—didn't speak any English at all. . . . So at first I would walk into a classroom and ask a student 'What did you do this weekend?' and either they wouldn't know what to say or wouldn't understand my question at all. Once I got past that and knew which lessons were good for which students, the job was extremely easy." Easy, however, doesn't mean boring. "There were so many students and opportunities to [run] the class however you wanted so it was really fun," shares an instructor. On top of that, instructors say the job can be rewarding. Says a veteran employee, "It's a very satisfying feeling, when a student passes a test or gets accepted to a foreign university, knowing that you have helped improve their communication skills."

Peers

"There is a lot of camaraderie" amongst the hundreds of young college grads Nova hires from the United States, England, Ireland, New Zealand, Scotland, Canada, South Africa, and Australia. A new hire enthuses, "Most people were right around my age—it was so fun having friends from all over the world and get[ting] to learn about their culture[s] as well. The people made the experience so amazing. It was fantastic." Echoes another, "People who start together in Japan seem to make lasting friendships that continue long after finishing the job. Many instructors go out after work and go on trips together." Nova employees also take the opportunity to enjoy Japanese nightlife, and tell us, "Pretty much everything you do after work, at least initially, is with the other teachers." According to Nova employees, "People are constantly going out and there is always something going on. Between karaoke or checking out a local pub, it seems like there [is] always something to do before work and on my days off."

Moving on

Those who choose to leave Nova most often so do in order to return to their home country.

Attrition

Although the company does not officially track their attrition rate, Nova Group estimates that 80 to 85 percent of their employees complete their first-year contract. In fact, "most people come with the intention of staying one year but, in fact, the majority sign on for a second contract." For those who stick it out, there are many growth opportunities within the company. A current manager affirms, "All foreigners in upper management started as regular instructors."

Best and Worst

While the company declines to offer specific examples of their best and worst employees, they say that some of their most successful entry-level instructors have "made astounding progress in the company and moved into important positions both in Japan and in the overseas recruiting office." In turn, they warn that students looking for an "extended holiday" should look elsewhere. In general, Nova's troublesome employees are those who "have trouble accepting that there are different ways of living and are at odds with the work ethic and lifestyle of Japan." An instructor explains, "People who were less happy than me seemed to have a problem with Japan—not the job."

OAKLAND TEACHING FELLOWS
TEACHING FELLOW

"One can never be bored in this profession. I find that when I feel slightly 'overwhelmed,' I then know that I have met an appropriate challenge."

The Big Picture

The Oakland Teaching Fellows program is designed to recruit talented teachers in math, science, and Spanish, as well as bilingual-elementary, physical, and special education; applicants need not have teaching credentials or even prior teaching experience to be hired. A "streamlined application and selection process" allows candidates to learn of their status relatively quickly. Comprehensive training prior to entering the classroom prepares Fellows to teach; and coordination with area colleges allow Fellows to earn their credentials while they work. The organization's website notes, "As a teacher, you can be the single most important factor in raising student achievement. As a Teaching Fellow, you will join a network of like-minded professionals dedicated to improving public schools." A current Fellow adds, "Teaching is very rewarding, and the pay is excellent for entry-level work in public service."

LOCATION(S) WHERE ENTRY-LEVEL EMPLOYEES WORK

Jobs are located in Oakland, California.

AVERAGE NUMBER OF APPLICATIONS EACH YEAR

The Oakland Teaching Fellows Program receives about 1,100 applications each year.

AVERAGE NUMBER HIRED PER YEAR

The program hires about 40 Fellows each year.

ENTRY-LEVEL POSITION(S) AVAILABLE

Available positions are for "first-year teachers in the Oakland Unified School District (OUSD) [who] enter through a highly selective program and teach in the high-need subject areas of math, science, Spanish, and bilingual-elementary, physical, and special education. Fellows earn a California Credential while teaching full-time."

AVERAGE HOURS WORKED PER WEEK

Fellows work about 40 to 60 hours per week.

AVERAGE STARTING SALARY

Starting salaries range from $38,777 to $43,980, "depending on education level and related course work. Fellows with previous teaching experience may start at a higher rate. Additionally, Fellows receive a stipend for completion of the Fellows Summer Training Institute, which they finish prior to entering the classroom."

Getting Hired

Those considering applying to the program should read all the information on the program's website to ensure that they meet eligibility requirements. Provided they do, they should then submit an online application form, including a resume, personal statement, and copies of all academic transcripts. Those who pass this level of screening are interviewed. For one component of the interview, candidates must prepare and teach a five-minute lesson. Before the Fellows Summer Training Institute begins, candidates must also pass "all required California teaching tests to finalize enrollment in the program."

One Fellow reports, "A teacher in Oakland Public Schools interviewed me. The tone was very cordial. She asked me why I wanted to teach; what led me to apply; how I would implement high expectations in my classroom; what my behavior management style was; what I would do if nothing seemed to work. It was clear to me [from the interview] that [the Oakland Teaching Fellows program] sought creative and resourceful individuals who wouldn't give up. They wanted people to be mentors and leaders."

Money and Perks

Teaching Fellows are paid on a fixed scale that "determines an individual's salary according to years of classroom experience and units of related course work." The organization notes that "bonuses for specific subject areas or contract signing vary from year to year and depend on an individual's qualifications." Top benefits include participation in the California State Teachers Retirement System (STRS), "financial planning assistance through the option to establish a 403(b) account," and "home-buyer assistance programs for Oakland teachers." Teachers also love "having the summer off" and "knowing that you are making a difference in someone else's life."

The Ropes

All candidates "begin their participation in the Oakland Teaching Fellows through a rigorous six-week training program generally beginning in June and aligning with the district's summer school calendar." During the program, "Fellows build a solid foundation and skill set through curriculum sessions led by successful teachers in target subject areas;" they also benefit from the "experience of observing and lead-teaching in summer school classrooms. Fellows learn how to succeed as newcomers in their first year of teaching, and benefit from research on the factors that have contributed to success for other first-year teachers in urban settings." A typical training day "begins with four hours of observation, practice teaching, or small-group work in summer school classrooms. During the hour-long lunch break, Fellows may discuss lesson plans or reflect on teaching practices with an experienced teacher or other fellows. The afternoon consists of around three hours of curriculum sessions with their Fellow advisor groups; during these, they build on skills related to practice teaching and plan for the year ahead. At the end of the day, they may attend a workshop on a specific teaching topic or meet with colleagues to plan upcoming lessons."

Day in the Life

Teaching Fellows have "the responsibilities of any teacher running a classroom." They spend their days "meeting the needs of their students; ensuring high standards for success in their classrooms; working with struggling learners; and building relationships with families, colleagues, and administrators important to the success of any student." One Fellow observes, "One can never be bored in this profession. I find that when I feel slightly 'overwhelmed,' I then know that I have met an appropriate challenge. This is why I chose this profession in the first place."

Peers

First-year teachers are incredibly busy managing their classrooms and preparing lessons; one Fellow explains, "I don't socialize that much with the Fellows because we are all swamped with work—but we have a great time when we do get together." When they can spare a minute to converse, Fellows find that they have a lot in common with one another. One writes, "I have found everyone to be very bright, motivated, and wanting to make a difference in students' lives as well as in their own lives. You have to be smart, flexible, and self-motivated to be able to do this job."

Moving on

Oakland Teaching Fellows is "a relatively young program," too new to have collected significant quantities of data on former Fellows. The organization notes that "to date, individuals who have not completed commitments to the program state personal reasons as the primary basis [for leaving]." Some find the job too arduous; one Fellow notes, "There is a big learning curve as a new teacher, and there is no way to avoid that. Different people react differently to that type of situation—whether they rise to the occasion or complain is all up to the individual."

Best and Worst

According to the organization, "The most successful first-year Oakland Teaching Fellows and teachers show a relentless drive for holding themselves and their students to the highest standards and overcoming obstacles to meet classroom goals. Successful teachers reach out to people and resources that will [have an] impact [on] the success of their students." They also "build relationships with other successful teachers, with the families of students, and with colleagues at their school site or in the Teaching Fellows Program. These individuals continually reflect on their teaching practices, actively seek ways to improve, and maintain a sense of perspective in the face of challenges."

OGILVY AND MATHER
ASSISTANT ACCOUNT EXECUTIVE AND ASSOCIATE

"Every day is unique, and there are always new challenges. That's what keeps this job exciting."

The Big Picture

"Ogilvy is extremely well known in the industry," which is what drives so many young graduates to seek a place among the agency's ranks. Dubbing itself the "most local of the internationals and most international of the locals," Ogilvy prides itself on "building brands" that boast small-scale and large-scale success. The company—which is driven by the advertising principles of its late founder, David Ogilvy—is known for its devout employees. One starry-eyed first job-ber raves, "I fell in love with the company based on their information session—the three presenters were professional but also extremely friendly and personable. They explained Ogilvy's history, showed tangible examples of the company's advertisements, and offset these presentation 'standards' with their own opinions about the company and what made it great." Another says that when she and other Ogilvy freshmen get together, "we mostly just talk about how lucky and fortunate we are."

LOCATION(S) WHERE ENTRY-LEVEL EMPLOYEES WORK

Ogilvy's headquarters are in New York City, with another 497 offices worldwide. Local country offices hire on site.

AVERAGE NUMBER OF APPLICATIONS EACH YEAR

Ogilvy receives 800 entry-level applications annually.

AVERAGE NUMBER HIRED PER YEAR OVER THE LAST FIVE YEARS

The company hires an average of 70 entry-level employees each year.

ENTRY-LEVEL POSITION(S) AVAILABLE

Newbies join the firm as assistant account executives (AAE) and associates. Ogilvy officials say, "The Associates Program is designed as a one-year rotational program that exposes the associate to the following disciplines: project management, planning, traffic, finance, production, and account management." The program allows the company to discover an associate's individual strengths while the associate determines "where his or her passion [lies] within the agency." It also allows the associate to learn the different aspects of how the business works in order to make him or her more rounded and knowledgeable for the future. AAEs "learn the discipline of client service and its function in the advertising industry. An AAE focuses immediately on one piece of business and is a part of a team responsible for understanding the client's business and coordinating the efforts of planning, media, and creative [content] to ensure the highest levels of service and creativity."

Getting Hired

Corporate officials explain that "each year, Human Resource Representatives from Ogilvy travel across the country to different schools and career fairs promoting our entry-level and training programs. This takes place in October. In February, on-campus interviews take place. Students are asked to apply online on their campus career management system (MonsterTRAK). Students must submit their resume, cover letter, and answer two mandatory questions. Ogilvy also hosts university visits at the agency. We give consideration to all applications." For the Associates Program, the company narrows down the candidates to twenty-four finalists. These finalists are invited to a challenging assessment day called "Super Saturday," an event designed to access the candidates' ability to deal with simulated situations and assess them against Ogilvy's core competencies. The process for assistant account execs (AAE's) isn't much easier. According to one AAE, "The interview/application process was extremely quick and exciting. I was initially interviewed by an HR manager. Once I had finished with her, I was sent to the fourth floor to meet with the DuPont account team. This began the interview marathon. I went on to meet two account executives, two account supervisors, and the client services director."

Money and Perks

Among Ogilvy rookies there are "complaints about low pay . . . especially given the fact that" many are stationed in the Big Apple, which is "such an expensive city." An AAE first jobber also notes, "Growth in terms of pay is difficult, and for some is hard to achieve." But these early financial woes are well worth it to get a foot in the door at one of the nation's preeminent ad agencies. As one newbie says, "Everyone mentions that they learn a lot, and that Ogilvy is a great place to begin their career." And the job comes with plenty of perks. For instance, Ogilvy employees "get a lot of time off," including "a whole week between Christmas and New Year's" and "Summer Fridays [which] end at 1:00 P.M. between July 4th and Labor Day." There are also "a lot of company-funded happy hours, discounted gym memberships, access to magazine/newspaper subscriptions for free, discounts at the company makeup store, and dinner/car service if you work more than ten hours" in a day.

The Ropes

"All new employees must attend new hire orientation," company officials say. The orientation, which takes place over a day and half, includes a "history of David Ogilvy and his agency, technology training, benefits summary, and an agency tour." While rookies describe orientation as "very standard," they assert that Ogilvy's "training program is pretty amazing." The Account Management Training Program (AMTP) is a training experience that provides a solid foundation that young employees build on throughout their years in the industry. One new hire explains, "Right away, you meet fifty [new hires] who are experiencing the same things you are. . . . Each week, we meet with different executives and department heads, [to hear] about what their department does and the type of responsibilities they [have]. We also meet with many members of senior management, who most people [find] to be very motivational." A fellow first jobber adds, "It is a very comprehensive program, and one of the top reasons I wanted to join Ogilvy above all other agencies."

Day in the Life

The workday in an ad agency can be hectic, to say the least. One fresh recruit at Ogilvy admits, "I do feel overwhelmed often. Especially in the beginning, I was extremely overwhelmed and stressed out with the volume of work." He adds, "Every day is unique and there are always new challenges. That's what keeps this job exciting. But, basically, I come into the office, and I already have many, many e-mails from the Asian markets, given the time-zone difference. I spend the first few hours replying to e-mails and focusing on the more urgent issues. I'm on the phone with clients to keep them in the loop and seek their advice on projects. I'm on the phone with local markets around the world managing their expectations versus client expectations on said projects. It's hectic and stressful. Each day is something new." A concurring colleague says, "A typical day at Ogilvy involves many surprises. No day is ever the same."

Peers

AMTP "involves fifty of the new AAEs [and] associates hired over the past several months," giving new hires plenty of opportunities to get to know one another. And what do they think about what they find? One newbie gushes, "Everyone here is extremely fun. You'll make a lot of friends really quickly. Once you meet your peers (and there are plenty of them), you will be hanging out with them at least a few times a week. It's a really fun environment." And as employees at the New York City headquarters note, "it doesn't hurt that our office is located in one of the busiest bar districts in NYC." But it's not all fun and games with this crowd. As a newbie says, "My peers are extremely smart, and I learn from them everyday."

Moving on

First jobbers leave Ogilvy to accept positions at other firms, to take a job in another industry, to return to school, to relocate, or to raise children.

Attrition

Only 2 percent of Ogilvy's recent-grad hires leave the agency before completing their first year. The camaraderie among new hires and the incredible training offered through AMTP are tough to walk away from. Still, young workers do "criticize Ogilvy on raises and promotions," saying that "everyone gets a raise or a promotion at a different time and no one likes feeling left behind. It generally takes a year to a year and a half to get a promotion." The largest frustrations felt by newbies, though, have more to do with the industry than the company itself. A first jobber explains, "When your friends all make huge salaries in banking, and your total salary after a raise doesn't even equal their bonuses, it's tough. It doesn't help that New York is such an expensive place."

Oxygen
Various Positions

"The perfect position to get started in the television industry."

The Big Picture

Once upon a time, aspirants to the television industry had to break in through one of the Big Three networks or one of their local affiliates. Now, thanks to digital cable, there are literally hundreds of television networks out there that serve every conceivable demographic. Oxygen is an "edgy" network for women that was co-founded by Oprah Winfrey, Geraldine Laybourne (formerly a big player at Nickelodeon), and the Carsey-Werner-Mandabach juggernaut (responsible for *Roseanne*, *Third Rock From the Sun*, *That 70's Show*, and *The Cosby Show*).

Location(s) where Oxygen Hires Entry-level Work

Headquarters are in New York, there are small offices in Los Angeles, Detroit, Chicago, and Dallas.

Average Number of Applications Each Year

Oxygen receives about 1,000 applications each year.

Entry-level Position(s) Available

Entry-level employees are hired as business and legal affairs assistants, community affairs associates, public relations assistants, research assistants, sales assistants, development assistants, marketing assistants, production assistants, department assistants, desktop support techs, and administrative assistants.

Average Hours Worked Per Week

Entry-level hires work an average of 40 hours per week.

Benefits Offered

Oxygen offers medical and dental coverage, as well as flexible spending accounts, life insurance, short-term and long-term disability, TransitChek, and 401(k) plans.

Contact Information

E-mail your cover letter and resume to jobs@oxygen.com or call the job hotline at 212-651-5687.

Getting Hired

Connections are critical in the entertainment industry, so it comes as no surprise that all the first jobbers we spoke with at Oxygen utilized previous contacts in the business to land their jobs. For some, the contact was someone met during an Oxygen internship, but just as many found their current positions because a family member or friend knew someone and was able to put in a good word. One first jobber explains, "I heard about it through a friend. It sounded like the perfect position to get started in the television industry." Because most hires arrive with a recommendation, the interview process is less grueling than at most places of employment. "I was interviewed by the vice president of Consumer Marketing and Affiliate Marketing," writes one marketing assistant, who continues, "The interview was very relaxed. Both sides were very excited to explore what [one another] had to offer. The first interview was very exploratory while the second was more finances and benefits."

Money and Perks

Start dates and salaries may vary, depending on the urgency to fill the position and the unique qualities the hire brings to the job. One newbie reports, "For me, the salary wasn't negotiable at all. I was told that I would have some influence over my job duties, but for the most part, that has yet to happen." Fringe benefits include four full weeks of paid vacation and "the CDs that you can take from the bin of unwanteds."

The Ropes

New hires can start at Oxygen at any time, and for the most part, they learn as they go, watching their bosses and trying not to foul things up too much until they master their jobs. Formal orientation occurs on or near the first day of work, "is three hours long, and features guest speakers from various departments throughout the company to provide new hires with an overview of Oxygen. The company mission statement is presented, and the group is also addressed by our CEO and COO." First jobbers also receive harassment training and a review of their benefits package during orientation. After that, "Your boss trains you. In my case, whenever I had a question she would sit with me until I figured it out. She was very patient. It probably took about a month to get acclimated and learn most of the ins and outs, which was mostly done by asking as many questions as possible."

Day in the Life

Oxygen hires first jobbers for a broad range of functions. What they do on a daily basis, how much autonomy they exercise over their work, and how likely they are to advance within the company all depends on where and for whom they work. First jobbers in small departments, for example, may enjoy a congenial work environment but have little chance for advancement, since few higher-ups leave the company. Among our survey respondents was a program coordinator who is "in charge of making sure that the correct episode or movie goes on the air at the correct time. I program them into the computer and keep the system updated with the correct series and their descriptions. I also keep track of what is going on at other networks and answer the viewer services line." We also heard from a marketing assistant whose responsibilities "are mostly administrative with some conceptualizing for consumer and marketing plans." A community affairs associate told us that "a typical day involves a lot of calls with nonprofits, note taking, arranging budgets, and transferring information from outside organizations within various company departments. Brainstorming and communication are always a big part of my day." All Oxygen employees benefit from an extensive formal mentoring program as well as a variety of informal mentoring apparatuses.

Peers

At Oxygen "there are opportunities for socializing after work," facilitated in part by "a bar downstairs from the office," but "it is mixed with all levels of employees," not just first jobbers. It's not a wild social scene, though, "because most of us are dead tired." Employees tell us that "the company is fairly relaxed and the people are easy to get a long with," and "it's a company mostly made up of young women, and it's great."

Moving on

According to Oxygen, "Entry-level employees who leave the company do so for another job opportunity or to switch career paths. For the most part, our entry-level employees do not leave but are promoted to other positions in the company." Some here complain that "it is hard to move up the corporate ladder because the company is so small and no one wants to leave their job." That drives some first jobbers to leave. Others "don't like the programming choices we put on air or are afraid we will become too corporate some day." Most, however, recognize that Oxygen is a pretty good gig and hope to stay on long-term.

PEACE CORPS
VOLUNTEER

"Peace Corps has the reputation of being where idealistic, liberal, young people go after college, but that's only
a small segment of the volunteer population. I know very
conservative married couples who serve, elderly individuals, former U.S. soldiers, and then your handful of liberal, recent college graduates as well."

The Big Picture

Assigned to posts in rural communities throughout the world, Peace Corps volunteers share stories of triumphs, failures, frustrations, and challenges as they struggle to adjust to life and make a difference as a member of this famous service program. Through ups and downs, Peace Corps volunteers say their unusual job affords unparalleled "opportunity to
truly see the world" and to "gain valuable leadership skills" in an international environment. Adventurous and self-motivated people tend to be most satisfied with their posts, saying they love the opportunity to "work as an incomparably
autonomous individual who is given nearly free reign to find projects that spark my interest."

LOCATION(S) WHERE ENTRY-LEVEL EMPLOYEES WORK

Peace Corps volunteers currently work in 75 countries around the world. In 2007, the Peace
Corps will offer new programs in Cambodia and Ethiopia.

AVERAGE NUMBER OF APPLICATIONS EACH YEAR

The Peace Corps Receives an average of 10,931 applications each year.

AVERAGE NUMBER HIRED PER YEAR OVER THE LAST TEN YEARS

On average, approximately 3,900 volunteers entered service each year over the last 10 years.

ENTRY-LEVEL POSITION(S) AVAILABLE

Entry-level hires work as volunteers.

AVERAGE STARTING SALARY

Peace Corps volunteers are unpaid, but basic living costs are covered.

BENEFITS OFFERED

Peace Corps volunteers receive medical, dental, and vision coverage. They also receive travel
to and from their assignment, student loan deferment, and two vacation days a month.

CONTACT INFORMATION

Call 800-424-8580 or go to www.peacecorps.gov/volunteer/recruit/regional.cfm.

Getting Hired

The first hurdle in becoming a Peace Corps volunteer is completing what can be an exceedingly long application process. A current volunteer jokes, "The application for Peace Corps felt like it was forty pages long. I'm sure it wasn't that long, but it took me a week or so to complete." In addition, the application requires "an interview with a recruiter, at least four references sent in separately, and a complete medical review." While 97 percent of Peace Corps volunteers have college degrees, it is not a requirement of the program. Instead, personal qualities, such as a "sense of adventure and a desire to help others" are the most important factors in a hiring decision. "Much of the interview was spent providing [me with] information on what life might be like in the Peace Corps. Especially the physical and emotional components of immersing yourself completely in another culture for two years," shares a volunteer. Adds another, "The interview asked about previous service experience, motivation for wanting to be a Peace Corps volunteer, international experience, hopes for your service, and about where, if given the choice, you would like to go in the world. The interview seemed to focus on looking at a person's motivations more than specific skill sets."

Money and Perks

The Peace Corps covers a volunteer's basic living expenses while participating in the program, including medical care and travel expenses to and from their post. Volunteers also receive $225 per month toward a "readjustment allowance," which they receive upon completion of their two years of service. Peace Corps volunteers may defer student loan payments while participating in the program, and "volunteers with Perkins Loans will receive a 15-percent cancellation of their outstanding balance for each year of their two years of service in addition to the deferment."

The Ropes

Peace Corps training begins at home, with a three-day orientation—basically, "a 'get-to-know-you' process, and a crash course in administrative matters." Next, volunteers fly off to their host country, where "trainees immediately are taken to a Training Hub where language, cultural, and technical training takes place for the next ten weeks." A volunteer elaborates, "We did almost 150 hours of language training, 80 hours of technical training, 25 hours of safety and security, and also medical training. These were all ran by Peace Corps staff in the main office or hired locals." In addition to language and technical training, the program usually includes, "diversity exercises, guest speakers, team building activities, and safety seminars." During this period, volunteers are required to live with a host family, an experience designed to augment their classroom instruction with an intimate initiation to the culture. For some, the home-stay is a difficult component of the program. A survivor admits, "For all of the cultural experience it helps you gain, it can be downright overwhelming at times." A former volunteer in Thailand shares this amusing story from his home-stay: "My height scared some of the children at first, but I tried to smile. When I hit my head on the ceiling at one point that brought some laughs and lightened the mood."

Day in the Life

Once they make it through the initial training period, Peace Corps volunteers head out to their field posts, usually located in rural and remote communities. Once in the field, volunteers have little contact with their peers, supervisors, or the Peace Corps organization. "Peace Corps doesn't offer much flexibility in where you work or your assignment, but the truth is that once you get to your site, your job is what you make of it," confides a volunteer. "You are the only person who motivates and evaluates your work," shares another. Adjusting to life in the Third World can be challenging. For example, a former English teacher tells us, "It was a lot of trial and error. My Kyrgyz wasn't that great and the kids didn't understand too much English. I didn't have any textbooks, only half of my chalkboard worked, [there were] not enough chairs/desks for the kids, and the electricity would come on when it wanted to." Another volunteer confides, "My initial responsibilities included trying not to get frustrated with my language ability, wishing my digestive system would just relax, and trying to tell myself that in time it would be easier." However, with time, perseverance, and ingenuity, many volunteers turn the situation around. "As I've gotten more comfortable in my community, become more familiar with how things work, and gotten to know more people, more opportunities for projects have presented themselves and my days have gotten much fuller," explains a volunteer. After hitting his stride, a volunteer in Thailand spent his days "at my desk in the local government office, riding my bike around my village hoping to have a chat with some rice farmers, standing in front of a class full of students helping to explain the proper way to use a condom, watching the local women weave cotton and talking about ways to improve their marketing, or even dressed up in traditional clothing and riding a float down the street during the annual rains festival!" While task lists vary by site, all Peace Corps assignments share one key component: "It's definitely not a cubicle job."

Peers

Think you know who you'll meet in Peace Corps? Think again. Current volunteers inform us that "Peace Corps has the reputation of being where idealistic, liberal, young people go after college, but that's only a small segment of the volunteer population. I know very conservative married couples who serve, elderly individuals, former U.S. soldiers, and then your handful of liberal, recent college graduates as well." Enthuses a volunteer, "Yes, the people are amazing—from all walks of life, [from] all regions of the U.S., from all forms of diversity, and [they are] all filled with a compassionate, curious heart for the world and its people." Volunteers assigned to the same country may only see each other every four-to-six weeks; even so, "there is a lot of camaraderie with other volunteers as they go through a lot of the same situations on the job." And, since volunteers often feel socially isolated in their communities, they lean heavily on other volunteers for support and friendship. Admits one, "After we moved to our sites, we got together almost every weekend to escape the loneliness. We partied like we were still in college, just in a different place."

Moving on

Peace Corps is a twenty-seven-month commitment. In most cases, volunteers complete their tours then pursue other opportunities.

Attrition

On average, 10 to 13 percent of Peace Corps volunteers leave service early each year. Of these, 74 percent were due to resignation and 17 percent were due to medical reasons. Peace Corps representatives tell us that, "Of the 74 percent [who resign], the two most common reasons reported from volunteers [are] family related/personal issues or the volunteer did not feel that Peace Corps service was a good fit for him/her."

Best and Worst

Without giving any specific examples, Peace Corps suggests, "Volunteers who come in with an open mind and who understand that other countries have their own values and traditions tend to be the most successful." Citing cultural and religious differences as common sources of friction between host countries and volunteers, Peace Corps officials insist, "Those volunteers who respect their new host culture, even if they do not agree with it, tend to be the most successful."

THE PEPSI BOTTLING GROUP, INC.

SALES MANAGEMENT TRAINEE AND OPERATIONS MANAGEMENT TRAINEE

"The training opportunities at PBG are phenomenal. PBG is invested in their employees and takes the time to develop managers such as myself into better managers, performers, and decision-makers."

The Big Picture

New hires at The Pepsi Bottling Group—or just PBG—are attracted by the company's "great reputation for brands and career growth." As one first jobber puts it, "If you perform and deliver results at PBG, the road is endless." PBG employment begins with the highly touted Management Training Program, a rotational "on-boarding process" that allows newbies to get a sense of how the entire company works. But the learning doesn't stop there. A fourth-year employee explains: "I consider every day, in some form or fashion, a day of training. Each day I am learning something new—whether it pertains to our customers or our business strategies, to our employees or consumers—which is preparing me for the next step."

LOCATION(S) WHERE ENTRY-LEVEL EMPLOYEES WORK

PBG operates 46 plants in the U.S.

AVERAGE NUMBER OF APPLICATIONS EACH YEAR

Each year, PBG receives approximately 3,000 entry-level applications.

AVERAGE NUMBER HIRED PER YEAR OVER THE LAST FIVE YEARS

On average, PBG brings in 125 entry-level employees annually.

ENTRY-LEVEL POSITION(S) AVAILABLE

Newbies enter PBG as either sales management trainees or operations management trainees. The company brass explains, "PBG's Sales Development Program and Operations Development Program offer recent college graduates an opportunity to enter our organization through eight-week and twelve-week training programs, respectively. Additionally, recruits complete informal on-the-job training for the first six months. These programs are designed to provide a foundation of knowledge to help recruits launch their careers in our organization, as well as to build their skills so they can be future managers and leaders."

AVERAGE HOURS WORKED PER WEEK

Newbies work 50 hours per week.

Getting Hired

The Pepsi Bottling Group's "Campus Development Program has solid relationships with more than sixty campuses across the United States. Every year, PBG Human Resources partners with PBG functional leaders and visits each campus to host informational seminars and job fairs—and to conduct on-campus interviews." This being said, PBG welcomes applications from students from any college or university. (Just visit PBG.com to apply.) What all successful candidates have in common is that they are "results-oriented, competitive, self-motivated people who possess a strong intellectual curiosity—plus great leadership and people skills." The hiring process often involves a few rounds of interviews. Recalling her first interview (conducted by two HR officers and a retail sales director), one first jobber states, "I was informed, in a very blunt fashion, [of] the tasks I would be facing as an entry-level employee. I was told that the work was not glamorous (more like blue-collar work), and that I would need to be able to lift twenty-five pounds repeatedly." But she also adds that in both rounds of interviews everybody "came across as both professional and sincere." PBG officials offer this insight into the kinds of questions that they pose to interviewees: "We ask candidates when they have had to analyze a complex problem, how they developed solutions to that problem, and how they communicated their recommendations to others. We also ask applicants to tell us about a time when they had to create enthusiasm around a project in order to motivate others to complete the task. Finally, we ask them to give us demonstrated examples of leadership (through clubs, sports, volunteering, etc.)."

Money and Perks

Newbies in operations receive a base salary; those in sales bring home a base salary plus commission. One way or another, PBG rookies start off with livable wages and have plenty of opportunities to move up in the company—in terms of both pay and responsibility. A PBGer who began his career with the Management Training Program twenty-two years ago and is now vice president of National Retail Sales for North America confirms: "I have seen that throughout my career the responsibility has come quickly and the pay appropriate for the responsibility." All "entry-level employees receive a sign-on bonus" to "jump-start their careers." Raises are typically given "after the first eight months of employment with PBG and are based on performance and business results." When it comes to perks, these employees enjoy the simple—but oh-so-important—things. A sales manager boasts, "PBG has an excellent 401(k) plan as well as superior health benefits." In fact, the 401(k) plan was recently enhanced. PBG now contributes 2 percent to employees' 401(k) plans, regardless of what the employee contributes. The company also matches, dollar for dollar, up to four percent of the employee's salary, depending on years of service.

The Ropes

PBG's orientation program, called "Fast Start," stretches over six months and combines departmental rotations, "job shadowing, classroom education, and experiential exercises."

"The orientation process at PBG was one I felt privileged to experience," says a first jobber who was particularly pleased with the chance to learn the ropes in a range of different departments. "PBG invested their time in ensuring that we were versed in various roles in the organization before we set foot on our own sales route. We spent approximately two to three weeks working cross-functionally with [employees] ranging from delivery drivers to warehouse foremen to key account managers and executive-level employees. We also spent several days reading and working scenarios out in our PBG on-boarding binders. These binders were [specifically designed for] building a foundation in the terminology, calculation, and sales strategies that we would soon be facing. It clearly defined our mission as well as our 'Rules of the Road,' which details what each of us at PBG are here to achieve." PBG also administers a range of mentorship programs that allow younger employees "to network with high-level executives."

Day in the Life

Early on, new hires devote plenty of time to the training program, which means shadowing veteran employees in different corners of the company, riding routes with members of various departments, and asking as many questions as they can think of. But it's not long before newbies ease into the workload of a full-time professional. Says one, "It was difficult at the beginning because of the complexity of the job and the amount of responsibility that is given to you." A colleague adds, "A lot of individuals are surprised about the amount of physical/grunt work." No, this is not a job spent hiding behind a computer screen. While there will be some of that, entry-level responsibilities range from managing merchandise to distributing it. This means that heavy lifting and (particularly in sales) client interaction come with the territory. (In fact, a rookie sales manager might have "twenty to twenty-five stores to service" each day.) The result is a dynamic environment in which new workers are "never bored [and] often overwhelmed." But that was all right for one former frosh, because she knew that her "work directly impacted the performance of our business, including profit, costs, and sales."

Peers

One first jobber says, "PBG is such a people-oriented business that I had no trouble making friends or meeting interesting people. The employees of PBG are also some of the most attractive people that I have seen in an industry. I know that may seem odd to say, but I'd be lying if I did not notice that when I was hired. The level of intelligence is also one that I find myself in awe of and I feel extremely lucky to be around such a bright group of folks on a daily basis." She adds, "There is a great camaraderie within PBG. . . . That's what makes working for [the company] so special. We here at PBG put a lot of hours into the work we do. [But] that's not to say that we don't go out and enjoy a happy hour or two."

Moving on

According to PBG officials, "Often, entry-level employees leave to pursue a graduate-school degree full-time. In addition, they may leave to take a position in another industry."

Attrition

Approximately one in every four new hires leaves PBG before the end of the first year. This is frequently caused by the multi-faceted nature of the work (as we mentioned earlier, this not your typical sit-at-a-desk management job). Fortunately, the Management Training Program gives fresh faces ample opportunity to figure this out. Those who do decide that PBG is for them tend to heap praise upon the training program. As one satisfied employee raves, "The training opportunities at PBG are phenomenal. PBG is invested in their employees and takes the time to develop managers such as myself into better managers, performers, and decision-makers."

Best and Worst

The Pepsi Bottling Group has seen a number of its one-time rookies rise to the ranks of senior management. First jobbers in the upper echelons today include the senior vice president of Global Sales and chief customer officer, the vice president for Consumer and Category Insights, the vice president of National Retail Sales for North America, the vice president for Manufacturing and Logistics, and the vice president for Food Service Operations.

PBG officials say, "Our least successful entry-level employees are those who do not possess a strong work ethic, leadership skills, communication skills, or intellectual curiosity."

PHILADELPHIA TEACHING FELLOWS
TEACHING FELLOW

"The School District of Philadelphia has so much that needs to be done within each and every school [that] there is definitely no extra time for boredom."

The Big Picture

The Philadelphia Teaching Fellows (PTF) program is in its second year, having just been launched for the 2004–2005 school year. The program seeks to recruit "a cohort of full-time new teachers in the school district of Philadelphia who fill high-needs vacancies in special education, math, science, English as a second language, and middle school subjects while working toward [obtaining] Pennsylvania [teaching] certification."

LOCATION(S) WHERE ENTRY-LEVEL EMPLOYEES WORK

Jobs are located in Philadelphia, Pennsylvania.

AVERAGE NUMBER OF APPLICATIONS EACH YEAR

Over the past two years, application numbers have hovered around 700.

AVERAGE NUMBER HIRED PER YEAR

The program hired 60 teachers to fill midyear teaching vacancies in February of 2005, and program officials now hope to recruit "75 to 100 teachers to fill vacancies at the beginning of the school year" and "50 to 75 teachers to fill midyear teaching vacancies."

ENTRY-LEVEL POSITION(S) AVAILABLE

New hires work as teaching fellows.

AVERAGE HOURS WORKED PER WEEK

Teaching Fellows work more than 35 hours per week.

AVERAGE STARTING SALARY

The base starting salary is $38,751, but "Fellows with a master's degree and those teaching certain subject areas receive additional pay. Bonuses and incentives may also be available."

BENEFITS OFFERED

Teaching Fellows have a choice of health insurance plans; they also receive dental, prescription, and vision coverage. Additional benefits include a pension, a 401(k) plan, and a pre-service Training Institute for which "Fellows are paid a stipend [to cover] living expenses."

CONTACT INFORMATION

Philadelphia Teaching Fellows
440 North Broad Street, Suite 112
Philadelphia, PA 19130
Tel: 215-400-8687
www.PhiladelphiaTeachingFellows.org

Getting Hired

Applicants to the PTF program must apply via the organization's website; a completed application includes a resume, a personal statement, and official academic transcripts for all college and university work. Applications are screened and notified of their status within two weeks. Those who clear this hurdle are invited to interview. One Fellow reports, "I was interviewed by current school staff and the PTF recruiters. The thought of the interview was nerve-wracking to me, since I had to prepare and present a class lesson to not only my interviewer, but also my Fellow [interviewee] group. However, it wasn't as bad as I had anticipated. The interviewer and my group were all welcoming and friendly and made me feel at ease throughout the whole process. After the group interview, we returned to speak with a PTF recruiter for a question-and-answer session at which all our concerns were addressed. Next, we met with a PTF recruiter one-on-one to talk about our interests specifically within teaching. I ranked my top three areas of interest, with computer science at the top." PTF maintains notification dates for its hiring decisions. Applicants for the fall program are typically notified in March; applicants for the winter program are typically notified in October. Those selected to teach "are supplied with an enrollment package." To finalize the process, candidates must pass state teacher tests (Praxis examinations) before entering the classroom as teachers."

Money and Perks

Teacher salaries are determined by strict schedules that vary slightly by district. Bonuses "may be offered for teaching in specific subject areas or schools. If this is the case, it will be clearly stated during the application process." Fellows love the work calendar, with its "many vacations, summers off, weekends off, and an early end to the work day."

The Ropes

Fellows enter orientation during two periods. The midyear replacement program begins in January; the summer program starts in June. Both training sessions consist of two parts: morning classroom teaching and observations and afternoon sessions led by a veteran teacher that cover "teaching strategies, managing student behavior, and understanding the diversity and culture in your school." One Fellow explains, "The month-long orientation process is very informative, yet at the same time very exhausting. The days are long. Every day I would wake up at 6:00 A.M., leave my house by 7:00 A.M., get to my cooperating school at 8:00 A.M. for student-teaching sessions, [eat] lunch from 12:00 P.M. to 1:00 P.M., then head over to the training institute for training from 1:30 P.M. to 7:00 P.M. Most of the training I received dealt with working in an inner-city school, working with inner-city students/administrators/parents, and class management. By the time I got home, ate, and did some of my homework, I was exhausted and ready for bed." In their first year as teachers, "Fellows begin a course of study for their Pennsylvania teaching certificate. Fellows are responsible for the cost of tuition for certification course work."

Day in the Life

Fellows are full-scale teachers whose responsibilities "are those of a classroom teacher." One Fellow reports, "A typical day begins at about 7:30 A.M., when I first get to school to begin setting up for the day. The kids come in and are picked up in the playground at 8:30 A.M., and classes begin by 9:00 A.M. Each Fellow teaches six periods a day, with one period for prep and one for lunch. The school day ends at 3:00 P.M., but most teachers stay in the building until at least 4:00 P.M.." Another adds, "The School District of Philadelphia has so much that needs to be done within each and every school [that] there is definitely no extra time for boredom. If you really enjoy what you are doing and want to help, you will find something or another to occupy your time."

Peers

Friendships are forged during the PTF orientation period, a time when Fellows are all together in one place. One Fellow observes, "I probably made more friends with members in my PTF cohort [than with members of] the staff at my school." In "high-needs" schools that are "largely staffed by Teaching Fellows, Teach For America [volunteers], and alternative certification teachers," the faculty is "largely young and idealistic," and "there is a lot of camaraderie. Collaboration and supporting [one another] is essential for survival." Most Fellows are too busy to enjoy a robust after-hours scene; when they do socialize, however, they find it "a good way to unwind, relax, and be yourself."

Moving on

The Philadelphia Teaching Fellows program is only two years old, so relatively few Fellows have left the program as of the writing of this profile. Those who did leave "cited personal reasons (moving from the city) as well as challenges [to] their school placement." One Fellow writes, "some of my peers came to quick conclusions that teaching wasn't for them after all. [This job] definitely opens your eyes and makes you realize whether or not [teaching] is for you."

Best and Worst

A successful Fellow is "intentional and reflective on his or her own professional growth. A successful employee is continually focused on the goal of increasing student achievement and takes responsibility for developing his or her craft to ensure success with regard to this goal. The successful employee welcomes feedback, seeking mentors in his or her school and beyond; seeking opportunities to observe and be observed; and constantly measuring the success of his or her strategies in terms of their ability to concretely raise student achievement in the classroom. This teacher is disciplined, consistently prepared, and is able to persevere when times are tough. This teacher fosters positive relationships with his or her principal and colleagues. This teacher is inspired by the students in his or her classroom and looks for opportunities to build meaningful connections with them, their families, and their communities."

THE PHOENIX COMPANIES, INC.
VARIOUS POSITIONS

"Phoenix is located in Hartford, the insurance capital of the world. The kind of actuarial exposure and opportunities available here are incomparable."

The Big Picture

The Phoenix Companies, Inc., "a leading life insurance, annuity, and asset management products provider for the affluent and high-net-worth," is a heavy hitter; the company ranks a spot on the Forbes Global 2000. The company's two main subsidiaries are Phoenix Life Insurance Company and Phoenix Investment Partners, Ltd. Phoenix's efforts to create a family-friendly, diverse work environment have been praised by Working Mother Magazine, the National Association of Female Executives, and the Anti-Defamation League.

LOCATION(S) WHERE ENTRY-LEVEL EMPLOYEES WORK

Entry-level hires work at the company headquarters in Hartford, Connecticut and at offices in Albany, New York and Greenfield, Massachusetts.

AVERAGE NUMBER OF APPLICATIONS EACH YEAR

The Phoenix receives approximately 1,400 applications for five of their key entry-level positions: actuarial assistant, client services representative, internal wholesaler, life new business account manager, and new business representative. An additional 1,000 applications are reviewed annually for a variety of other entry-level positions.

AVERAGE NUMBER HIRED PER YEAR

During the past year, the Phoenix hired approximately 60 entry-level employees for the five positions listed above and an additional 75 employees for other entry-level positions.

ENTRY-LEVEL POSITION(S) AVAILABLE

Five key entry-level positions available for recent college graduates are: actuarial assistant, client services representative, internal wholesaler, life new business account manager, and new business representative. A variety of other entry-level positions are also available; among these are internal investment consultant, internal sales support representative, and sales completion specialist.

AVERAGE HOURS WORKED PER WEEK

Full-time employees work 40 hours per week.

AVERAGE STARTING SALARY (BY POSITION)

In 2005, actuarial assistants earned $50,000–$70,000 per year; client services representatives earned $32,000–$38,000 per year; and new business representatives earned $36,000–$45,000 per year.

Getting Hired

Phoenix requires all job seekers to submit applications online. After that, "a corporate recruiter reviews candidate resumes and selects individuals to call who appear to be a strong fit with position requirements. Candidates are assessed by phone and in person." The company also recruits on many campuses and accepts applications from students at all colleges and universities. The company notes that "technical skills for specific professions may include strong math ability for actuarial students and finance/accounting for other disciplines. Excellent written, verbal, and interpersonal skills are necessary to partner with other professionals, departments, and customers. A strong focus on customer satisfaction is a plus." One successful hire describes the on-site interview process: "There was a dinner interview on the night I arrived in Hartford. It was quite informal but gave me an opportunity to learn more about the company. It also gave me an idea about the skills they require for the position. The next morning, I had a series of five interviews. Each interview focused on a different aspect of my resume. There were a few technical questions based on my finance background, but in general, the interviews were very friendly and relaxed."

Money and Perks

"Job offers are competitive within the industry," company officials note. That said, initial offers are not always negotiable. One recent hire explains, "When I started may have been negotiable, but the offer worked well for me, so I never tried to negotiate." One employee reports having been unsuccessful in trying to negotiate a higher starting salary. But fear not: Regular salary reviews and increases "coincide with performance reviews." Those in the Actuarial Development Program also earn raises "as a result of passing rigorous actuarial professional exams." One ADP participant notes, "The exam raises and exam bonuses are liberal. The pay package is attractive to begin with and keeps getting better with the exam raises." The company also notes that "a few entry-level positions are eligible for a 5–10 percent bonus." Some employees consider the job location a big perk; one such employee writes, "Phoenix is located in Hartford, the insurance capital of the world. The kind of actuarial exposure and opportunities available here are incomparable." Another plus: The Asset Management and Life Operations "work closely together. This gives [employees] the opportunity to work in a life insurance company with a very strong investment side. Actuaries are ultimately financial professionals. Hence, having access to a complete investment branch within the company inevitably expands one's fiscal knowledge base."

The Ropes

An orientation kit is given to new hires before they start working. One first jobber writes, "Orientation lasted about two hours, [during which] they informed us of all the benefits offered by the company and [of] how to register/sign up for our selections. They also reviewed the office tools employed by the company and how to navigate them. After orientation, my boss was called to come get me." And that's it; after that, it's time to get to work. A series of one-on-one trainings follow [during] the subsequent weeks and months; the specific training content depends on the employee's job functions in the company.

Day in the Life

Phoenix brings new hires on board in a number of areas. Noteworthy positions include actuarial assistant, internal wholesaler, and client services representative. Actuarial assistants are part of an elite "intensive development opportunity" that "seeks to recruit, train, and develop business professionals with strong actuarial aptitude for a progression into technical and managerial roles at Phoenix." Daily life involves "interdepartmental rotations generally lasting eighteen to thirty months;" these may include work in life and annuity pricing and product development, individual financial reporting, investments, strategic planning, investor and rating agency relations, underwriting, corporate finance, and enterprise risk management. Internal wholesalers "partner with and support the external sales team to distribute and sell individual annuity products to independent financial planners, regional brokerage firms, and banks. [They must be able] to develop strong interpersonal working relationships with wholesalers and advisors. Candidates must be able to multitask and produce results," as well. Client service reps handle client inquiries on annuities and life insurance; they also "assist advisors and clients through education of products and by resolving problems."

Peers

It's easy for first jobbers here to make "some very good friends" among their peers because of the "great camaraderie," which is bolstered by "social events, happy hours, etc. that allow us to spend time with [one another] outside the office." One actuarial newbie reports, "We sometimes plan out something to do over the weekend. Since there are only fourteen actuarial students, it's a close-knit community. The fact that we are all going through the same exam process automatically makes people connect. We often eat lunch together at the cafeteria; it's a great way to get to know everyone on a personal level." Human resources "organizes various events from time to time;" for example, "recently we had the whirly ball event that was a lot of fun." First jobbers also report that "the work environment is great. It's relaxed, and everyone is willing to help you."

Moving on

Company officials tell us, "When employees leave Phoenix, most often it is for a new job or to relocate to another area of the country. Other reasons are too diverse to categorize." The Phoenix has undergone a structural change over the course of the past three years, during which it morphed from a mutually held company into a stockholder entity. This, too, "has led to a change in workforce composition." "Company statistics suggest that about one-third of Phoenix's work force has been with the company for fewer than two years, and another third have been with the company for [a period of] three to five years."

Attrition

Of the 190 college graduates Phoenix hired in the year prior to our survey, 177 were still with the company. Current employees explain why some leave: "Most people are concerned with the current environment of corporate change and consolidation happening within the industry."

Best and Worst

The best example of a successful entry-level employee who has advanced within the company is "Dona Young, Chairman, President, and CEO," who "has been with The Phoenix for twenty-five years. She began as a summer law intern and has risen steadily the top of The Phoenix!"

PIER 1 IMPORTS
VARIOUS POSITIONS

"After eighteen years, I still enjoy coming to
work every day. The environment is positive, enthusiastic, and motivational."

The Big Picture

Pier 1 Imports, a specialty retailer of imported decorative home furnishings and décor, does not have a structured college-hire program; but the company "does hire candidates directly out of college for positions based on their academic background and internship/work experience." Many begin their Pier 1 careers as sales associates in stores, an experience that provides them with "valuable knowledge to bring to the corporate home office," at which they may ultimately end up working in allocations and logistics, human resources, finance, customer relations, ISD, marketing, merchandising, or store operations. There are also significant growth opportunities within the organization's retail stores and distribution centers.

LOCATION(S) WHERE ENTRY-LEVEL EMPLOYEES WORK

Pier 1 has its corporate headquarters in Fort Worth, Texas. There are distribution centers in Savannah, Georgia; Ontario, California; Mansfield, Texas; Baltimore, Maryland; Columbus, Ohio; Chicago, Illinois; and Dupont, Washington. Pier 1 has more than 1,100 stores nationwide.

ENTRY-LEVEL POSITION(S) AVAILABLE

Pier 1 has various positions available for entry-level hires.

AVERAGE HOURS WORKED PER WEEK

Employees work an average of 37.5 hours per week (at the home office).

BENEFITS OFFERED

Pier 1 offers a medical PPO as well as dental and vision coverage. Additional benefits include a 401(k) program, stock purchase program, paid time off, associate discounts, flexible spending accounts, educational assistance, and holiday gift dollars.

CONTACT INFORMATION

Learn about job opportunities at Pier 1 by visiting www.pier1.com/jobs.

Getting Hired

Many first-jobbers come on board at Pier 1 via the company's retail outlets. A large proportion of the first jobbers we contacted at the home office had begun their careers as sales associates; they frequently checked the job postings at the Pier 1 website until they found an opening that suited their talents and goals. The company tells us that it seeks candidates "who are customer- and solutions-oriented, collaborative, enthusiastic, and flexible. We look for effective communication skills, strong interpersonal ability, and passion and excitement for the work that they do." The standard interview consists of behavioral-based questions. These are intended to elicit the past successes of candidates and in turn, determine their potential for success in the future. "We focus on customer orientation, problem solving, teamwork, communication skills, business knowledge, and questions that are technically specific to the position for which they are interviewing."

One first jobber hired in allocations explains, "Two managers interviewed me for the position. Since it was obvious that I had no previous allocations experience, the questions were more related to my work ethic, ability to learn, etc. There were some behavioral questions (e.g., 'Name a time when…') and some questions about my school experiences and how I handle certain situations. I was told that I would be informed within a week or so, and several days later I was offered the job by the staffing department."

Money and Perks

For most starting positions at Pier 1, "salaries/wages are nonnegotiable and work off a tight job grade/pay scale." Raises are "merit- and equity-based" and are awarded annually. Major perks include a benefits package with a 401(k) plan, medical benefits, stock purchase plans, stock options, associate discounts, and vacation time. One first jobber writes, "The coolest thing about this company is that they offer so much to their employees. It is hard to pick one, but the employee discount is probably the best fringe benefit." Workers also love "Holiday Dollars," which are distributed to associates every November and may be spent at Pier 1 and Pier 1 Kids stores. For many, "the biggest benefit of working for Pier 1 [is] the atmosphere and environment." "After eighteen years," writes one veteran employee, "I still enjoy coming to work every day. The environment is positive, enthusiastic, and motivational."

The Ropes

New hires at the home office undergo a half-day orientation that "covers company policies, new hire paperwork, employee relations issues (such as drug abuse policy, sexual harassment, etc.), the Employee Assistance Program, and building and systems security." Subsequent training occurs on the job. One allocations analyst reports, "I received training first from my manager. She got me on my feet so I could start doing daily tasks. Over the next twelve weeks, I received training with many different analysts, each focusing on a different part of the department functions. By the end of the twelve weeks, I had some familiarity with everyone's job functions and a more in-depth representation of our department." Since so many first jobbers enter the company as sales associates, they literally learn the business from the ground up. One first jobber who worked his way up from floor sales notes, "training lasted about a month. It involved every aspect of my job, from receiving freight to processing the shipments, merchandising, and customer service. I was given feedback on a daily basis."

Day in the Life

Day-to-day responsibilities at Pier 1 vary considerably among first jobbers, who are brought into all areas of the company. Most enter positions with few important responsibilities; they learn, they watch, they network, and ultimately they parlay their time and efforts into a better job with more responsibilities—sometimes within the same area of the company, sometimes not. One first jobber who began as a help-desk specialist (i.e., telephone support contact for stores and customers) "gradually worked up to a morning shift (preferred shift for me) and was then promoted to supervisor of the team. I supervised the group for just over one year, and I then applied for a position in a different group of IT—the backup and recovery group. I have been working with the business continuity group for almost one year now."

Peers

First jobbers can be found throughout the Pier 1 empire, so there's not a well-defined first-jobber network here. One newbie writes, "There is a lot of diversity with my peers. We're similar in some respects, but very different overall. I think this has been helpful for me; it's kept me open to others' ideas and perspectives." Another reports, "There are often after-hours activities available, but first jobbers here at the company must be socially active and forward to be included in these activities."

Moving on

Ironically, one of the problems with working at Pier 1 is that employees like the place a lot. "There's a lack of upward movement due to the fact that so many people are happy here; and management jobs do not open up that often," explains one first jobber. This sends some ambitious career-seekers off in search of employment elsewhere. Most, however, stay. They appreciate that "the company is wonderful about taking care of its employees. The company provides a great work-life balance, and most people are satisfied with this."

Best and Worst

Pier 1 sent us typical success stories rather than a best or worst. Here's one: "P.B. began her Pier 1 career in the stores, working as a Pier 1 store associate in Texas. After a year, she was promoted to assistant manager, and about two and a half years later, she moved on to the corporate office as a customer relations representative. After a year as a customer relations representative, armed with her advertising/marketing degree from the University of North Texas, P.B. moved into the marketing department." "My job is incredibly fun," she reports. "I have been able to apply my knowledge from the store and from the call center to about every decision I have had to make."

PRICEWATERHOUSECOOPERS

PRICEWATERHOUSECOOPERS 🅡

ASSOCIATE

"It's amazing how much training and resources they have available for you to perform the best quality audit."

The Big Picture

A large and well-respected public accounting firm, PricewaterhouseCoopers LLP (PwC) offers entry-level positions to students with backgrounds in accounting, taxation, auditing, or computer science/MIS. Many PwC applicants say they were immediately drawn to the "fast-paced environment, diversity of learning experiences offered, ability to learn how to provide value to clients, exposure to all facets of a company, and ability to work with [their] peers in teams." Once on the job, they enjoy the prestige of working for one of the "Big Four" in accounting, as well as the firm's commitment to providing "continuous technical, management, and leadership development."

LOCATION(S) WHERE ENTRY-LEVEL EMPLOYEES WORK

PwC hires at 70 different locations in the United States.

AVERAGE NUMBER OF APPLICATIONS EACH YEAR

PwC receives up to 23,000 applications for entry-level positions each year.

AVERGE NUMBER HIRED PER YEAR OVER THE LAST TEN YEARS

On average, PwC hired 2,813 entry-level employees per year. In both 2005 and 2006, the firm hired more than 3,000 entry-level employees.

ENTRY-LEVEL POSITIONS AVAILABLE

Recent grads are hired as associates in all of the organization's client-service business lines: assurance, tax, and advisory.

AVERAGE HOURS WORKED PER WEEK

New associates usually work between 40 and 60 hours per week.

PERCENTAGE OF ENTRY-LEVEL HIRES STILL WITH THE COMPANY AFTER THREE, FIVE, AND TEN YEARS

PwC conducted a study in 2004, which "confirmed that work/life balance is a critical retention factor, and that we tend to lose many of our employees at the Senior Associate level (anywhere from two to four years from hire)." As a result, the firm made a commitment to improving work/life quality for its employees. Over the past few years, the turnover rate for all employees has dropped from 26.5 percent to approximately 16 percent.

AVERAGE STARTING SALARY

Depending on their job title and location, associates receive a salary of $50,000 to $59,000 per year. Salaries, however, do vary by city, based on specific geographic market needs.

Getting Hired

Many students participate in summer internships at PwC and some are pleased to be offered full-time jobs during their exit interviews. Aside from those lucky candidates, PwC recruits "new hires at more than 200 colleges on a regular basis, based on the quality of the educational program." According to PwC, the ideal candidates are "people who are able to deliver against our strategic priorities of People, Quality and Profitable Growth," qualities which are best tested in "a behavioral-based interview that brings out the competencies our people have exhibited under certain circumstances." Since PwC places a great deal of importance on the interview, serious candidates should come prepared to answer questions about themselves, their goals, and their area of technical expertise. A candidate shares his experience: "During my interview, the partner's questions were very direct, asking about the decisions I had made that brought me to the accounting profession. He also inquired about my interest in public accounting and specifically PwC." Another recounts, "I was once a telemarketer, so the interviewer asked me if I ever had to deal with a difficult person on the phone, and of course I had a story to support the answer to this question. Then she asked if we could role-play what I said to potential customers. We actually reenacted a call." Later, candidates are often invited to dinner or to a day at the office, where they are further interviewed for the position. However, survivors reassure us that "the day of the office visit was much more relaxed and was more about the firm showing its true self to me and me showing my true self to the firm."

Money and Perks

In addition to their salaries, entry-level employees are eligible for special performance bonuses meant to provide "on-the-spot recognition for contributions above and beyond expectations." Besides the money, PwC offers an excellent and comprehensive benefits package to its employees, including perks like "nice discounts on car and home insurance." PwC also encourages its diligent staff to lead a balanced lifestyle. In the summer, a "Flexible Fridays program allows staff to take a full or partial Friday off after working at least forty hours prior to that."

The Ropes

All new employees at PwC are required to attend a general firm orientation and training, during which "the main pillars of proper conduct and ethics [are] presented to the new hires in a dynamic environment which also include[s] team building and internal networking activities." It is during this training that employees are introduced to the firm's core values, technical methodologies, and "all of the ins and outs of the basics you need to do your job, such as time-and-expense reporting, how to use your e-mail, etc." According to one recent hire, "By the end of the sessions new employees are fully prepared to perform [their] duties." Once on the job, new hires continue to receive instruction and feedback from their coworkers and managers. An employee attests, "My bosses are the managers, directors, and partners that I interact with on a daily basis. PwC has set up a positive coaching environment where we, as associates, are able to learn from everyone around us." While PwC does not offer a typical mentorship program, "each of our 29,000 staff, including new hires, are assigned to a partner in what we refer to as our Partner Connectivity efforts," a program that helps "every person to have a one-on-one relationship with a leader in the firm." Even as new employees transform into more seasoned professionals, the educational opportunities continue. "It's amazing how much training and resources they have available for you to perform the best quality audit," claims a former new hire.

Day in the Life

"As a new hire your roles and responsibilities are usually assigned during the initial team meetings of each engagement," explains a PwC newbie. However, "over time, associates are assigned more challenging areas of the engagements or multiple tasks." A first year employee attests, "When I was first hired I would often be given an assignment with specific instructions. Now that I have more experience I have more options regarding my assignments and providing my own instructions." While "most assignments for entry-level employees focus on auditing lower risk areas of an engagement," employees say that their work "is the foundation [on] which the audit opinion will be based" and is therefore indispensable to the firm's work. Eventually, new employees are "expected to be more analytical, understand the relationship between accounts, investigate differences/exceptions on [their] own, and communicate directly with clients."

Peers

"PwC hires the best and brightest people from around the globe," and, from day one, "there is a large sense of camaraderie with other first-year associates." In fact, a newbie tells us that the training week "is similar to freshman orientation; before its completion you will have met over a hundred people, and built lifelong friendships." As time progresses, "the ability to share experiences, laughs, and stories is a vital part of this job." "They are the kind of people I look forward to working with, going to dinners with, taking road trips with, or inviting to weekly poker games. My peers are some of my best friends," admits an employee. While many staffers say they encounter kindred spirits amongst their coworkers, they also find a wide range of interests in their peer group. Jokes a staffer, "Even though we have much in common, like enjoying balancing our checkbooks, we also have a lot of unique interests that make lunch conversation interesting."

Moving on

When staff leave PwC, the most common reasons they cite in their exit interviews include pursuing work in another career field, improving the balance between work and home life, returning to school, and personal reasons.

Attrition

Only 6.5 percent of entry-level employees leave PwC in their first year.

Best and Worst

When discussing their best entry-level employee, PwC reps point to Dennis Nally, the current U.S. Chairman and Senior Partner. Mr. Nally was recently interviewed for PwC's campus paper, during which he advised new hires that "demonstrating maturity and intelligence is not necessarily having all the answers all the time, but knowing when to ask when you don't know." On the other hand, PwC says "lack of maturity, leadership and communication skills, and integrity are the real career derailers."

THE PRINCETON REVIEW
VARIOUS POSITIONS

"I was extremely impressed by my training. In fact, I was so impressed that I e-mailed all those who had trained me, to let them know just how impressed I was and to thank them for spending the time to work with me in such a welcoming way."

The Big Picture

The Princeton Review—or TPR, as insiders call it—is top dog when it comes to helping "students, parents, and educators achieve the best outcomes at all stages of their educational careers." The company maintains its reputation by producing a steady diet of educational reference, test-prep, and career resources—in print and on the web. The company also offers standardized test courses countrywide. As you might expect, TPR breeds a culture of life-learners—a point emphasized by the annual "educational stipend" each employee receives. One new hire gushes, "The Princeton Review seems to value education for education's sake, and I am sincerely thankful for that!"

LOCATION(S) WHERE ENTRY-LEVEL EMPLOYEES WORK

The company is headquartered in New York City, though entry-level opportunities are available "across the country."

AVERAGE NUMBER HIRED PER YEAR OVER THE LAST FIVE YEARS

On average, TPR brings in around 150 new hires each year.

ENTRY-LEVEL POSITION(S) AVAILABLE

The Princeton Review hires recent college grads for a variety of positions: assistant marketing manager, research assistant, call center representative, helpdesk operator, production editor, department coordinator, sales assistant, HR administrator, benefits administrator, and assistant director of operations. Though "each new hire has responsibilities that vary with his/her particular position," all newbies seem to agree that "there is no typical day here at TPR."

AVERAGE HOURS WORKED PER WEEK

The average TPR work week lasts 45 hours.

AVERAGE STARTING SALARY

A first jobber's annual salary is typically around $35,000.

Getting Hired

The Princeton Review primarily uses the Web (its own site plus other job-search portals) to get word out about entry-level job openings. According to a first jobber, "The application process was easy. There was an online application form; I uploaded my resume and cover letter, and then I submitted the application. I then received a call two days later for a phone interview." If all goes well during the phone screening, an applicant is typically invited to the nearest TPR office for an in-person interview. Employees who've been through the process assure us that it's not a traumatizing experience. Says one, "The entire tone of the [first] interview was very cordial as we went over my education and experience. . . . The second interview was very cordial and relaxed as well, with my [interviewers] focusing more on my personality than my experience." Other newbies echo this sentiment, noting that the "laid-back yet professional" tone of the interviews allowed them to shine. But one recent hire notes that the relaxed vibe can also cause a little confusion: "I remember being concerned about what to wear to the interview because The Princeton Review is such a casual company. As their website proudly boasts, the only requirement is that you 'must have something on your feet.' I ended up checking with my interviewer to see what type of attire would be appropriate and she told me that casual attire would be fine."

Money and Perks

"I'm not sure about pay, but I do feel like there is room for growth in responsibilities," says an HR newbie. Others concur, noting that a rise in ranks doesn't promise "more money, but it is good for the self and the resume." Still, each employee is up for a yearly bump in pay. As company officials explain, "We have annual performance and salary reviews. At this time the performance of the employee is evaluated and, based on the performance and budget, increases are granted." Employees are also on the receiving end of a barrage of fringe benefits. "Summer Fridays (a half day on Friday during the summer), beer Wednesdays (an hour-long break on Wednesdays during the summer to 'relax'), and the annual meeting (a week-long paid vacation to some tropical destination to discuss the company and have seminars) are just a few." New hires also rave about the "casual dress code," "the free bagels on Friday," and "the $2,000-per-year educational stipend" to be used on any educational venture, regardless of whether or not it pertains to work. And, of course, TPR classes are on the house.

The Ropes

Within a few weeks of joining the company, new hires participate in a three-hour orientation that goes "over the company history, benefits, and our systems." Aside from this, the exact shape of the on-boarding experience depends on the site, the job, and the supervisor. An assistant director in New York gushes, "I was extremely impressed by my training. In fact, I was so impressed that I e-mailed all those who had trained me to let them know just how impressed I was and to thank them for spending the time to work with me in such a welcoming way. The training was extremely clear and organized and consisted of a lesson or two per day over the span of a week." An assistant director in New Jersey, however, says that his training experience "can be described as a trial by fire. As bad as that may sound, it is a fun learning process."

Much of the on-the-job training occurs through frequent interactions among new hires and their direct supervisors. While TPR doesn't "have a formal mentoring program," company officials note that "the HR department would be happy to recommend members of upper-level management for our entry-level employees to meet with."

Day in the Life

"Let me begin by saying there is no such thing as a typical day at The Princeton Review," a recent college grad says. "All throughout the day, one project can be interrupted by another just from a simple phone call that could end up leading to a half-hour long project." This means that the abilities to multitask and manage time are critical at TPR. As one newbie explains, "You really don't have time to be bored when it comes to professional development of any kind. The correct word is challenged. It's a challenge to stay on top of all that may come your way. I look at the job at hand as being in the driver's seat. When you are out on the road, in an ideal world, you would only have to keep your eyes on the road, stay in your lane, and everything is fine as long as you obey these rules. But this isn't the case; when you drive you have to watch for potential dangers in the road and rely on common sense and applied knowledge to get you to your destination. It's the same here [but] your job is really never done. New challenges arise daily, but it's all about how you pace yourself." Though the specific duties of a new hire depend on the position, it's fair to assume that all newbies will become very familiar with terms like SAT, GRE, GMAT, MCAT and LSAT.

Peers

One employee who's only been at TPR for five months tells us, "I cannot say enough good things about the people I work with. I have already made friendships that I know will last beyond my employment here. We constantly talk and joke throughout the day, which is great because it makes the day go much quicker—and more pleasant." Another says, "We're all irreverent, silly, intelligent, and witty. It's great to finally work in an environment where people are like-minded and have like interests." The social atmosphere at the workplace often carries over into after-hours activities—particularly in the big-city locations. "We have been known to go out after hours, but that is not just with first-year employees," explains an NYC first jobber. "The crowd is normally mixed when it comes to the amount of years worked at TPR." A freshman employee in Philadelphia adds, "We like drinking. The bar is our support group."

Moving on

When first jobbers leave TPR, "most say they have found a better opportunity elsewhere"—often within the publishing or education industries. Employees sometimes enroll in graduate or professional school as well.

Attrition

The staff at The Princeton Review is composed of individuals from a wide variety of educational backgrounds with a variety of professional aspirations. This, in part, explains the dynamic environment that so many young employees extol. But it also explains why first jobbers move on to pursue other professional or educational goals. One recent hire, who plans to leave the company in a few years, explains, "While this job is a great foot in the door and I'm thankful for this chance, it's a corporation. . . . Ideally, I'd like to work [at] a small liberal arts university." A colleague says, "I graduated with a degree in journalism and professional writing and that is where my heart is and it's the field I hope to be in one day." But whether they plan to leave in two years or stay for life, most first jobbers agrees that TPR "is a great place to work."

PRINTING FOR LESS
TECHNICAL SERVICE REPRESENTATIVE

"The job is very different [from] any other job that I know of. PFL has basically rolled customer service, commercial pre-press, graphic design, consulting, and business management into a single position."

The Big Picture

Printing For Less (PFL) is an online seller of full-color printing products; their product line includes brochures, catalogs, cards, newsletters, and stationery. The primary entry-level position at PFL is that of technical service representative (TSR). This job offers many opportunities to advance; a company rep notes, "Some entry-level TSRs have moved quickly into leadership roles on our three-person self-directed teams within a few months of graduating from the training program. TSRs also may assist on project work in developing new products and services."

LOCATION(S) WHERE ENTRY-LEVEL EMPLOYEES WORK
The headquarters are in Livingston, Montana.

AVERAGE NUMBER OF APPLICATIONS EACH YEAR
Printing For Less receives 1,400 applications each year.

AVERAGE NUMBER HIRED PER YEAR
Printing For Less hires thirty entry-level employees per year.

ENTRY-LEVEL POSITION(S) AVAILABLE
Entry-level workers begin as technical service representatives (TSR).

AVERAGE HOURS WORKED PER WEEK
Entry-level employees work 45 hours per week.

PERCENTAGE OF ENTRY-LEVEL HIRES STILL WITH THE COMPANY AFTER THREE, FIVE, AND TEN YEARS
Eighty percent of entry-level employees remain with the company past the three-year mark.

AVERAGE STARTING SALARY
Entry-level hires earn $34,000 per year.

Getting Hired

The vetting process for new hires at PFL is "very rigorous," according to those who have successfully navigated it. It begins with an online application; those deemed worthy of further consideration undergo a "top-grading" interview approach, which begins with a forty-five-minute, four-question prescreening interview (which may include questions such as: How did you learn about our company? What are your career goals? What are you good at? What are you not good at?). Next comes "the first structured interview process," a three- to four-hour ordeal in which candidates review their past successes and failures. Then comes "the assessment and reference phase, which includes a personality assessment, a math test, technical evaluations, and reference checking (references must be previous supervisors or managers)." Then you're done, right? Not quite. Finally, "HR schedules the second round of interviews, [in which] the candidate meets with several department and senior managers and observes a TSR at work." One successful applicant writes, "The process was very rigorous. I spent two hours with the HR department during my first interview. We took a tour of the facility, and the HR director sat down with me to explain the extensive database and the roles and responsibilities of the position that I was applying for. My second interview lasted a total of seven hours. I met with everyone from the HR department and the president of the company, the VP of business development, and executive members of the IT department and management team. The whole thing was very thorough. What I really liked about all of this strenuous interviewing is that each person made sure to give me [a] personal testimony about why he or she liked PFL and what makes him or her excited about coming to work every day."

Money and Perks

Most first jobbers at PFL felt they had little leverage to negotiate salary; start dates here are largely determined by the company's orientation schedule. All employees "are eligible for company bonuses. Bonuses may be earned quarterly and are based on overall company performance in meeting sales revenue and other performance goals for the quarter." One employee notes, "The best benefit is having the chance to gain experience and have a successful career while living in a place like Bozeman, Montana. This area offers skiing, hiking, hunting, and some of the best fly fishing in the world. PFL pays me a salary that lets me enjoy all of this. They also offer discounts on lift tickets at the local ski hills and host an annual company whitewater-rafting trip and a golf scramble. This is a great place to live."

The Ropes

PFL starts new hires with a four-month training program; new cohorts are initiated every three or four months. One first jobber reports, "The program included instruction on customer file processing, customer relationship management, phone sales and skills, and database navigation. Plus, we all learned about twelve new high-end design programs used by graphic designers around the country. The training was presented by current and former TSRs who had been successful in their positions and knew the material well. This was great because they also gave us insight [into] what we would experience when we were actually on the job."

Day in the Life

Entry-level TSRs at PFL handle "customer service and sales via phone and e-mail, digital file processing using graphics software applications, order processing, and quality control." One TSR writes, "The job is very different [from] any other job that I know of. PFL has basically rolled customer service, commercial pre-press, graphic design, consulting, and business management into a single position." A typical day for a TSR "includes coordinating with teammates to strategize [about] how we could best handle forty or more customer phone calls and the same volume of customer e-mails; process twenty or so customer orders from beginning to production; and meet all of our high-level objectives, which typically included something like 'increase our customer conversion rate' or 'reduce latency between order entry and order approval.'"

Peers

PFL "doesn't hire anyone [whom supervisors] wouldn't want to be friends with," and "as a result, we have a great corporate culture." PFL first jobbers are "smart, cool, highly motivated, and high performing. They are great to hang out with at work or on the weekends." There is an especially strong bond among workers who went through training together; explains one, "You spend four months together training, and a lot of the time, you do social activities such as lunches, dinners, weekend activities, etc."

Moving on

PFL is "a young company that has only been hiring entry-level technical service reps for their first post-college job for three years." The company reports that more than "90 percent of those are still with the company," a solid record of employee retention. The low turnover rate is attributable to the "many growth opportunities within our company. The few [who] have left accepted jobs in other industries or pursued other educational opportunities."

Attrition

About one in twenty first jobbers leaves PFL before finishing at least one year with the company. An HR rep writes, "The most common reason for turnover at PFL is [the] pace. We are operating a high-growth, fast-paced company with virtually no downtime. While [PFL] provides employees [with] plenty of excitement and opportunities for career development, not everyone can consistently and effectively function at that pace at all times. Second to that would be just a change in lifestyles and personal plans, i.e., moving out of the Montana area, going back to school, [attending to] family needs, etc."

Best and Worst

The company reports, "One college grad we hired showed such competence and drive that he was able to catch up and graduate with a training class one month ahead of him; was placed on a front-line team immediately after training; became a highly successful team lead; and was promoted to production manager and later marketing manager in less than two years."

The worst first-jobber ever "did not complete the training program. The biggest challenges she had here were the demands for excellent listening (both to customers and team members), coachability, and reliability. Employees who are not team-oriented and motivated for personal and professional growth have difficulty fitting in and are not well suited for our company culture."

PROCTER & GAMBLE
VARIOUS POSITIONS

"New hire roles vary according to function, but all have tremendous early responsibility built into their work."

The Big Picture

Procter and Gamble (P&G) is one of the nation's corporate giants and makes products for personal care, beauty, health, house cleaning, and baby care. The company offers entry-level positions in just about every area essential to its business.

LOCATION(S) WHERE ENTRY-LEVEL EMPLOYEES WORK

"P&G is a promote-from-within company; [this] means that we hire primarily from college campuses for both commercial and technical functions. Depending on the year, we will hire between 2,000 and 3,500 [entry-level employees] globally, of which about 25 percent are located in the United States. Of the people hired in the United States, about half are based in the greater Cincinnati area and half in subsidiary company, plant, or field sales locations throughout the country."

AVERAGE NUMBER OF APPLICATIONS EACH YEAR

"We typically receive [more than] 240,000 applications each year, all of which are electronically processed via our candidate management system."

AVERAGE NUMBER HIRED PER YEAR OVER THE LAST TEN YEARS

"P&G has averaged 725 management hires per year in the U.S. over the last ten years with a high of 1,100 and a low of 450."

ENTRY-LEVEL POSITION(S) AVAILABLE

"Entry-level positions typically exist across all functional areas, including marketing, finance, accounting, [taxation,] legal, marketing research, sales, engineering, purchases, research and development (which includes a number of PhD scientists) human resources, etc. In addition, we have a large number of nonmanagement positions in administrative and technical areas, most of which require college-level educations. For example, we hire a significant number of researchers who are four-year degreed people with majors in the physical and life sciences."

AVERAGE HOURS WORKED PER WEEK

"The average work week varies by function within [the] business unit. The company uses flex time and other flexible work arrangements to help people maintain balance in their lives. Managers typically work about 50 hours a week with variation to meet important deadlines."

Getting Hired

P&G takes the scientific approach to hiring; company representatives note, "The criteria we use for hiring is directly linked to our success drivers competency model that was developed by interviewing our top management, a sample of 1,600 employees from every region of the world in which we operate, [and] a sample of our alumni, customers, and investors. This effort is sponsored and led by our Global Talent Supply organization." The model calls for candidates who have "integrity, brainpower, and demonstrated leadership. They should be collaborators [and] embrace change. They must communicate persuasively and clearly. They must have an appetite for results and a flair for innovation. We expect mastery of their learned discipline." Applications are fielded online on the corporate website and supplemented by recruiting trips to around fifty campuses; top applicants "are invited to [visit] with the company [for a day]," during which they "tour the city, tour the facility, and have the opportunity to meet with new hires (one to three years) during lunch and in one-on-one situations." During the visit, applicants also "have a behaviorally-anchored interview by a panel of three people and go through some form of cognitive assessment." One first jobber cautions, "The tone of the interview was intense and serious. They wanted specific examples of how I was successful in previous roles that I have been in." Those who make it through the intense interview process tend to be very happy with the offers they receive.

Money and Perks

P&G offers solid starting salaries; one first jobber reports, "Their offer was much higher than the other offers I had." The same first jobber especially appreciated the company's flexibility: "At the time I was brought in, the business unit recruiting me was looking to fill several positions in engineering. My initial offer was for a position in a field that did not interest me. I made my hiring department aware of my preferences, and they were able to place me in one of the departments that appealed [more] to me." Other perks (which may vary widely by department and function) include flex time, travel opportunities, and discounts.

The Ropes

The company has "an extensive [orientation] process that starts [on] acceptance of our offer, utilizing a new hire pre-start website. Once a new hire is in the company, the join-up period lasts for one year and is centered around three major training events that give people exposure to [one another], top management, functions, business units, company history and principles, and more. The events are fun, interactive, and thorough." Training sessions range from "one-day to one-week programs on such topics as company policy, inclusion training, women in engineering, or technology-related training." Subsequent training "is both formal and informal, offered by outside vendors, agencies, and upper management. All focus [is] on building business understanding early to help make an impact."

Day in the Life

First jobbers at P&G often find themselves waist-deep in responsibility almost from the get-go. As company officials put it, "New hire roles vary according to function, but all have tremendous early responsibility built into their work." Our survey respondents confirm this assertion; one writes, "When I was first hired, I was given three different projects to work on, each on a different product. This allowed me to know three different product lines very quickly. I was given clear direction and full reigns and was responsible for all results. My manager wrote a work plan with me that described my responsibilities. This work plan included a list of key contacts, in my own and other functions, for each project that he suggested I meet with for join-ups. These contacts became an integral part of the project team, and their collaboration helped to make me succeed. Essentially, I was given the tools and the contacts to get the work done and the rest I was responsible for."

Peers

For most first jobbers at P&G, there's "tons of interaction with new hires, including training and social events (informal and formal) on a weekly basis." One newbie reports, "About once a month there would be a happy hour or other event that allowed us to interact with others in their first year. There is also a sense of camaraderie within my group. I enjoy working with the others in my group, and occasionally we meet up outside of work." In the larger offices, "it is difficult not to run into others and have a quick chat in the halls because of the cubicle environment," while engineers in the field tell us that "during plant visits, experiments comprise long days and sometimes long weeks, so [people] get to know [one another] very well while traveling. During these trips [people] eat all meals together and often have long commutes to and from work."

Moving on

Although "many stay for a career" at P&G, occasionally workers do move on. The Cincinnati location in particular sees some workers move on. "It's a conservative, family-oriented city with employment opportunities [that] are less robust than [those in] Chicago or New York. This is sometimes an issue," company representatives inform us.

Attrition

Less than 1 percent of first jobbers leave P&G within twelve months of being hired, according to company officials.

Best and Worst

"All of our CEOs started as first jobbers," P&G representatives tell us. "We have had many great leaders. We believe our current CEO, Mr. A. G. Lafley, is an example of the kind of leader we produce, and [that he] will be one of the very best we have ever had." The worst first jobbers were "the people who joined P&G with skills, capabilities, and values that were not consistent with the culture of the company."

QUALCOMM
VARIOUS POSITIONS

"One of the best advantages of their management structure is that all my managers are engineers so they actually know what I am talking about. They aren't looking for the buzzwords. They are looking for solidly engineered designs."

The Big Picture

A leader in the wireless telecommunications industry, QUALCOMM is headquartered in sunny San Diego and annually recruits for more than 300 entry-level positions, primarily in engineering. Recognized by the San Diego Business Journal as "one of the best companies to work for in San Diego" and rated one of Fortune's "Best 100 Places to Work" for eight consecutive years, QUALCOMM expects all of its employees, regardless of experience, "to be a productive member of the team they join." Employees appreciate the opportunity to make a tangible contribution to the company, as well as the company's relaxed dress code and flexible work hours.

LOCATION(S) WHERE ENTRY-LEVEL EMPLOYEES WORK

QUALCOMM's headquarters are located in San Diego, California. The company also has offices in San Jose, California; Boulder, Colorado; Austin, Texas; Cary, North Carolina; Bedminster, New Jersey; Concord, Massachusetts; Bangalore, India; Hyderabad, India; Farnborough, UK; Cambridge, UK; Seoul, Korea; Tokyo, Japan; Beijing; China; Shanghai, China; Nuremburg, Germany; Frankfurt, Germany; and Taipei, Taiwan.

AVERAGE NUMBER OF APPLICATIONS EACH YEAR

QUALCOMM receives upwards of 10,000 applications per year.

AVERAGE NUMBER HIRED PER YEAR OVER THE LAST TEN YEARS

Typically, there are spots for roughly 250 new graduates per year.

ENTRY-LEVEL POSITION(S) AVAILABLE ENTRY

The majority of recent grads work as software engineers, systems engineers, hardware engineers, test engineers, financial analysts, and IT engineers.

AVERAGE HOURS WORKED PER WEEK

New employees work 40 hours per week.

AVERAGE STARTING SALARY

Salary depends on major and degree level (BS, MS, or PhD); average salaries for recent college graduates range from $60,000 to $90,000.

Getting Hired

QUALCOMM recruits at about fifteen North American college campuses; however, all applicants—even those from targeted schools—must apply via their website. When scanning for qualified candidates, the company places a lot of stock in personality, saying they look "for employees that represent our core values: Innovate, Execute and Partner." However, the most attractive candidates are those "that have the technical skills required of the position but also a passion for wireless communications." Applicants usually interview with six to eight working engineers, who test them on their technical knowledge and education. A QUALCOMM engineer details, "I was interviewed by a manager and hardware engineers—the same people I'd be working with if I had a full-time position. Each interview lasted forty-five to sixty minutes and consisted of a brief introduction and a lot of design-related questions." Another confers, "I had to go through a series of six forty-five-minute interviews with engineers. The interviews were casual, and most of the questions were hardware-design related." While on-the-spot engineering questions certainly sound intimidating, current employees say the interview process is consistent with the high standards that the company expects from their employees. Explains one, "QUALCOMM is very much a place where they expect you to hit the ground running—hence, why the interviews are very technical (you have to pick things up very quickly)."

Money and Perks

While most new engineers readily accept their introductory offer from QUALCOMM, "employees are eligible for raises twice per year." Strong performance is readily reflected in financial rewards, as "raises, stock options, and bonuses are based on individual and business-unit performance." In addition to their fancy benefits package, QUALCOMM offers a number of perks to its employees. Shares one satisfied employee, "My favorite is the 'Q-Life' department, which is dedicated to enhancing the balance between an employee's work life and personal life or social life. They always have classes they offer to employees at a discount, including dancing, golfing, and surfing." Employees also love the amenities at the QUALCOMM offices, including "gyms on site that are free to employees," as well as a pool and libraries.

The Ropes

QUALCOMM orientation, a "four-hour affair on the first day of your employment," provides a basic introduction to the company, during which "HR goes over a few things such as the company hierarchy, the intranet, dress code, etc." It only lasts for a half-day, after which "your manager picks you up and takes you out to lunch. After that, you are introduced to your team, at which point they take over and show you what you'll be doing." These simple steps comprise, more or less, the entire training program at QUALCOMM. As the company hires intelligent young people with a background in engineering, most new employees are able to jump right into their assignment without too much ramp-up. Explains a new engineer, "There is no formal training when you start. The team lead or whoever you're working directly for will show you what you're working on and point you to some resources which will help you get started. After about one or two days, you'll be given tasks at which point you just ask questions when needed." Another echoes, "I received very little training, but when

I don't know how to do something, I just ask my coworkers." While most QUALCOMM engineers are confident self-starters, they concede that the company's "training" policy may not work for everyone. One newbie agrees, "I'm the type that asks lots of questions so the 'open-door policy' works really well for me. The problem lies in the fact that you have to ask the questions. If you're the type that doesn't like to ask questions, the 'open-door policy' doesn't work at all."

Day in the Life

Thrown directly into the fire, new engineers at QUALCOMM say the first few weeks of work can be highly intense. A new engineer confides, "Initially, the job was very stressful—mainly because of looming deadlines and the sheer complexity of the spec that needed to be implemented in hardware." Over time, however, he says, "Things have calmed down significantly. . . . I have a strong understanding of the hardware and spec and am confident in my abilities." Once brought up to speed, new engineers are important parts of the team, involved in strategy meetings and working on vital aspects of their team's project. A newbie adds, "One of the best advantages of their management structure is that all my managers are engineers so they actually know what I am talking about. They aren't looking for the buzzwords. They are looking for solidly engineered designs." This common ground may also be the reason why QUALCOMM managers allow their engineers so much autonomy, including a totally flexible work schedule. An engineer relates, "It's nice for me to be able to run errands in the morning and show up around 10:00 or 11:00 A.M. (and then stay late). Without this I would be stuck on so many issues. If I'm feeling ill I can just VPN into work and work from home."

Peers

"My design peers are very smart. In terms of work ethic and goals, they are very much like me," explains an entry-level engineer. There is a great deal of camaraderie amongst teams, and the company places emphasis on developing peer relationships. An employee in QUALCOMM's San Jose office reports that they "have team-building events every month." In addition, the company operates a Peer Mentor Program designed "to help ease this transition [from school to the workplace] and ensure effective on-boarding. Each new employee will be assigned a Peer Mentor whose role is to allow for a comfortable, more informal environment in which the employee can ask questions and receive information about the office culture, norms, and the everyday (mostly unwritten) procedures and policies that help explain how things really get done."

Attrition

QUALCOMM's annual turnover rate averages about 4.5 percent for employees of all levels. While some employees plan to pursue an advanced degree in the future, through the company's tuition reimbursement program a career at QUALCOMM and a graduate degree aren't mutually exclusive.

QUICKPARTS
VARIOUS POSITIONS

"Because this is a small, growing company, I feel there is plenty of room to grow and develop. Since we are still growing, there is a flexibility to create new procedures and programs that allows for lots of room for growth."

The Big Picture

Quickparts is a business-to-business e-vendor that uses proprietary software to custom-generate price quotes on parts production. In other words, if your business needs a machine part custom-made, Quickparts can find the producer for you and get you a good price on it. First jobbers work in a variety of areas for this up-and-coming company, whose Atlanta location is a definite plus for many city lovers.

LOCATION(S) WHERE ENTRY-LEVEL EMPLOYEES WORK

The company has offices in Atlanta, Georgia and Huntsville, Alabama.

AVERAGE NUMBER OF APPLICATIONS EACH YEAR

Quickparts receives 1,600 applications per year.

AVERAGE NUMBER HIRED PER YEAR

Quickparts hires 14 entry-level employees per year.

ENTRY-LEVEL POSITION(S) AVAILABLE

Entry-level hires work as software developers, inside sales representatives, project managers, and territory accountants.

AVERAGE HOURS WORKED PER WEEK

Entry-level hires work an average of 45 to 50 hours per week.

PERCENTAGE OF ENTRY-LEVEL HIRES STILL WITH THE COMPANY AFTER THREE, FIVE, TEN YEARS

Twenty-five percent of entry-level hires are still with Quickparts after three years.

AVERAGE STARTING SALARY (BY POSITION)

Software developers earn $38,000–$42,000; inside sales representatives earn $35,000–$40,000; project managers earn $38,000–$42,000; and territory accountants earn $28,000–$32,000.

Getting Hired

Quickparts posts job openings online, both at its own website and at various internet job sites (e.g., Monster.com and AJCJobs.com). The Human Resources Department here "practices a process called Topgrading, which focuses on filling all open positions with an 'A' Player. Our hiring manager (the future team member's supervisor) and human resources work closely together to make sure that the position is clearly defined and candidates are evaluated accordingly." After screening resumes, HR conducts a brief telephone interview with likely candidates; if that goes well, "we have them fill out an employment application in preparation for on on-site half-day interview. During this step, the candidate interviews with several members of our team, covering everything from high school to college to work experience (even if it is unrelated to the position) to future plans and goals. Also during this step, the candidate will take several assessment tests (personality, computer skills, verbal, and quantitative tests)." The process is designed to yield "future leaders who are aligned in positions that correspond with their passions and goals."

Money and Perks

Terms of employment at Quickparts are negotiable "to a small degree," first jobbers tell us, especially with regard to start time. Salary and job description are far less negotiable, our survey respondents agree. Quickparts "conducts salary reviews on an annual basis. We don't believe in giving team members raises based on tenure. We are strong believers in pay for performance." To that end, "All team members are eligible for bonuses, depending on which department the team member is in. All bonuses are based on exceeding the performance goals of the department and are clearly outlined at the beginning of the year."

New hires agree that "Quickparts University is the best benefit to the employees now and in the future inside or outside of Quickparts. QPU is a program by which we continue learning about business and technology through a set curriculum, and in doing so, [earn] raises on top of our normal increases." Sample courses include Telephone Customer Service, Negotiation Skills, Marketing Strategies, "A" Player Attitude, Dealing with Change, Personal Finance, Delegation, Open-Book Management, and Stress Management. "Upon completion of each degree, the team member receives a $2,000 salary raise," the company reports. Employees also love the "many company events, parties, and free lunches" that Quickparts provides.

The Ropes

Orientation at Quickparts begins at HR, where "the team member learns about the company's history, culture, and expectations and is free to ask any questions about his or her role in the company. This part of orientation typically lasts one to two hours. The remainder of the day is spent with the team leader, who takes the new team member around to personally meet everyone. The team member then finds out in more detail the requirements and expectations for his or her role and will [then] begin a two-week extensive training period."

Day in the Life

Many first jobbers begin at Quickparts as sales representatives. One writes, "My responsibilities entailed engaging new customers for the first time and working on the smaller projects as they came up, as well as assisting the area manager with his duties." For another, a typical day consisted of "calling and working with prospective customers to see how we could better fit the needs that they have for projects. I was also tasked with follow-up on old quotes and [with] helping customers [who] had questions [about] our online store." Others enter via the finance department; one such first jobber writes, "My responsibilities were to reconcile vendor bills, input invoices, and manage projects financially. A typical day would include entering twenty to thirty-five invoices, followed by reconciliation of vendor bills, and ending with reviews of projects."

Peers

Quickparts "is a very young company" with "a lot of camaraderie among young workers, but without excluding older employees." First jobbers are impressed with how "smart, interesting, and different" their peers are; one area rep writes, "I have very intelligent team members, and several are friends I spend time with outside of the office on a regular basis. Even my direct boss is a friend with whom I have developed an extremely close mentor-type relationship." There isn't much of an after-hours scene here, though, since "some of the new people are married and have kids," explains one first jobber.

Moving on

When they do leave Quickparts, first jobbers cite their desire "to pursue a passion that could not be fulfilled at Quickparts." A company representative notes, "Given our company's size, we have only had a few team members decide to leave our company. They left to pursue professional and educational aspirations in financial services, acting, law, and entrepreneurship."

Attrition

About 15 percent of first-jobber college grads remain with Quickparts for fewer than twelve months. Because the company is relatively young, the average tenure of first jobbers here (1.52 years) does not accurately reflect the company's turnover rate. In fact, a substantial number of first jobbers who started their careers with Quickparts are still with the company. There are compelling reasons to stick around. As one employee notes, "Because this is a small, growing company, I feel there is plenty of room to grow and develop. Since we are still growing, there is a flexibility to create new procedures and programs that allows for lots of room for growth."

Best and Worst

The director of HR at Quickparts tells us that "We have a team member who has been a star in our finance department and on his most recent performance review expressed his desire and goals to do more analysis work. When an opening for a business analyst position was available, we promoted this team member to this opening. He didn't have the education we required for the position (MBA), but he has expressed a desire to go back to school to get his MBA. He also has a track record at Quickparts of excelling and being a leader in finance."

RANDOM HOUSE
VARIOUS POSITIONS

"It's entirely energizing to stay ahead of trends and get a glimpse at innovative writing as authors are creating it and as it winds its way into the mainstream."

The Big Picture

Find, develop, edit, print, and market books just like the one you're holding now! Entry-level positions in all facets of the publishing industry await you at Random House, a bellwether of the world of book publishing.

LOCATION(S) WHERE ENTRY-LEVEL EMPLOYEES WORK

Jobs are available primarily in New York, New York; the company also hires for individual publishing imprints in Colorado Springs, Colorado and Roseville, California. "Additionally, we have operations centers in Westminster, Maryland and Crawfordsville, Indiana; these handle distribution and other critical support services. Entry-level employees are hired at all of these locations," company officials report, adding that "as the world's largest trade book publisher, Random House also operates in Canada, the United Kingdom, Australia, Korea, Japan, India, New Zealand, and South Africa. Random House also encompasses some of the leading publishing houses in Germany, Austria, Spain, Argentina, Mexico, Chile, Colombia, Venezuela, and Uruguay."

AVERAGE NUMBER OF APPLICATIONS EACH YEAR

Random House receives 25,000–30,000 applications in the United States per year.

AVERAGE NUMBER HIRED PER YEAR

The company hires about 200 people per year in the United States.

ENTRY-LEVEL POSITION(S) AVAILABLE

The company tells us that "for college grads interested in a career in book publishing, Random House offers an enormous range of opportunities. Entry-level employees usually start out at the level of 'assistant' and not only work in traditional publishing areas such as editorial, marketing, and publicity, but also in production, sales, information technology, finance, human resources, subsidiary rights, new media, and other areas." A one-year associate program "for entry-level hires who are uncertain as to which area they want to join but are committed to publishing" is also available. In this program, associates rotate among various departments for one year; after that period, most stay on to take a permanent position at the company.

AVERAGE HOURS WORKED PER WEEK

Entry-level hires work 35 hours per week.

AVERAGE STARTING SALARY

Starting salaries are competitive by publishing industry standards.

BENEFITS OFFERED

PPOs, EPOs, and HMOs are offered; employees must contribute, "but the company pays the majority of the cost." There are also options to participate in dental, disability, life insurance, flexible spending accounts, the 401(k) program, pension program, tuition reimbursement, and profit sharing. Additional benefits include a very generous vacation benefit (four weeks per year after your first year!), paid parental leave, child care benefits, physical fitness reimbursement, a pre-tax account for transportation expenses, and a work/life assistance program.

CONTACT INFORMATION

To apply for a job, visit www.careers.randomhouse.com.

Getting Hired

Random House officials note, "Most obviously, we look for employees in our publishing and sales divisions who are passionate about books. Beyond that, we also look for individuals who take initiative, possess strong communication skills, and work effectively with others." The company recruits on campuses at certain colleges and also accepts applications via its website. Some new hires attribute their employment success to a post-college publishing course experience; one such employee writes, "I definitely think that having my resume come from the director of the Columbia Publishing Course was crucial in helping me to get an interview." That said, a substantial proportion of entry-level employees have not taken a publishing course. The vetting process includes a two-stage interview. One associate recalls, "My first interview was with human resources. The tone of the interview was very positive and friendly. I was asked about my educational background as well as my work experiences. I was then invited for further interviewing. I interviewed with several people, one from editorial and others from sales and marketing. All of these meetings were very informative and confirmed the positive impression of the company that had been established earlier." After that, it's a waiting game. According to one newbie who cleared the interview stage, "When a position became available that would allow me to utilize my major, I was asked if I'd be interested, and I was. I was hired about six months after my initial contact."

Money and Perks

Starting salaries at Random House are "the most competitive in the industry," according to one employee. Still, this is publishing, which is "by no means a gold mine," jokes one worker. Avid readers and others will enjoy the many perks of working at Random House. These include "getting to read interesting books months before they come out. It's entirely energizing to stay ahead of trends and get a glimpse at innovative writing as authors are creating it and as it winds its way into the mainstream. Getting to go to book events and movie premieres and meeting literary greats is also wonderful." One boasts, "Since I've started working here, I've encountered Joan Didion, John Updike, and Billy Collins [and many other important authors] who help shape our culture." Random House employees also enjoy "incredible" medical coverage and "unparalleled" vacation time—including the week off between Christmas and New Year's. Employees praise the physical fitness reimbursement program as "generous." Company representatives report that "many entry-level employees benefit from Random House's highly decentralized organizational structure. This enables each of its publishing divisions to maintain the ambience and creative and entrepreneurial autonomy of a small company, while enjoying all the resources and operational support of a market leader."

The Ropes

Orientation at Random House is a relatively brief affair. One employee explains, "The orientation process was quick—just one morning, [for] about three hours." Another reports that the orientation session gave "a very general overview of all our benefits, vacation policies, sick days, etc." Beyond that, this employee writes that she "received a half-day computer session [in which she learned] how to use a complicated program designed for our contracts system." Most agree that the bulk of training takes place on-the-job "on an as-needed basis." One notes, "my managers went out of their ways to give me varied tasks so that I could learn new systems." Another newbie reports that "come lunchtime [on the first day], I was already in my office, reading manuscripts and answering the telephone and communicating with authors. Publishing moves so fast that it is necessary to hit the ground running and learn as you go." Random House also has a weekly Luncheon Seminar series, in which executives from various departments share information about their areas of expertise, their career paths, and their workgroups. The series typically concludes annually with a talk by Peter Olson, Chairman and CEO.

Day in the Life

Random House offers entry-level jobs in editorial, production, publicity, marketing, sales, rights, HR, finance, customer service, and warehouse operations, so the daily experiences of new hires vary greatly. Those who enter through the Associates Program rotate among various jobs within a particular division. This path has its plusses and minuses; one employee who took this route explains, "As an associate, I was placed in an entry-level position for a period, after which I would move to a new position. At the end of the one-year program, I was expected to select a permanent position. The program's goal is to give a new employee a better understanding of the different work environments within a single publishing house." Associates praise the variety of their positions, though one cautions that it "could have been very boring if I had not been assertive about getting new jobs and tasks." That said, the Associates Program positions new hires well for permanent positions; in the words of one former associate, "It was definitely a great advantage to already be sitting on the bench versus still trying to get into the stadium."

Even for entry-level hires who start out as assistants, many note that they "don't really have a typical day." One editorial assistant writes, "When I first started, my responsibilities leaned more toward clerical work—copying, writing up rejection letters and reader reports, reading lots of slush submissions, answering phones. However, I also took my downtime during this slower period to ask lots of questions of the other assistants, read up on industry news, and read my bosses' previous titles to find out what types of books they were interested in." Another notes that there was some flexibility for her to plan her days: "I was able to organize my time myself, when I wasn't scheduled for a meeting, as long as I completed my projects on time."

Peers

"There is tremendous camaraderie among first jobbers at the company," writes one newbie. "From the minute I walked to my new desk, people came to introduce themselves and offer help in my settling in." Another newbie writes, "I have made quite a few good friends within the company, and they are a lot like me—outgoing and social, but still really interested in books, literature, current events, and the like." Another chimes in, "Because the industry has an apprenticeship culture ('everybody started as somebody's assistant' is a favorite axiom), it often feels like half the company is under twenty-five. I have lunches or happy hours with other twenty-somethings almost daily." In particular, "the Associates Program offered a ready-made group of people to become friends with, and by rotating, I met most of the first jobbers in the imprint."

Moving on

Entry-level jobs at Random House are designed to lead to better positions within the company. Many young workers stay to pursue their careers in publishing. "A major reason for voluntary departures is often to attend graduate school," note company officials, who also cite "relocation, career change, and personal reasons" as reasons why some employees leave the company. One entry-level employee notes that "there is plenty of room to grow in terms of pay and responsibility," though some report that promotion occurs faster in some imprints than in others. While "people complain about the workload and relatively poorer pay of publishing," they "also love the culture."

Attrition

Personal relationships are important in publishing, and many who leave do so because they don't enjoy working for their superiors. "Enjoyment of one's entry-level job is directly proportional to how much one enjoys one's supervisor, professionally and personally," points out one successful entry-level employee. Other people leave because they are "not satisfied with the level of responsibility allocated to them." Still others note a publishing industry trend: "Sometimes a move is necessary after a few years (generally four to five) in order to progress. As there is generally little movement once you reach the higher positions in editorial, it is often beneficial to move in order to be promoted, no matter how much you enjoy your current company."

RAYTHEON COMPANY
VARIOUS POSITIONS

"I've had the opportunity to do many different things during my career, from marine data collection on a seismic survey vessel in the North Sea to technical writing, training and development, and staffing."

The Big Picture

Raytheon is one of the world's biggest defense and aerospace technology systems suppliers. Its enormity allows engineers to work in virtually any area that interests them. From geospatial weather satellites and electronic tolling systems to radioactive material detection portals, Raytheon's engineers are known for working on cutting-edge technology.

LOCATION(S) WHERE ENTRY-LEVEL EMPLOYEES WORK

"Nationwide. Our 55 locations that hire co-ops/interns and full-time entry-level employees include the following metropolitan areas: Boston, Massachusetts; Falls Church, Virginia; Los Angeles, California; Southern California; Dallas, Texas; Tucson, Arizona; Denver, Colorado; St. Petersburg, Florida; Ft. Wayne, Indiana; and Indianapolis, Indiana."

AVERAGE NUMBER OF APPLICATIONS EACH YEAR

"Our electronic resume process logged 23,000 domestic United States entry-level candidates in Fall 2004 and Spring/Summer 2005."

AVERAGE NUMBER HIRED PER YEAR OVER THE LAST TEN YEARS

"Raytheon grew to its current state through mergers and acquisitions in the late 1990s. The average number of entry-level hires for recent college graduates has been over 1,000 per year since then."

ENTRY-LEVEL POSITION(S) AVAILABLE

"[There are anywhere from] 1,000 to 1,200 available positions. Predominately, openings are for engineering positions in hardware, software, and systems designs of large, complex defense and commercial electronic systems. Raytheon fills the greatest number of openings with candidates who majored in electrical engineering, computer engineering, and computer science. [They] also hire graduates with the following majors for technical positions: mechanical engineering, math, aeronautical/aerospace engineering, physics, [and] material science. Raytheon recruits graduate engineering degree candidates from select universities to participate in a rotational engineering leadership development program. Finally, [they] hire candidates with majors in human resources, marketing, and finance/accounting/business for leadership development programs in support [and] functional organizations such as business development, communications, contracts, finance, human resources, information technology, and supply chain management."

Average Hours Worked Per Week

"Most recent college graduates are [placed in] salaried positions. Hours worked vary according to individual program and phase [of project]. Employees average 40 to 50 hours per week, but the greater focus is doing what is required to get the job done. Many employees enjoy a flexible work arrangement and are on a 9-80 work week (nine-hour days for eight days and one eight-hour day in a two week period with every other Friday off)."

Average Starting Salary

"Raytheon offers competitive salaries for new college graduates based on a number of criteria, including work location, degree level and major, academic qualifications, and work experience. Recent salary offers were $47,000–$65,900 for technical degrees and $36,000–$50,000 for nontechnical degrees."

Benefits Offered

"At Raytheon, we understand the importance of rewarding our employees for all they bring to the table. For a general overview of the health care, income protection, investment/retirement, and work/life benefits as well as some of the extras available to eligible Raytheon employees worldwide, please refer to our recruitment website at rayjobs.com/campus." Additional benefits include income protection (disability coverage, basic life insurance, accidental death and dismemberment insurance, and business travel accident insurance), investment/retirement plans (pension, savings, and investment plans, and [a] stock program), work/life (flexible work schedule, paid time off, holidays, dependent care reimbursement account, adoption assistance, employee assistance program, and business casual attire), and extras (educational assistance, internal job transfer system, relocation assistance, home and auto insurance, matching gifts, Raytheon Scholars Program, same-sex domestic partner benefits, and discounts).

Contact Information

Visit the website at www.rayjobs.com/campus. Candidates are asked to submit their resume online.

Getting Hired

Raytheon recruits most aggressively at "twenty-three universities nationwide; these 'strategic schools' are valued [because of] our hiring history, potential to produce numbers of targeted graduates, and potential to produce females and minorities in our targeted degree majors. They also have research capabilities in technologies of interest to our businesses. We actively recruit on campus at approximately 100 schools. All candidates are referred to our campus recruitment website, where they can search for opportunities, complete a profile, and attach their profile to the jobs of greatest interest and match for them. This would include any candidates from schools where we may not actively recruit." One engineer who landed a job explains how he did it: "I submitted a resume at the job fair and then was contacted by Raytheon for an on-campus interview. The on-campus interview was done with one interviewer, and it lasted about twenty minutes. It was a scenario-based interview; the interviewer would ask 'what would you do?' questions based on scenarios. Also, there were questions about my greatest accomplishments in college and what specifically useful classes/projects I [completed] in college. After the on-campus interview, which consisted of thirty-two people from every department at the school, Raytheon invited four of us to a second round of interviews at Raytheon. In addition, there was a 'get acquainted' dinner the night before, a plant tour, and an information session before the interviews [at which] we were given an overview of Raytheon, and the initial work for our security clearances was begun. After the plant tour and lunch, a second interview was held. There were two interviewers in this session, but the questions were basically the same as the on-campus interview. The interview was longer, approximately forty-five minutes, and more time was set aside to allow me to ask any questions that I had. About three weeks later, I received a job offer from Raytheon. My later understanding was that the second interview was more of a formality, and that the real cut point for getting a job offer was made during the on-campus interviews."

Money and Perks

Raytheon offers competitive salaries, so the first jobbers we surveyed saw no need to negotiate pay; they also tell us that start time and location are sometimes negotiable. One writes, "I was given a six-month time window for when I wanted to start. The salary was not negotiable. However, the salary I was offered was $5,000 higher than any other offer I received, so there was no incentive for me to try to negotiate a higher salary. I felt the offer I was getting was more than fair." Company officials note that "salary increases are an integral part of an annual performance evaluation process. Increases are based on individual performance and company factors." Top perks include relocation allowances and the flexible work schedule.

The Ropes

Raytheon newbies are introduced to their new workplace through a brief orientation, which lasts anywhere between half a day and two days, depending on their placement in the company. One entry-level employee writes, "The initial orientation was an introduction to the company, company policies, security polices, and so on. Although it was necessary, it was no fun." Some engineers report subsequently taking formal classes, but most of them tell us that the majority of their training came from their bosses. One engineer explains, "I didn't receive any streamlined training. I was assigned to work on a project with another engineer the afternoon of my first day at work. He told me what we were working on and what he thought the next steps should be, and I basically jumped right in. I had enough theoretical and practical experience that a few questions were all I needed to be helpful. After a few days my boss and coworkers trusted that I knew what was going on, and they started to let me suggest ideas and initiate experiments." Another engineer agrees: "Aside from a few training classes, all of which took place months after I started working, all of my training has been informal, 'ask-my-mentor' type training."

Day in the Life

Raytheon hires engineers and support staff in a variety of areas. Company representatives tell us that "New technical hires work in a wide variety of assignments ranging from production support, design upgrades, full-scale program design and development, advanced developments for concept demonstration, and pure technology development. In all cases, new grads work with experienced lead engineers, and it is common to have an additional senior engineer designated as mentor." Engineers must also be prepared to work independently; as one tells us, "When I was first hired, I had to design a graphical user interface in Matlab. I had absolutely no idea how to do this, so first I had to gather as much info as I could from the Web and books. Not many people I asked had any experience with it, so I basically had to teach myself how to do it, but that was probably a good first experience because I learned that I could do something on my own with minimal help from others." Company representatives point out that engineers have responsibilities that people may not normally anticipate, such as "the requirement to present and defend designs at a design review, develop documentation, work with tenured technicians, source parts and deal with vendors, workout at one of our 'on-site' athletic facilities, participate in a community affairs/outreach events at a local school, etc. The ability of new grads to perform well in these additional tasks is what separates successful engineers from those who become disenchanted with their role and/or Raytheon in general."

Peers

Most of the new engineers we spoke with tell us that there were "very few entry-level engineers" in their particular area, making it hard to develop a peer network. One first jobber found a solution: "A small unit of young engineers had posted e-mails and established a company-sponsored social group, which did help me get acquainted with other new hires. This enabled me to increase social interaction after-hours." Those who do have contact with other newbies enjoy the experience; one writes, "All of us play sports and drink together. I still have lunch every week with some of the other new guys at the other two facilities."

Moving on

Raytheon at one time lost a substantial number of first jobbers, but that has changed in recent years. Company representatives explain, "Early this decade, Raytheon lost many recent hires to the lures of very large salary increases and stock option hiring bonuses from now-defunct high tech companies." These days, most Raytheon workers are in it for the long haul. One veteran writes, "While twenty-seven years sounds like a long time, it would place my tenure at third of four people in a small row of offices in the staffing systems and university programs office in Dallas. I've had the opportunity to do many different things during my career, from marine data collection on a seismic survey vessel in the North Sea to technical writing, training and development, and staffing. This becomes one of the greatest strengths of a corporation the size of Raytheon: the ability of its employees to use internal job mobility to change assignments and even locations to facilitate personal career vitality. For many years, I have listened to experienced line workers, whom we have assembled to share meals with new hire candidates, remark that once they had decided what they really wanted to do, all they had to do was ask."

Best and Worst

The best first jobber, Raytheon tells us, was "a guy hired from California Polytechnic University—San Luis Obispo, with a bachelor of science degree in industrial engineering, named William Swanson. Why? He is now Raytheon chairman and chief executive officer."

REPUBLICAN NATIONAL COMMITTEE
VARIOUS POSITIONS

Perks include "getting to help with all of the political aspects in Washington: campaign, convention, and other events," and the "exposure and contacts" employees make.

The Big Picture

As an employee of the Republican National Committee (RNC), you will help solicit political donations, coordinate "get out the vote" drives, formulate the Republican platform, produce issue advertising, and devise election strategies.

LOCATION(S) WHERE ENTRY-LEVEL EMPLOYEES WORK

Employees of the RNC work in Washington, DC.

ENTRY-LEVEL POSITION(S) AVAILABLE

Various support staff positions are available to entry-level hires.

AVERAGE HOURS WORKED PER WEEK

New hires work 40 or more hours per week.

PERCENTAGE OF ENTRY-LEVEL HIRES STILL WITH THE COMPANY AFTER THREE, FIVE, AND TEN YEARS

First jobbers typically stay for one election cycle, then use contacts made during their tenure to find other party/political jobs.

CONTACT INFORMATION

Contact your local Republican party office, via www.gop.com/contactus.

Getting Hired

You've got to hang around the grapevine to get a job at the RNC. All but one of the employees we spoke with told us that they learned about their jobs through personal contacts (the remaining first jobber, who works at GOP TV, was recruited). If you're active in the College Republican National Committee or with your state party organization, you're probably connected enough to find out about job opportunities at the RNC. One newbie writes, "I found out through the Wisconsin state party. It was the perfect job for me—I wanted to move to DC to work in press and for a Republican. It had all three. Initially I passed my resume to everyone I knew at the state and national party. It was more word of mouth that helped me get the initial interview. The interviewer just asked [about] my background [and] told me what the job entailed, and I told them how I could carry out the necessary tasks. I called two weeks later to follow up, and we scheduled another meeting two days later [during which] I was hired."

Money and Perks

New hires at the RNC have some flexibility in defining their roles in the organization but find little wiggle room in negotiating start time, location, or salary. Most don't care; one writes, "I didn't put up much of a fight about anything because the job was what I wanted." Perks include "getting to help with all of the political aspects in Washington: campaign, convention, and other events," and the "exposure and contacts" employees make.

The Ropes

"There is no specific orientation process" at the RNC; it varies from hire to hire. For one newcomer, it was "one afternoon during my first week, mostly 'company' policy and insurance issues." For another, it was "a couple of hours on the first day," mostly just meeting the other staffers and getting settled in. Subsequent training is similarly informal. "I was shown around and trained by my boss's assistant, and it was 'learn as you go,'" explains one first jobber. "A guy who had held the position a year ago was very helpful," offers another. A third advises, "Learn quickly!" The reason for this apparent lack of structure? One fresh hire opined, "Obviously everything moves very quickly right now, including hiring and placement. Jobs develop because there is a need for the function, not because a title is empty."

Day in the Life

Support staffers at the RNC often find their days filled with administrative duties; they "answer phones, make copies, put press releases up on newswire, and handle any additional administrative tasks people have in the office. [They] also help plan events and communication in the office." Those who make a solid impression quickly gain more responsibility and eventually move up the organization's hierarchy. While they "spend very little time with high-level executives personally, it's not uncommon to see the chairman roaming around downstairs talking to my bosses." Our first jobber at GOP TV has a radically different itinerary; he "coordinates reporters and crews, daily news feeds, and live-shot requests, liaises with capitol and presidential administration officials to plan and set up interviews for news and special feature programming, and creates pitches and coordinates outreach and pitching efforts on behalf of GOP TV with national and local media."

Peers

RNC staffers tell us that "there are many opportunities to meet other coworkers. We do have happy hours, for example." One entry-level employee writes, "There is a good social scene and overall respect and camaraderie. RNC staff members are wonderful people!" They don't distinguish between first jobbers and more senior staff, though; there's "nothing special because we are first jobbers."

Moving on

RNC staffers tend to move on after the given election cycle during which they were working ends. All of them will try to move onto other jobs within the world of party politics.

RESULTÉ UNIVERSAL
RECRUITER AND ACCOUNT MANAGER

"There is literally unlimited earning potential for new employees. The more job orders they fill and the more clients they satisfy, the more money they make."

The Big Picture

Resulté Universal is a Texas-based consulting and staffing services firm that "helps clients achieve their business goals through strategic investment in human capital." According to Resulté's website, the firm's consulting services division "deploys tactical teams to solve clients' critical business problems." Its staffing services division allows the company to deliver "top talent for contract, contract-to-hire, and direct-hire opportunities." First jobbers here recruit candidates to meet both client staffing and internal needs and help develop the firm's relationships with current and future clients.

LOCATION(S) WHERE ENTRY-LEVEL EMPLOYEES WORK

Employees work in Dallas and Houston, Texas.

AVERAGE NUMBER OF APPLICATIONS EACH YEAR

Resulté receives 1,000 applications each year.

AVERAGE NUMBER HIRED PER YEAR

Resulté currently hires just five entry-level employees each year, but the firm plans to increase the program size in the near future.

ENTRY-LEVEL POSITION(S) AVAILABLE

Resulté hires entry-level employees as recruiters and account managers.

AVERAGE HOURS WORKED PER WEEK

Entry-level hires work 50 hours per week.

AVERAGE STARTING SALARY

Recruiters and account managers earn $30,000–$35,000, plus commission.

BENEFITS OFFERED

Resulté offers health and dental coverage as well as life insurance. Disability is paid at 75 percent after 90 days of employment. Additionally, employees are eligible to contribute to the 401(k) program after one year of employment.

Resulté Universal
5151 Belt Line Road, #455
Dallas, TX 75254
Tel: 972-448-7070
Fax: 972-448-7059
E-mail: jobs@Resulté.com.

Getting Hired

Resulté "has an entrepreneurial environment." "If you work hard and produce, you have a lot of personal freedoms," reports one first jobber in recruiting. The firm seeks candidates who are a good fit for its corporate culture—people who are "competitive, intelligent, creative, and driven. They are people who can separate themselves from the crowd. An ideal employee at Resulté needs to be flexible, motivated to overcome obstacles, and great with people to get the job done successfully." Resulté "generally posts jobs online;" after all, "the type of candidate we are looking for needs to be well versed [in] computers to effectively use our patented system for qualifying, delivering, and managing contingent resources. Our internal recruiters, who are usually searching for qualified IT and accounting/finance professionals, use their skills to find the best prospects for their new coworkers. Once the prospects are narrowed down, the candidates are brought in first for a face-to-face interview with two to three recruiters or account managers in the division for which they are applying. The candidates who pass that round will interview with the division recruiting and account managers. Finally, a select few will meet with the three company partners, and the entire group decides which person will be the best fit for the organization." One successful hire notes, "Resulté Universal has a long interview process that allows everyone on the team to make a decision on a prospective employee."

Money and Perks

Starting salaries and wages are "somewhat negotiable" at Resulté, first jobbers here report. In addition to base pay, "entry-level recruiters and account managers are eligible for commissions at the same rate that the more senior employees earn. There is literally unlimited earning potential for new employees. The more job orders they fill and the more clients they satisfy, the more money they make." Raises "are given annually based on revenue and activity and quality goals, [such as] number of interviews, number of filled job orders, and customer satisfaction level. Teamwork, mentoring activities, and volunteering for special projects are also taken into consideration for raises."

Top perks include "a great Christmas party and an annual trip for high performers," plus quarterly events called "Gold Club outings." Gold Club events may include "racing Mustangs on a professional track, visiting an amusement park, or taking a helicopter tour of the city." Finally, "employees who meet certain requirements get to attend the annual company trip, which in the past has included a cruise to New Orleans and Cozumel, a trek through the Costa Rican rainforest, and lounging on the beach in Cancun."

The Ropes

Orientation at Resulté "typically lasts a week. It starts with a tour of the office and an introduction to all of the new employee's coworkers. Next, the employee will be introduced to Resulté, and one of the partners will present the state of the company and explain our history, our patented methodology, and where we fit [into] the marketplace. Then, a representative from the IT department will demonstrate how to use our proprietary systems for general tasks like scheduling appointments and e-mail and provide the new employee with all of the technology he or she will need, such as a laptop and a Blackberry. The majority of the first day is spent in formal training on the new employee's role—what's expected, the processes for achieving goals, and the Resulté way of doing things.

The rest of the week consists of attending short team meetings every morning to discuss the focus for the day and job shadowing." During the shadowing period, the new hire "spends several hours with each of the team members in the same position, so account managers will shadow all the other account managers in their division, and recruiters will shadow all the other recruiters in their division. This allows the employee to get different perspectives and form a more complete view of his or her role and the company while getting to know team members. Because recruiters and account managers work as a team to provide skilled employees to the clients, new recruiters will spend a day with the account manager division lead, and new account managers will spend a day with the recruiter division lead."

Day in the Life

Account managers work with current clients and also seek out new ones. Job duties include creating and implementing a successful sales plan, maintaining positive relations with current and prospective customers, and seeking new opportunities for Resulté to expand the services it provides to current clients.

Recruiters "source, screen, and evaluate candidates." One recruiter writes, "A typical day entails routine follow-up calls and check-up calls to ensure that all candidates are aware of where they are in the process. [We are also responsible for] calling new candidates, interviewing them, and submitting them [as applicants for] various positions, as well as setting up any interviews between the candidates and clients. Finally, [we receive] feedback about candidates and from candidates about their feelings on an opportunity."

Peers

"There is a big after-hours social scene among all employees" at Resulté, and this provides "a good and popular way to get new people to come out and meet their coworkers. Many people even hang out on the weekends." First jobbers feel their peers "are a lot alike in terms of their personalities and general attitude. We work well together because the atmosphere allows people to ask questions and be open."

Moving on

According to Resulté, "Few employees leave voluntarily, but many of those who have [done so] have gone on to start their own staffing companies."

Attrition

Resulté loses less than 10 percent of its college-grad first-jobber population within twelve months of hiring. Most who leave do so "because they were not able to meet our performance requirements." The firm tells us that such employees "generally go to work for a competitor." The average tenure of a Resulté first jobber is three years.

Best and Worst

Resulté identifies IT Recruiting Manager K. S. as an exemplar of a successful first jobber, reporting that she "was hired straight out of college with no experience in the industry. Because of her willingness to learn and her competitive drive, she quickly moved up the ranks and was promoted over more senior recruiters. In just a few short years, she has gone from knowing nothing about staffing to managing a team of eight responsible for more than $7 million in revenue in 2004 and has consistently exceeded her stated individual and team goals."

Unsuccessful first jobbers "are the ones who don't seem to have the ability or the initiative to solve problems and come up with answers and solutions on their own. A Resulté employee has a high degree of control when it comes to taking action to satisfy a customer. A new hire needs to be able to make decisions, defend those decisions, [be accountable] for mistakes, and do whatever is necessary to correct any mistakes that are made."

SCHLUMBERGER
FIELD ENGINEER AND RESEARCH, DEVELOPMENT, AND MANUFACTURING ENGINEER

Schlumberger

Good first jobbers "learn early on how to strike a good balance between their work lives and their personal lives. A candidate who thrives in the face of challenge and takes an objective view of the long-term prospects will generally do very well."

The Big Picture

Are you an engineer seeking entry into the world of bubblin' crude? You know, black gold? Texas tea? If so, here's your invite. Join Schlumberger, "a recognized technology leader providing products, services, and solutions to the oil and gas exploration and production (E&P) industry."

LOCATION(S) WHERE ENTRY-LEVEL EMPLOYEES WORK

"We recruit where we work worldwide, in approximately 100 countries, virtually everywhere you find oil and gas. In the United States, approximately 30 percent of the field engineers (FE) hired will start employment in an international location. Most research, development, and manufacturing engineer (RPM) hires work in one of the United States facilities."

AVERAGE NUMBER OF APPLICATIONS EACH YEAR

The company receives roughly 4,000 applications for the field engineer position and 1,500 for the RDM position (both in the United States).

AVERAGE NUMBER HIRED PER YEAR OVER THE LAST TEN YEARS

The company hires 200 FEs and 50 RDMs, yearly.

ENTRY-LEVEL POSITION(S) AVAILABLE

"Schlumberger mostly hires engineers and technical professionals. The two main types of positions are for field engineers and research, development, and manufacturing engineers."

AVERAGE HOURS WORKED PER WEEK

"Field engineers do not work a typical eight-to-five office schedule; the jobs often have long shifts (more than twelve hours per day) and/or odd hours. Time off is not on the normal weekend cycle; there is either a planned schedule (something like nine days on, three days off) or a minimum amount of days off per month (four). Research, development, and manufacturing engineers have a more typical schedule, with longer hours during peak project times, an average of 40 to 60 hours per week, with weekends off."

Getting Hired

Schlumberger recruits "on forty-nine United States campuses, including most of the top engineering schools. Students from other schools are open to apply through our online system, and many come to us through the referrals of current employees." The company seeks a complement of skills in its new hires, including technical aptitude, problem-solving skills, self-motivation, and interpersonal skills. First interviews are conducted by phone or on campus; subsequent interviews are held at company offices. The company notes that "because the FE job especially is quite different than the average engineering job on offer, attendance at the pre-interview information session the night before is critical." A field engineer reports that her first interview was with a recruiter on campus: "Questions asked ranged from how I handle stress to what activities I was involved in. About a week after the initial interview, I was contacted [and told] that I was a candidate for a second interview. Two months later, I was given a list of interview dates, and asked to pick the most convenient ones for me. It was a two-day interview, including a tour of one of the training centers, an overview of the company and positions available, and all of it was done in a relaxed manner."

Money and Perks

Field engineers "are promoted two separate times [during the training program] before finally being promoted to general field engineer. Each time the base salary increases incrementally. Each service segment also has an operational bonus structure based on its service delivery model. It can be highly dependent on work location and operational activity, but in general, there is extremely high growth potential in the second and third years as the engineer assumes higher levels of responsibility." Research, development, and manufacturing engineers receive "bonuses and promotions linked to performance." New recruits tell us that "the job offer is generally negotiable in terms of start date. However the actual location, salary, and position are set." Perks include a new laptop, extra allowances for engineers placed overseas, and bonus pay.

The Ropes

Orientation at Schlumberger lasts for ten days. Here's how one engineer described the experience: "The orientation process began in Houston for initial training into the Schlumberger lifestyle. Beginning on a Tuesday, the new hires spent five days covering company history, IT issues and setup, introductions to available resources for seeking help in anything, an introduction to the oil-field setup, and issued proper personal protective equipment and a drug test. The next five days were spent in driver training near Tulsa, Oklahoma." Other components of orientation include "health and hygiene training from a certified Schlumberger instructor and alcohol and drug awareness training from an outside contractor." Training is an ongoing process throughout an engineer's tenure with the company; one worker offers, "I have spent [more than] nine months in Schlumberger training schools since coming to work for the company."

Day in the Life

Research, development, and manufacturing positions frequently require an advanced degree; most offer entry-level positions as "sustaining engineers, responsible for sustaining and improving a variety of projects," gradually earning more responsibility and gaining more independence over time. For field engineers, the position that is more often available to recent college grads, "there is not much of a typical day." One new hire reports, "When I was first hired, I was assigned a supervisor to shadow and learn from, so I was on call with his schedule, which meant working about seventy hours a week. On any given day, I would be on call. When I was called in, I had an hour to report to the office and prepare for the job. Over time, I have been given an exponential amount of responsibility. In four months I've progressed from being an observer on the job to nearly running the entire job when on location." Another FE adds, "I had to get dirty (every day!) with the operators and work like an operator to learn and appreciate the equipment and the operators' job responsibilities before I could sit in the big seat and run a job (you don't get as dirty there)." Field engineers love "the early responsibility, in-depth training, and the ability [really to] put engineering theory into application. And over the longer term, the diversity of career opportunities is really the most attractive aspect. We call it 'borderless careers,' and it means people have the option to move fairly fluidly between businesses, functions, and locations."

Peers

Contact with other field engineers is inevitable, given the isolation of some work environments. One writes, "I work offshore; therefore I live, eat, sleep, and work two weeks at a time with the same people. They become family and great friends." Another agrees: "There is a good amount of contact with other first jobbers. There are two other people who fall into this category [where I work]. As far as after-hours social interaction, we get together when we can, but that time is limited. At work, we spend some time together depending on how the rotations work out." Off the rigs, peer-to-peer contact at Schlumberger "depends on the location. Some new hires spend a lot of time together at work and outside of work, and some do not. I [seldomly] spend time with peers outside of work. We spend so much time together at work that I try to spend time with other friends or family [on] my off-time."

Moving on

Those who leave Schlumberger early "will [most likely enter] completely different industries. Those who stay on and gain a bit more experience will often go to operators (oil and gas companies) and to a lesser extent our competitors and other oil field services companies." Most people view Schlumberger as a good place to build a career. As one field engineer tells us, "If I have the opportunity to leave the company for an interesting position [that] I feel I can do well in, then I will. However, I will not leave intentionally to work for another service company. I would like to continue my career here if the opportunities within the company allow me that opportunity."

Attrition

Attrition rates are relatively high for field engineers; about one in five can't handle the long hours, the stress, and the separation from family and friends. As one field engineer puts it, "The first few [reasons for leaving] that come to mind are the hours, schedules, and locations. We work twenty-four hours a day, seven days a week, and we do not stop for holidays. You do not have a schedule to follow and almost all locations are remote. You don't see many oil rigs in tourist-type locations." Research, development, and manufacturing engineers, who work under more conventional conditions, are much less likely to quit.

Best and Worst

Good first jobbers "learn early on how to strike a good balance between their work lives and their personal lives. A candidate who thrives in the face of challenge and takes an objective view of the long-term prospects will generally do very well." Less-than-ideal new hires "tend to be those who are less prepared for the transition into full-time job independence."

SEAMLESSWEB
VARIOUS POSITIONS

"In a company this small, everyone's job is unique, and no individual's day-to-day routine looks anything like another's."

The Big Picture

Those looking for opportunities in "an extremely fast-paced and growing company, as opposed to a large established corporation," should seriously consider applying for a position at SeamlessWeb. SeamlessWeb provides companies and individuals with a Web-based system for ordering from restaurants, caterers, florists, gift-basket purveyors, and other local vendors. In fact, the service was so well received that SeamlessWeb launched a consumer site for individuals to order at home or anywhere. The company serves individual customers and corporate clients in New York City; Washington, DC; Chicago; San Francisco; Los Angeles; Philadelphia; Stamford; Greenwich; and Jersey City and is rapidly expanding to serve corporate clients in other major cities. Not surprisingly, SeamlessWeb was ranked the number four fastest-growing privately-held company in the country by *Inc.* magazine. According to one employee, SeamlessWeb "has literally tripled in size in the last year."

LOCATION(S) WHERE ENTRY-LEVEL EMPLOYEES WORK

SeamlessWeb's headquarters are in New York City; the company also has several regional offices.

AVERAGE NUMBER OF APPLICATIONS EACH YEAR

SeamlessWeb receives 4,000 applications each year.

AVERAGE NUMBER HIRED PER YEAR

SeamlessWeb hires 15 entry-level employees each year.

ENTRY-LEVEL POSITION(S) AVAILABLE

Entry-level employees start as inside and outside sales associates, junior account managers, marketing associates, member support representatives, and accounting/human resources assistants.

AVERAGE HOURS WORKED PER WEEK

Entry-level employees work 40 hours per week.

PERCENTAGE OF ENTRY-LEVEL HIRES STILL WITH THE COMPANY AFTER THREE, FIVE, AND TEN YEARS

More than 85 percent of entry-level hires remain with the company after the three-year mark, and just about 85 percent stay on past five years.

AVERAGE STARTING SALARY

Entry-level employees earn $30,000 per year.

Getting Hired

SeamlessWeb reports that successful applicants "must be enthusiastic and have a desire to succeed as well as exhibit strong communication and follow-through skills. We try to avoid applicants who are not passionate about our product and the growth potential of SeamlessWeb." As at many small, nascent companies, the application process is relatively informal. One successful applicant recounts, "My initial interview was held in one of the VP's apartment in NYC. The VP was in sweats and a T-shirt when he interviewed me. Some [may] have seen this setting as a negative when reviewing a potential employer, but I saw it as the sign of a company that knew it was going places and didn't feel the need to impress anyone. [There] was very much a 'You'll be lucky to join us' attitude, [and] I appreciated [that]. I was brought back for a second round of interviews with the VP of firm sales, the department [within which] I was applying for a job, and [also with] the CEO. Both these individuals were founders and had gone to law school together. They were young, motivated, and demonstrated tremendous vision and sheer brilliance in answering my onslaught of questions about the company, its history, and its path for the future."

Money and Perks

Starting salaries are negotiable, first jobbers here tell us, and can be augmented with performance-based raises and performance-based bonuses. Some sales positions are commission-based. Perks include "free samples from New York City's finest delivery restaurants," a 401(k) pension plan, the "relaxed dress code," and "the chance to work with a great team every day."

The Ropes

As in the interview process, informal is the operative word concerning orientation at SeamlessWeb. One first jobber explains, "SeamlessWeb is a small company that does not have a human resources department, so our 'orientation' was not an official outlined process, but rather a [series] of meetings and [observation experiences] that helped us to learn more about the logistics and operations of the company." Another adds, "The training process was just as informal as the interview process. There was no training manual, and there was no [set] schedule. It was a hands-on, learn-by-observing-the-pros, be-proactive-and-ask-lots-of-questions process." Employees report having to be proactive "to get questions answered." But, one notes, "being the type of person who [dislikes being] micromanaged, I enjoyed the freedom and the fact that they put the success and speed of the training program in my hands. The training program [foreshadowed] my position [in that it had] an abundance of freedom and the understanding that only my proactive efforts and motivation to excel would bring success; nothing would be handed to me."

Day in the Life

A number of the first jobbers we spoke with began their SeamlessWeb careers performing data entry, customer service, database maintenance, filing, and receptionist duties. They tell us it was a good way to learn the business and find a place within it. They then moved on to take jobs in marketing and sales, where their days involved working directly with restaurants and corporate clients to build the business and publicize the SeamlessWeb brand. In a company this small, everyone's job is unique, and no individual's day-to-day routine looks anything like another's.

Peers

First jobbers at this "young and energetic company" enjoy "a lot of after-hours contact with other employees," though "in some cases, people choose to keep their office and social lives separate." One employee observes, "A few times a month we tend to get together for drinks or activities outside of the office, some of us who happen to be closer friends, even [get togethers] on the weekends. We try to include everyone, including those from other departments and teams so that everyone can get to know [one another]. I think there is a level of cliquishness between some of the people who have been here longer and developed friendships when the company was smaller; but for the most part, everyone gets along both in and out of the office." The overall vibe is "friendly," and "there is a feeling of family because everyone is so close."

Moving on

Because SeamlessWeb is a small company with lots of growth potential, first jobbers aren't anxious to move on. Many realize that they are joining what could potentially soon be a big and booming business. Because of this, they may have opportunities for advancement that are relatively rare in the first-job world. Those who leave generally do so because they're not interested in the SW business itself; some leave to go to graduate school.

Attrition

The company reports that about 5 percent of first jobbers leave SeamlessWeb within twelve months of taking a job here.

Best and Worst

The company tells us "We have had many very successful entry-level employees. The most successful are those who started either after graduating college or even working part-time as data entry clerks while still attending school. People who started with SeamlessWeb five years ago in an entry-level capacity are now running or helping to manage areas of their departments."

And the least successful SW hire? "An employee came in and didn't want to take the time to learn the core requirements of the company. He just wanted to push ahead without having the proper foundation."

SEARS
RETAIL MANAGEMENT DEVELOPMENT PROGRAM

"This was the longest training program available (among recruiting retailers), which I found attractive. To me, it meant that Sears would be investing time and money [in] me, thus giving me the information, tools, and background I would need to be successful in my first assignment."

The Big Picture

"Sears has everything!" That's what this venerable retailer claimed in one of its early slogans; after its merger with former competitor K-Mart, the assertion rings truer than ever. We've been assured that the company's well-regarded management training program will not change as a result of the K-Mart deal.

LOCATION(S) WHERE ENTRY-LEVEL EMPLOYEES WORK

Candidates select from six geographic regions that cover the U.S. In each region, multiple metro markets are available and select stores are identified for training locations.

AVERAGE NUMBER OF APPLICATIONS EACH YEAR

The company receives 1,200–1,500 applications per year.

AVERAGE NUMBER HIRED PER YEAR OVER THE LAST TEN YEARS

The company hires 150 entry-level employees each year.

ENTRY-LEVEL POSITION(S) AVAILABLE

Entry-level hires enter the Retail Management Development Program.

AVERAGE HOURS WORKED PER WEEK

New hires work 40 to 50 hours per week.

AVERAGE STARTING SALARY

The starting salary is $36,000 per year, plus an annual target incentive.

BENEFITS OFFERED

Sears offers HMO and PPO plans. The company provides dental insurance, health care flex spending accounts, disability insurance, life insurance, business travel insurance, a 401(k) plan, Sears discounts, tuition reimbursement, education loans, daycare flex spending account, vacation, and flex time off.

Getting Hired

Sears recruiters look for "demonstrated leadership skills and abilities, as well as a strong interest in the program and company" through a "structured candidate assessment process" that "utilizes both business representatives as well as human resources professionals." The company recruits on thirty-two core college campuses and also considers internal referrals and unsolicited candidates, who may apply via the Internet. One successful hire reports, "The first-round interview was held at my college campus. It was about forty-five minutes long. I was interviewed by a Sears rep sent by Chicago. She was absolutely pleasant and quite relaxed. The tone was very professional, and she focused on my abilities and skill sets rather then my limited job experience or my nontraditional major. I was e-mailed the following week to congratulate me on my interview and was invited to Chicago for the second and final round of interviews. I was allowed to pick the date of my trip. The interview day began at 6:00 A.M. We had a series of interviews for most of the morning as well as simulation activities. The day ended at 8:00 P.M. I was exhausted. It was a very impressive process. It made me want the job even more because I felt as though I was interviewing for something much larger." (Sears officials note that final interviews are typically scheduled from 7:00 A.M. to 4:00 P.M.)

Money and Perks

Retail Management Development Program trainees start at $36,000 per year and "are eligible for an annual incentive based on the following: Sears earnings per share and Full Line Store Balanced Scorecard (a metric combining customer, people, sales, and profit goals)." After twelve months, successful trainees are "promoted into an assistant store manager assignment" and receive a commensurate raise. Popular perks include the associate discount; one trainee points out, "This company is involved in many facets of retail, and in one way shape or form the discount for me has been very beneficial." Another notes, "Besides the discount, the best benefit from this program is the opportunity to run around with the high-level managers, both on the store and district level. As a result, as a new ASM, I am not intimidated by the district or regional staff because I [have] always worked with them and [am] familiar with their expectations."

The Ropes

Orientation begins in Hoffman Estates, Illinois (a suburb of Chicago), where trainees are flown to attend a full-day session at a Sears training store. Here, trainees complete the requisite paperwork and benefits overview, then are trained in eLearning, an Internet-based training tool that preps trainees for upcoming rotations. Team-building activities take up much of the afternoon, along with an overview of the program, a career-planning workshop, and a Q-and-A session. Subsequent training occurs online and on the job, with a rotational system ensuring that trainees learn all aspects of the business ("We work in each department of the store for two weeks to a month," reports one participant). Most are "impressed by the depth of the training program offered by Sears. This was the longest training program available (among recruiting retailers), which I found attractive. To me, it meant that Sears would be investing time and money [in] me, thus giving me the information, tools, and background I would need to be successful in my first assignment."

Day in the Life

The day-to-day life of management trainees varies with their rotational assignments, "shadowing experiences that include time in all selling and nonselling aspects of a Sears Full Line Store." Trainees also perform two special assignments "that will challenge their leadership skills. Each assignment will last three to four months and include goals in alignment with the Balance Scorecard." One trainee sums up her experience in the program: "My responsibilities were generally the same throughout the entire program. Phase one consisted of me shadowing all five assistant store managers. I worked with them, did their reports, conducted their walk-throughs, assisted with customer opportunities, etc. I essentially lived their lives for at least two weeks each. I then followed each of their leads (hourly managers/sub managers); I learned how they supported their ASM and how they contributed to the team as a whole. Phase two consisted of two special assignments. I assumed the role of a lead in both a hardlines and softlines position. I took ownership of specific departments and reported to a specific ASM."

Peers

Trainees report that the size of their peer network depends greatly on their placement. Those in larger districts enjoy a large group of contemporaries. One trainee reports, "I instantly became friends with the other trainees and younger management staff in my district. We frequently meet for dinner or karaoke throughout the week." Those in smaller districts have relatively few peers in their own age group. A trainee from the hinterlands warns, "My advice for new trainees would be to really consider where you are asking to be assigned. Your area will become your new home. In the world of retail, most managers are older, with families, etc. Your social life is dependent on what you bring to the table, who your other trainees are, and where you ask to be assigned."

Moving on

Trainees who move on usually do so "for multiple reasons, but most revolve around career fit." Top motivators include "selecting a line of work other than retail," "returning to school," "moving to a competitor within the retail industry," and "personal reasons, including location issues." A typical trainee writes, "I think I will probably want to continue my education at some point and perhaps to go forward in higher level jobs in the company or I may take another route all together."

Attrition

Less than 10 percent of Sears Management Development trainees don't remain through the end of the first year. Those who do leave "talk about how they feel the work-life balance that Sears promotes is only for [the] corporate office. They complain about the hours and the crazy schedule." There were concerns in the past that trainees were not well connected to the company's suburban Chicago headquarters, but a change in corporate personnel has improved the situation. Nowadays, "trainees really have the potential to accelerate quickly if they work hard and are willing to demonstrate their capabilities."

Best and Worst

According to the company, "There are several high-potential leaders at Sears who began their careers in the Retail Management Development Program. Common keys to their success include [having] tremendous passion for the business, [being] highly results-driven, and [cultivating] expertise in performance management."

Sherwin-Williams Company
Management Trainee

"One of the greatest things about this job is that you learn something every day. After six years, I still draw [on] things I learned during the first six months, and I continue to learn more every day."

The Big Picture

Sherwin-Williams, one of the nation's leading names in paint, painting supplies, wallpaper, and chemical coatings, offers college grads a thorough training program that transforms them from eager greenhorns into store managers in one brief, but intense, year.

Location(s) Where Entry-level Employees Work

Sherwin-Williams has 3,100 stores throughout North America.

Average Number Hired Per Year over Last Ten Years

The company hires between 450 and 500 people per year.

Entry-level Position(s) Available

New hires work as management trainees.

Average Hours Worked Per Week

New hires work 44 hours per week.

Average Starting Salary

New hires earn a base salary in the low- to mid-30s (depending on location), plus quarterly bonuses.

Benefits Offered

Sherwin-Williams offers various choices in company-paid health insurance (with small employee co-payments), dental insurance, and eye care. Additional benefits include a stock savings plan, a 401(k) plan with company match, company-paid pension plan, tuition aid, sickness and accident leave, paid holidays, and vacation.

Contact Information

Visit www.sherwin.com, click "Careers," and then click "Career Paths."

Getting Hired

With the job market as tight as it has been the past few years, candidates have been taking increasingly novel approaches to distinguishing themselves from their fellow candidates. One successful hire at Sherwin-Williams recalls, "I focused on my cover letter, knowing that whoever read it would continue to my resume if I conveyed intelligence, structure, and personality, which are vital in a sales position. I sent my resume to the headquarters, and it made its way to the human resources director, who was the first person to interview me. I sent a shoe wrapped nicely in a box with a note on top that read 'Thank you for letting me get my foot in the door.' Since the interview process can be nerve-wracking, the strong cover letter and the ice-breaking shoe helped me feel a little calmer and more confident." Once your foot is in the door, interviewing at Sherwin-Williams is a three-stage procedure. One who survived all three stages explains, "During my first interview with human resources, I felt the tone to be very professional but not too rigid. I was impressed that the interviewer was selling the company to me as much as I wanted to sell myself. He asked me questions about how I had handled situations in the past concerning customers and about setting and achieving goals and multitasking. His questions were all positive and directed toward my past work and school experiences. He explained to me the path I would take both with the interview process and upon being hired, as well as how the MTP (Management Training Program) worked. Following this interview I met with the district manager of the area where I would start, and finally, with the vice president of sales of the same division. The second interview had the same tone, but had more specific questions applicable to the job and the management training program. The third interview felt like more of a formality and a get-to-know the company interview. During this interview, I was officially offered the job."

Money and Perks

At Sherwin-Williams, "All employees receive annual merit increases, plus bonuses. At such time, a trainee is promoted to manager or representative (about one year after being hired), there is a substantial promotional increase, [and] bonus potential increases threefold." Start date and location can be negotiable, if the company has numerous openings at the time of hire. Salary is not negotiable. Most first jobbers agree that the best perks are "the paid vacation time and the 401(k)."

The Ropes

New management trainees spend their first six weeks on the job "in a training store learning the basics of the business. Trainees are provided with videos and literature to help familiarize them with benefits, policies, and procedures. The training store manager is specifically trained in training techniques and is compensated, in part, on the success of the trainees. It is the responsibility of the training store manager to orient the trainees, introduce them to employees and customers, and ensure that they are familiar with policies and procedures and are aware of the resources available to them as new employees. After six weeks in a training store, trainees participate in one week of classroom training at their division-training center. The third phase of training entails being assigned to a store as an assistant manager." One former trainee writes, "The entire orientation process lasted about six months. During this time I completed courses that helped with all aspects of the job, including product knowledge, quality control, financial reports, managing employees, and time management. I also worked in several different stores. This helped me get to know not only the people in my area, but also the market. The START (Store Training and Reference Tool) courses and books, floating around and working in different stores with different managers, and a week of training at the headquarters helped me to develop during the orientation process. One of the greatest things about this job is that you learn something every day. After six years, I still draw [on] things I learned during the first six months, and I continue to learn more every day."

Day in the Life

A current management trainee tells us, "When I was first hired, my biggest responsibility was to focus on training, learning all I could about my own duties as an assistant manager as well as [about] my employees. I needed to know where the stock went and how to put it away, how to order, how to delegate tasks, and what tasks needed to be done; doing everything from mopping the floor to filling orders to helping customers find what they need[ed] for their project was included in a typical day; [and] understanding the paperwork and what needed to be done was important so that I could learn how to prioritize and manage my time on the job. Another great thing about this position is that there are not many 'typical' days. Every day is different with different tasks to complete and new things to learn." One former trainee who has since moved onto a management position notes, "At first, product knowledge is the toughest part of the job. However, over time your knowledge in products grows, and you then have to start learning your customers. You learn that each customer is completely different from the next. In this industry, you may see a person once a year or twice a day. The goal is to know what customers need no matter how often you see them." As time progresses, trainees "take over the tasks of the assistant manager. These tasks include making collection calls, fulfilling orders, staffing the store, and managing accounts payable."

Peers

One Sherwin-Williams management trainee says, "[We] make lifelong friends during the management training program week [at division headquarters]. They are from different parts of the country, and we still keep in touch. I see them all once a year during the National Sales Meeting in Nashville, Tennessee." Once back at their jobs, however, they don't see other trainees regularly; one explains, "Since I was the only MTP in my district, I had very little exposure to other people [across] the country in my position. However, other employees throughout the district were very welcoming to me. I have had many opportunities to interact with other employees on a social basis as well as [for] business. The mix between the two has made my first six months very enjoyable." First jobbers tell us that Sherwin-Williams has a congenial work vibe; one notes, "Friends are easy to make at Sherwin-Williams. Each day it gets hectic and chaotic. By busting your butt and getting the job done, everyone is brought together as a team. My best friend works at Sherwin-Williams!"

Moving on

Sherwin-Williams carefully tracks former employees. Although the employee turnover rate is low (in the single digits), company officials tell us that out of all who leave, three-quarters of people leave for other job offers; about one in eight leave for personal reasons; and about one in ten leave for other reasons." Company representatives report that the vast majority of people leave to "start their own business, take a sales job in another industry, become a painting contractor, or go back to school." Those who stay say they like the fact that many different opportunities are available within the company. One writes, "Sherwin-Williams allows its employees to wear many different hats. If I wanted to get into the marketing side, I could choose to go to marketing. If I wanted to go into corporate management, I could have that opportunity. The fact is, with Sherwin-Williams you have the opportunities to grow into the position that [best fits] you."

Attrition

Some folks can't hack it in Sherwin-Williams' Management Trainee Program; one who could says, "I found, and still find, that those people who drop out of the program or are dissatisfied are not ready to work. Most people were expecting to put on a tie and sit behind a desk after college. I felt like my strong work ethic set me apart from them, and I enjoyed my success." The job is certainly demanding; as one trainee tells us, "I guess the most common complaint that I have heard is being frustrated about not being able to learn fast enough. What is interesting is that I have never heard anyone complain about the program itself, but only about their own ability or inability to learn the products."

Best and Worst

The most successful first jobber ever, Sherwin-Williams tells us, is "John Morikis, who entered the program in 1984 and is now president and chief operating officer of the Sherwin-Williams Company."

STARCOM
MEDIA ASSOCIATE

STARCOM MEDIAVEST GROUP

"Some days will be absolutely crazy, while others are quite slow. I have never felt I couldn't get help from someone if I had too much to do, though."

The Big Picture

Starcom is one of the giants of brand communications, an industry that offers services in media management, multicultural media, internet and digital advertising, and beyond. Clients include beer companies, consumer packaged goods, high-tech businesses, and just about every other business you can think of.

LOCATION(S) WHERE ENTRY-LEVEL EMPLOYEES WORK

Entry-level employees work in Chicago, Illinois and Los Angeles, California.

AVERAGE NUMBER OF APPLICATIONS EACH YEAR

Starcom receives about 3,000 applications each year.

AVERAGE NUMBER HIRED PER YEAR OVER THE LAST TEN YEARS

Starcom hires about 100 entry-level employees each year.

ENTRY-LEVEL POSITION(S) AVAILABLE

Entry-level employees are hired at the media associate level.

AVERAGE HOURS WORKED PER WEEK

New hires work 40 to 50 hours per week.

PERCENTAGE OF ENTRY-LEVEL HIRES STILL WITH COMPANY AFTER THREE, FIVE, AND TEN YEARS

Half of entry-level employees remain with the company after three years.

AVERAGE STARTING SALARY

Starting salaries range from $28,000 to $32,000.

BENEFITS OFFERED

Benefits include medical, dental, vision, tuition reimbursement, short-term disability, long-term disability, life insurance, fitness center memberships (very low cost), immediate 401(k) participation and company matching, an employee assistance program, paid vacation, paid holidays, personal legal assistance (low cost, through vendor partner), paid wedding leave and paternity leave, a commuter spending account, a health reimbursement account, a dependent care account, company charity match, adoption assistance, and international travel assistance for all full-time employees.

Getting Hired

Starcom recruiters seek hires with "strong verbal and written communication skills, strong math and analytical skills, and a passion for work in the media industry." Applications are accepted "either online or through campus visits. If there is a strong fit with the candidates' backgrounds and interests and our recruiting needs, they would be contacted to start the interview process." Interviews "focus on questions surrounding communication (both verbal and written), teamwork, relationship building, knowledge of and interest in the media industry, quantitative skills, critical thinking, problem solving, innovation, and creativity." One successful hire describes the process: "My first interview was with an agency director over the phone. [It] was very casual. I was very comfortable, and we spent the majority of the time talking about my experiences and how they relate to a work environment. I was given ample opportunity to be myself and really sell myself through to the company. About a week after my first interview, I was then invited back for second round, which subsequently took place a month and a half later in Chicago. I, along with about 100 other students, came to Starcom for a day full of interviews. I had interviews with five different people at different levels of experience. These interviews were a bit more tense, not as comfortable, and the questions were a little harder. After the interviews, we went out to lunch with the other applicants and a manager. This was great because it was a relaxed environment and I was able to ask any questions I had about the company."

Money and Perks

First jobbers agree that starting salaries are "not negotiable," but they appreciate what they get in return. Most are philosophical about the situation; one newbie writes, "That is how this industry is. We don't make much less than the industry standard; I just feel we may work more than the rest of the industry." In addition to gaining valuable career experience, newbies "are wined and dined by vendors, and your social calendar is constantly booked with sporting events or after-work parties/concerts/festivities." One worker writes, "On any given occasion, a vendor could take me out to sushi for lunch, out for a manicure, dinner, limo ride, or Cubs game, or [give me] an invitation to a media party where we get to drink all night free while listening/dancing to a band, singing karaoke, and eating a full-buffet dinner. These 'perks' are definitely icing on the cake." The company itself also provides "lots of perks. Every December, the company gets together for its huge annual holiday party. The entire day is filled with incredibly fun stuff, including drinking at bars, big-ticket raffle prizes, and watching the executives perform skits." There are also many programs designed to make newbies to feel like they're part of the Starcom family. These include mentorship programs, affinity groups, training classes and brainstorming sessions, community volunteer opportunities, health management programs, "brown bag" meetings with the CEO, and more.

The Ropes

Every new associate at Starcom is automatically enrolled in "Connections College," a fourteen-week formal training program introducing him or her to the world of media and consumer engagement. "This program strongly differentiates us in the marketplace, is considered a competitive advantage, and is often a primary reason why candidates want to work here," one first jobber explains. The classroom curriculum covers a number of media business basics, including techniques for analyzing and boosting a client's business; developing consumer insights; reaching today's multitasking marketplace; media "activation" (how advertising can come to life across every single viable ad medium, from traditional to digital); and gauging consumer captivation. The College is not just a series of presentations. Participants' discussions and exercises teach them such skills as brainstorming, creative thinking, teamwork, negotiating, and relationship building. At the end, each team presents to a room of directors a complete plan for their brand, from start to finish.

Day in the Life

"Every day is very different" for media associates at Starcom, the company's only entry-level position for media professionals. That's due in part to "an excellent rotational program where one can move from a specific department to another." The three main groups for associates are strategy groups, which "create and present media plans to clients" to meet their advertising needs; activation groups, which "invest client budgets with media vendors in the most effective and efficient way" and monitor advertising buys to ensure that they run as ordered across digital and traditional media; and specialty groups, which focus exclusively on "one medium or type of advertising," such as multicultural media, Internet marketing, out-of-home marketing, international media, TV programming, or entertainment marketing. One media associate observes, "Some days will be absolutely crazy, while others are quite slow. I have never felt I couldn't get help from someone if I had too much to do, though. And if things are slow, I usually ask for an extra mini-project or volunteer for something that needs to get done in the group."

Peers

Starcom "is full of young, vibrant, engaging people just like myself," making "the transition into the work environment easy because you are starting with people just like yourself who are just out of college and new to the work world." Accordingly, there is "a lot of camaraderie amongst first-jobbers. You grow very close to one another because you begin training together, you are in the same life-stage as one another, and you have similar life experiences. Many people get together after work for social events, shopping, drinks, and even intramural athletic teams."

Moving on

Those few who leave Starcom do so to "pursue advanced education on a full-time basis, professional careers outside of the media industry, opportunities at other media agencies, or for personal reasons." Company representatives note, "People who want to work in the media industry tend to stay here long-term."

Attrition

Only about 10 percent of Starcom newbies don't remain with the company through the end of the first year.

STARWOOD HOTELS AND RESORTS
VARIOUS POSITIONS

STARWOOD
HOTELS & RESORTS

Hospitality, Starwood representatives note, "is very much a hands-on business, and we look for business professionals who also know how to work with customers, have a guest-service ethic, and know how to lead those who serve the guest."

The Big Picture

Starwood Hotels and Resorts Worldwide, Inc., "one of the leading hotel and leisure companies in the world," is the proprietor of such world-famous facilities as St. Regis, the Luxury Collection, Sheraton, and Westin. Although a relative newcomer to the field, Starwood is a major player and has entry-level positions available in a broad range of areas, including the coveted and more competitive positions at corporate headquarters as well as on the front lines at Starwood's various hotels.

LOCATION(S) WHERE ENTRY-LEVEL EMPLOYEES WORK

Entry-level employees are hired to work almost anywhere. Starwood has more than 700 properties worldwide.

ENTRY-LEVEL POSITION(S) AVAILABLE

Line-level, supervisory, coordinator/administrative, assistant manager, and manager positions are available in the following departments: sales, accounting, guest services, catering/convention services, rooms, food and beverage, six sigma, and other corporate management positions in IT, legal, hotel management, real estate, and revenue management.

AVERAGE HOURS WORKED PER WEEK

People may work 35, 40, and 47.5 hours per week, depending on title, corporate/property, and union status.

AVERAGE STARTING SALARY

"[Salary] starts at $10 [per hour] for interns and goes up from there. [The] typical entry-level management [salary] is $32,000–$36,000, depending on region and hotel. We have a very competitive compensation structure and continually compare our structure against our competitors and other industries."

Getting Hired

"While Starwood has a centralized college relations program through which approximately thirty college graduates enter, college recruiting is not the primary way people join Starwood." For those seeking corporate jobs with Starwood, "a big plus is an early, demonstrated interest in the hotel and hospitality business through a hotel-school education—summer internships in hotels, resorts, and other customer-focused businesses." Hospitality, Starwood representatives note, "is very much a hands-on business, and we look for business professionals who also know how to work with customers, have a guest-service ethic, and know how to lead those who serve the guest." Because of the high demand for corporate jobs with Starwood, the company "only recruits for the small-management training and internship programs from a core group of ten hotel schools and, currently, two business schools. Students from other schools are encouraged to contact hotels local to their homes or schools to inquire about available internships [and entry-level positions] throughout the year." One successful hire reports, "I was explicit in my cover letter and stated that this was the job I wanted; it was my top choice, and if given an offer, I'd accept on the spot. I think this really helped my application." The hiring process for property positions is less formal; one accounts-payable employee who works at a hotel learned of the position through a college professor, sent her cover letter and resume, and underwent a "very laid-back, carefree" interview. No matter what position you're applying for, all respondents agree that your cover letter and resume are important.

Money and Perks

Starwood representatives advise, "The hospitality industry in general does not have the reputation for very high entry-level salaries, but, with time, it is known for great bonuses, the opportunity to work in different locations in the country (or world) throughout one's career, and the opportunity to be associated with a very old, yet also very exciting industry." The best fringe benefit, first jobbers here agree, are "the Starwood HotRates!!! Cheap five-star hotel rooms. I'd never be able to travel like this right out of college, but I stay at the top hotels in the world for next to nothing."

The Ropes

Participants in Starwood's corporate management training program go through a number of rotations, allowing them to learn all the different responsibilities within a certain area of the company. Company representatives explain, "The program is a twelve-week rotational training through all departments of the hotel with a concentration in one of three areas: food and beverage, rooms, or sales. At the completion of the program, each participant is placed in a position of responsibility at the same hotel where the management-training program was completed." The experience starts with "an informal orientation process. For me, it entailed one day of touring our hotels in New York, New York and a couple of days learning about how Starwood's systems work and what each group does within STARS [Starwood Technology and

Revenue Systems, the program in which this employee was enrolled]." The newbies we spoke with agree that "most of the real learning comes on the job." For positions at Starwood's properties, the orientation and training process is less prescribed and is specific to the position. For example, one such employee took classes on how her hotel "stands out from other [Starwood] properties." Another respondent took "classes pertaining to customer service and guest satisfaction, computer programs, [and] property management systems as well as brand standards."

Day in the Life

Corporate management trainees agree that "the learning curve is pretty steep. You start right away on projects. A typical day includes some meetings, preparation for an upcoming presentation, and a dialogue with my boss around the issues that have come up and how we need to tackle them." Contact with Starwood higher-ups is fairly frequent; one employee in strategy explains, "We are always invited to meetings where we have done work to support the conclusions. We are encouraged to speak at meetings." Employees at Starwood properties seem less overwhelmed by their day-to-day tasks; for one employee in accounting, it is "pretty straight forward. I work from nine to five." A Whatever/Whenever agent—an aptly named position—agrees: "With each passing day, my resposibilities increase."

Peers

The first jobbers we spoke with describe a pretty subdued peer network at Starwood. One person working at a hotel tells us, "We have special cocktail time within our property once [a] month; [this] allows us to interact with people from other departments, and we spend time together, like one hour, including lunch break. It all depends [on] what kind of event we go to, but generally three hours in a week." People at corporate headquarters tell us that "the groups here are pretty small. There's not really an after-work scene, since the main office is in White Plains and most of us live in the city. It becomes difficult to coordinate and motivate when we commute. But we get together for special events and whatnot."

Moving on

Starwood does not track data on former employees. People we spoke with still work at Starwood and plan to remain there. They tell us that those with complaints "sometimes have problems with their specific bosses" and "wish there would be a little more training at the beginning."

STATE FARM
VARIOUS POSITIONS

"State Farm promotes a good work-life balance. Employees are encouraged to be open about their workload and be honest if they are feeling overwhelmed."

The Big Picture

"Insurance and financial services are not glamorous professions, but they're stable, and both provide valuable services." It's the grown-up world in all its glory, and State Farm is one of the biggest players in the game.

LOCATION(S) WHERE ENTRY-LEVEL EMPLOYEES WORK

Entry-level hires work across the nation and in parts of Canada.

ENTRY-LEVEL POSITION(S) AVAILABLE

"State Farm has many positions that can be considered entry-level, but the most hiring activity occurs for positions in our claims and underwriting operations. In addition, we have a very large systems (information technology) department [in which] we hire many recent college graduates for entry-level positions."

AVERAGE HOURS WORKED PER WEEK

The hours vary widely by position.

AVERAGE STARTING SALARY

"Starting salaries can vary by the skill sets that a candidate brings to the position and by the geographical location of the job."

BENEFITS OFFERED

State Farm offers PPO and HMO plans, medical, dental insurance, and long-term disability. It also has a 401(k) program, employer-funded retirement plan, tuition reimbursement, professional education opportunities, Select-A-Gift (a holiday gift benefit), adoption assistance, LifeWorks (an employee assistance program), childcare assistance, and business casual dress.

CONTACT INFORMATION

"Visit the 'Careers' section on www.statefarm.com to submit your resume for a job or internship, to find out where we will be recruiting on campus, and to learn more about our benefits. Visit the 'Zone Offices' link in the 'About State Farm' section to find office addresses and phone numbers for the State Farm office nearest you."

Getting Hired

State Farm recruits on a number of college campuses; prospective employees may also search for job openings and post a resume via the Internet. Interviews are conducted in several stages. One successful applicant explains, "The tone of the first interview was professional, and it was directed with open-ended questions. Some of the questions that were presented are 'Tell me about yourself. Why do you want to work for State Farm?'" Those who clear this hurdle receive a second interview, generally with their prospective boss. One first jobber reports, "During the second interview, most of the questions asked were scenario questions, such as, 'What would you do if you had an angry policyholder?' or 'Describe a situation [in which] you resolved a conflict with a customer and what the outcome was.' When responding to those questions, I tried to answer them as clearly as possible and elaborate on the answer. When faced with a question of a situation I had never encountered, I was honest with the interviewer in saying that I had never been in such a situation, but I [also] answered the question hypothetically. Throughout both interviews, I showed confidence and advised both interviewers that I was in here for the long haul; I was interested in a career, not a position."

Money and Perks

First jobbers report that there's minimal room for salary negotiation from the outset. There are, however, opportunities to qualify for raises and incentives that can quickly increase one's earnings. Location is more negotiable, a benefit of the company's size and widespread presence. Newbies appreciate the generous benefits package, which includes "retirement [plans] and different paid absences [for such events] as personal family leave, doctor or dentist appointments, and sick leave among others." They also love the extracurriculars; one writes, "There are several clubs and sport groups that have been created for employees."

The Ropes

Training varies from job to job and from site to site at State Farm, with a few constants. New hires start with your standard orientation: They meet superiors, fill out paperwork, and learn about benefits, compensation, and corporate philosophy. The real training begins on the second day and continues for the first few months of an employee's tenure. One claims rep explains, "In training, we learned from the very basics of insurance terminology to the actual claim-handling process. We worked in a classroom setting, studying material on different subjects such as property and casualty, medical terms, auto inspections, legal concepts, etc.; we were then tested. We later learned to work the software used to handle claims. Later we learned hands-on by actually handling claims—the easier ones initially and progressing into the more complex ones, always with our trainer/boss by our side. The training lasted three full months. At the completion of those three months, we traveled to State Farm's headquarters offices in Bloomington, [Illinois], where we received two additional weeks of training. This trip made me connect with our home office and be even more proud of my company."

Day in the Life

Daily life varies depending on the particular entry-level job. The four major entry-level positions are claim rep, which involves screening potential customers for risk level and working directly with State Farm agents; business analyst, which involves "serving as a liaison between business areas or the IT department"; and systems analyst, which focuses on the technical aspects of State Farm's business. Training in all areas is extensive, and first jobbers happily report that "State Farm promotes a good work-life balance. Employees are encouraged to be open about their workload and be honest if they are feeling overwhelmed. I have had to turn assignments down before because of my workload. I was never reprimanded when I had to do this."

Peers

"The culture here is employee-oriented," first jobbers tell us, noting that "flexible work schedules are available, it is business casual dress, and surrounding stores and restaurants have discounts for State Farm employees. The list goes on." The peer network is strong, "and it doesn't only include [those] under twenty-five and first jobbers. Almost all come out to happy hours and other events."

Moving on

According to company data, "The top five reasons for departures from State Farm are 'another opportunity,' 'retirement,' 'employment agreement expired' (this is when someone is hired temporarily for a specified period of time), 'returned to school,' and 'no reason given.'" State Farm does not track first jobbers independently of other employees, but notes that "recent data shows that voluntary turnover at State Farm is lower than the industry average."

Attrition

"For the most part, people at State Farm are very happy and proud to work for the company," explains one first jobber, adding that "clear evidence of this is the longevity of most employees at State Farm. It is not unusual to see people [who] have been working for the company for thirty to thirty-five years. In my opinion, that says a lot." Those who bail out sometimes do so "because they do not like the current position they are in. I do not think that they are unhappy with the company itself." The same employee adds that "State Farm is an excellent company because they provide ways for employees to move within the company. If a person is unhappy with [his or her] current position, I believe that [he or she has] opportunities to improve on this if [he or she wants] to take action."

Best and Worst

State Farm tells us that "successful candidates vary in skills and competencies. We look for individuals who are good at what they do and want to continue to develop. In positions dealing directly with our policyholders, people who want to help others and care about providing quality service do the best. An interest in learning about our industry (insurance and financial services) is important as well." Poor employees demonstrate "an inability to be flexible and lack of desire to learn and grow."

STATE STREET
VARIOUS POSITIONS

"State Street is a huge company with tons of room for growth, both professionally and monetarily. The career path at State Street is endless."

STATE STREET.
For Everything You Invest In™

The Big Picture

State Street, a leader in the financial services industry, hires scores upon scores of college grads every year. The pay is relatively low, but the work is challenging, the learning opportunities numerous, and the chances for advancement even more so. A solid benefits package further sweetens the deal.

LOCATION(S) WHERE ENTRY-LEVEL EMPLOYEES WORK

"State Street is a global organization, and we have entry-level opportunities at most of our twenty-five offices worldwide. The largest percentages are currently within our corporate headquarters in Boston, Massachusetts and its environs. Additionally, there are entry-level opportunities in our other State Street locations, including some of our European locations."

AVERAGE NUMBER OF APPLICATIONS EACH YEAR

State Street receives 3,000–4,000 applications each year.

AVERAGE NUMBER HIRED PER YEAR

State Street hires 1,000 entry-level employees each year.

ENTRY-LEVEL POSITION(S) AVAILABLE

The majority of entry-level hires at State Street take positions as portfolio administrators, portfolio accountants, and mutual fund accountants. Other entry-level positions are also available in specialized areas across the organization.

AVERAGE HOURS WORKED PER WEEK

New hires work 36.25 hours per week, with some overtime.

AVERAGE STARTING SALARY

Entry-level employees earn salaries in the low $30,000s.

BENEFITS OFFERED

State Street offers seven medical and two dental plans to choose from. Employees also receive vision care and may take advantage of flexible medical spending accounts. Additional benefits include life insurance, long-term disability, pre-tax transportation accounts, salary savings program, a 401(k) program, retirement plan, generous vacation, educational assistance, adoption assistance, and work/life programs.

Getting Hired

State Street posts job openings on various posting websites worldwide, at colleges across the nation, and on its own website. Many of the first jobbers we contacted found their positions through these resources. The firm also "has a strong campus-recruiting program at a diverse population of schools across the nation" and "[gives] consideration to all applications, whether [they're] from a target school or outside of our current list of schools." Ideal candidates are "hard working, customer-focused, determined, engaging, creative team players with global knowledge, [who demonstrate] integrity and strong computer skills." Interviewers look for "an understanding of what the candidate knows about State Street and why he/she would be a [good] fit for the organization and the position. We also ask what the candidate is looking for in his/her next job to see if it fits what we look for here. We ask about skills and interests, as well as experience." One successful hire recounts her experiences: "I was contacted for a phone interview/screening approximately three weeks after I submitted my online application and cover letter. At that point I scheduled my interview, which took place in Quincy, Massachusetts. I had two interviews (with current managers), both of which involved a set group of questions. Most of the questions were stated in the following way: 'Tell me about a time where you. . . .' It was up to me to fit in as many of my own experiences and qualifications without going through my resume piece by piece. I tried not to talk about only my job experiences, but my leadership ones as well."

Money and Perks

"Salary is not negotiable" at State Street, fresh hires tell us; but there "can be some flexibility about start date." Entry-level employees are not eligible for bonuses, though they become eligible for them as they move up the hierarchy. They are eligible for performance-based pay raises, promotions, and overtime pay. Of the many perks offered, first jobbers praise the 401(k) package and the tuition reimbursement program; of the latter, one writes, "I am currently working on my MBA, and State Street recently created an alliance with Suffolk University so that they pay for my class upfront. I do not have to wait until the course is over to get reimbursed."

The Ropes

New fund accountants, portfolio accountants, and portfolio administrators at State Street all undergo extensive "required training programs prior to going on the floor/to the business unit for [which] they are hired. The program is an overview of State Street: who we are in the industry and what our role is in the market." The program also gives new hires "a place to learn our proprietary system and understand both the basics of the job and how to apply these basics in a real life environment. It is also builds a foundation so [that] when the new hire is on the floor, he or she can much more easily adapt to the position." One portfolio administrator reports, "Training was a several weeks-long process. It was done in a classroom environment, and it included quizzes and homework. There was a great deal of group work; we also had many simulations in which we were able to work through typical requests/procedures ourselves. We were graded on our ability to meet deadlines and perform with accuracy."

Day in the Life

State Street hires the majority of its first jobbers in three positions: mutual fund accountant, portfolio accountant, and portfolio administrator. Accountants spend their days occupied with such "daily processing" chores as "reviewing ledger accounts, verifying financial statements, and delivering monthly pricing reports." As their expertise increases, their duties expand to include "auditing the work of coworkers, taking on ad hoc requests, taking on additional projects and reporting, and training new employees." Portfolio administrators are "responsible for the daily processing of all cash and securities transactions to a series of mutual fund accounts. This includes: forecasting cash flow to the client, monitoring the physical movement of securities purchased and sold, and posting all portfolio and shareholder activity onto State Street's mainframe accounting system. Weekly and monthly reporting is also required."

Peers

State Street hires lots of people fresh out of college. One first jobber explains, "That is one of the great things about this company when you are coming right out of college: There are a lot of young people working there, and it [presents] a great opportunity to make new friends. The nature of the job allows a lot of bonding. Everyone goes to lunch at the same time, and the entry-levels, the seniors, and some of the managers tend to stick together." The initial training program provides an instant common bond for those starting here. As time goes on workers enjoy "a definite after-hours scene, [though] it depends some on the office that you work out of. I think those located in Boston tend to go out after work a lot more than the Quincy workers."

Moving on

Those who are unhappy at State Street grumble about the relatively low starting salaries and heavy workloads. One first jobber acknowledges, "Many of State Street's competitors who have local offices pay better." What grousers fail to realize, according to their more sanguine peers, is that "this job is a great stepping stone to a successful future. State Street is a huge company with tons of room for growth, both professionally and monetarily. The career path at State Street is endless." One newbie writes, "State Street probably offers more opportunity to move up and expand your knowledge than our competitors do."

TARGET CORPORATION
VARIOUS POSITIONS

"The company places a very high value on education. No matter how well you do your job, if you don't have a college degree, you will only go so far in the company."

The Big Picture

Although most of the country regards Target as "the new kid on the block"—especially in relation to its downscale rival Wal-Mart—this giant discount department store chain has been in existence since 1962. The company traces its roots back even further, to the Dayton Dry Goods Company, founded in 1903. Throughout its history, Target has earned a solid reputation both for contributing to its host communities and for creating a hospitable work environment for its employees.

LOCATION(S) WHERE ENTRY-LEVEL EMPLOYEES WORK

Corporate hires work in Minneapolis, Minnesota; the company has stores in many cities.

AVERAGE NUMBER HIRED PER YEAR OVER THE LAST TEN YEARS

Target employs more than 273,000 people in 47 states.

ENTRY-LEVEL POSITION(S) AVAILABLE

Target offers entry-level positions in all areas of the company.

BENEFITS OFFERED

"[Benefits include] dollar-for-dollar (up to 5 percent of your salary) matching of our 401(k); company discount at all stores; savings on prescriptions; and flexible work schedules. Target has specific benefits programs, but they share a focus on flexibility, family, and financial security."

CONTACT INFORMATION

Apply online at www.target.com.

Getting Hired

Target employees caution that "Target considers only resumes that are submitted to Target.com and Monster.com online; there's a Team-Member Referral program, but anyone referred to the company through a current employee still has to apply online." An exception is made for people who are recruited at campus events; students must submit resumes directly to the campus career center; you can learn more about these events at the Target website. The interview process "is the same style used by many other employers. First, there is a phone interview [conducted] by a human resources recruiter, then a formal interview with the human resources recruiter; afterward applicants have an interview with two of the people who would be managing [them], followed by an informal meeting with the national head of [their] department. The tone of the interviews are serious but friendly." One particular applicant "was asked job-related questions, such as

'Describe your past job experience. Why do you think you are right for this position?' Other questions that were also asked were geared toward finding out about my personality." One first jobber notes, "One thing about Target—the company places a very high value on education. No matter how well you do your job, if you don't have a college degree, you will only go so far in the company. Many people want to advance but can't because they didn't go to college. Although many entry-level jobs seem mundane to someone with a college degree, you have to start somewhere—and you'll move up if you stick it out, demonstrate a work ethic, and have a degree." Target seeks "a diverse workforce to reflect the communities we serve."

Money and Perks

Most of the terms of employment at Target are negotiable, first jobbers tell us; as in all such cases, the more you bring to the table—and the less competition there is for jobs (such as when the economy is strong)—the better chance you have of negotiating a higher starting salary. As employees move forward, "It's hard to get a pay increase at any time other than at annual reviews. We're reviewed twice a year—the annual is in March."

The Ropes

All Target employees start their tenure with the company with a half-day orientation class. One first jobber writes, entry-level employees find out "a lot about Target, what is acceptable (protocol, etc). A lot was geared toward harassment, benefits of Target, what they're trying to do to improve Target, and its history." In many areas of the company, subsequent training is handled by fellow employees on a "need to know" basis. One newbie explains, "My training was conducted by the three individuals [who] I work directly with. Since my position was open, they all helped to train me on the procedures, day-to-day activities, [and] all of the technical equipment that I would be working with." Some formal classes in technical areas, such as computers, are required of new workers in certain areas; these classes constitute part of the employee's formal work day.

Day in the Life

First jobbers work in all areas of the giant Target world. We spoke with first jobbers in many different departments doing a wide variety of jobs. All of them say that they quickly assumed important responsibilities and that they felt their managers and bosses offered them sufficient support to get their jobs done. According to company representatives, workers benefit from "a fun and challenging work environment," one that rewards "performance-driven risk takers."

Peers

Of the entry-level employees in several different areas and functionalities at Target, all of them agree that at Target "people are really friendly. The company is full of young twenty-somethings." One writes, "We do things outside of work. We're going bowling tonight, for example." Another notes, "All of us get along and do happy hours regularly. Target has several touch football teams in the fall and baseball teams in the summer." Many do volunteer work together as well; one newbie reports, "Target does a ton for the community. I volunteer once a week at a local school, just reading to kids. There are always ways to get involved in the community, and that's been a good way to meet Target people who aren't in my department (and to get out of the office for awhile to do something helpful and fun)."

TEACH FOR AMERICA
CORPS MEMBER

TEACHFORAMERICA

"I had never before had the opportunity to be surrounded [by] and work with people that were all determined to be successful and wanted to achieve that success for the betterment of others and the society as a whole. It really was a life-changing experience for me."

The Big Picture

Teach For America's goal is straightforward: to "eliminate educational inequality." The organization strives toward this goal "by building a highly selective national corps of outstanding recent college graduates—of all academic majors and career interests—who commit two years to teach in urban and rural public schools in our nation's lowest-income communities." Corps members say that "the opportunity to have a significant and direct impact on such an important issue right away" is what makes Teach For America so unique and appealing. One first jobber says, "After my two years as a Teach For America corps member, I had so many more doors open to me both inside and outside the organization. So many of our nation's top graduate programs and employers actively seek out Teach For America alumni because of the level of challenge and ability required to be a successful teacher in the challenging situations in which we teach."

LOCATION(S) WHERE ENTRY-LEVEL EMPLOYEES WORK

Teach For America sends corps members to 25 locations, ranging from New York City to rural South Dakota to New Orleans.

AVERAGE NUMBER OF APPLICATIONS EACH YEAR

In 2006, Teach For America received around 19,000 applications. Organization officials note, "Over the last few years, applications for Teach For America have increased significantly." They expect this growth to continue as the corps size will strategically expand through the year 2010.

AVERAGE NUMBER HIRED PER YEAR OVER THE LAST FIVE YEARS

Numbers vary annually. This said, Teacher For America officials "anticipate placing a corps of 3,100 in the fall of 2007."

ENTRY-LEVEL POSITION(S) AVAILABLE

Recent college grads join Teach For America as corps members (AKA teachers). Each day, corps members serve as teachers in low-income pockets of the nation. Corps members rank Teach For America locations in terms of "highly preferred," "preferred," and "less preferred." In 2005, Teach For America was "able to place 96 percent of accepted applicants in one of their highly preferred sites and 99 percent in one of their highly preferred or preferred sites."

Getting Hired

If you want to join Teach For America, you have to first buy into its mission. After all, working in one of America's most hard-luck schools is no walk in the park. Successful applicants are typically recent college graduates "who have a proven leadership record (whether in school, work, or extracurricular activities) and who demonstrate leadership qualities such as the ability to influence and motivate others and the ability to persevere through difficult challenges." Becoming a corps member begins by submitting an online application; if Teach For America officials like what they see, they invite the candidate to participate in a phone interview with a member of the Teach For America selection team. The most promising candidates are then invited to a full-day, in-person interview which includes teaching a sample lesson, completing a problem solving activity, participating in a group discussion, and interviewing one-on-one with a Teach For America staff member." The entire day lasts about six hours." Teach For America officials add, "Although our program is selective, applicants are not competing against other applicants for a fixed number of positions. . . . Given the enormity of the problem we're addressing, we feel a moral imperative to grow."

Money and Perks

At Teach For America, "corps members teaching in urban sites typically have higher [annual] salaries, starting at $28,000 and reaching a high of $44,000. Corps members in rural sites, who make between $25,000 and $33,000 [a year], tend to have more discretionary income because the cost of living is disproportionately lower in these sites." Corps members, who tend to be driven more by social conviction than salary heft, offer no complaints about the paychecks. The job comes with perks, too. A former corps member notes, "It was nice to receive $9,400 [in AmeriCorps education award funds] to pay back loans—in addition to my regular salary." Loan deferment, too, is nice. But by the far the biggest "perk" is the work itself. One corps member tells us, "I had sixty kids who treated me like I was famous every day." Another adds, "Teaching children how to read—there is no better feeling."

The Ropes

Teach For America operates "rigorous five-week summer preparation institutes in Atlanta, Houston, Los Angeles, New York City, and Philadelphia," which offer "practice, observation, coaching, and study" in the art of teaching. Thinking back on her orientation in Los Angeles, a corps veteran says, "I had a curriculum specialist train me on all of the basics of teaching: classroom management and culture, literacy, etc. for part of the day. For the other part of the day I worked with a corps member advisor who coached me individually to improve my lesson plans and my actual performance in the classroom. In the evenings there were a variety of other staff members who provided workshops and small-group learning opportunities to develop specific skills that I was working to improve." While orientation gets two thumbs up from most of the participants, corps members say that you can't "fully prepare yourself until you actually get into the classroom." One veteran of the program suggests that the best way to prepare for the Teach For America experience is to "visit a corps member's classroom before" joining the organization.

Day in the Life

The life of a corps member is the life of a school teacher, which often means early to work and late to arrive back home. Here's how one former corps member describes his daily routine: "A typical day involved arriving at school at 6:45 A.M., tutoring in the morning, teaching from 7:45 A.M. to 2:15 P.M., tutoring after school, coaching until 4:30 P.M., grading papers or attending classes/workshops in the late afternoon, [and] calling parents or talking with students to help with homework in the evenings." Another corps member says, "My job was to take fourth-grade students that were at a first- or second-grade level and ensure that they progressed at least a year and a half to two years in the one year I had with them. To do this, I had to work long, exhausting hours." Initially, it's not unusual for corps members to feel a little overwhelmed. But an old hand assures, "By October I felt that I knew what I was doing and by December everything was smooth sailing."

Peers

Corps members tell us they are "inspired and humbled by the incredible people [they have] the opportunity to work alongside." One corps member even gushes, "I had never before had the opportunity to be surrounded [by] and work with people that were all determined to be successful and wanted to achieve that success for the betterment of others and the society as a whole. It really was a life-changing experience for me." Just because the days are so busy doesn't mean corps members can't find time to hang out together. "I interacted with other corps members constantly," insists a veteran. "Nearly all of my friends there were corps members, and we socialized together all the time."

Moving on

Sixty percent of Teach For America alumni "have remained in the field of education as teachers, principals, education-policy advisors, and leaders and staff of education reform organizations." Graduate school, professional school, and careers in business, law, medicine, and journalism are other avenues alumni pursue. Whatever field they ultimately pursue, alums remain dedicated to tackling critical issues surrounding school systems within low-income communities.

Attrition

Corps members that do not complete their two-year commitment typically discover that they're not cut out for the challenging circumstances and ambitious goals associated with the job. That said, the overwhelming majority (between 85 and 90 percent) of corps members return for the second year. Corps alums note that the "deplorable state of education" for "children growing up in low-income communities" can make "the everyday challenges and realities of a teacher often overwhelming and frustrating." But Teach For America administrators add, "Some of our corps members tell us that, although there are certainly days that are extremely difficult, the commitment that they make to their students to help them receive the education they deserve compels them to persist."

Texas Teaching Fellows
Teaching Fellow

> "Despite the demanding workload, many praise their positions for providing them with the opportunity to do worthwhile, rewarding work."

The Big Picture

Like many states, Texas has a relatively hard time recruiting teachers in mathematics, science, special education, and bilingual education. The mission of the Texas Teaching Fellows program is to address the shortage of teachers in these areas by attracting "the most talented and outstanding professionals from all walks of life" and getting them "to commit to teaching in the state's critical shortage subject areas." The organization's website points out that "teachers do need to have a record of university course work focused on the subject area(s) [that] they would like to teach. Candidates interested in the areas of math and science should have academic backgrounds specifically in the areas of math and science, [however]. Candidates interested in teaching bilingual education, special education (at the elementary level), English as a second language, or elementary (limited positions) should have well-rounded academic backgrounds." This brand-new program had its inaugural year in 2005–2006.

Location(s) Where Entry-level Employees Work

Teaching Fellows work in Dallas, Texas.

Average Number of Applications Each Year

Texas Teaching Fellows receives 1,000 applications each year.

Average Number Hired Per Year

The program hires 100 employees each year.

Entry-level Position(s) Available

This program seeks to hire teachers in "hard-to-staff content areas" (such as math, science, special education, and bilingual education).

Average Hours Worked Per Week

Teaching Fellows work 55 hours per week.

Average Starting Salary

The average starting salary is $37,000. "Fellows teaching special education, math, bilingual education, and science can expect their salaries to either start at a higher level or be augmented by a stipend."

Getting Hired

The Texas Teaching Fellows program "is designed for individuals without a background in education or previous education course work." The program seeks "recent college graduates and career changers who can demonstrate leadership and achievement, analyze situations thoroughly and [then] generate effective strategies, and assume accountability for reaching outcomes despite obstacles."

To apply, "candidates must complete and submit an online application and attach a resume and personal statement describing why they want to become teachers, particularly in a high-needs content area. Applicants must also provide the program office with copies of official college transcripts. Applicants are notified within two weeks of their application status [about whether they have been granted an interview]. After the interview, candidates are notified of their selection status within two weeks." One Fellow reports, "After being accepted into the program, I still had to interview with the school district and principals." Candidates must also pass state teacher tests before they start to teach.

Money and Perks

As in most states, teacher salaries in Texas are set by law; they are based on a formula that takes into account "years of experience, [level of] certification, content specializations, and level of education." Teachers may earn bonuses "when sponsoring an extracurricular activity or teaching in a specific content area." Opportunities to earn extra money by "tutoring in an afterschool program or teaching during summer school" are also available. Fellows tell us that their favorite perks are "the summers off" and "doing what I love for a living."

The Ropes

TTF is "a fast-track certification program, [and so] training and certification requirements are condensed into one year. All Fellows begin their formal participation in the TTF program during a Summer Training Institute, which begins in late May. During the Institute, Fellows participate in seven rigorous weeks of training [that focus] on two domains: classroom management and culture and instructional design and delivery. During the summer, Fellows also participate in student-teaching under the watchful supervision of experienced summer-school teachers. District-specific orientation occurs once the Fellow is hired and attends New Teacher Training prior to the beginning of the school year."

Once the school year begins, "Fellows continue their professional development by participating in content seminars. These seminars are conducted by experienced district teachers and equip Fellows to translate their current content knowledge into high-quality lessons and instruction. Seminars are hosted two times per month and serve as a support mechanism for fellows."

Day in the Life

Fellows have "all the responsibilities of a [traditional] classroom teacher." One special education teacher reports that "there is a lot of paperwork in the beginning of the year [as well as] lots of scheduling, planning, and testing. Eventually you get to teach." Another Fellow warns, "There is not time to do everything my school wants me to do (update my website, plan good lessons, plan good learning goals, attend meetings/seminars, [and] other tidbits) [as well as] get ready for class each day. I [also] take home work to do (either grading tests/labs and/or lesson-planning)." Despite the demanding workload, many praise their positions for providing them with the opportunity to do worthwhile, rewarding work.

Peers

Texas Teaching Fellows "are all different, but great in their own ways. We are all smart and capable." Fellows are willing to share insights and information; one writes, "Some of us have the same students and have helped [one another] out to understand those students. I have used ideas from other class lessons and in classroom management from other teachers." Outside the classroom, "there are some after-hours events [to which] everyone is always invited." One teacher reports, "We have gone to football games and dinners together. It has been nice to have those people around to vent and share!"

Moving on

Those who have left the Texas Teaching Fellows program to date "have cited personal reasons," the organization tells us. The program is too young to have accumulated significant data on former Fellows. A program organizer notes, "We anticipate that those who leave classroom instruction will do so to further their careers in another educational capacity (e.g., [to become] principals, counselors, or specialists)."

Best and Worst

The most successful Fellow to date, we're told, is "a gentleman who consistently models the characteristics of a successful employee and teacher. He proactively takes responsibility in his learning of new and [traditional] effective teaching strategies and [in] understanding the larger classroom concepts. He continually seeks out additional guidance through mentors, TTF staff, and his school colleagues to improve his teaching skills and abilities. A man of constant optimism, he fosters effective relationships with both his principals and his colleagues."

Among the least successful Fellows was someone who "consistently remained inflexible and continually created negative relationships [with] students."

TGI FRIDAY'S
MANAGER AND ASSISTANT MANAGER

The management training program at Friday's takes place over the course of a fourteen-week period during which a future manager "spends time in each hourly level position learning those specific jobs as well as shadowing a manager and ultimately performing management-level tasks."

The Big Picture

TGI Friday's management-training program rotates future managers through all the hourly wage positions in one of its restaurants to teach them the ropes. It's a whirlwind tour that lasts a scant fourteen weeks, culminating in the trainee's ascension to the captain's chair. Graduates say it's a great way to learn the chain restaurant business quickly as well as an excellent means of getting ahead in parent company Carlson Restaurants (which also owns the Pickup Stix chain of Chinese eateries).

LOCATION(S) WHERE ENTRY-LEVEL EMPLOYEES WORK

"We operate in 48 states, primarily east of the Rockies."

AVERAGE NUMBER OF APPLICATIONS EACH YEAR

"We review and receive over 500 applications a year for entry-level management jobs."

AVERAGE NUMBER HIRED PER YEAR OVER THE LAST TEN YEARS

TGI Friday's hires 15 to 20 entry-level management trainees per year.

ENTRY-LEVEL POSITION(S) AVAILABLE

New hires work as assistant managers and managers.

AVERAGE HOURS WORKED PER WEEK

New hires work 55 hours per week.

AVERAGE STARTING SALARY

New hires earn $38,000 per year.

BENEFITS OFFERED

"We offer several different medical, dental, and vision plans." Additional benefits include vacation, a 401(k) plan, purchased time off, long-term disability insurance, and a complimentary dining discount.

Getting Hired

TGI Friday's "visits specific colleges each semester to participate in career fairs, on-campus interviewing, and classroom presentations. Students from other colleges can apply online at Fridays.com or send a resume to the college recruiter." The next step in the process is a personality-profile assessment; "If the result of the assessment fits our profile, then the candidate interviews with a general manager and spends time observing in a restaurant," company representatives tell us. "Finally, the candidate would interview with a director of operations. An applicant can be discontinued at any point during the interview process." Sound daunting? A successful applicant makes the experience sound a little less so. He writes, "I did not do anything specific to help me get an interview, but I did have some good experience. I was interviewed by the college recruiters over the phone and given personality tests. I was then interviewed by a few of the general managers from the local stores. After that I was interviewed by the regional manager. The interviews were all good; they asked me what I had done in the past, where I thought I would go with Friday's, what types of things I was looking to accomplish, and a lot of questions about my critical thinking skills. A few days later I was offered a position. From start to finish, the process took roughly two weeks."

Money and Perks

According to the trainees we spoke with, "start date, location, and salary are all negotiable" at TGI Friday's. One notes, "Everything that was explained to me during the interview process [captured] how [the process actually] happened. I was told once I completed the internship and made the move to management [that] all I would have to do was talk salary and location; no additional training would be necessary. I also did research at school [regarding] similar jobs and what students were offered in terms of jobs and salaries, and the offer seemed pretty high." Regarding raises, "each manager's compensation is assessed yearly through a performance evaluation compared with a salary range. Average raises are 4 percent." Asked which fringe benefits they most enjoyed, trainees responded, "Free meals during shift[s], being able to make [our] own schedule, and bonuses. If we hit pace dollars or pace percent or if we hit our sales goal, we get a certain percentage of money in return. It's done quarterly, and it's a great incentive to manage responsibly and to pay attention to what is going on around you at all times."

The Ropes

The management training program at Friday's takes place over the course of a fourteen-week period during which a future manager "spends time in each hourly level position learning those specific jobs as well as shadowing a manager and ultimately performing management-level tasks." One graduate of the program explains, "I was trained on every hourly position, both 'front of the house' and 'back of the house,' and then learned all management functions and procedures. I learned about food cost, beverage cost, and the different parts of the income estimate. When I learned the hourly stations, I was trained by hourly employees, and when I trained on the management functions, the general manager as well as the rest of the management staff trained me." Besides familiarizing the manager with each worker's role in the restaurant, the training regimen yields another valuable benefit; one manager explains, "If the restaurant ever gets so busy that someone needs help, I am able to assist in any position we have!"

Day in the Life

Once the training period is over, management trainees drop the trainee designation and start managing. Here's how one describes her responsibilities: "I was placed in a high-volume store and given the bar as my department. Aside from the typical management duties of running a shift, I also have the responsibility of beverage cost. I have to ensure that we hit our budgeted weekly/monthly/yearly beverage cost percentages. I also have the ultimate responsibility for the bar staff—hiring, promoting, training, and developing their abilities to take care of the guests—and the overall cleanliness of the bar. On a typical day, I start out with a pre-shift meeting with my employees for the shift, letting them know our sales projections, sales contests, any additional expectations, and what I would like to see on our shift. I then spend a majority of my time out on the restaurant floor talking to guests and making rounds to ensure the shift is running clean and smooth. If necessary, I help out in the kitchen or at the door when needed, running sales reports on a frequent basis to help keep the staff positive and motivated. At the end of the shift, I am responsible for the collection of any monies and the closing of the daily computer reports and functions. I then check out the employees to ensure they closed everything down, and it all looks clean."

Peers

Sitting atop the hierarchy (or food chain, if you will) of a restaurant can be a lonely job; as one manager explains, "I don't have interaction with any first jobbers. Sometimes I hang out with other managers, but that is like once a month." Accordingly, "there are no after-hours social scenes. However, I do interact with my management team every single day. We communicate on a daily basis about the day-to-day operations of our job. I spend a lot of quality time with them at work. I don't spend much time outside of work with them. I would much rather go home and spend time with my family and my dogs. The only time I communicate with others outside of work is through voice-mail to keep lines of communication open amongst us."

Moving on

People leave Friday's for a variety of reasons; for some, it's "not what they expected," while for others the "work-life balance" doesn't suit their goals. Some people, according to company representatives, have "unrealistic expectations of life after college." Some head for other industries, while others seek work at restaurants that do not keep late hours (TGI Friday's stays open until 2:00 A.M., some trainees consider this a drawback).

Attrition

Friday's representatives tell us that "due to the interview and recruiting process, less than 5 percent of [their] first jobbers leave within twelve months."

Best and Worst

A great management trainee "is able to network and use their resources to better understand the business and the company, while successfully adjusting to the pace of the business." The worst, "besides the employees who are no longer part of the organization due to bad business/professional decisions," are "those who were unable to keep up with the pace of our business."

TURNER BROADCASTING SYSTEM
VARIOUS POSITIONS

A TimeWarner Company

> "It's nearly impossible to describe a 'typical' day" at Turner. That's the beauty of television: I never knew what to expect! I could be writing copy one minute [and] rushing to an emergency session to make a reel for a VP's presentation the next."

The Big Picture

For great television experience and the chance to get a "foot in the door at CNN," you can't beat Turner Broadcasting System's highly sought-after training programs. Recent grads are eligible to participate in one of three entry-level programs: CNN Video Journalists, Turner Trainee Team (T3), and Braves Trainees (a gateway to a career in professional sports broadcasting). It isn't easy to get the job, but the lucky stiffs who score a spot are thrilled to work at a "top news network and learn from the best in the business," while enjoying a work environment that is "fast-paced, challenging, and a place where eager employees [can] grow and advance their careers."

LOCATION(S) WHERE ENTRY-LEVEL EMPLOYEES WORK

Most entry-level employees work at Turner headquarters in Atlanta, Georgia; however, positions are also available in Los Angeles, California; Washington, DC; Chicago, Illinois; New York, New York; and many other domestic and international locations.

ENTRY-LEVEL POSITION(S) AVAILABLE

Turner operates three paid trainee programs: the CNN Video Journalist program, the Turner Trainee Team (T3), and Braves Trainees. These three programs are designed to provide "hands-on experience and training" to entry-level hires hoping to pursue a career in television production. In addition, there are entry-level positions at the assistant and coordinator level in departments such as production, programming, marketing, human resources, public relations, sales, and operations.

AVERAGE HOURS WORKED PER WEEK

Almost all entry-level employees work 40 hours or more per week.

Getting Hired

If you think working in television sounds like fun, you're not alone. To stand out among the thousands of applications that Turner receives, successful candidates go the extra mile. An associate producer shares her tactics: "I color-coded my resume, cover letter, demo reel, and references to match the packet I sent in. I felt like it would literally stand out in a pile of applications." Others take unpaid internships or freelance work to get their foot in the door. A current video journalist started out as a freelancer, explaining, "They were ignoring my e-mails and phone calls because of the volume of applicants for the VJ position. Since I was working freelance, I had the ability to e-mail people from inside and meet with them. I finally got the interview after much persistence." Even if you don't go to such extremes, a lot of applicants have experience in television from courses they've taken or through internships, so submitting samples of your work is par for the course. "I submitted a demo reel of projects I had worked on in school and at other professional internships along with a script that displayed how my writing was a good fit for the department," explains a current T3 trainee. Once they are granted the elusive interview, however, most say the process becomes more gentle. An associate producer claims, "One of the senior producers interviewed me and she was extremely professional, but informal at the same time. She asked me questions ranging from past experience to why I thought I was the best candidate for the job." Another entry-level employee describes her interview as "very casual but thorough." She goes on, "It felt like everyone was really trying to get a feel for my personality. They asked about my work experience but also a lot about my interests and [the] activities I enjoyed."

Money and Perks

While salaries aren't spectacular (and are also a carefully guarded secret), newbies say, "You are pretty much happy to just be getting into the company anyway you can." Plus, Turner employees have their share of perks, not the least of which are "free tickets to Braves, Thrashers, and Hawks games!" TBS employees also "get discounts on all kinds of retail, travel, [and] attractions around Atlanta."

The Ropes

For employees working in Atlanta, there is a short orientation session on the first day of work. Thereafter, new trainees are sent directly to their department where they have a few weeks to learn the job by shadowing current employees. A T3 associate producer explains, "The person who held my job before me trained me. She basically continued doing her job for a week and I watched her and then gradually started taking over her responsibilities." A video journalist describes a similar process: "Training is about three weeks and you work with different VJs throughout each day." However, he also warns, "You'll need to pay attention and jump in as much as you can to practice because once you're on your own, mistakes are not really tolerated by directors and anchors; it's embarrassing to make a mistake so focus, focus, focus." While almost all training takes place on the job, "The company offers classes to all new employees to introduce them to the technology." A newbie reassures us, "Even though it was a lot to learn at once, they gave me the tools and information to understand the system."

Day in the Life

Scattered throughout the organization, entry-level employees fill any number of responsibilities at Turner. A T3 production assistant says her duties include "ordering movies and screeners for producers, going down to the studios to make dubs and compilation reels, organizing the library, archiving tapes, [and] working with other departments in delivering spots." In contrast, a CNN video journalist says a typical day includes "floor directing, teleprompting, and delivering scripts to anchors for CNN domestic, CNN Headline News, and CNN International." Even so, "It's nearly impossible to describe a 'typical day' at Turner." Exclaims an enthusiastic newbie, "That's the beauty of television: I never knew what to expect! I could be writing copy one minute [and] rushing to an emergency session to make a reel for a VP's presentation the next." One thing is for certain: No matter what you are doing, you must do it well. New staffers warn us, "It's an extremely competitive environment and you have to work hard to set yourself apart from your peers."

Peers

"I found people who were just as ambitious and could have stimulating discussions while in a fun work environment. Generally, people worked as a team, and having exceptional work friends made the job so much better," enthuses a Turner employee. "I have made some pretty good friends within the T3 program because we're all the same age and going through the same phase of life," agrees a new hire. In fact, employees tell us the environment is particularly conducive to making friends, since "so many people are coming in from out of town [and] looking to meet new people in the area." Despite camaraderie on the job, the demanding and variable work schedule limits the after-hours social scene. Even so, employees assure us, "If someone suggests it, there are always people up for going out after work."

Moving on

Even after fighting so hard to get in, there are sometimes good reasons to leave Turner. The number of career development opportunities is limited. Explains a VJ, "You do have to work your way up and there aren't as many open positions as people wanting to get promoted so there may be a bottleneck at certain times of the year." What's more, the company prefers to see their employees move on—at least temporarily. A video journalist explains, "I hear it is encouraged to move on, get other experiences, and come back. CNN does seem to like variety." A production assistant confers, "I've heard it said several times that the best way to move up in this company is to leave for a short term and [then] return." However, hopeful new hires also note that "bosses at CNN are very often long-time CNN employees which means they were once in entry-level positions usually with CNN."

UNITED TECHNOLOGIES CORPORATION
VARIOUS POSITIONS

"There is always plenty of room to grow within the various UTC companies. Since UTC also pays for their employees to continue their education, employees can develop and grow on the company dime."

The Big Picture

UTC is a heavy hitter, a $37 billion company with a product line that includes Carrier heating and cooling, Hamilton Sundstrand aerospace systems and industrial products, Otis Elevators, UTC Fire & Security systems, UTC Power fuel cells, Sikorsky helicopters, and Pratt & Whitney aircraft engines. Beyond the scores of entry-level engineering positions available at UTC, the company also has a Financial Leadership Program (FLP) and an IT Leadership Program (ITLP) that provide a two-year rotational training experiences to promising college grads in business and computer science.

LOCATION(S) WHERE ENTRY-LEVEL EMPLOYEES WORK

Entry-level employees work in Hartford, Connecticut; Farmington, Connecticut; and East Hartford, Connecticut.

AVERAGE NUMBER OF APPLICATIONS EACH YEAR

UTC receives 700–800 applications for entry-level positions each year.

AVERAGE NUMBER HIRED PER YEAR

UTC hires 75 to 80 entry-level employees each year.

ENTRY-LEVEL POSITION(S) AVAILABLE

The company has many engineering jobs; it also has a Financial Leadership Program (FLP) and an IT Leadership Program (ITLP).

AVERAGE HOURS WORKED PER WEEK

Entry-level employees work 40 hours per week.

AVERAGE STARTING SALARY

Starting salaries are, HR officials note, "comparable by functional area with the NACE Senior Salary Survey."

BENEFITS OFFERED

UTC offers "medical and dental coverage," which are "available after 30 days of employment." Additionally, "employees build their own plans." Additional benefits include an Employee Scholar Program (100 percent payment of tuition and textbooks and time off to study); retirement plan; pension (available after one year, vested after five years); vision care discounts; and vendor discounts.

CONTACT INFORMATION

Prospective applicants are encouraged to visit UTC on the Web at www.utc.com/careers.

Getting Hired

UTC's offices are located near several major universities, and the company draws on these resources to populate a broad range of internships and co-op positions. A solid number of college graduates who ultimately take full-time jobs at UTC start in these positions. Others check job openings and submit their resumes online. The company does not generally conduct on-campus interviews; instead, it "encourages students to attend a variety of alternative activities that they participate in on campus (career fairs, sponsored workshops, student group events) as a means of engaging with our representatives. This allows us to consider a larger number of candidates than a typical campus interview schedule would allow. Only a few select programs schedule campus interviews." Those invited to a UTC business for an interview can expect "behavioral interviewing methods that give candidates the opportunity to share with us examples of past work/experiences that relate to our core competencies. We are trying to determine individuals' fit within our organization [and] learn about their backgrounds and what they would bring to UTC." One UTC engineer writes, "During my interview I was asked about my classes in specific areas, how I have worked with teams, and what area of engineering would I be most interested in working in. I received a call a couple of weeks later asking me to come to Pratt & Whitney's campus for another interview. Two managers from different disciplines interviewed me. Again, I was asked about my experiences with working in teams, my strengths and weaknesses, and the areas and/or disciplines [in which] I would be most interested in working. I also asked many questions about opportunities at Pratt & Whitney and [about] how Pratt & Whitney supports their employees to achieve their goals within the company. Knowing about the company and having questions is very important."

UTC recruits on targeted campuses for its IT and Financial Leadership Training programs, both of which accept applications online. The screening process for these is similar to the process outlined above for conventional hires.

Money and Perks

Job offers at UTC are "somewhat negotiable," in that "it is possible to have multiple offers from different divisions." Once an applicant settles on a position, though, salary and job definition are pretty much set; however, start time can be negotiable, according to some newbies we surveyed. Raises "occur yearly based upon the performance of the organization." Perks include "a great Employee Scholar Program that pays for your tuition, fees, and books for any graduate or undergraduate degree you want to pursue, regardless of your job function or responsibilities. They even give you paid time off from work to do homework or to work on projects that are school related, and [the company also] gives you a stock bonus when you complete your degree. So even though I had to work all day I was still able to continue my education and not at my own expense."

First jobbers also love "the opportunity to travel outside of the continental United States on business, [often] to visit suppliers and/or remote offices. There are a lot of travel opportunities in some departments and groups."

The Ropes

"Specified orientation varies by business unit or program, though each employee is a part of the new employee orientation conducted by HR," UT officials tell us. One young engineer notes, "Orientation lasts for half a day. You meet other new hires, and then you go over the company history, organizational structure, and benefits packages available to you (health care, dental, life insurance, etc.). You also fill out any paperwork that was missing in your file. Afterward, your supervisor picks you up and takes to you to your work location."

Ongoing training includes "classes that specialize in job functions or programs you need to do your daily work, as well as generalized courses like the Seven Habits of Highly Effective People to help your professional proficiency."

Day in the Life

The daily routines of UTC first jobbers vary tremendously, as the company brings college grads on in many different divisions and departments. Participants in the leadership programs perform rotations; finance trainees rotate departments every six months; and IT trainees rotate every nine months. Trainees in both finance and IT perform tasks that teach them skills in project management, business analysis, and decision-making.

Peers

UTC is a sizable company, and accordingly, the experiences of new hires here vary greatly among the different divisions and departments. Some engineers report that they participate in "a New Hires Club, [in which] there are always events going on and opportunities to hang out after work and on the weekends. It also allows us to get to know [one another] and help those that are [even] newer than [we are]." One newbie writes, "Some of my coworkers are my old college buddies, [and] some are my friends from high school. We share similar interests, watch similar TV shows, hang out in similar locations after work. And even if we don't, I can still talk to anyone in my group about things outside of work." Others, however, experience less camaraderie on the job. One writes, "I'm the youngest person in the office, so I haven't made many friends at work [whom] I can connect with outside of work. Most of the people I work with (or for) have kids only a few years younger than I am."

Moving on

Those who leave United Technologies often do so "to pursue new opportunities" or "to relocate due to a change in family status." Some here "criticize their workload," complaining that "we need more bodies in the office to accomplish the work without putting such a workload strain on the employees." Still, most stick around here a long time, in part "because there is always plenty of room to grow within the various UTC companies. One could move up in levels or receive bonuses and/or awards for working hard on certain projects. One could also move from working in engineering to the [business] side of the companies. Since UTC also pays for their employees to continue their education, employees can develop and grow on the company dime."

Attrition

UTC reports that "We have a strong retention rate, in particular with our entry-level employees who converted (i.e., those who were previously interns (INROADS) or co-ops with us). For INROADS, the retention rate is 80 percent."

UNITED WAY OF NEW YORK CITY
VARIOUS POSITIONS

"Each day you get to leave work with the fact that somewhere in this city you have impacted someone's life in a positive way."

The Big Picture

According to their mission statement, the United Way of New York City addresses "the root causes of critical human care problems in order to achieve measurable improvement in the lives of the city's most vulnerable residents and communities." As one first jobber says, this means "that each day you get to leave work with the fact that somewhere in this city you have impacted someone's life in a positive way." UWNYC offers a terrific launching pad for new college grads who are looking to make not only a paycheck but also a social difference. As organization officials say, all employees must possess "honesty, integrity, compassion, and a commitment to serving the disadvantaged of New York City."

LOCATION(S) WHERE ENTRY-LEVEL EMPLOYEES WORK

All new hires work in New York, New York.

AVERAGE NUMBER OF APPLICATIONS EACH YEAR

The average number of applications received each year for entry-level positions is 250.

AVERAGE NUMBER HIRED PER YEAR OVER THE LAST FIVE YEARS

The average number of entry-level employees hired each year is seven.

ENTRY-LEVEL POSITION(S) AVAILABLE

UWNYC's entry-level positions include fundraising manager, program associate, IT associate, administrative assistant, dispatch attendant, and junior designer.

AVERAGE HOURS WORKED PER WEEK

All employees, including new hires, work 35 hours per week.

PERCENTAGE OF ENTRY-LEVEL HIRES STILL WITH THE COMPANY AFTER THREE, FIVE, AND TEN YEARS

After three years, 50 percent of all entry-level employees are still with the organization.

AVERAGE STARTING SALARY

Starting salaries average between $35,000 and $40,000 per year.

Getting Hired

UWNYC does not target particular colleges for recruitment, though "if a specific academic requirement has been identified, the position may be posted at local colleges and universities with an excellent reputation for graduating students with a discipline in that field." Otherwise, all jobs are posted on the organization's website and application materials are emailed to resume@uwnyc.org. By all accounts, the interview process is simple, often involving one agency interview with an HR screener, and another with management from the appropriate department. Here's how one first jobber recalls his experience: "The person I interviewed with was the Human Resource Manager. She made me feel very comfortable and I began to feel as if I wasn't on an interview, but rather having a discussion with a friend. After interviewing with HR, I was called back to interview for two positions within the organization. At that point I had met with both hiring managers and my general sense was that they both went out of their way to make me feel comfortable and explained the positions to me very thoroughly." What sort of questions are posed during these interviews? "One question," say UWNYC officials, "that is asked of all entry-level applicants is where the applicant sees him or herself within the organization in two to three years. This question is used to assess the applicant's goals and aspirations as well as to begin formulating a path for the growth and development of that individual." Interviewers also like to know that applicants have a strong understanding of what UWNYC is all about. As an administrative assistant notes, "I felt very comfortable during my interview [because] I had researched the company by visiting their website . . . . This was good preparation because they asked if I knew about the organization."

Money and Perks

Newbies—who typically bring in between $35,000 and $40,000 a year—aren't too preoccupied with money. And that's a good thing—as a nonprofit, service-based organization, UWNYC is often looking outward rather than in. The majority of the staff (including all entry-level hires) is "not eligible for bonuses at this time." While "all employees are given raises once a year," the heft of these raises is "largely dependent upon the budgetary capacity. At that time, the department heads are given a pool of funds that are allocated based on the performance of each employee." The job does come with its perks—most notably, tuition reimbursement. This kicks in after one year on the job.

The Ropes

"It was a day to remember," says a newbie, recalling his UWNYC orientation. Why? Because he learned "how UWNYC works, and how the staff is working together to help build a better NYC." That said, the organization's orientation is a relatively quick affair, lasting "approximately forty-five minutes" and covering "the organization's history and mission, the employee handbook, [the] number of employees, the different departments within the organization, [and] what is expected of [each] employee." There's also a second phase of orientation which occurs at "a quarterly organization-wide gathering where representatives from each of the departments describe the nature of their work." The ins and outs of the position are primarily learned through on-the-job training. An official "Buddy System" aids this process by giving newcomers two veterans to whom they can go with questions and concerns. One first jobber notes that he also took classes for three different software programs, business writing, and administrative assistant techniques—and "all of the trainings were paid for by the organization."

Day in the Life

From top to bottom, what keeps the staff at UWNYC ticking is the belief that they are each integral pieces in an organization that brings a lot of good to the world. A first jobber who got her start as an administrative assistant says, "I felt like what I did really mattered to the organization. Although many people see copying and filing as grunt-work, I think you can take that and still feel like you're making a difference. If files are not maintained correctly then your customer database may not be updated, which makes providing a service to people in need less efficient. If you fail to copy relevant documents, how do you keep track of what a customer or organization has received in the form of service or/and funding?" Of course, not all rookies spend their days maintaining files. Other entry-level duties include building campaigns and relationships to benefit the organization's fundraising efforts; supporting "the development, implementation, and oversight" of community programs; handling "administrative support and mailroom and carpool services as well as office security and warehouse and inventory maintenance"; and designing and producing UWNYC's "print and electronic communications."

Peers

One thing all employees at UWNYC have in common is that they're "compassionate towards each other." A sense of social awareness and a belief in the organization's service-oriented goals bind these colleagues as well. While newbies describe their fellow newcomers as "smart" and "cool," they say there's not much out-of-the-office socializing. A program associate remarks, "The only real contact with other newcomers to the organization was made at the orientation. There was no social networking after hours."

Moving on

First jobbers most frequently leave UWNYC to go to graduate or professional school, to move to a new location, or to take a job with a nonprofit organization that offers greater opportunity "for direct interaction with those being serviced."

Attrition

As we noted above, one of the primary reasons that entry-level hires decide to leave UWNYC is to find a position that offers more face-to-face contact with those in need; administrators explain that this reflects "the discrepancy that often exists between commonly held expectations of the structure of nonprofit organizations and the method of indirect customer service utilized by the UWNYC, which strengthens and supports organizations servicing those in need." Despite this frustration, UWNYC reports that very few of its first jobbers leave before their first year is complete.

Best and Worst

UWNYC officials say, "The most successful entry-level employee demonstrated dedication to the organization and 100 percent accountability for her work by continuously providing work of a high quality and by picking up the slack of other employees whenever necessary."

On the other side of the coin, "The least successful entry-level employee did not identify with the mission and values of the organization. This employee also displayed a poor attitude and was unpleasant to work with."

VALPAK
ACCOUNT EXECUTIVE

"The sky is truly the limit. Depending on how much you want to work, you can potentially generate an enormous amount of business."

The Big Picture

A subsidiary of media giant Cox Enterprises, Valpak is a forty-year-old media company specializing in direct mail and on-line advertising. Valpak distributes coupons through its blue envelope to more than 500 million households annually, and operates Valpak.com—the largest local coupon site on the internet. After completing a $200 million facility in 2008, Valpak will look to fill 500 sales positions per year. The company appeals to ambitious, self-motivated, and spirited people—"it's nonroutine, the schedule is flexible, and there is a tremendous opportunity for growth." Entry-level staffers say Valpak offers "a great opportunity for someone starting out," as "the experience you get is priceless." A new employee details, "I started this job without any sales or advertising experience. I have truly learned so much as a Valpak sales rep and I have also become familiar with many types of businesses and their operations."

LOCATION(S) WHERE ENTRY-LEVEL EMPLOYEES WORK

Of the 191 independently-owned Valpak franchises and 11 corporate-owned offices, about 60 percent have entry-level job openings.

AVERAGE NUMBER OF APPLICATIONS EACH YEAR

In the past 15 months we received 9,870 applications through our internet sites.

AVERAGE NUMBER HIRED PER YEAR OVER THE LAST TEN YEARS

Between 500 and 650 account executives are hired each year, 50 percent of whom are entry-level.

ENTRY-LEVEL POSITION(S) AVAILABLE

Valpak hires entry-level employees for the role of account executive, a position primarily responsible for selling marketing and direct-mail services to local business owners.

AVERAGE HOURS WORKED PER WEEK

Entry-level hires work 40 to 45 hours per week.

AVERAGE STARTING SALARY

The average starting salary for entry-level hires at Valpak is $30,000 plus commissions and bonuses. First jobbers usually take home between $40,000 and $50,000 annually, depending on performance.

BENEFITS OFFERED

Benefits offered vary by office, but usually include health, dental, and disability insurance, as well as a 401(k) plan.

Getting Hired

All Valpak's entry-level positions are on the sales team. Since the position requires certain innate qualities such as good listening skills, professionalism, and high energy, Valpak gives each applicant a computer-based personality test designed to gauge their ability in sales before inviting them to a personal interview. During the interview, the strongest candidates demonstrate natural ability and interest in sales, and get extra points if they ask "specific questions about the company and the opportunity." Interviewees recall "a mix of casual conversation and typical "interview-type" questions," with the aim of getting to know the candidate on a personal level. Valpak has approximately 200 locations throughout North America, so most of the hiring process takes place within each individual office. While some candidates are interviewed by corporate representatives, most have a face-to-face with their future boss before they get offered the job. As a result, new hires say they already have a good idea of what they will do and who they will work with at Valpak after the interview process.

Money and Perks

Valpak's base salary is nothing spectacular; however, the generous commission schedule only increases with your years of experience at the company. A veteran employee boasts, "I can give myself a raise at any point by working harder and selling more." In addition, entry-level employees are eligible for "bonuses based on exceptional performance." Many employees tell us that an unexpected benefit of the job is the "relationships on both a personal and business level" that they develop in the local business community. Enthuses a Valpak employee, "I get excellent service and know exactly where to go." Employees also appreciate occasional office events and extras such as "tickets to sporting events."

The Ropes

For the most part, Valpak sales execs are trained on the job. Explains a newcomer, "My boss interviewed me and worked closely with me for about two weeks after I was hired. He guided me through several daily exercises and assignments, took me out into the field on some of his sales calls, and offered a lot of coaching and advice." Adds another, "Within the first two weeks I [had] trailed . . . each member of the team. . . . I learned different approaches and techniques from each person. I took these techniques and began creating my own style. After a month, I felt unified and part of the team." In addition to on-the-job training, all entry-level employees participate in a company-wide orientation and training, held at headquarters in Largo, Florida. Most employees begin working in their home office and later attend the training, usually several weeks or months after they have started at their franchise. Offering the chance to meet other entry-level sales reps while simultaneously receiving instruction in sales techniques, new staffers say the Largo training is indispensable and a lot of fun. Gushes a current employee, "The methods and strategies I developed through the course of the formal orientation program have proven to be very effective in my position at Valpak, and undoubtedly will serve me well throughout my career."

Day in the Life

After trailing peers and training with managers, Valpak account execs are ready to build up their own client base. Employees explain, "At first you don't have a lot of clients, so your duties are more cold-calling and telemarketing." Trying to build up a new client base with no previous sales experience can be a challenge, but a newbie reassures, "Whenever I would feel overwhelmed I had a huge amount of support from my sales support, sales manager, and colleagues." Over time, Valpak account execs say their responsibilities widen to include more than just sales calls. On any given day, you might find them "staying abreast of the competition and how they compare to our organization; setting appointments with and giving presentations to business owners; planning mailings; and designing ads with clients," as well as following up on campaign successes and collecting on accounts. Most importantly, as they acquire clients, an account exec's "focus shifts more to managing existing accounts and not so much so on prospecting and acquiring new accounts." Employees warn that there's "plenty of room to grow in terms of pay, but not so much in terms of responsibility. . . . [However], depending on how much you want to work, you can potentially generate an enormous amount of business." While account exec's keep busy, the "schedule is extremely flexible" at Valpak.

Peers

Since most franchises (with the exception of larger offices such as New York, Chicago, and Los Angeles) only hire one new employee at a time, many entry-level staffers say, "The only time I have contact with other new employees on my level is when I attend a company training event or something of that nature." Even so, some have "developed lasting friendships" at Valpak corporate events and trainings. Also, most Valpak offices are fairly close-knit, and employees tell us, "In times of hard work and achievements, the office celebrates together [through] an after-hours social scene."

Moving on

According to Valpak, "Most people will leave in the first twelve months if they find that the field of direct sales is not suited to them. This is the primary reason for attrition."

Attrition

Valpak experiences a normal loss of entry-level reps who discover that direct sales is not for them. The company emphasizes that theirs is a "get-rich-slow process," best suited to professionals with the patience to build up and maintain a big client list.

Best and Worst

When asked to name a model employee, Valpak reps point to Dave Ireland, who "joined Valpak of Virginia just over a year after he graduated from Florida State University in December, 1991 as an entry-level AE. Today, he is a partner [in] two Valpak Franchises—Valpak of Charlotte (North Carolina) and Valpak of Maryland (Rockville, Maryland). His career path took him [from] entry-level AE into management then to franchise ownership over the past thirteen years." They also make mention of Kevin Johnson, an LA-based sales rep who started out as an entry-level employee in 1995 and earned more than $150,000 (with a base salary of just $31,000) in 2005.

VH1
VARIOUS POSITIONS

It's a great place to start in television production, especially for fans of pop culture." It also offers numerous opportunities "to make contacts and to try on a lot of different hats."

The Big Picture

"The wonderful thing about VH1 and a lot of cable networks is that they give young people a real hands-on chance to make television that wouldn't be afforded to them at a network," explains one first jobber, who adds, "They also, by nature, don't pay as well, but the work environment and experience you'll accrue there is worth it." There you have it; at VH1, you'll have the opportunity to learn—learn how to select, produce, and market programming to adult music fans—and learn how to live on a relatively tight budget.

LOCATION(S) WHERE ENTRY-LEVEL EMPLOYEES WORK

Entry-level hires work in New York, New York.

ENTRY-LEVEL POSITION(S) AVAILABLE

There are various positions available to entry-level hires.

AVERAGE HOURS WORKED PER WEEK

New hires work more than 40 hours per week.

CONTACT INFORMATION

Visit https://jobhuntweb.viacom.com/jobhunt/main/jobhome.asp, click on the "Job Search" link, then highlight VH1 in the "Channels" column. There is also a "Jobs" link at the bottom of the screen at www.VH1.com.

Getting Hired

Persistence is key to success in broadcasting, our VH1 entry-level employee correspondents tell us. One writes, "In the film business, it's always said, 'It's all who you know.' Bull pucky! It's all [to whom] you extend your friendship, your support, and your best effort." I can't think of another profession where they don't care if you have two heads, dark green complexion, and no eyes. If you can do your job, they don't care about anything else. Where one went to school? No concern. Whom one is married to, it may get you a few doors opened, but if one isn't passionate and successful, out the door they go. It's all about the moment. Not yesterday or tomorrow, but what can you do now. I love that philosophy. Only now matters." Or maybe it is who you know; another of our correspondents writes, "I sent in my resume; my brother, who worked at VH1, passed it on; the interview was casual and comfortable. The head of VH1.com interviewed me, and he asked my familiarity with certain software." The company posts openings at the Viacom website; jobs at other Viacom broadcast companies can be browsed on the same site.

Money and Perks

"Nothing seemed too negotiable" in VH1's job offer to our first timers, and this makes sense; as one employee puts it, "Since there's no shortage of people who want to work in television, the moment you've put in your time at a place like VH1 and start applying for more lucrative network television jobs, there's dozens of hungry young kids ready to take your place. To this end, some [may] say that cable networks serve as kind of a bush league to the free-access networks." Another newbie adds, "In the beginning there was no negotiation for pay or when and where one worked. One had nothing to barter with, but after having experience one could negotiate all of the above." The best perks of working at VH1 are "the casual atmosphere" and "the parties. At the end of a show's season, there's always a party, and one gets to get crazy and hang with the creative pulse of the entertainment industry."

The Ropes

Orientation at VH1 "lasts about half a day. It mostly covers benefits information." After that, first jobbers often find themselves on their own. "It's the only way to learn," writes one assistant editor at the network. "I love being in over my head, and any chance I get I try to chew off way too much." To get up to speed, the editor "learned as much before and after work as I could. I asked coworkers for help when I couldn't figure [a] problem out. I learned [that] if one constantly asks for help, people tend to not give it; but if one attempts to go at it by oneself, people will . . . help out."

Day in the Life

First jobbers are scattered throughout VH1, performing all the various support jobs necessary to run a television channel. Those we spoke with logged and digitized video, edited rough cuts of programs, performed clerical duties, conducted research, and assisted the development of programming. All told us that those who asked for more responsibility were given it and that they were recognized and rewarded if they succeeded. One writes, "I would recommend that any recent college graduate get their start at MTV Networks [VH1's parent company]. You'll probably have as much responsibility at your level as you want, and as they often promote from within, you'll rise through the ranks with other people you'll see again later down the road. It's a great place to start in television production, especially for fans of pop culture." It also offers numerous opportunities "to make contacts and to try on a lot of different hats."

Peers

First jobbers at VH1 share the same ambitions and many of the same interests, so it's no surprise that many "make most of [their] friends at work. All of [them] are heading in the same direction: up." As one first jobber tells us, "There's definitely a strong bond between people working in show business. It comes from following dreams, and everybody understands you're going after the big prize because they're doing the same thing. And putting yourself out there like that brings everyone together." The company holds "after-hours parties for special occasions" and other similar events to "encourage camaraderie."

Moving on

VH1 first jobbers usually either move up the corporate ladder at Viacom, or they move on to other jobs in television.

WASHINGTON MUTUAL
PACE MANAGEMENT TRAINEE

"Throughout my training I was surrounded with experienced individuals who helped me enhance the skills I already had while developing the new skills I was learning."

The Big Picture

Washington Mutual's PACE (Premier Achievement of Career Employees) program prepares entry-level employees for a career on the bank's management team. Participants like the fact that Washington Mutual takes a "proactive approach to developing employees" and tell us that the program provides an excellent "opportunity for fast advancement and the development of a new skill set." After completing the twelve-month course, PACE Trainees apply for assistant manager positions at a branch, experiencing a pleasant upswing in their responsibilities and salary. However, the PACE program can be a gateway for many leadership roles in the organization, not just in management. Both trainees and management reassure us that "there are so many positions within the company, not just in the branch environment; there really is something for everyone."

LOCATION(S) WHERE ENTRY-LEVEL EMPLOYEES WORK

Washington Mutual operates the PACE program in Arizona, California, Colorado, Connecticut, Florida, Georgia, Idaho, Illinois, Nevada, New Jersey, New York, Oregon, Texas, Utah, and Washington.

AVERAGE NUMBER OF APPLICATIONS EACH YEAR

The PACE Program receives roughly 600 applications per year.

AVERAGE NUMBER HIRED PER YEAR OVER THE LAST TEN YEARS

Exact statistics are not available; however, Washington Mutual tells us that 900 new managers have graduated from the PACE program since 1986.

ENTRY-LEVEL POSITION(S) AVAILABLE

Washington Mutual hires recent grads as management trainees in the PACE program. The program is an intensive 12-month-long training on all the bank's functions and services, and paves the way for a career in bank management.

AVERAGE HOURS WORKED PER WEEK

PACE Trainees are on the job 40 hours a week.

PERCENT OF ENTRY-LEVEL HIRES STILL WITH THE COMPANY AFTER THREE, FIVE, AND TEN YEARS

Eighty-five percent of PACE management trainees are still with the company after five years.

Getting Hired

While the PACE program is entry-level, its participants will eventually fill important roles within the company; therefore, Washington Mutual is understandably picky about who they hire. Recruiters aren't necessarily looking for candidates with previous bank or financial experience, though those experiences are helpful. Instead, leadership qualities and sales experience seem to be the most important factor in a hiring decision. A PACE Trainee explains, "They felt that they could teach all of the bank processes to anyone, but they were looking for the right type of person who would have a great attitude, [be] outgoing, . . . perform well under pressure, and . . . handle many tasks at one time." A candidate states that "Washington Mutual interviews were quite different from other interviews I have experienced," as the company has a specific question-and-answer format to which you must adhere. A successful candidate summarizes, "Answers should explain the situation/task experienced, application/answer to the situation/task, and results achieved." But don't let these precise requirements scare you off. During the interview process, Washington Mutual upholds its nationwide reputation for friendliness. A recent hire reassures, "I was made to feel comfortable, the interviewer was upbeat; they seemed excited about their job. . . . In no case was I left wondering what the next step would be."

Money and Perks

"Washington Mutual invests a large amount of money into their management trainees"; however, PACE participants admit that the investment isn't reflected in their salaries. Participants also lament the fact that "during the PACE program, you are not eligible to receive compensation for the products you sell." However, once they have completed the program, PACE trainees are valuable resources and are compensated as such. A new assistant manager attests, "My pay jumped up considerably when I graduated from the program and was hired on as a management team member." Remarkably, PACE trainees are eligible to receive "full benefits from the company while in the program." They also appreciate a "couple [of] fun days [during] the year where we got to get together as a PACE group and go out and do something fun together for the day." A PACE Trainee remembers the following outing: "The trip we took to Seattle for the PACE national convention was amazing. The company flew us there, put us up in a wonderful hotel, and introduced us to the company executives including the CEO. We were also given an opportunity to meet PACE trainees from all over the country."

The Ropes

After attending a basic, two-day orientation to the company, trainees officially begin the PACE program. An extensive twelve-month course, PACE introduces its participants to every aspect of Washington Mutual's business and banking services. The training includes tellering, new accounts, consumer lending, small business banking, operations, and "an internship phase where we were with the management of the branches." For each phase in the program, "You go to a training session for the rotation at hand. Then you go into a branch and apply what you learned." A trainee recalls, "We trained throughout the entire twelve months of the program. We attended training classes, and when we were not in an official training class we were training in a branch." As an integral part of the training, PACE participants rotate for training at various local Washington Mutual branches. Explains a PACE grad, "When we switched phases, we switched branches as well. So we had a whole new management team as well as [new] employees inside the branch that we had to work with."

Day in the Life

Needless to say, there is no typical day in this year-long program, as every few weeks bring a new set of challenges and responsibilities. In fact, "In the PACE program, every few months you have a first day." A PACE trainee swears, "One thing we were always told about Washington Mutual was that the only thing we could be certain about was that everything would always change. This is very true." In general, PACE employees are in "training classes at least 30 percent of the time" and training at a branch with the remainder of their time. Responsibilities vary, and "in the branch we could be working on a variety of tasks, including processing deposits/withdrawals, opening new accounts, processing loans, interviewing applicants with another manager, performing monthly audits on the branch, working with customers, writing performance reviews, etc. In this line of work, your day can vary quite often." While most like the stimulation, employees also say that the "floating could become overwhelming. As soon as you were settled and familiar with your workplace, you were on to the next branch." However, Washington Mutual's friendly staff and supervisors do everything possible to support beleaguered management trainees. Reassures a PACE graduate, "Throughout my training I was surrounded with experienced individuals who helped me enhance the skills I already had while developing the new skills I was learning."

Peers

From day one, PACE participants find they have a lot in common with their friendly colleagues. "I have never been more at ease with a group of strangers before. It did not take long for us all to become great friends," says one satisfied employee. Another shares, "I did not have one person that I did not get along with within the program and it was nice going through the same things at the same time with these individuals as we were all open and honest and were able to share our feelings with one another on how we were doing in our phases." While PACE participants are usually assigned to different branches during their training, they tend to maintain contact and meet "about once per month" for lunch or dinner. Many find these relationships prove useful in the workplace. Says a current manager, "The wonderful thing about the program is it has built-in networking, so I now know twenty-one assistant financial center managers that I can ask for help, advice, whatever. It's really great."

Moving on

Washington Mutual employees say it's possible to move on to a new career without actually leaving the company. A former PACE trainee shares: "Washington Mutual provides many different job opportunities. . . . [When], after two years of management, I realized that it wasn't exactly for me, I was able to transfer into something that I truly enjoy." Those who stay on the management path say the sky is the limit. "Meeting past PACErs and hearing their stories of moving throughout the company are very encouraging. Several former PACErs have gone on to hold top positions throughout the company and many in a very short period of time," enthuses a current PACE trainee.

Attrition

The average yearly graduation rate of the PACE program is 91 percent.

WELLS FARGO
VARIOUS POSITIONS

"With the amount of work that is being done, if an individual has any initiative whatsoever, the management team is quick to respond, and you can often receive incredible opportunities merely by asking."

The Big Picture

There are about 160,000 team members at Wells Fargo; this profile focuses on the approximately 200 positions available each year in the bank's professional development programs for recent college graduates. These programs offer project- or rotation-based training to provide broad-ranging exposure to the many facets of Wells Fargo's business; in this way, they allow first jobbers to select the career path best suited to their tastes and talents.

LOCATION(S) WHERE ENTRY-LEVEL EMPLOYEES WORK

"There are more than 300 potential locations available, though most positions are clustered around our primary cities of employment: San Francisco, California; Minneapolis, Minnesota; Phoenix, Arizona; and major cities in Texas."

AVERAGE NUMBER HIRED PER YEAR OVER THE LAST TEN YEARS

Wells Fargo HR officials note that they hire "on average, 200 team members per year" in their various professional development programs.

ENTRY-LEVEL POSITION(S) AVAILABLE

Professional development programs include the following: Audit Rotational Development Program (audit services), Business Banking Associate Program (business banking), Finance Associate Development Program (corporate finance), Information Technology Associate Program (internet services group), Leadership Development Program (technology and operations), Financial Analyst Program (wholesale banking), and Leadership Pipeline Program (wholesale), and Wells Cap Analyst Program (wholesale).

AVERAGE HOURS WORKED PER WEEK

"New hires work about 40 to 50 hours per week, with the chance of having to work longer hours during a large project."

AVERAGE STARTING SALARY

"Starting salaries vary by position, [and] they also vary by program depending on geographic location, prior work experience, market reference point for the function, etc. Overall, our programs ranged from $41,000 to $65,000, plus a sign-on bonus and benefits, in 2006."

Getting Hired

Wells Fargo interviews on many campuses each year and "reviews applications from hundreds of campuses nationwide. Wells Fargo hired students into these programs from approximately forty campuses this year." Applications are also accepted online. Wells Fargo seeks out team members "who share our core values." These include ethics, customer satisfaction, leadership and personal accountability, and diversity." "Interviews are conducted in two stages; the first is typically handled by a recruiter, and the second, by one or more managers." Wells Fargo advises prospective applicants "to be well versed on the company," as candidates who are "tend to be the strongest." "We make it easy by providing much of the information a candidate needs to know on our website." A few entry-level employees we spoke with noted that "some of the interviewing questions were pretty difficult; they were trying to get a feel how you handled yourself under pressure." One, for example, reports that questions he found "particularly hard (and thought-provoking) were: 'If you were a product, what would you be, how would you market yourself, and how much would you cost?' as well as 'What would your enemy say about you?' Another newbie who had "three interviews with senior executives and an on-the-spot presentation in one day" called her interview process "intense, exciting, and memorable."

Money and Perks

Raises "vary based on team member performance, potential relocations, etc." According to people we spoke with, location and start date are negotiable for some positions, while starting salary and bonuses are less likely to be open to discussion. According to HR officials, "salary reviews are conducted in conjunction with performance reviews on an annual basis." There may, however, be "exceptions to this, depending on start dates and individual business practices. Increases are dependent on individual performance [as well as] company performance." Although Wells Fargo offers generous benefits, many newbies focus on the intangible perks. "The best fringe benefit has been working with all of the great people in my group. They have made the work fun and exciting while also an educational experience," boasts one. "I've enjoyed becoming very involved in the community by attending numerous sporting events, shows, luncheons, etc. That's been the best perk," notes another.

The Ropes

Every professional development hire this year will participate in Wells Fargo's Class of 2007 program, "a six-month corporate-level program focused on broadening their understanding of Wells Fargo—its businesses, values, and strategy—and helping them build their professional network at the peer and executive levels. The highlight of the year is a two-day forum in San Francisco, where participants are introduced to our chief executive officer and leadership team." Professional development programs also involve rotational training, supplemental classroom training "to build in-demand skill sets," and mentoring. One participant in the business banking services program writes, "I have received extensive training from many different avenues, including, but not limited to, my boss, classes, online tutorials, and my mentor. The training was on accounting, office applications, credit underwriting, treasury management, sales, and personal growth." While new hires appreciate the availability of resources, most note that the bulk of their training was "on the job, from the existing group of analysts of associates." One also notes having taken "a couple of accounting classes from the local city college [as a] supplement."

Day in the Life

Profiles detailing a typical day in the life for most appear at the company's website. Still, one employee notes that he "never really had a typical day, but felt challenged on most assignments." The rotations that many newbies make provide "a good opportunity to try different job functions and see what would be a good fit." One explains that "we're sent out to all rotations to learn, to network, to seek out projects; it's a very developmental program. On the micro-level, I'm in charge of my own development [so I can] do the best job I can do while learning." Still, first jobbers warn that "some rotations will not be as exciting as others; this will vary on personal interests as well as assigned hosting managers. Many times the assignments can be overwhelming." As one trainee tells us, "There is such an incredible breadth of learning resources, such as online training, that there was no time to be bored. With the amount of work that is being done, if an individual has any initiative whatsoever, the management team is quick to respond, and you can often receive incredible opportunities merely by asking."

Peers

Entry-level employees' peer network and social scene at Wells Fargo "is dependent on work location and rotation group." Newbies characterize their peers as "very smart and talented," "outgoing," and "very welcoming and willing to help out when aid is requested." That said, many work with only a few other new hires, so there isn't much of an after-hours scene. As one first jobber tells us, "Being straight out of college, I still enjoy all of the things that college kids do. Most of my coworkers are older and live a more domestic lifestyle than I do. But they are wonderful people, and I truly enjoy spending my days with them and spending nights and weekends with my friends." Trainees stay in touch through "numerous networking events" and "constant telephone contact." Additionally, "there are a number of events scheduled so that first jobbers can socialize;" most such events are "organized by [program] managers."

Moving on

Wells Fargo tracks information about where its trainees end up if they leave the bank, but informs us that "this information is gathered during exit interviews, which are confidential." None of the employees we spoke with offer any further insight on this subject, except to say that some leave to pursue MBAs. As the numbers above attest, most people stick around for at least three years, and with the depth and breadth of experience in financial services that they are likely to receive during their tenure, many will be well positioned for other jobs in the industry.

Attrition

Wells Fargo tells us that "there are usually no more than two program participants who drop out of a program in any given year. Generally, a dropout that early on has to do with an unusual or unexpected personal situation. We find that it's rarely a reflection of the program." Employees agree; one tells us, "Everyone that I have spoken with seems extremely satisfied with the job. All of us appreciate the amount of responsibility that we are given and have been able to maintain a good balance between our work and outside lives."

Best and Worst

"One of our recently retired executive vice presidents started with Wells Fargo as a proof operator, a person who visually verifies that cashed checks have accurate information, before being referred into one of our programs. At [the job from which he retired], he oversaw a business line that was responsible for approximately 30 percent of Wells Fargo's earnings, and [he] reported directly to our chief executive officer."

WILLIAM MORRIS AGENCY
ASSISTANT AND TRAINEE

"For every career in Hollywood, it's the best place to start and to learn quickly. They run Hollywood; they have all the information."

The Big Picture

In operation for more than a century, William Morris Agency is the oldest and largest talent and literary agency in the world, and industry insiders consider it to be one of Hollywood's two most powerful agencies today. Its agents represent all "above the line" talent, including actors, writers, directors, producers, musicians, comedians, hosts, and a variety of companies (many entertainment entities and others seemingly unrelated to Hollywood) that have interests that can be furthered using the agency's extensive experience and connections in the industry. The three main departments in which assistants work are television, motion picture, and music (there's also a noteworthy consulting department in Beverly Hills, and a significant theater department in the New York office). Even though the pay could be better and the hours for assistants are many, "it's known as one of the best places to start, whether you want be an agent, producer, filmmaker, whatever. It's the graduate program in entertainment." Expect to work hard, earn little, get yelled at a lot . . . and love it.

LOCATION(S) WHERE ENTRY-LEVEL EMPLOYEES WORK

Entry-level hires work in Beverly Hills, California; New York, New York; Nashville, Tennessee; Miami, Florida; and London, England. The vast majority of entry-level employees start in Beverly Hills or New York.

ENTRY-LEVEL POSITION(S) AVAILABLE

New hires work as assistants or trainees.

AVERAGE HOURS WORKED PER WEEK

First jobbers work from 40 to 60 hours per week.

AVERAGE STARTING SALARY

According to our respondents, the starting salary is not much. One new hire goes so far as to call it unlivable, but another says that if you can handle a humble lifestyle for a little while, you can even manage to save a little dough.

BENEFITS OFFERED

One first jobber writes, "I received a basic HMO-type medical plan, for which I had to pay a small monthly fee. I had the option of paying more for a far superior PPO plan, but the additional cost did not justify the benefits for most healthy twenty-somethings." Additional benefits include two weeks' vacation and paid sick leave.

CONTACT INFORMATION

Visit www.wma.com/o/careers/wmacareers/.

Beverly Hills	New York City	Nashville
Human Resources	Human Resources	Human Resources
William Morris Agency, Inc.	William Morris Agency, Inc.	William Morris Agency, Inc.
One William Morris Place	1325 Avenue of the Americas	2100 West End Avenue, #1000
Beverly Hills, CA 90212	New York, NY 10019	Nashville, TN 37203
Fax: 310-859-4205		

(The Beverly Hills office is the only one that accepts fax submissions.)

Getting Hired

Competition for assistant and trainee positions is fierce. One first jobber notes, "There are two application processes—one for those who have industry connections and one for those who do not. The former almost always are offered interviews; the latter almost never are. I originally sent my resume directly to the human resources department, and I was fortunate to be offered an interview. (Incidentally, I was offered an interview only after I followed up with a phone call after faxing my resume, and I highly recommend that everybody do this.) I met with two people from the human resources department, and they seemed to have two primary concerns. First, they wanted to make sure I knew what I was getting myself into (low pay and high stress in a fast-paced environment). Second, they wanted to make it clear that I would have virtually no contact with celebrities. While I was waiting for them to get back to me with a job offer, I did my homework and found an alumna from my college who worked there. I faxed her my resume, and the next thing I knew, I had an interview with an agent she knew. That agent offered me a job, but he also introduced me to the gentleman who eventually became my boss."

Money and Perks

Like most highly desirable gateway jobs, entry-level offers at William Morris are essentially a take-it-or-leave-it affair. One assistant writes, "Most things were not negotiable. I had the option of starting the week after I was given the offer or the week after that. The salary was set, and I was expected to do what my boss told me to do." Assistants start at about $500 per week and can earn overtime; trainees earn about $400 per week and don't earn overtime pay, "[though] they surely work overtime hours." The perks are good; one first jobber reports, "Although people often work on the weekends, the work is often semi-enjoyable (reading scripts, attending social events, etc.) and does not require people to come into the office." Another plus is that "you can get into any party in Hollywood. You have access to anybody in entertainment." One trainee sums it up this way: "The perks are fun. The in-office desk is pretty tedious and can oftentimes be awful, but you will always have better stories than your friends. 'Yeah, I was hanging out with Martin Sheen. Yeah, I was hanging out in the skybox with DiCaprio.' It becomes a way of life. The glam wears off eventually, though, and it becomes a job. If you want to be an agent, you stay focused and stay at the agency."

The Ropes

For assistants, "the orientation process is about a week long. Along with the other people starting that Monday, you attend computer-training sessions and a variety of meetings with people from human resources. When you're not in formal training, you're working alongside an experienced assistant on your new boss's desk." Training is "mostly trial and error, [though] sometimes your predecessor will spend a few days training you." One assistant explains, "Once I earned my boss's trust, he would often take me aside and give me mini-tutorials on different aspects of his job. Almost daily, we would have informal discussions about things I read in the trade papers, questions I had about the business, interests I had in my boss's phone conversations, etc. This was unusual, though; most agents don't make the time to become a formal mentor to their assistants." Trainees often start in the mailroom. One writes, "They threw you in there right away. Orientation and training comes in bits and pieces. You [do] an afternoon of computer training for two hours, then [you're] back in the mailroom. Then a day or two later you'd do phones for forty-five minutes, then back. It last[s] over a few weeks, but each specific session [is] very brief." A trainee adds, "You learn by doing, [by] getting in people's faces, and [by] asking if you can help them. The benefit of starting in the mailroom is that you get a chance to decide what area of the department you want to work in. Television, new media—you get a chance to decide, and you go and jockey for position, trying to get out of the mailroom and get a desk when it opens up. That's when you really start your formal training on how to become an agent. The mailroom is basically boot camp."

Day in the Life

Assistants serve as agents' gophers. "I was little more than a glorified secretary when I began my job," writes one. Trainees do all the other grunt work at the agency, and in terms of sheer quantity, it usually well outweighs the assistants' responsibilities. Trainees traditionally have the inside track on opportunities to advance within the agency. One assistant explains, "More is often expected from trainees, but more is offered to them (in terms of future possibilities) as well. I think trainees have a slightly better chance of being promoted to agents—after all, they were handpicked from the start. It's a bit like honors classes in high school—it's not impossible to get into an Ivy League school without being in all the honors classes, but if you're playing the odds, you're going to bet on the kids in the honors classes." One trainee disagrees; he says, "It used to be that the only people that'd get promoted were the trainees. My class and those after me have found that you're no more likely to get promoted [as a trainee] than as an assistant. The only value is that you're able to pick your path. As an assistant, you have to go where the opportunity is." Regardless of their point of entry, successful first jobbers soon find themselves with growing responsibilities. One writes, "By the end of my first year, I was my boss's right-hand man. If he was unavailable, I might be asked to listen in on a phone call in his place. Experienced assistants will tell you that they do pretty much everything that their agents take credit for. Admittedly, this is an exaggeration, but only slightly so."

Peers

"There is a great deal of contact and camaraderie" among William Morris Agency's first jobbers, "but there is also a bit of competition, especially among trainees." One trainee agrees: "Some peers become your best friends, [and] some become your enemies. There's more competition in a mailroom between the trainees than any other job in Hollywood. You can't trust anyone. The desk will be opening up, and it won't be on the board. So oftentimes there'll be a couple people there, and you'll get screwed out of it if you're not on top of your game." The after-hours scene "is fairly large." Many people view after-hours socializing as part of the job. One trainee writes, "It's not a job where you punch in, punch out, and go home. I would get home on average at 11:00 P.M. [or] 11:30 P.M., and I'd be out till 4:00 A.M. sometimes. You should always have dinner or drinks to schmooze."

Moving on

"People who leave the agency find success at studios, production companies, management companies, publicity houses, other agencies, and as personal assistants to the stars. The list of possibilities is virtually endless." As one assistant puts it, "for every career in Hollywood, it's the best place to start and to learn quickly. They run Hollywood; they have all the information."

Attrition

Many of those who leave the agency do so because they grow disillusioned with the industry, while others decide that they would rather work in a different facet of the industry. Producing is a popular aspiration among people who leave these days, for example; and many who leave pursue creative executive positions at studios. Some "point out that the place is not especially friendly toward women and minorities. . . . People displeased with the agency also argue that, due to the very low salaries for trainees, only applicants from wealthy backgrounds are able to remain on the trainee track long enough (usually four-plus years) to have a shot at being promoted to agent. And even then, your chances are quite slim." It's important to note, however, that in regard to these issues the William Morris Agency is not unique among talent agencies. The most powerful executives in the most powerful entertainment companies continue to be mostly white males these days. Also, the agency does seem to make an effort to hire significant numbers of women and minorities into entry-level positions; it's just that most of them tend to leave the agency before they are promoted to agent.

YMCA
Director, Coordinator

In addition to enjoying a flexible schedule with plenty of responsibility, Y directors like knowing "they are a front line for helping to meet
people's needs."

The Big Picture

The largest not-for-profit community service organization in the United States, the YMCA provides community-based health and human services at more than 970 centers nationwide. The Y works in collaboration with schools, hospitals, churches, and courts to provide a variety of programming, from child care to adult wellness. Young college grads often fill the role of program director, helping to administer special programs, camps, or daycare at the Y. In addition to enjoying a flexible schedule with plenty of responsibility, Y directors like knowing "they are [at the] front line . . . helping to meet people's needs."

Location(s) Where Entry-level Employees Work

There are over 970 YMCA's throughout the United States, contributing over 3,400 branches. Globally, YMCAs are present in over 120 countries and serve 14,000 communities.

Entry-level Position(s) Available

Most entry-level positions at the YMCA are at the director or coordinator level, and in areas such as youth development, aquatics, youth sports, child care, fitness, and wellness. According to YMCA reps, many new employees "begin their YMCA careers as directors or coordinators then pursue a senior director certification through training and other professional development."

Average Hours Worked Per Week

Usually 40 to 50, though hours are determined at each local YMCA.

Average Starting Salary

Annual starting salary for entry-level hires ranges from $29,300 to $36,600.

Benefits Offered

Entry-level employees receive medical, dental, and disability insurance; a funded retirement plan; flexible work schedules; subsidized child care; YMCA facility usage; tuition reimbursement; time off; training and education; and professional development.

Contact Information

For more information about YMCA jobs, e-mail recruitment@ymca.net or call 800-872-9622 ext. 2772. To search open positions, visit www.ymca.net.

Getting Hired

YMCA maintains "relationships with numerous colleges and universities around the country and strives to connect local YMCAs with college partners in their geographic area." In fact, many students begin their affiliation with YMCA before graduating from college, taking jobs at a facility while they complete their studies, or taking courses in the YMCA Professional Development Program (Springfield College in Springfield, Massachusetts and Lindenwood University in St. Charles, Mississippi even allow students to receive academic credit for these courses). A current employee attests, "I strongly believe that what helped me most with getting an interview was going through the YMCA program at GWU [Gardner-Web University]. I was given such a strong recommendation from [my previous supervisor], and I had already completed many management training courses that help directors in the YMCA." When screening candidates, reps from the organization emphasize, "Character counts at the YMCA, where our core values of caring, honesty, respect and responsibility are practiced every day." They also look for individuals willing to uphold "an atmosphere of inclusion for all members of the communities they serve." While these standards are global, YMCA does most of its hiring on a local level. Most interviews are conducted by a YMCA's CEO or other staff, and hiring decisions are made at the site. A successful candidate affirms, "I was first interviewed by phone with the CEO, then I was invited to a face-to-face interview with the CEO and the other professional staff members."

Money and Perks

In addition to a comprehensive benefits package, YMCA employees enjoy the ability to use YMCA facilities at no cost. A staffer also points out, "I have a 12-percent retirement plan, which from what I have seen in other organizations is very good!" On the job, working conditions are particularly agreeable for certain employees. For example, a Youth and Teen Director enjoys "being able to spend two to three hours a day beside the pool" during the summer months. A YMCA camp director who is also a resident of the camp describes his enviable position: "I have no bills. None. All my housing, food, transportation, etc. are paid for by [the] camp because I live here."

The Ropes

"Each local association establishes its own orientation process," and all training takes place on site and under the direction of the association's CEO. However, "many local associations utilize the YMCA of the U.S.A.'s New Employee Orientation Tool, a computer-based training module designed to provide new staff insight into the history and scope of the YMCA movement." In addition, staffers must complete a number of job-specific classes that prepare them for and protect them on the job. Says one, "My orientation process was basically given to me the first week of my job where I had to go through all of the CPR, First Aid, Child Abuse Prevention, and other required programming." Another shares the following laundry list of training modules: "I took computer training, 'Making the Difference' training, Child Abuse, Risk Management, CPR, First Aid, Blood Borne Pathogen . . . everything . . . to make me suitable to work with kids." After that, most training takes place on the job, and employees say they receive minimal instruction or supervision from the higher-ups. However, on a company-wide level, there are plenty of opportunities for professional education. "The YMCA has a great program to help directors advance all the way to a CEO level" through training courses and seminars. A current employee shares, "I feel like there is plenty of room to grow within this organization. There are trainings constantly that I am able to attend and I am in the process right now of achieving my senior director certification."

Day in the Life

The YMCA grants a great deal of responsibility to its new staffers, providing little direct oversight and trusting their staff to use judgment and ingenuity on the job. A new director shares, "I was not under strict supervision . . . . [Rather], from the first day I started, I was given the freedom to do what I saw necessary to help this organization." While typical responsibilities depend on your specific position, most new program directors are expected to oversee and manage many aspects of the program. A director of a summer camp near Dallas explains his duties: "I was told to hire staff, work on staff training for the summer, and recruit campers. I would work on marketing: set up college visits, make flyers, schedule summer camp activities." A youth-and-teen director explains his daily line-up: "I was responsible for all youth and teen programming and budgeting. I was able to run a successful day camp program and also create and maintain new and existing programs. Typical days depending on the season are spent between my office in the morning and out coaching a youth sport or working with area teens in the afternoons." Needless to say, so much responsibility at your first professional position can be a little daunting at first. A new employee confides, "'Overwhelmed' is a small word next to the feeling. My job is not hard . . . there is just so much to do. So many tiny pieces." Another staffer shares her words of advice: "I have also learned to leave work at work when I go home. I have learned that working in a nonprofit organization means there is always plenty of work that needs to be done. I would work eighty hours a week and still have more work that [wouldn't] get done."

Peers

As with much nonprofit and humanitarian work, YMCA employees share a strong sense of camaraderie with and respect for their fellow employees. These sentiments are especially evident in residential settings. A camp director tells us, "We eat together, we are all neighbors, and we help each other. If the kids in my program [don't] get fed because the meat isn't cooked . . . I am sure going to get back there and put my gloves on." Whether or not you'll make close friends on the staff depends on your association's location and size. While some recent grads say they are the youngest person at their center, other say, "I get along quite well with my coworkers, we are all around the same age and we are all good friends."

Attrition

As of May 2006, 47 percent of the entry-level staff hired since May 2004 were still with the organization.

INDEXES

ALPHABETICAL INDEX

INDEX BY INDUSTRY

Education (for profit)

Education (nonprofit)

Energy

Environmental Activism

Finance

Food Service

Health Care

Hotel & Leisure

Insurance

International Service

Legal

Media

Technology (defense)

Technology (nondefense)

ABOUT THE AUTHORS

Ron Lieber writes the "Green Thumb" column in the Money & Investing section of the *Wall Street Journal's* Weekend Edition and also writes about travel and food for other sections of the paper. He has written about career issues for *Fast Company* and helped write the first package of stories for *Fortune Magazine's* list of the 100 Best Companies to Work For. His first book, *Taking Time Off,* encourages students to take a year off before or during college. The book, coauthored with Colin Hall, was a New York Times bestseller in 1996 and is available in an updated edition from The Princeton Review. His second book, *Upstart Start-Ups,* is about young entrepreneurs. He lives in Brooklyn with his wife, Jodi Kantor, who writes for the *New York Times,* and his daughter, Talia.

Tom Meltzer is a freelance writer who has taught and written materials for The Princeton Review for eighteen years. He is the author of eight books covering such diverse subjects as United States history, government and politics, mathematics, and the arts, and he is a contributing author to the *Best Colleges* and the *Best Business Schools* guidebook series. Tom is also a professional musician and songwriter who performed for many years with the band 5 Chinese Brothers and who currently writes, performs, and produces *The Princeton Review Vocabulary Minute* podcast. He attended Columbia University, where he earned a bachelor's degree in English, and currently lives in Durham, North Carolina, with his wife, Lisa, and their two dogs, Daisy and Lebowski.

NOTES

NOTES

NOTES

NOTES

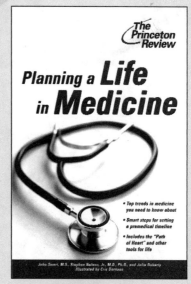